Captive Hearts

Shojo Beat

Story & Art by
Matsuri Hino

Vol. 3

Captive Hearts
Vol. 3

CONTENTS

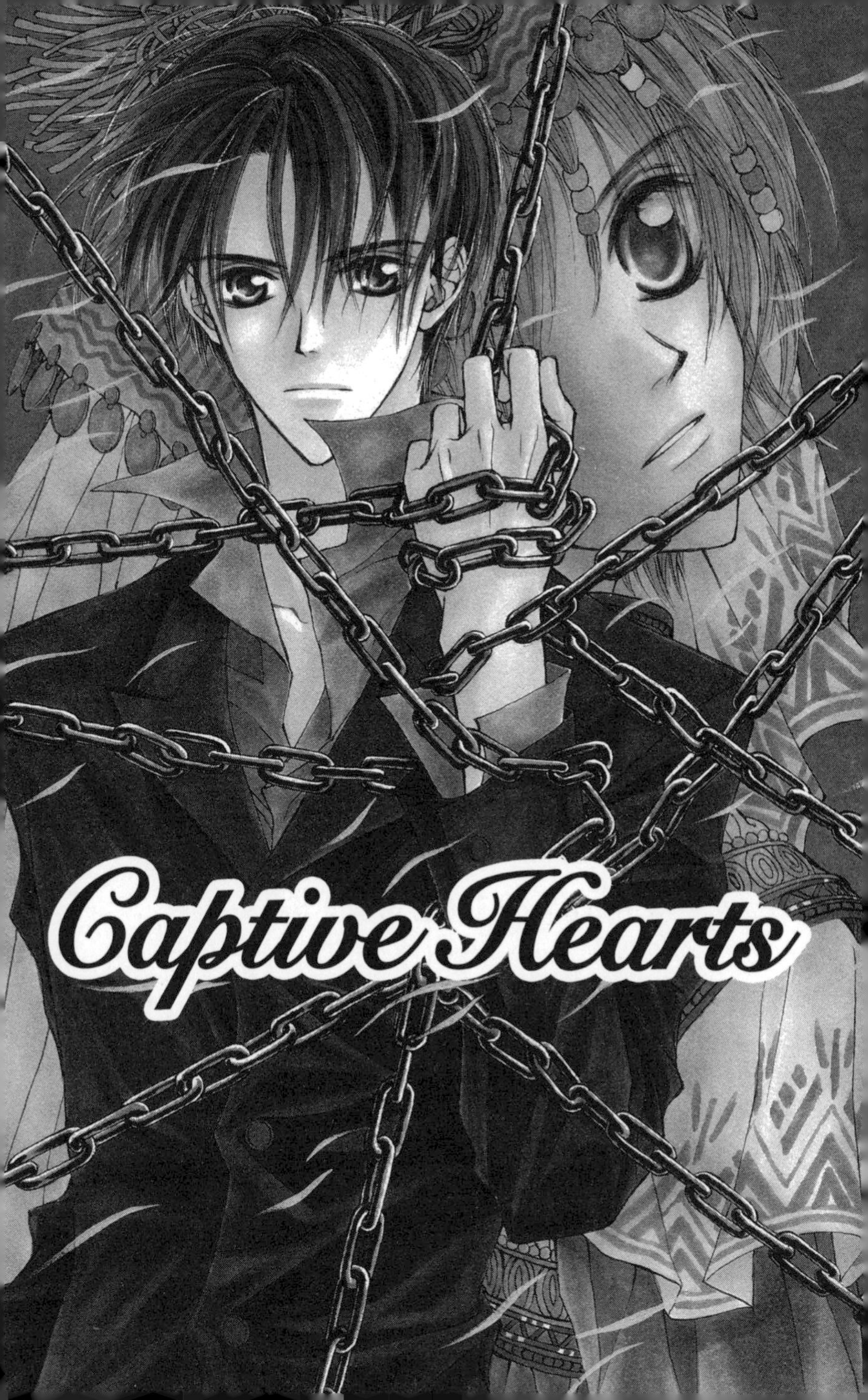
Captive Hearts

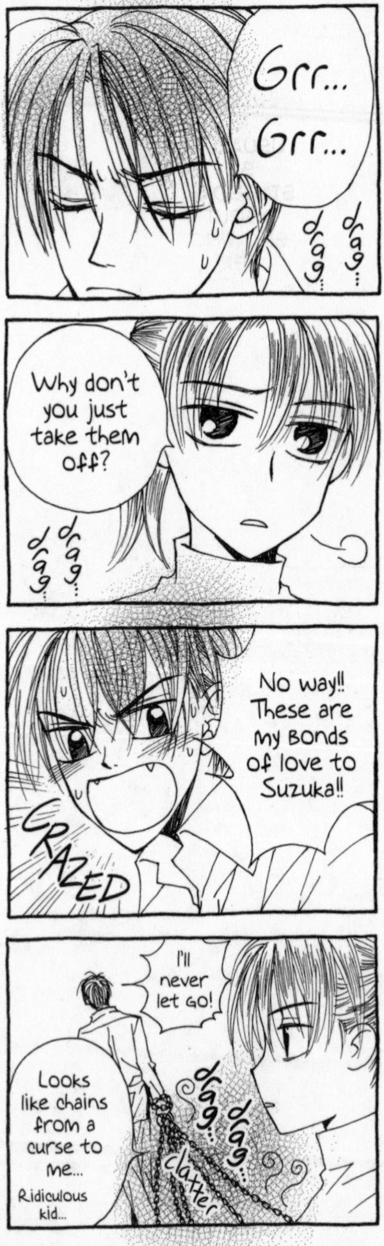
Grrr... Grrr...
drag drag...
drag drag...
Why don't you just take them off?
drag drag...
drag drag...
No way!! These are my bonds of love to Suzuka!!
CRAZED
I'll never let go!
Looks like chains from a curse to me...
Ridiculous kid...
drag drag...
drag drag...
clatter

A ridiculous manga...

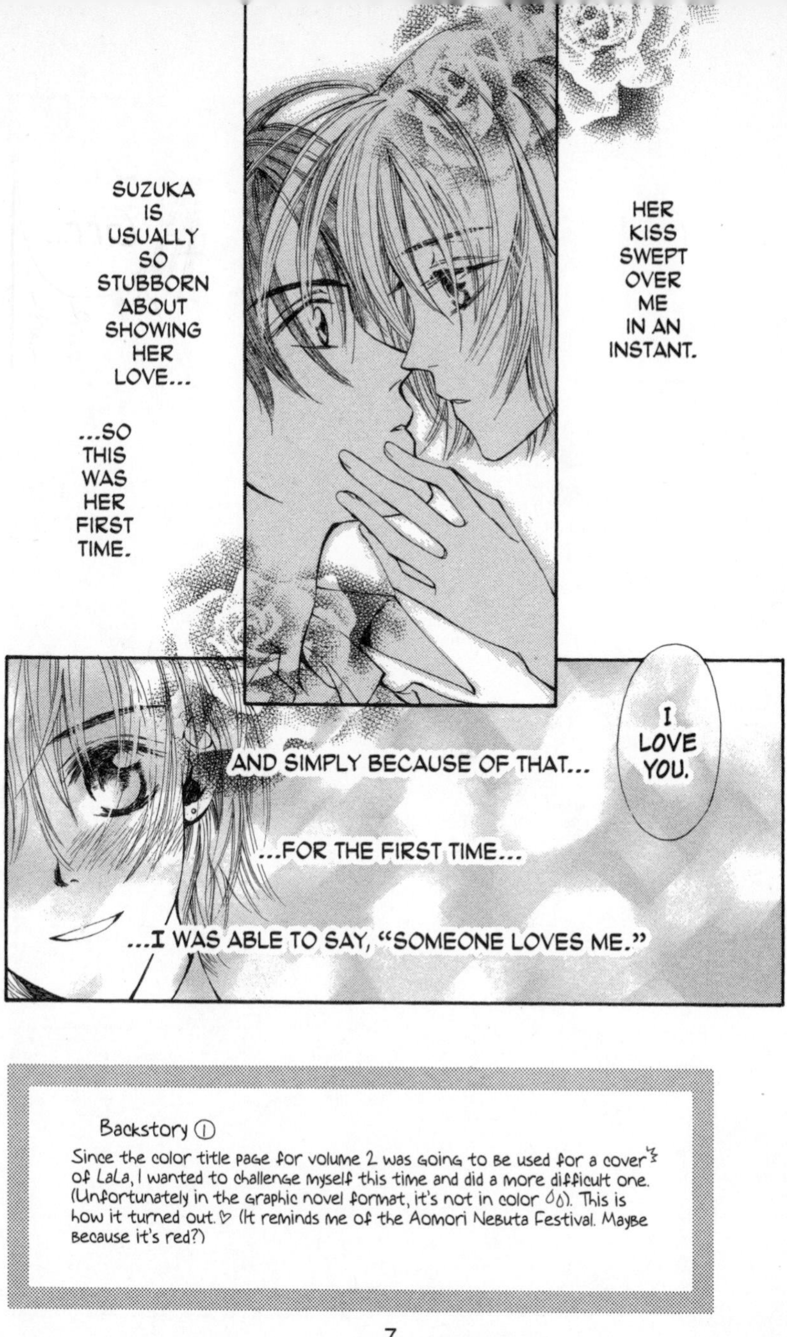
HER KISS SWEPT OVER ME IN AN INSTANT.
SUZUKA IS USUALLY SO STUBBORN ABOUT SHOWING HER LOVE...
...SO THIS WAS HER FIRST TIME.
I LOVE YOU.
AND SIMPLY BECAUSE OF THAT...
...FOR THE FIRST TIME...
...I WAS ABLE TO SAY, "SOMEONE LOVES ME."

Backstory ①

Since the color title page for volume 2 was going to be used for a cover of LaLa, I wanted to challenge myself this time and did a more difficult one. (Unfortunately in the graphic novel format, it's not in color). This is how it turned out.♡ (It reminds me of the Aomori Nebuta Festival. Maybe because it's red?)

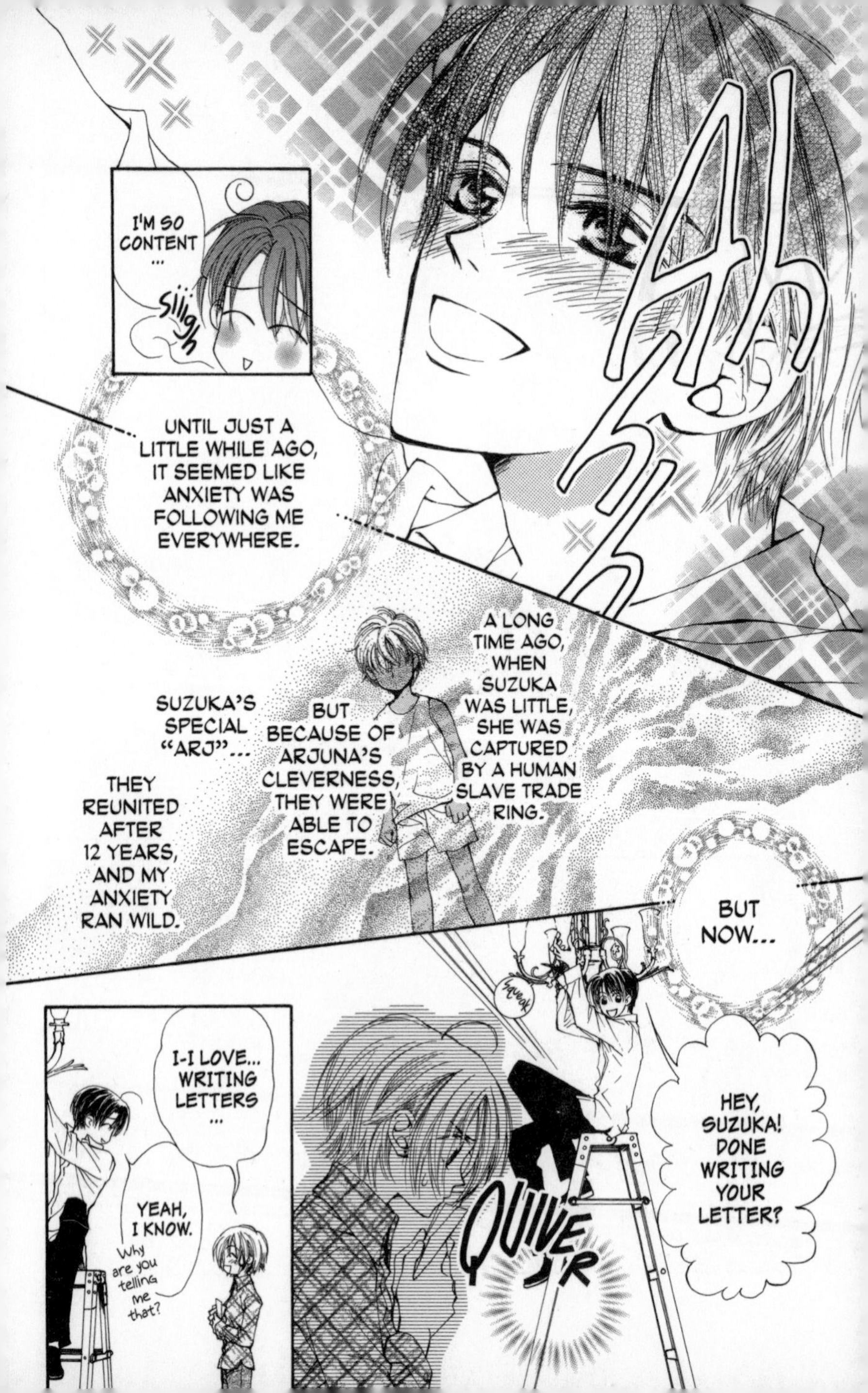
Ahhh
I'M SO CONTENT ...
Siiigh
UNTIL JUST A LITTLE WHILE AGO, IT SEEMED LIKE ANXIETY WAS FOLLOWING ME EVERYWHERE.
A LONG TIME AGO, WHEN SUZUKA WAS LITTLE, SHE WAS CAPTURED BY A HUMAN SLAVE TRADE RING.
BUT BECAUSE OF ARJUNA'S CLEVERNESS, THEY WERE ABLE TO ESCAPE.
SUZUKA'S SPECIAL "ARJ"...
THEY REUNITED AFTER 12 YEARS, AND MY ANXIETY RAN WILD.
BUT NOW...
Squeak
HEY, SUZUKA! DONE WRITING YOUR LETTER?
QUIVER
I-I LOVE... WRITING LETTERS ...
YEAH, I KNOW.
Why are you telling me that?

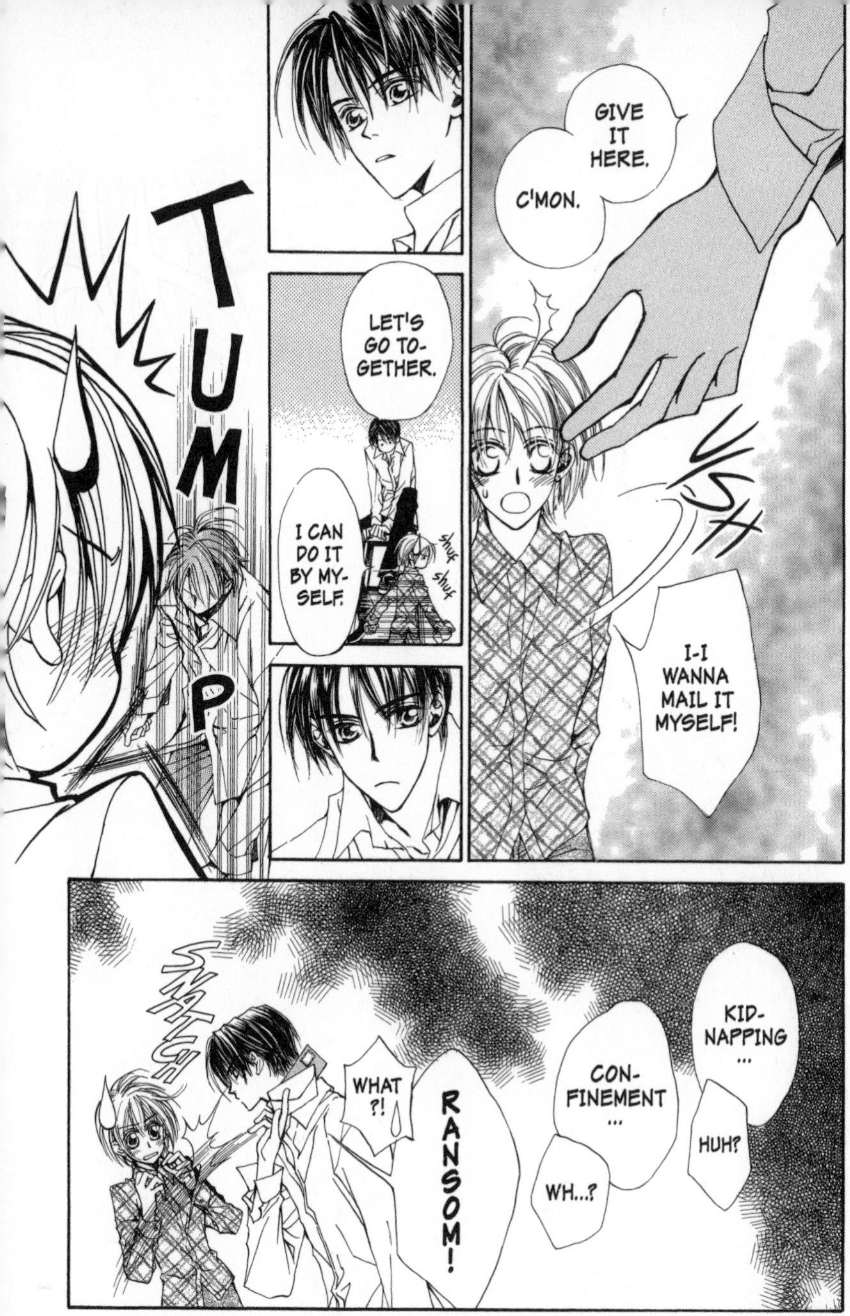
GIVE IT HERE.
C'MON.
VSH
I-I WANNA MAIL IT MYSELF!
LET'S GO TO-GETHER.
shuf
shuf
I CAN DO IT BY MY-SELF.
TUMP
KID-NAPPING...
HUH?
CON-FINEMENT...
WH...?
RANSOM!
WHAT?!
SNATCH

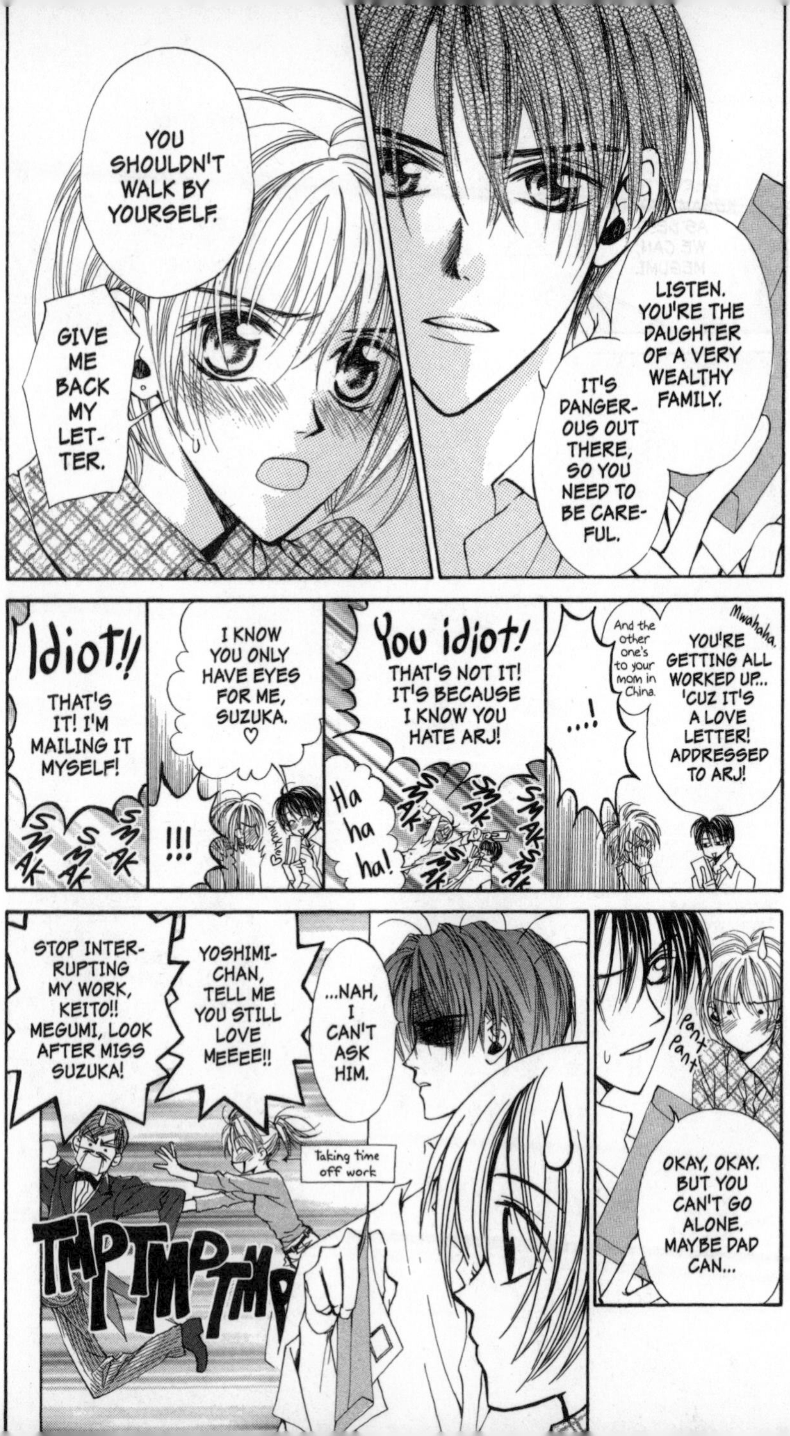
LISTEN. YOU'RE THE DAUGHTER OF A VERY WEALTHY FAMILY.
IT'S DANGER-OUS OUT THERE, SO YOU NEED TO BE CARE-FUL.
YOU SHOULDN'T WALK BY YOURSELF.
GIVE ME BACK MY LET-TER.
Mwahaha.
YOU'RE GETTING ALL WORKED UP... 'CUZ IT'S A LOVE LETTER! ADDRESSED TO ARJ!
And the other one's to your mom in China.
...!
You idiot!
THAT'S NOT IT! IT'S BECAUSE I KNOW YOU HATE ARJ!
SMAK SMAK SMAK SMAK
Ha ha ha!
I KNOW YOU ONLY HAVE EYES FOR ME, SUZUKA. ♡
!!!
Idiot!!
THAT'S IT! I'M MAILING IT MYSELF!
SMAK SMAK SMAK
Pant Pant
OKAY, OKAY. BUT YOU CAN'T GO ALONE. MAYBE DAD CAN...
...NAH, I CAN'T ASK HIM.
YOSHIMI-CHAN, TELL ME YOU STILL LOVE MEEEE!!
STOP INTER-RUPTING MY WORK, KEITO!! MEGUMI, LOOK AFTER MISS SUZUKA!
Taking time off work
TMP TMP TMP

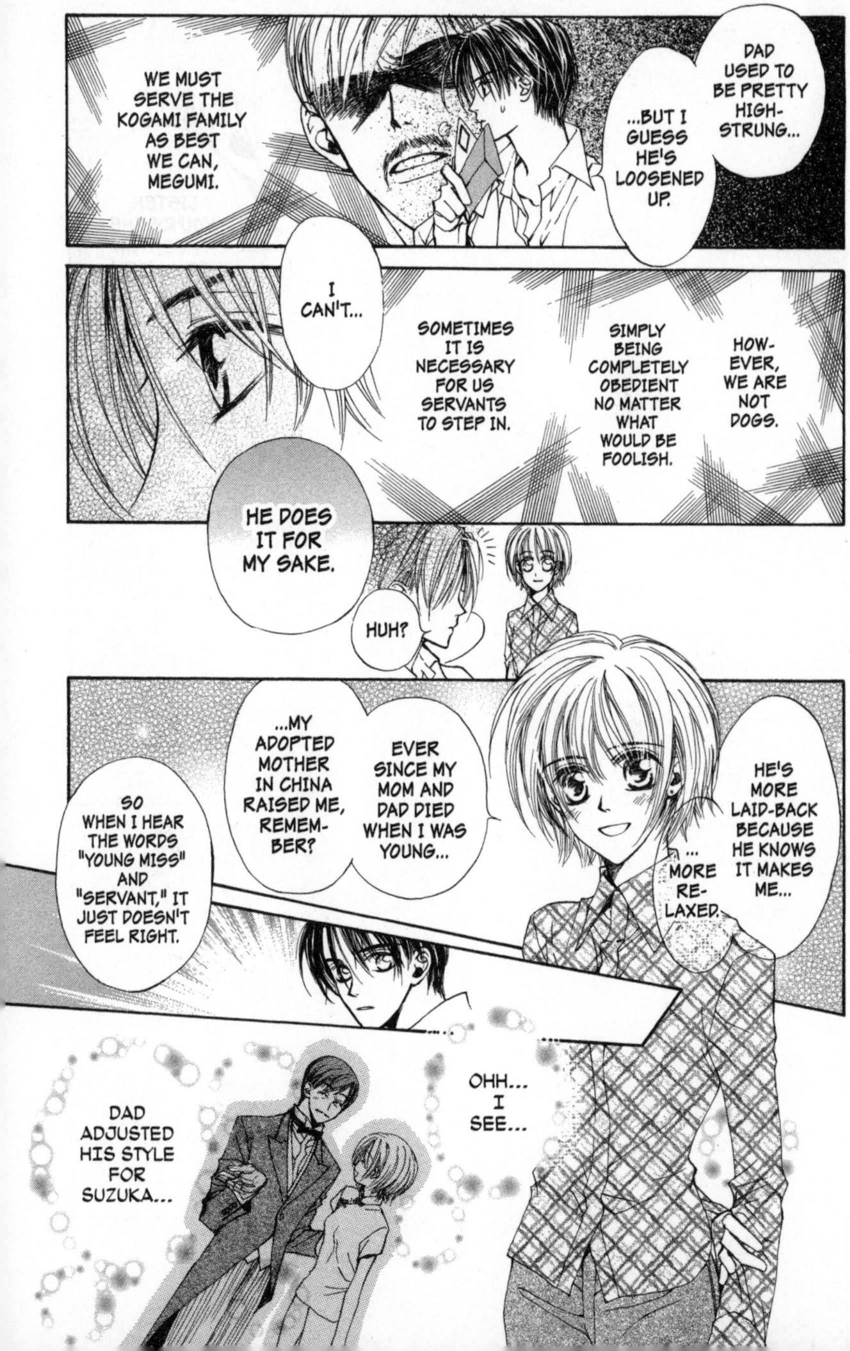

DAD USED TO BE PRETTY HIGH-STRUNG...
...BUT I GUESS HE'S LOOSENED UP.
WE MUST SERVE THE KOGAMI FAMILY AS BEST WE CAN, MEGUMI.
HOW-EVER, WE ARE NOT DOGS.
SIMPLY BEING COMPLETELY OBEDIENT NO MATTER WHAT WOULD BE FOOLISH.
SOMETIMES IT IS NECESSARY FOR US SERVANTS TO STEP IN.
I CAN'T...
HE DOES IT FOR MY SAKE.
HUH?
HE'S MORE LAID-BACK BECAUSE HE KNOWS IT MAKES ME...
...MORE RE-LAXED.
EVER SINCE MY MOM AND DAD DIED WHEN I WAS YOUNG...
...MY ADOPTED MOTHER IN CHINA RAISED ME, REMEM-BER?
SO WHEN I HEAR THE WORDS "YOUNG MISS" AND "SERVANT," IT JUST DOESN'T FEEL RIGHT.
......
OHH... I SEE...
DAD ADJUSTED HIS STYLE FOR SUZUKA...

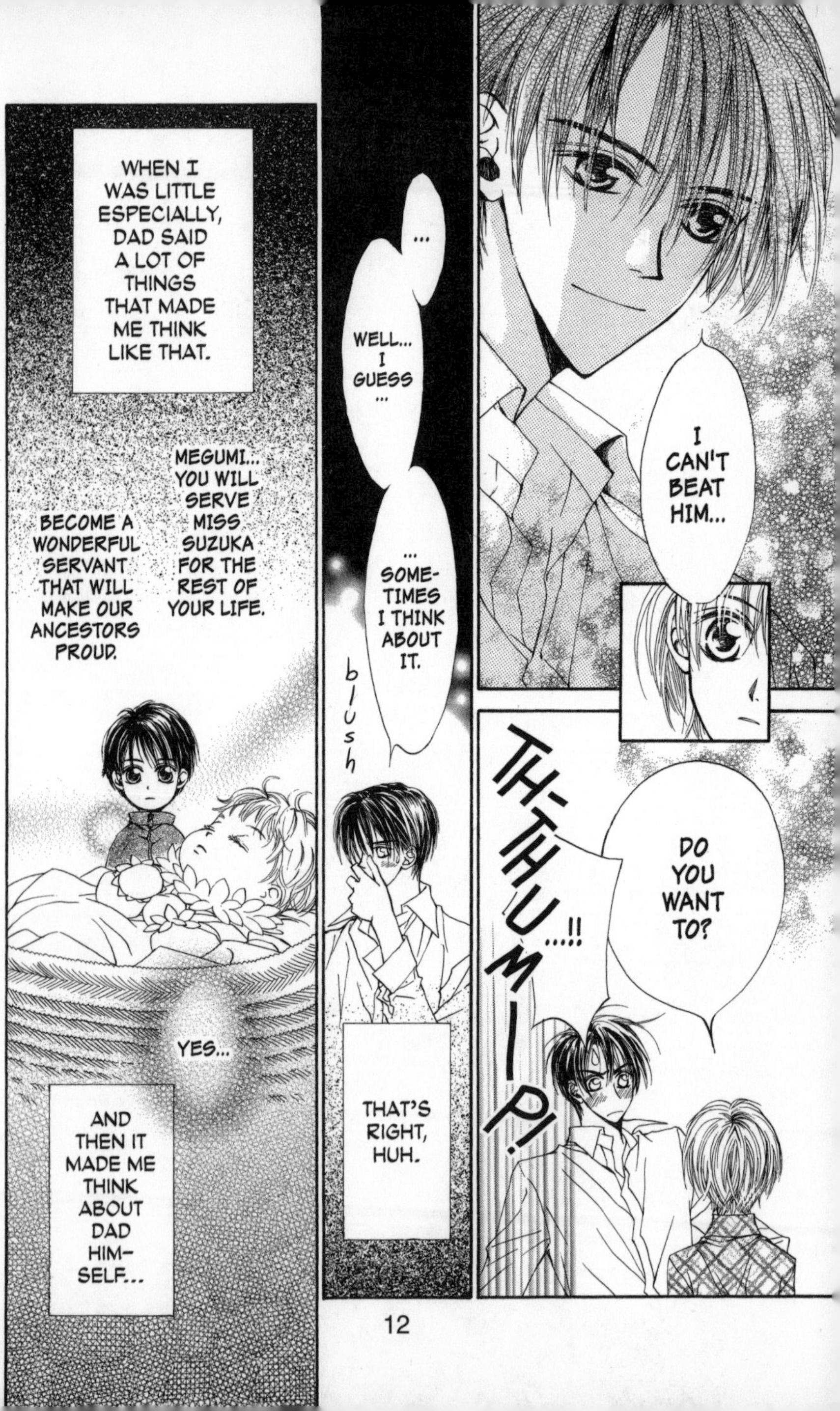
I CAN'T BEAT HIM...
DO YOU WANT TO?
TH-THUMP!
...!!
...
WELL... I GUESS...
...SOME-TIMES I THINK ABOUT IT.
blush
THAT'S RIGHT, HUH.
WHEN I WAS LITTLE ESPECIALLY, DAD SAID A LOT OF THINGS THAT MADE ME THINK LIKE THAT.
MEGUMI... YOU WILL SERVE MISS SUZUKA FOR THE REST OF YOUR LIFE.
BECOME A WONDERFUL SERVANT THAT WILL MAKE OUR ANCESTORS PROUD.
YES...
AND THEN IT MADE ME THINK ABOUT DAD HIM-SELF...

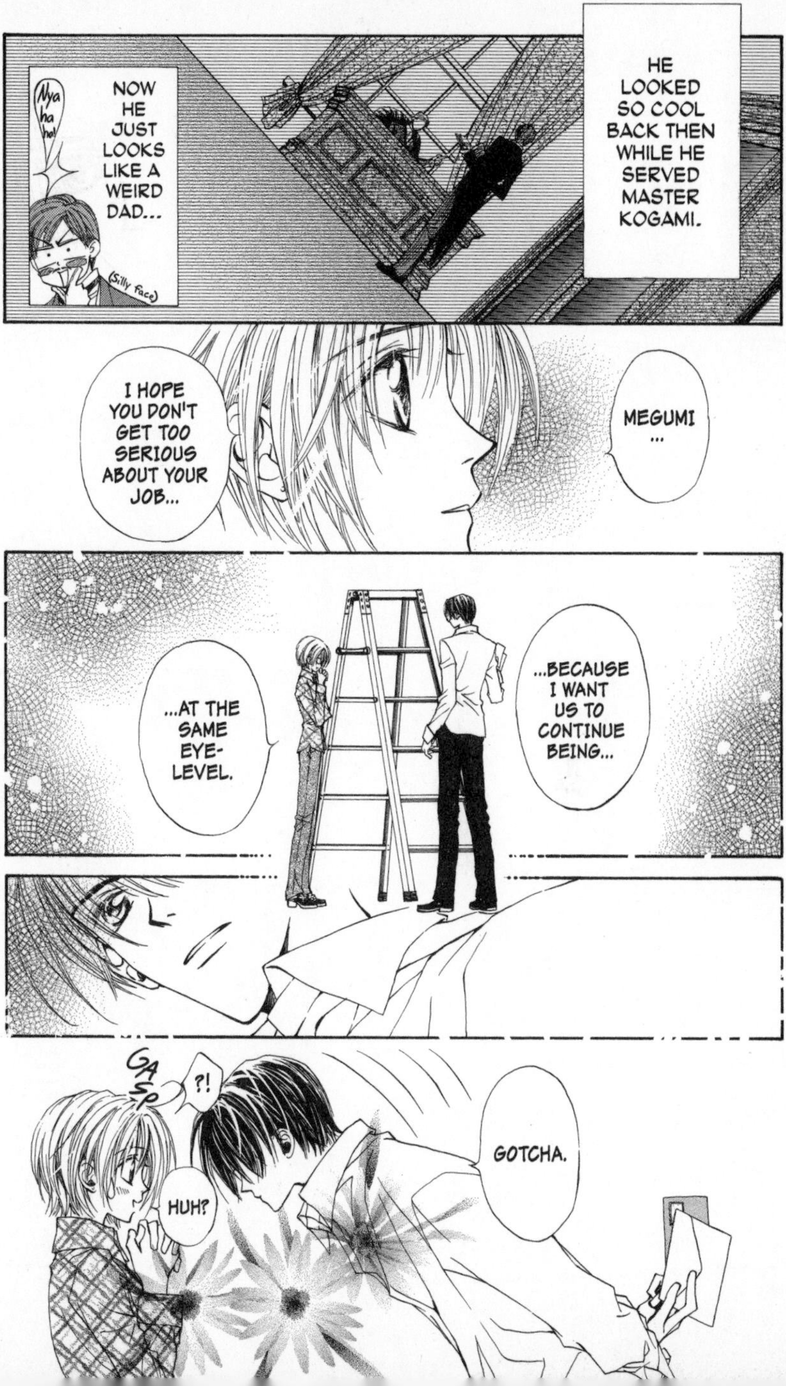
HE LOOKED SO COOL BACK THEN WHILE HE SERVED MASTER KOGAMI.
NOW HE JUST LOOKS LIKE A WEIRD DAD...
Nya ha ha!
(Silly face)
MEGUMI...
I HOPE YOU DON'T GET TOO SERIOUS ABOUT YOUR JOB...
...BECAUSE I WANT US TO CONTINUE BEING...
...AT THE SAME EYE-LEVEL.
GOTCHA.
?!
GASP
HUH?

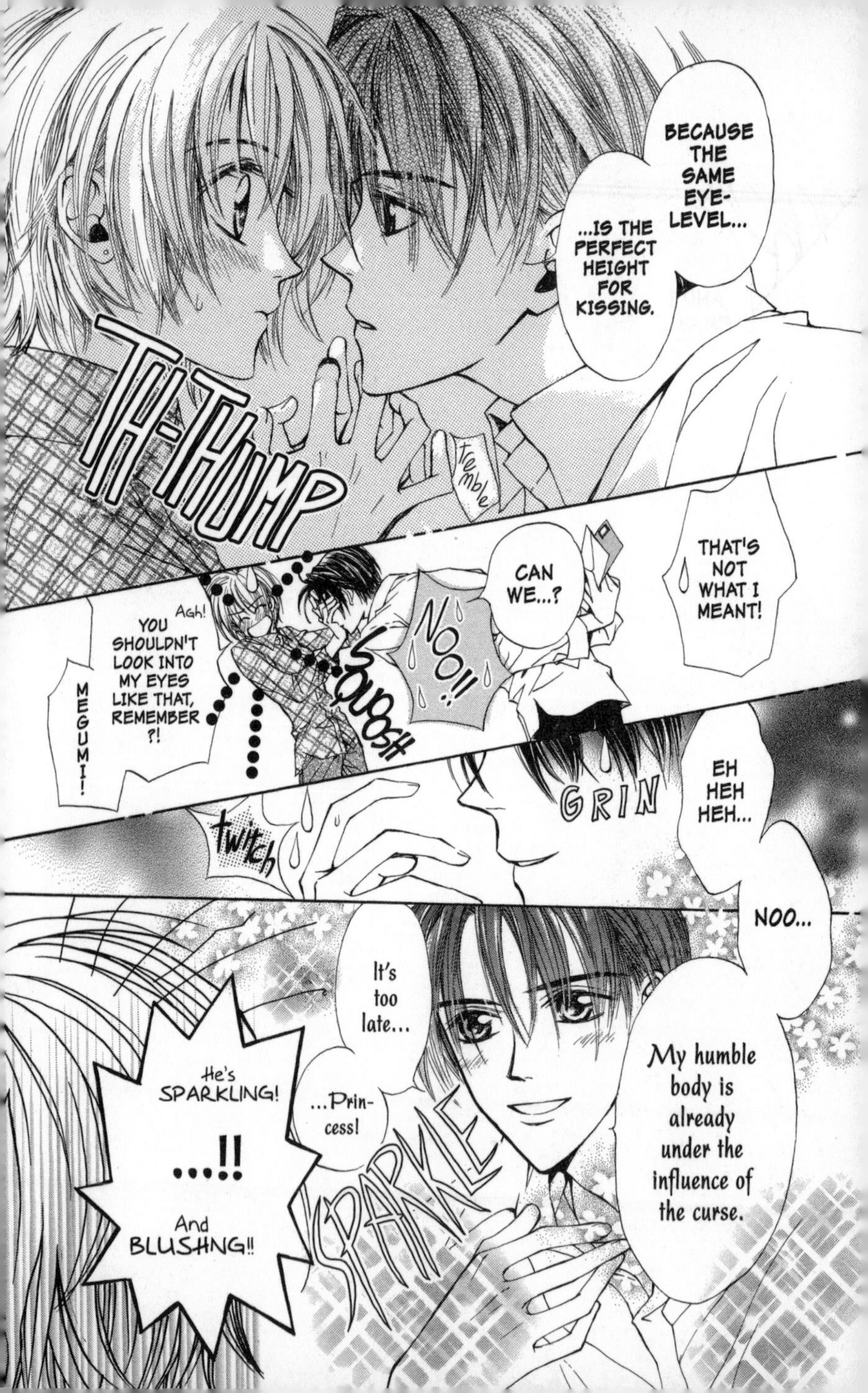
BECAUSE THE SAME EYE-LEVEL...
...IS THE PERFECT HEIGHT FOR KISSING.
TH-THUMP
tremble
THAT'S NOT WHAT I MEANT!
CAN WE...?
NOO!!
SQUOOSH
Agh!
YOU SHOULDN'T LOOK INTO MY EYES LIKE THAT, REMEMBER?!
MEGUMI!
EH HEH HEH...
GRIN
twitch
NOO...
My humble body is already under the influence of the curse.
It's too late...
...Prin-cess!
SPARKLE
He's SPARKLING!
...!!
And BLUSHNG!!

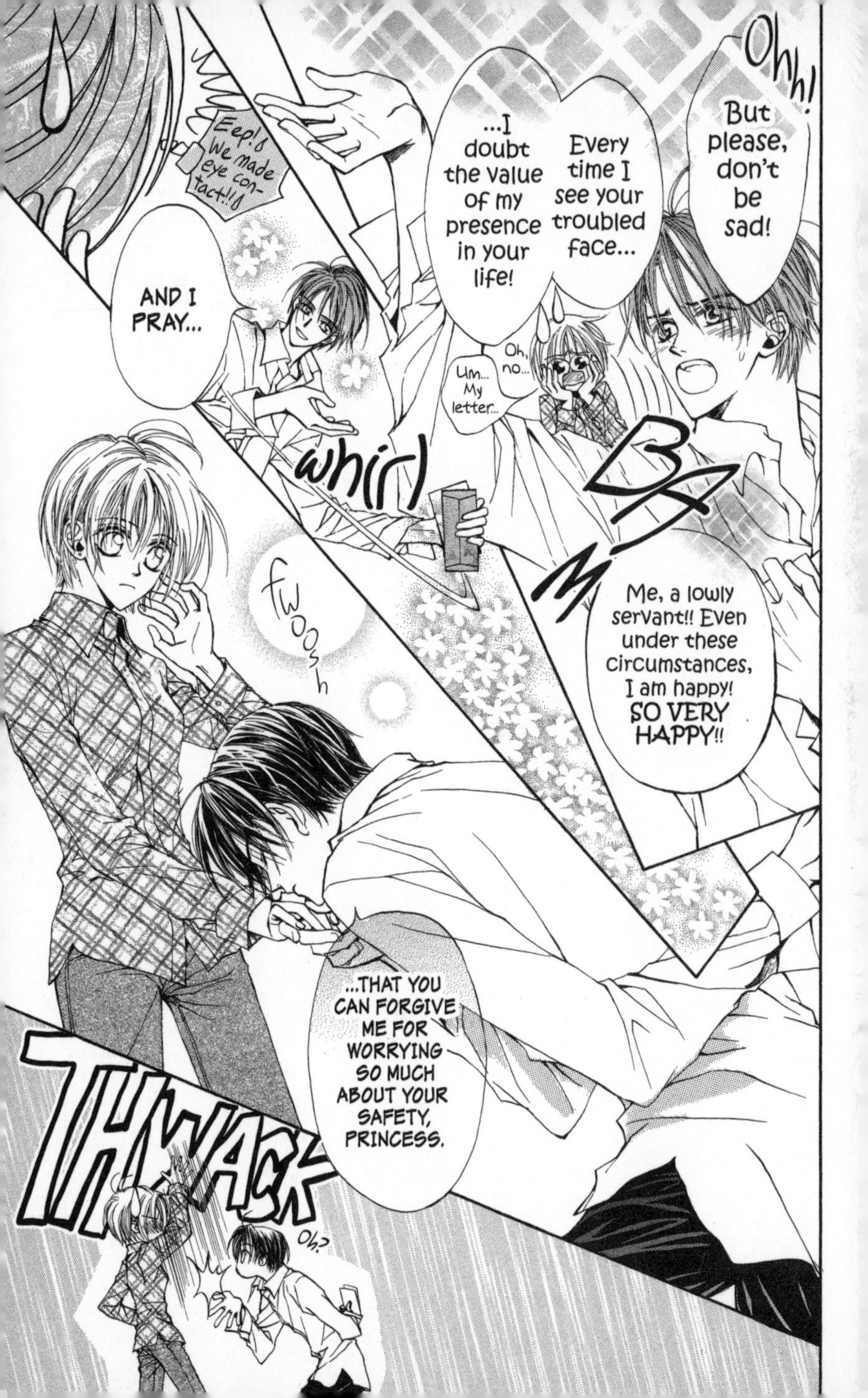
Ohhh!
But please, don't be sad!
Every time I see your troubled face...
...I doubt the value of my presence in your life!
BAM
Me, a lowly servant!! Even under these circumstances, I am happy! SO VERY HAPPY!!
Oh, no...
Um... My letter...
Eep!♪ We made eye contact!!♪
AND I PRAY...
whirl
fwooosh
...THAT YOU CAN FORGIVE ME FOR WORRYING SO MUCH ABOUT YOUR SAFETY, PRINCESS.
THWACK
Oh?

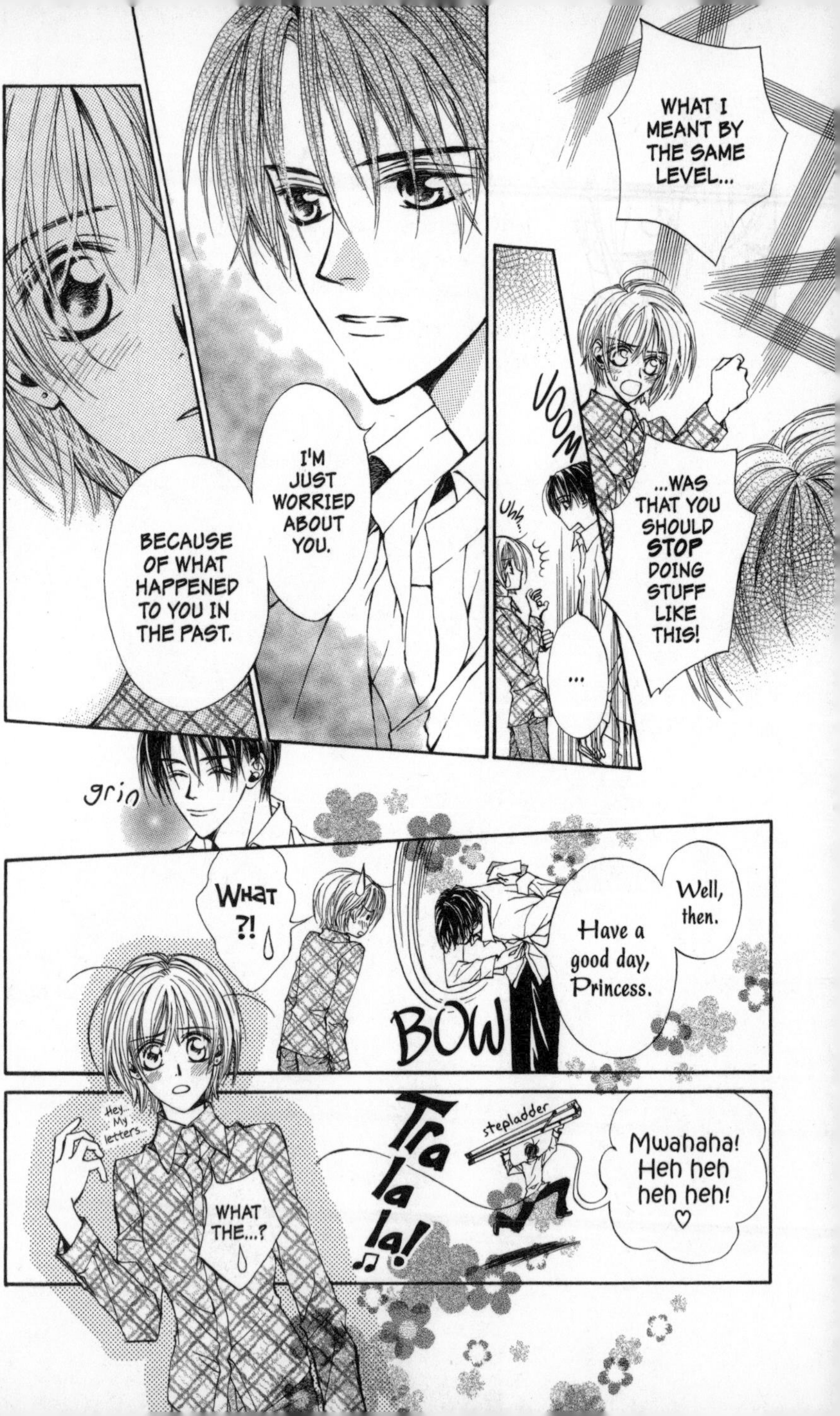
WHAT I MEANT BY THE SAME LEVEL...
VOOM
...WAS THAT YOU SHOULD STOP DOING STUFF LIKE THIS!
Uhh...
...
I'M JUST WORRIED ABOUT YOU.
BECAUSE OF WHAT HAPPENED TO YOU IN THE PAST.
grin
Well, then.
Have a good day, Princess.
BOW
WHAT ?!
Mwahaha! Heh heh heh heh! ♡
stepladder
Tra la la! ♫
Hey.. My letters...
WHAT THE...?

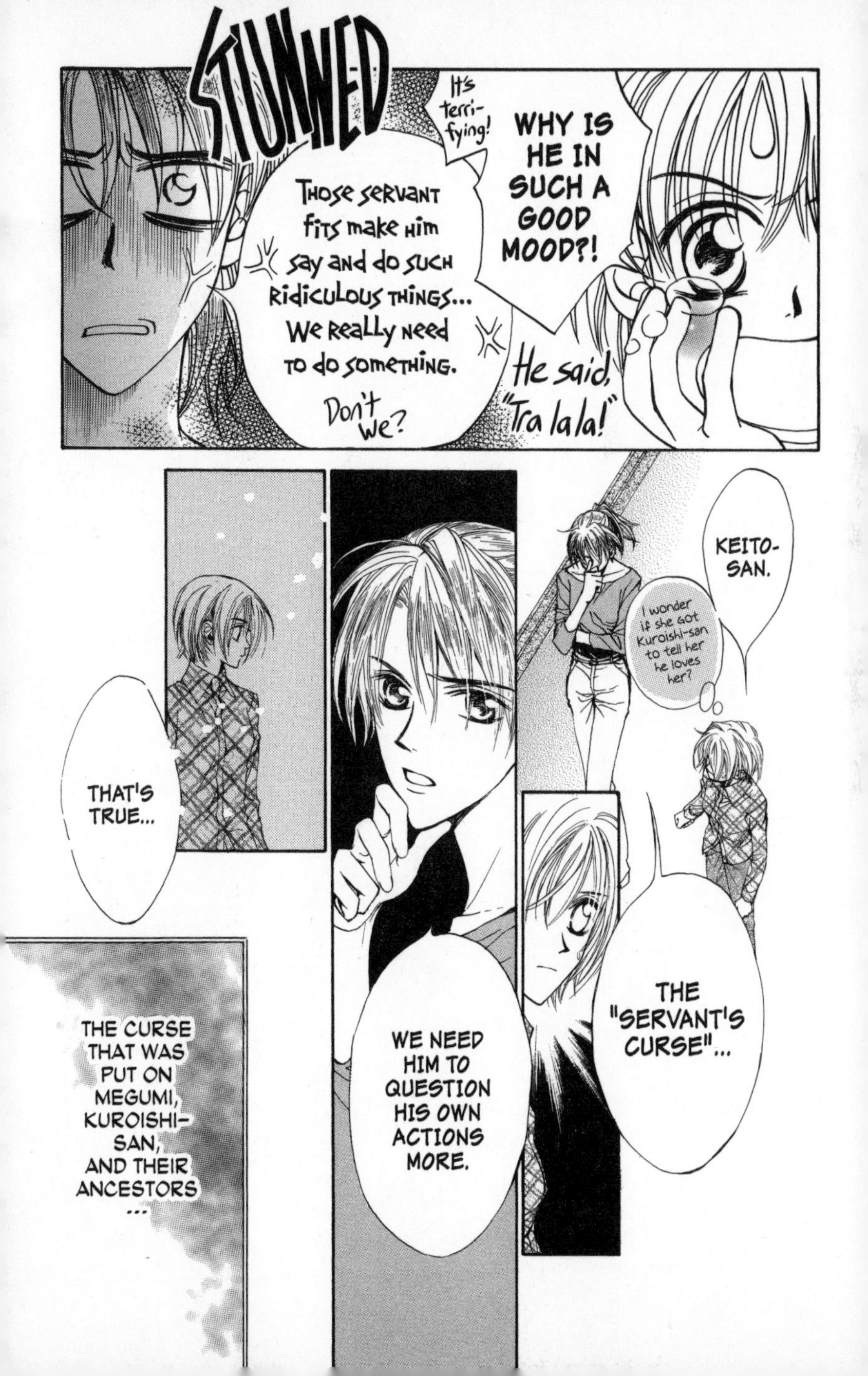
WHY IS HE IN SUCH A GOOD MOOD?!
He said, "Tra la la!"
It's terri-fying!
Those servant fits make him say and do such ridiculous things... We really need to do something.
Don't we?
STUNNED
KEITO-SAN.
I wonder if she got Kuroishi-san to tell her he loves her?
THE "SERVANT'S CURSE"...
WE NEED HIM TO QUESTION HIS OWN ACTIONS MORE.
THAT'S TRUE...
THE CURSE THAT WAS PUT ON MEGUMI, KUROISHI-SAN, AND THEIR ANCESTORS...

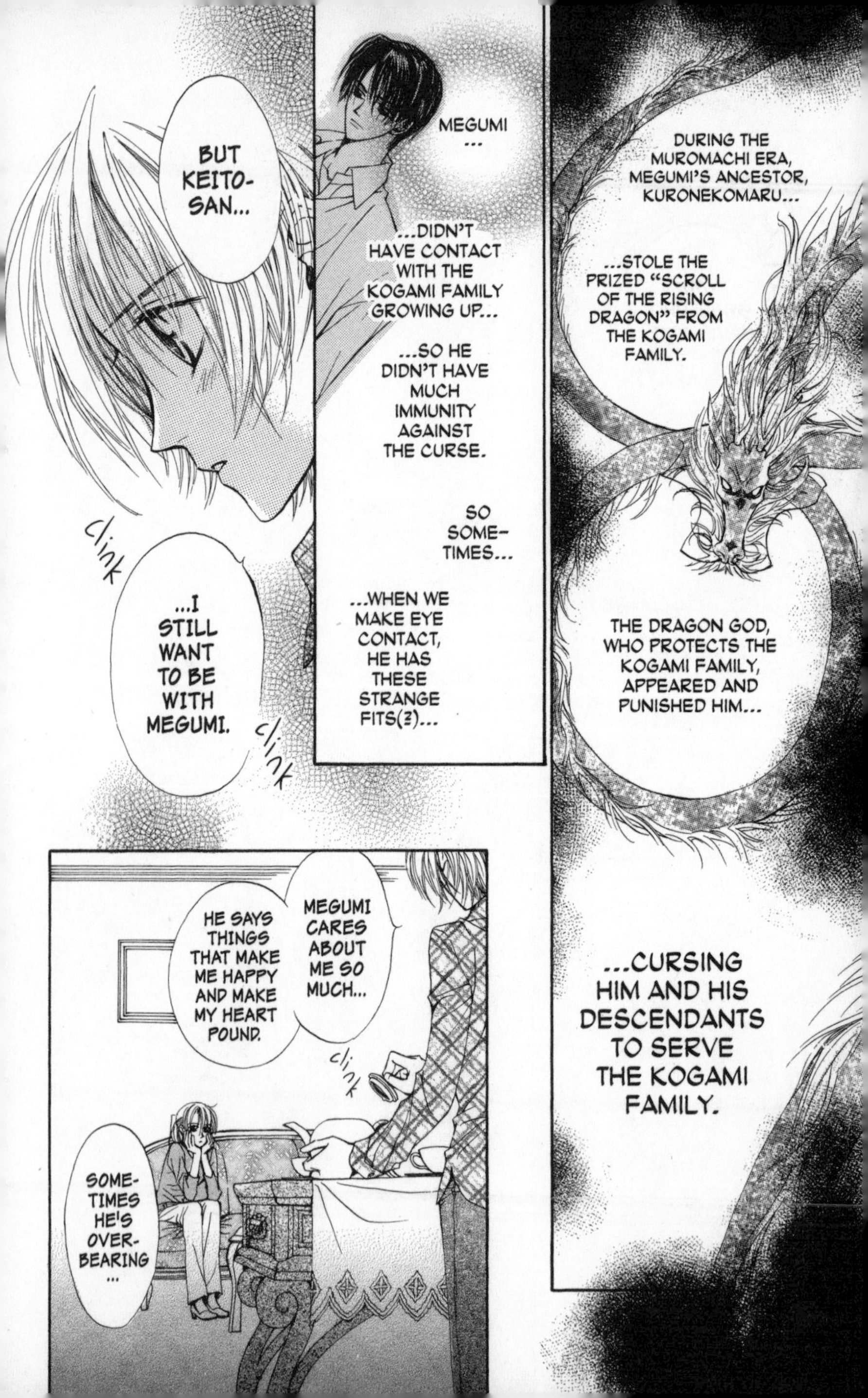
DURING THE MUROMACHI ERA, MEGUMI'S ANCESTOR, KURONEKOMARU...
...STOLE THE PRIZED "SCROLL OF THE RISING DRAGON" FROM THE KOGAMI FAMILY.
THE DRAGON GOD, WHO PROTECTS THE KOGAMI FAMILY, APPEARED AND PUNISHED HIM...
...CURSING HIM AND HIS DESCENDANTS TO SERVE THE KOGAMI FAMILY.
MEGUMI ...
...DIDN'T HAVE CONTACT WITH THE KOGAMI FAMILY GROWING UP...
...SO HE DIDN'T HAVE MUCH IMMUNITY AGAINST THE CURSE.
SO SOME-TIMES...
...WHEN WE MAKE EYE CONTACT, HE HAS THESE STRANGE FITS(?)...
BUT KEITO-SAN...
clink
...I STILL WANT TO BE WITH MEGUMI.
clink
MEGUMI CARES ABOUT ME SO MUCH...
HE SAYS THINGS THAT MAKE ME HAPPY AND MAKE MY HEART POUND.
clink
SOME-TIMES HE'S OVER-BEARING ...

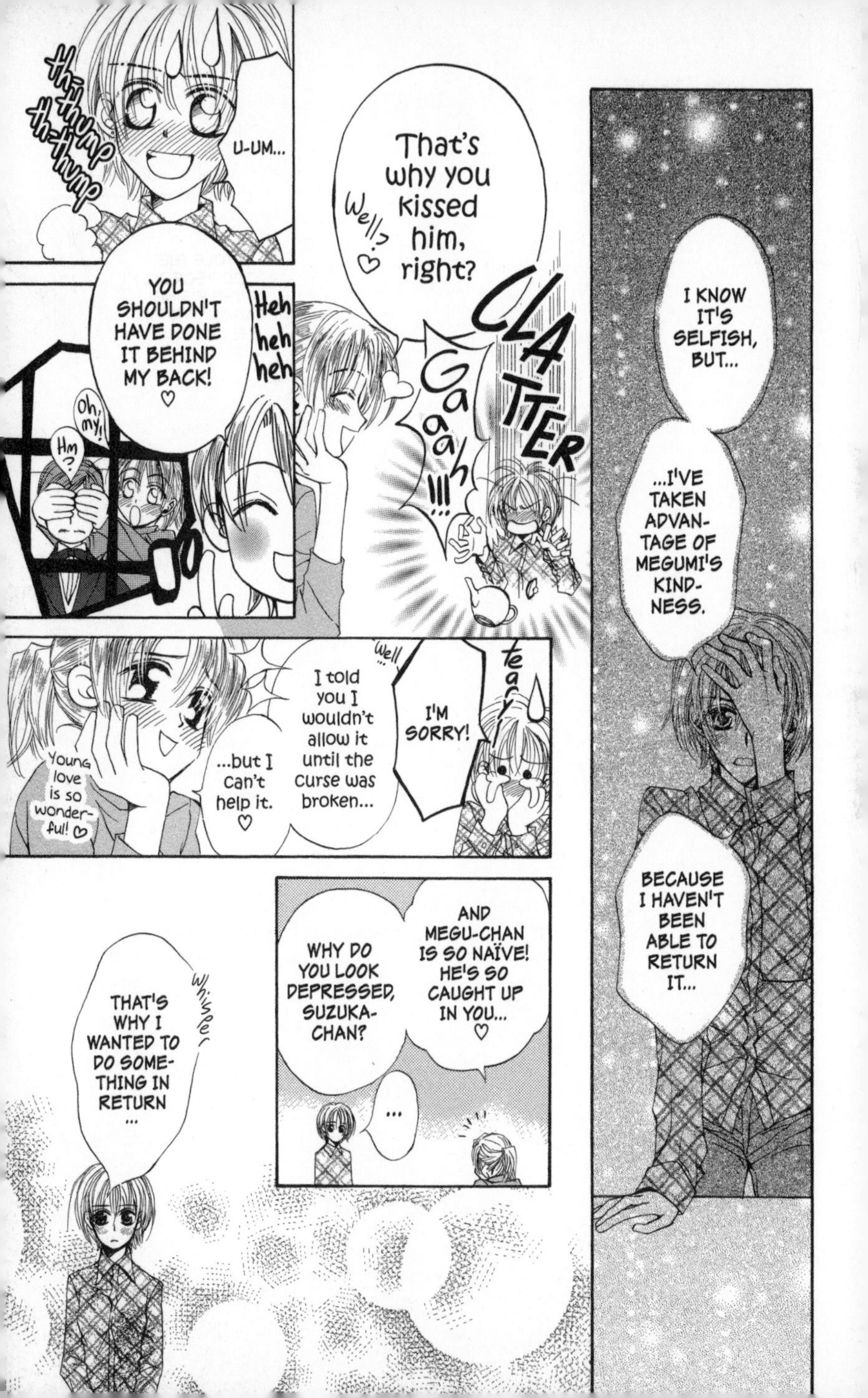
That's why you kissed him, right?
Well!? ♡
U-UM...
th-thump th-thump
CLATTER
Gaaah!!!
YOU SHOULDN'T HAVE DONE IT BEHIND MY BACK! ♡
Heh heh heh
Oh, my!
Hm?
teary
I'M SORRY!
Well...
I told you I wouldn't allow it until the curse was broken...
...but I can't help it. ♡
Young love is so wonderful! ♡
AND MEGU-CHAN IS SO NAÏVE! HE'S SO CAUGHT UP IN YOU... ♡
WHY DO YOU LOOK DEPRESSED, SUZUKA-CHAN?
...
I KNOW IT'S SELFISH, BUT...
...I'VE TAKEN ADVANTAGE OF MEGUMI'S KINDNESS.
BECAUSE I HAVEN'T BEEN ABLE TO RETURN IT...
whisper
THAT'S WHY I WANTED TO DO SOMETHING IN RETURN...

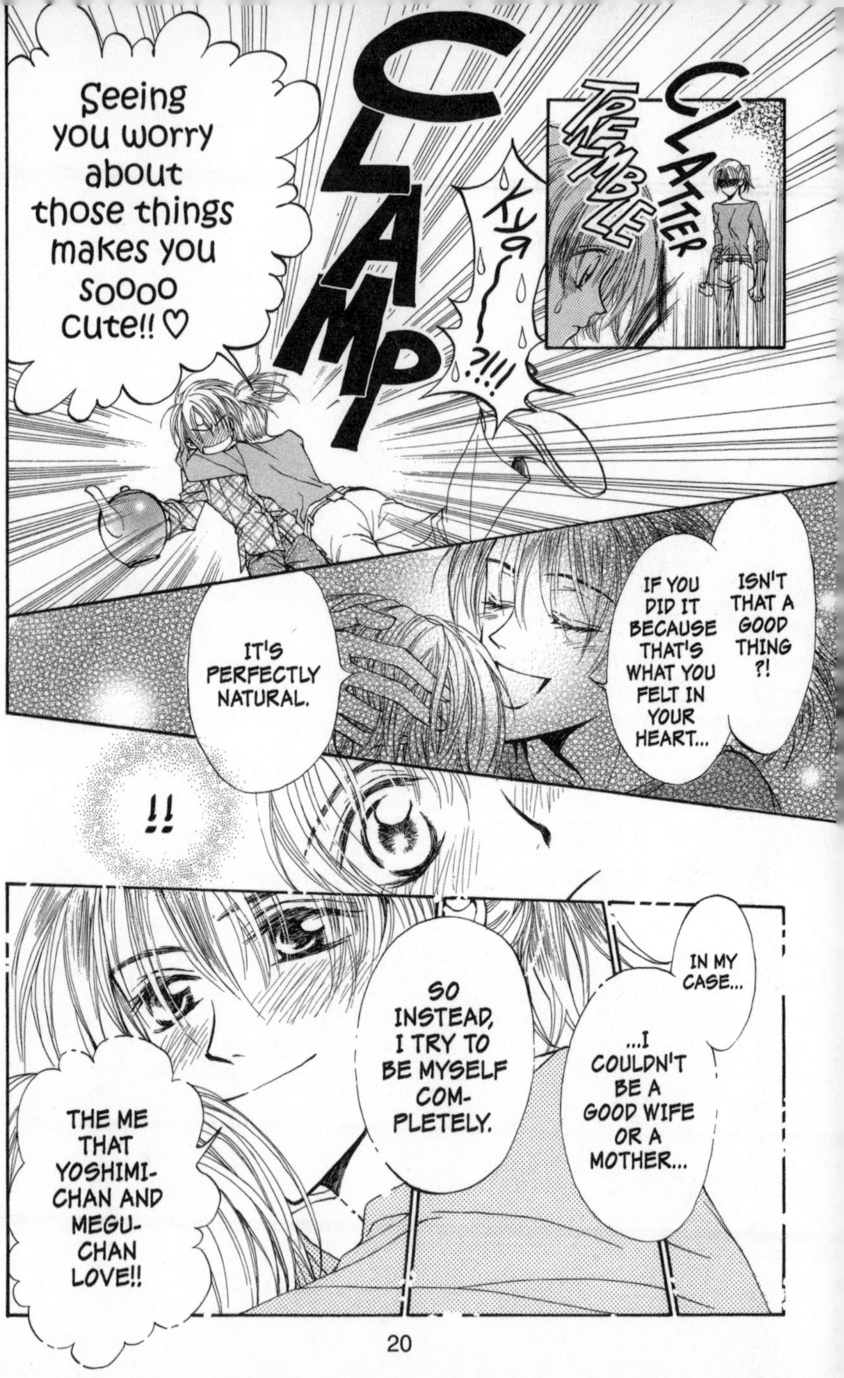
CLATTER
TREMBLE
Kya—
?!!!
CLAMP
Seeing you worry about those things makes you soOOO cute!! ♡
ISN'T THAT A GOOD THING ?!
IF YOU DID IT BECAUSE THAT'S WHAT YOU FELT IN YOUR HEART...
IT'S PERFECTLY NATURAL.
!!
IN MY CASE...
...I COULDN'T BE A GOOD WIFE OR A MOTHER...
SO INSTEAD, I TRY TO BE MYSELF COM- PLETELY.
THE ME THAT YOSHIMI- CHAN AND MEGU- CHAN LOVE!!

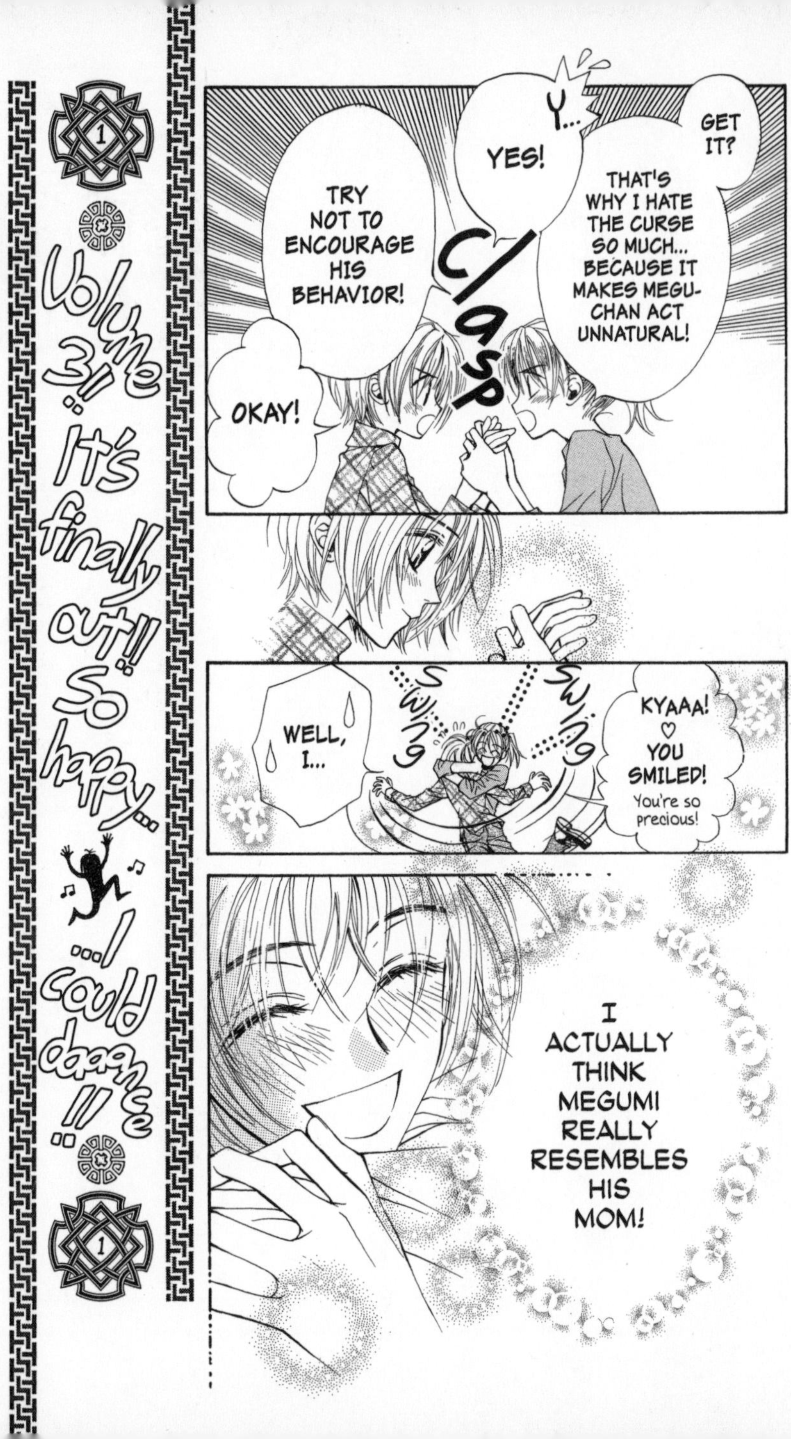
GET IT?
Y... YES!
THAT'S WHY I HATE THE CURSE SO MUCH... BECAUSE IT MAKES MEGU-CHAN ACT UNNATURAL!
TRY NOT TO ENCOURAGE HIS BEHAVIOR!
Clasp
OKAY!
KYAAA! ♡ YOU SMILED! You're so precious!
Swing
Swing
WELL, I...
I ACTUALLY THINK MEGUMI REALLY RESEMBLES HIS MOM!

Volume 3!! It's finally out!! So happy... ...I could daaance!!

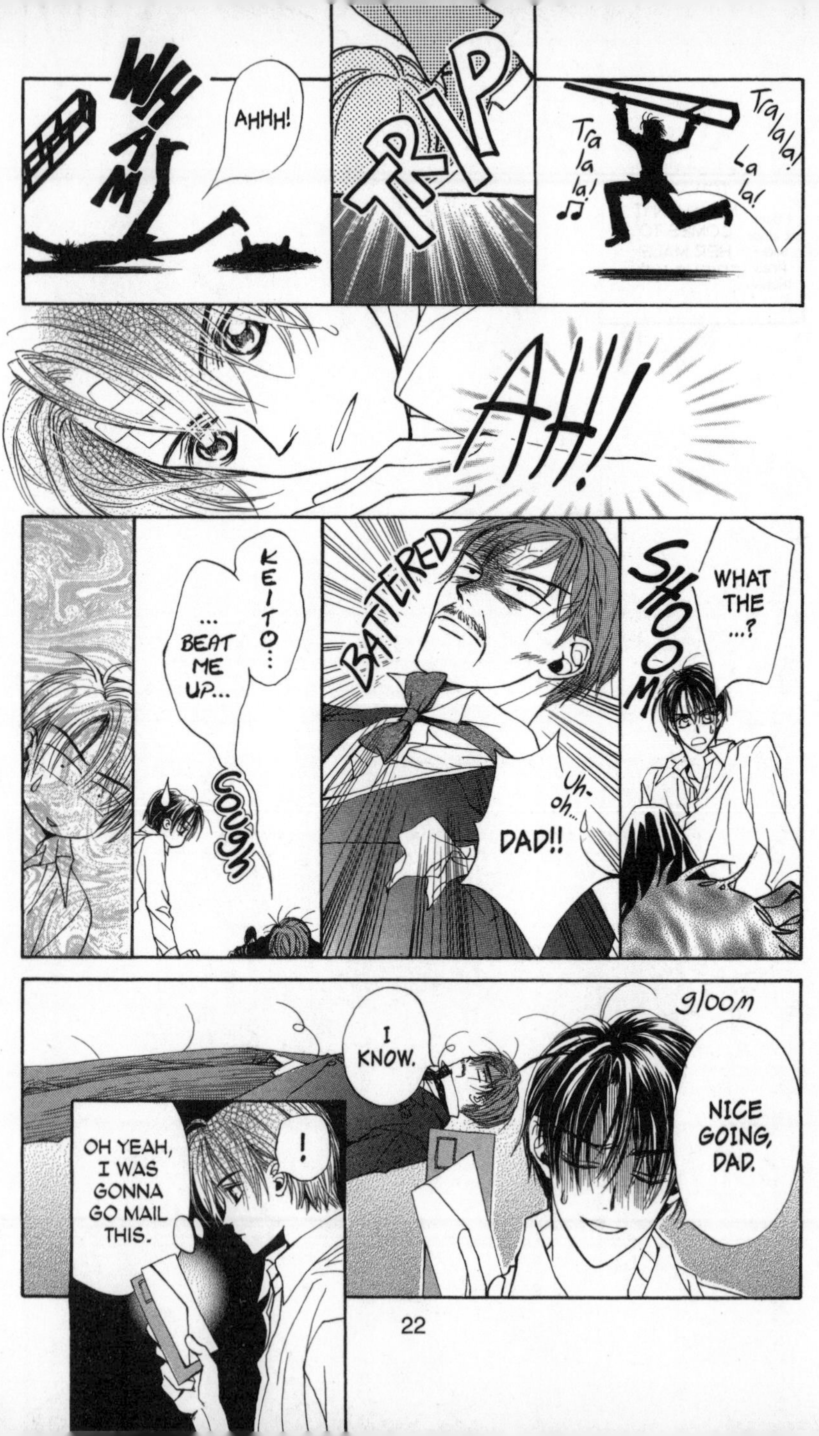

Tralala! La la!
Tra la la! ♪
TRIP
AHHH!
WHAM
AH!
WHAT THE ...?
SHOOOM
BATTERED
Uh-oh...
DAD!!
KEITO... ... BEAT ME UP...
COUGH
gloom
NICE GOING, DAD.
I KNOW.
!
OH YEAH, I WAS GONNA GO MAIL THIS.

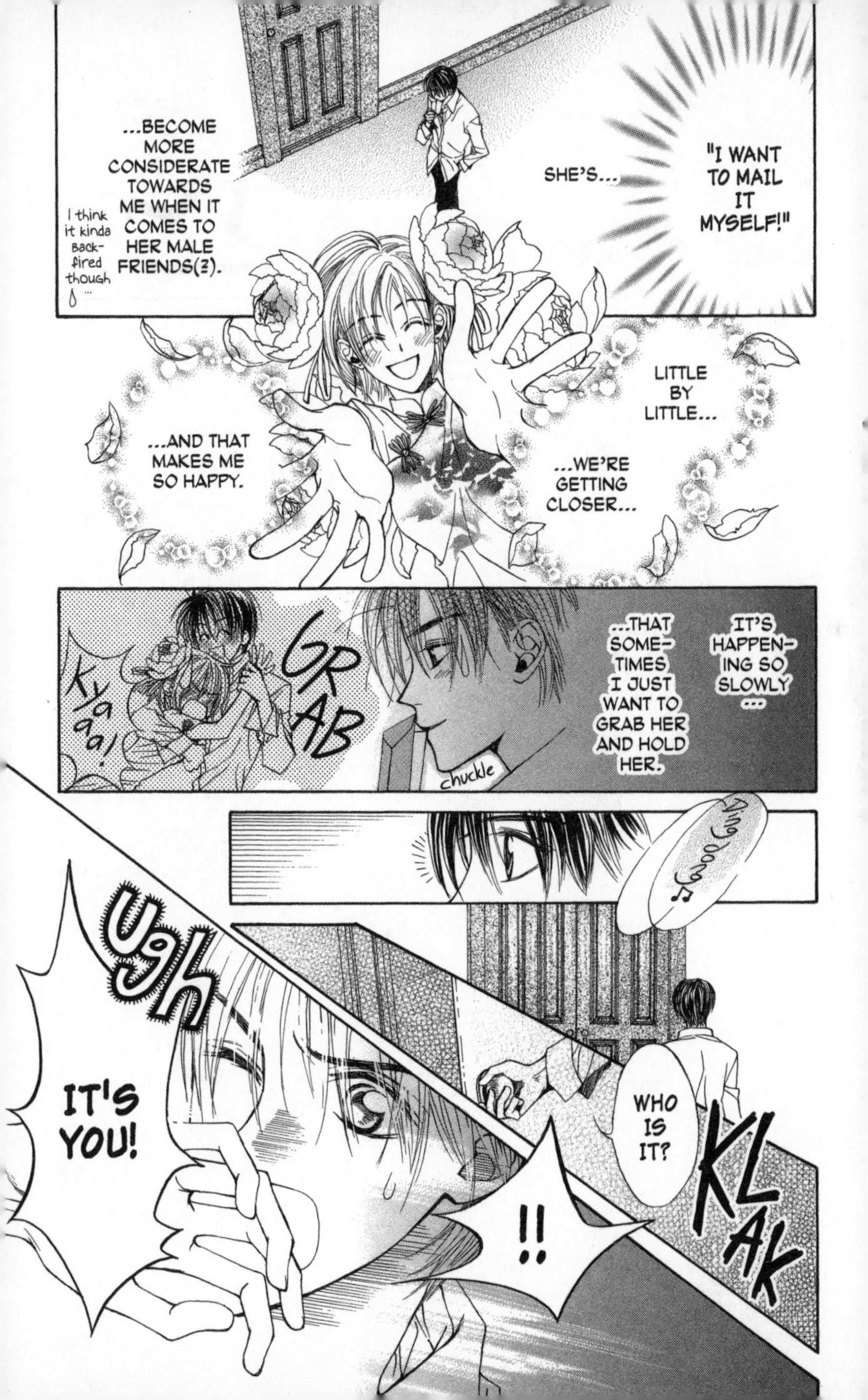
"I WANT TO MAIL IT MYSELF!"
SHE'S...
...BECOME MORE CONSIDERATE TOWARDS ME WHEN IT COMES TO HER MALE FRIENDS(?).
I think it kinda Back-fired though ...
LITTLE BY LITTLE...
...WE'RE GETTING CLOSER...
...AND THAT MAKES ME SO HAPPY.
IT'S HAPPENING SO SLOWLY...
...THAT SOMETIMES I JUST WANT TO GRAB HER AND HOLD HER.
chuckle
GRAB
Kyaaa!
Ding dong♪
WHO IS IT?
KLAK
!!
Ugh
IT'S YOU!

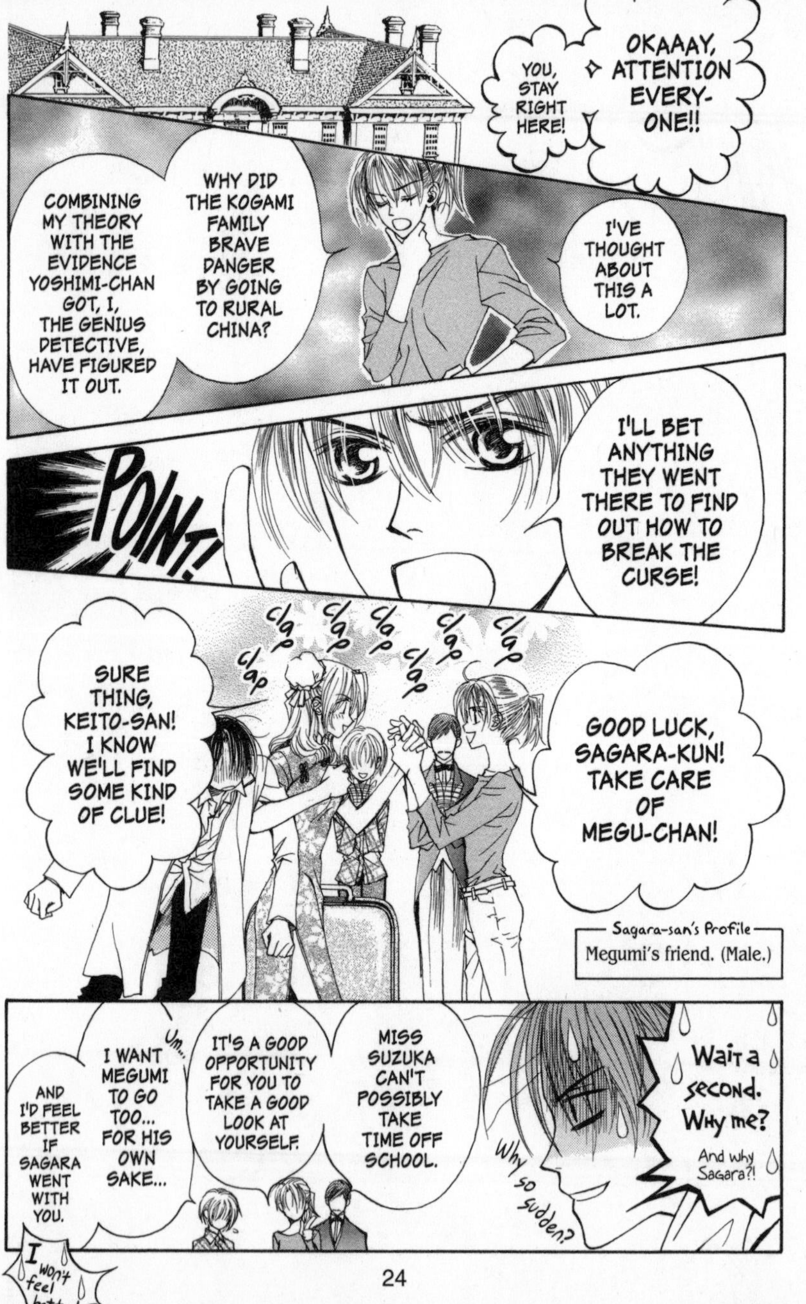
OKAAAY, ATTENTION EVERY-ONE!!
YOU, STAY RIGHT HERE!
I'VE THOUGHT ABOUT THIS A LOT.
WHY DID THE KOGAMI FAMILY BRAVE DANGER BY GOING TO RURAL CHINA?
COMBINING MY THEORY WITH THE EVIDENCE YOSHIMI-CHAN GOT, I, THE GENIUS DETECTIVE, HAVE FIGURED IT OUT.
I'LL BET ANYTHING THEY WENT THERE TO FIND OUT HOW TO BREAK THE CURSE!
POINT!
GOOD LUCK, SAGARA-KUN! TAKE CARE OF MEGU-CHAN!
clap clap clap clap clap clap clap
SURE THING, KEITO-SAN! I KNOW WE'LL FIND SOME KIND OF CLUE!
Sagara-san's Profile
Megumi's friend. (Male.)
Wait a second. Why me?
And why Sagara?!
Why so sudden?
MISS SUZUKA CAN'T POSSIBLY TAKE TIME OFF SCHOOL.
IT'S A GOOD OPPORTUNITY FOR YOU TO TAKE A GOOD LOOK AT YOURSELF.
Um...
I WANT MEGUMI TO GO TOO... FOR HIS OWN SAKE...
AND I'D FEEL BETTER IF SAGARA WENT WITH YOU.
I won't feel better!

Story

Our story is set at Seisou Academy, which is split into the General Education School and Music School. One day Kahoko, a Gen Ed student, encounters a music fairy named Lili, who gives her a magic violin that anyone can play. All of a sudden, Kahoko finds herself in the school's music competition with good-looking, quirky Music School students as her fellow contestants! Kahoko eventually comes to accept this daunting task and actually finds herself enjoying music. And now the first round is about to begin...!

DON'T TELL ANYBODY ABOUT WHAT YOU JUST SAW.

YOU MEAN THE PIANO ...?

sigh...

...

WHY...?

Previously ...

Kahoko has managed to find an accompanist, a dress, and even a musical piece that is appropriate for the theme of the first round, "A Beginning." Kahoko also discovered that her fellow Gen Ed student Ryotaro is a phenomenal pianist, but he makes her swear to keep his talents a secret. Now the first round is finally about to begin...

The music fairy Lili, who got Kahoko caught up in this affair.

La Corda d'Oro

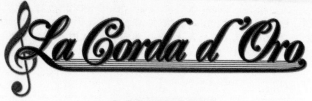

CONTENTS

Volume 3

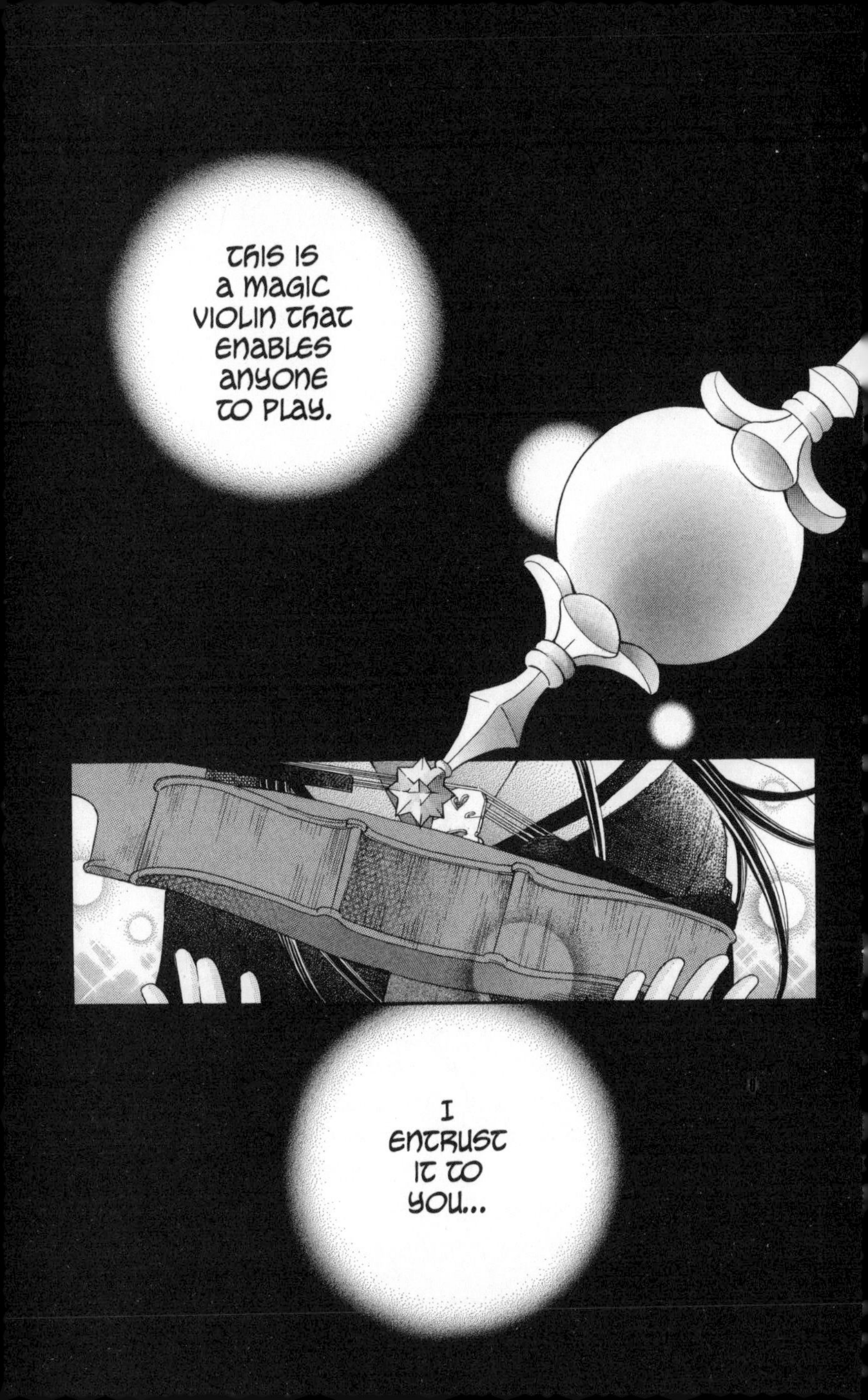
THIS IS A MAGIC VIOLIN THAT ENABLES ANYONE TO PLAY.
I ENTRUST IT TO YOU...

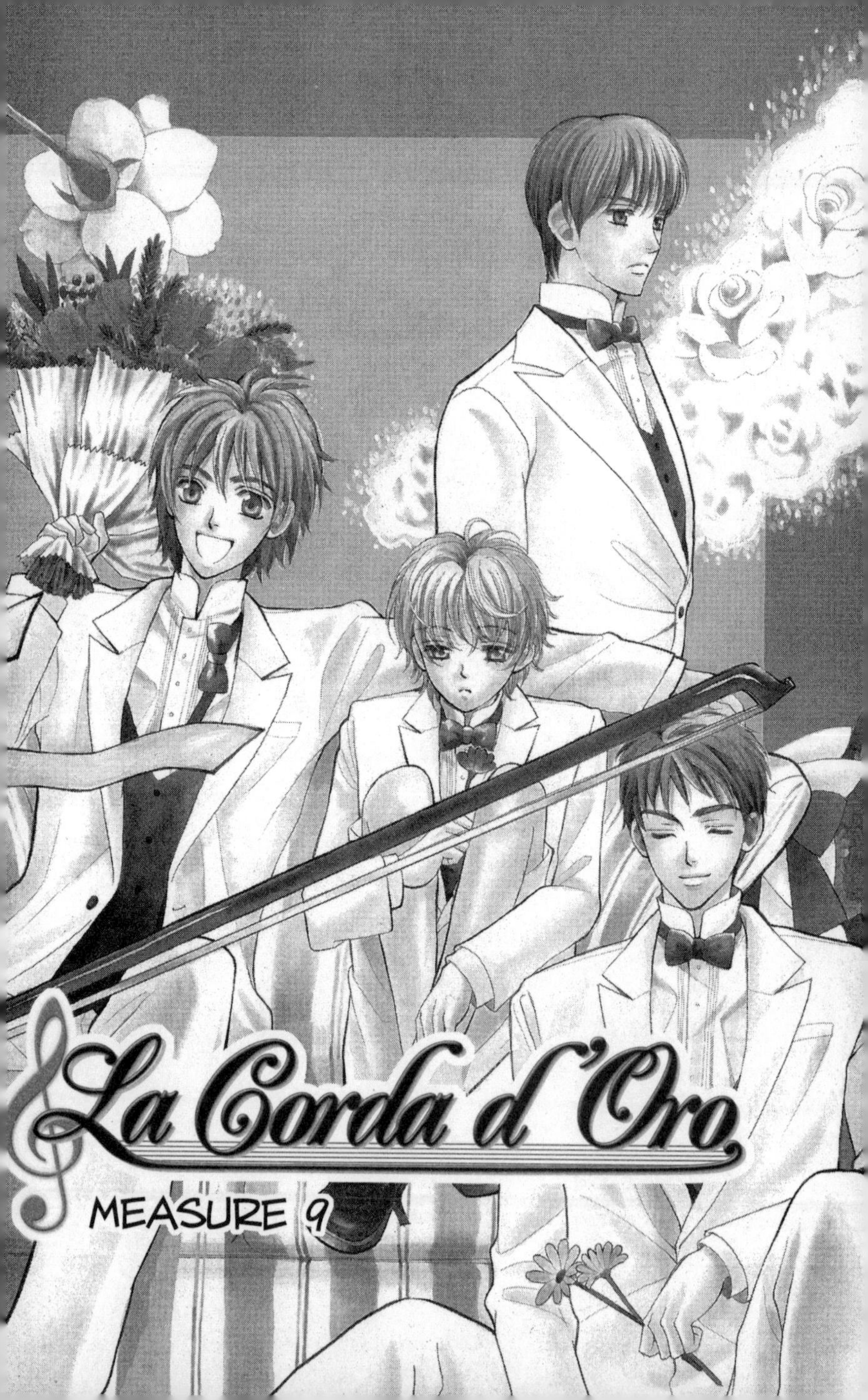
La Corda d'Oro
MEASURE 9

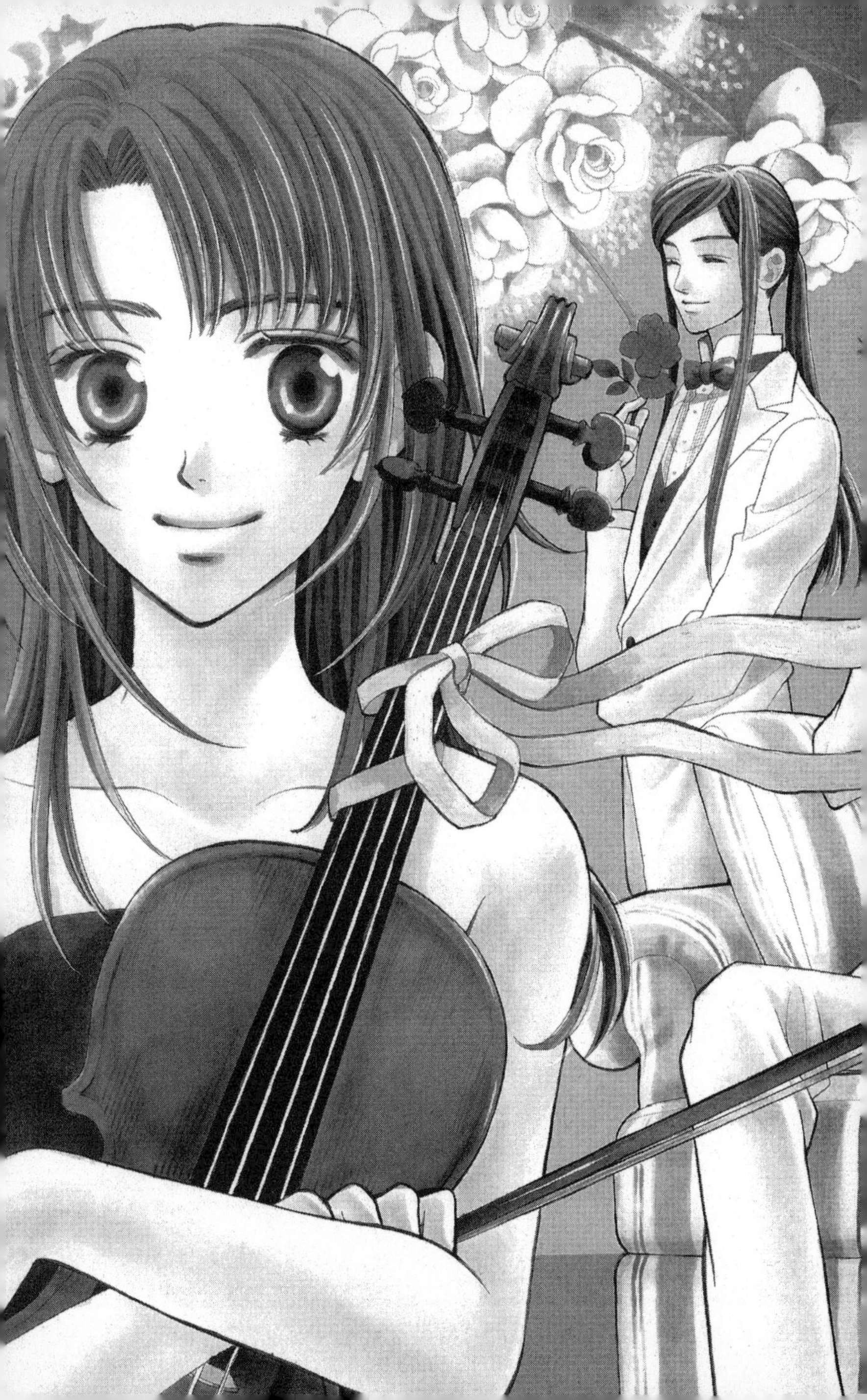

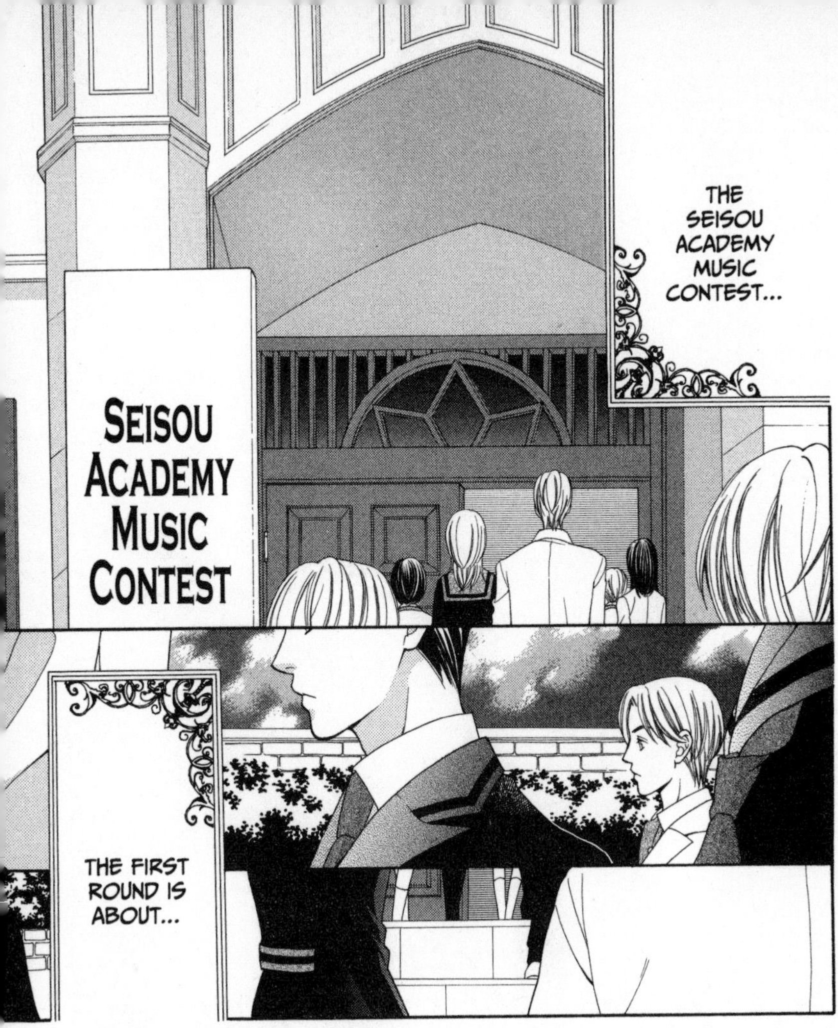
THE SEISOU ACADEMY MUSIC CONTEST...
SEISOU ACADEMY MUSIC CONTEST
THE FIRST ROUND IS ABOUT...

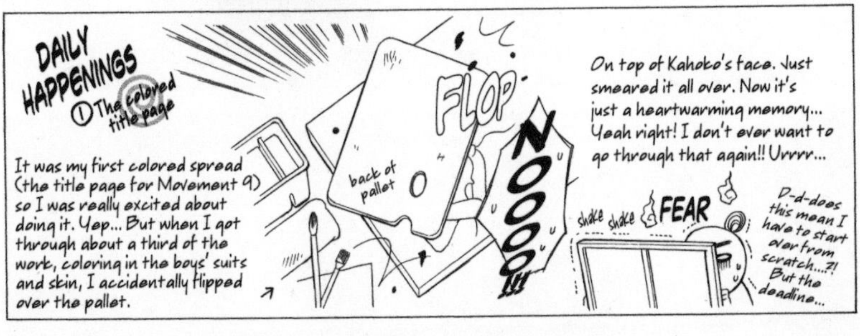
DAILY HAPPENINGS
① The colored title page
It was my first colored spread (the title page for Movement 9) so I was really excited about doing it. Yep... But when I got through about a third of the work, coloring in the boys' suits and skin, I accidentally flipped over the pallet.
back of pallet
FLOP
NOOOOO!!!
On top of Kahoko's face. Just smeared it all over. Now it's just a heartwarming memory... Yeah right! I don't ever want to go through that again!! Urrrr...
shake shake
FEAR
D-d-does this mean I have to start over from scratch...?! But the deadline...

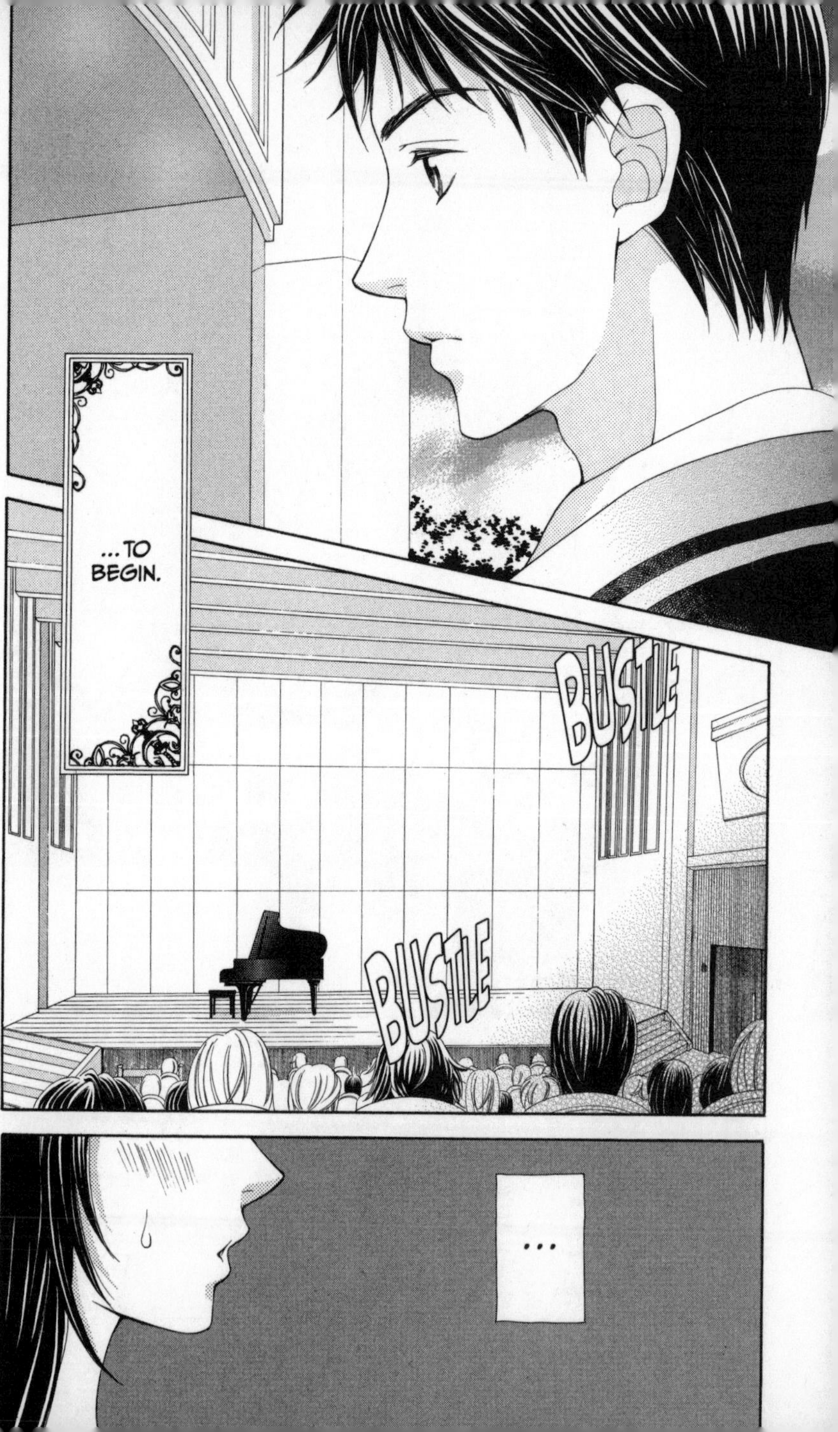
...TO BEGIN.
BUSTLE
BUSTLE
...

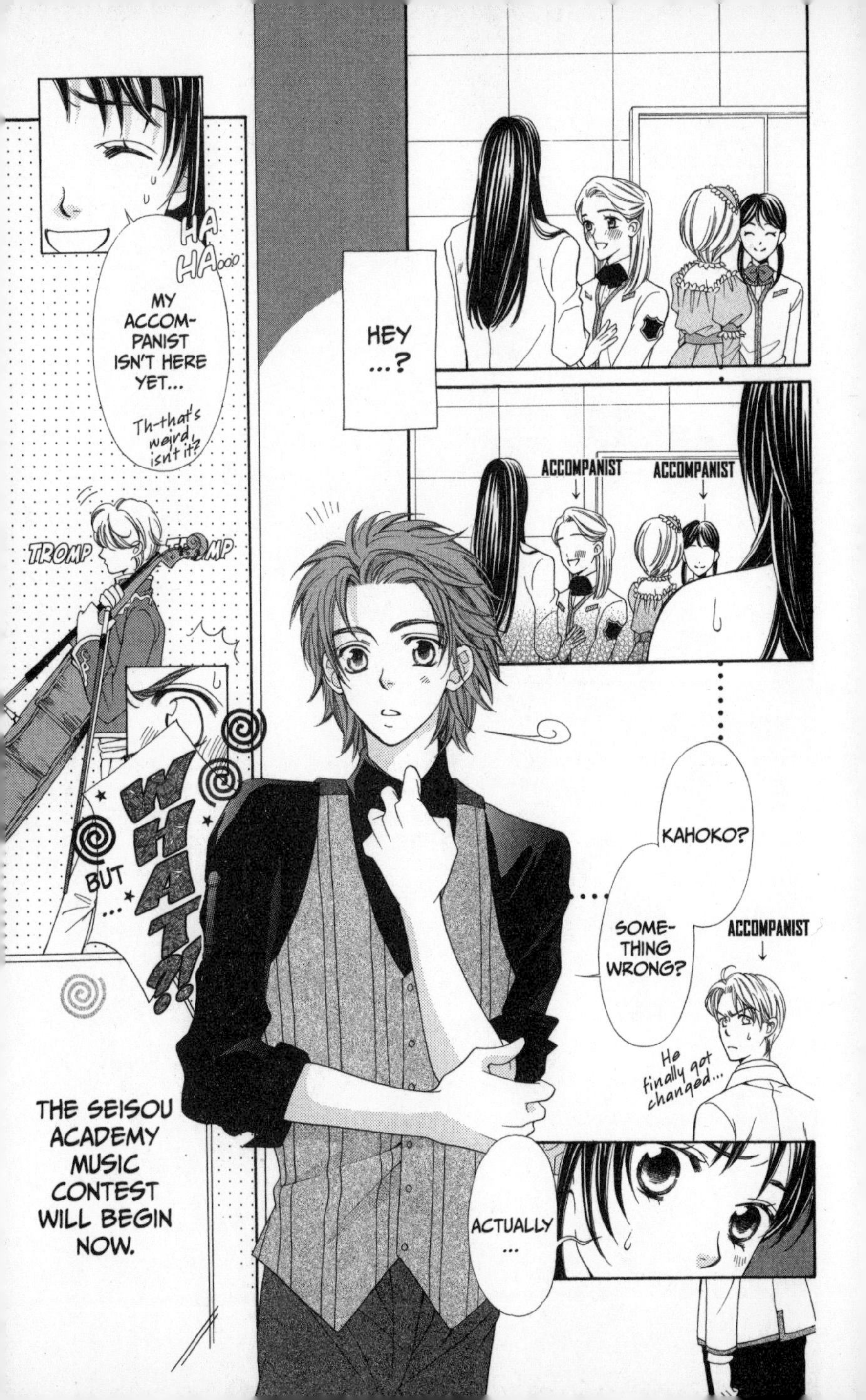
HEY ...?
ACCOMPANIST
ACCOMPANIST
KAHOKO?
SOMETHING WRONG?
ACCOMPANIST
He finally got changed...
ACTUALLY ...
HA HA...
MY ACCOMPANIST ISN'T HERE YET...
Th-that's weird, isn't it?
TROMP TROMP
WHAT?!
BUT ...
THE SEISOU ACADEMY MUSIC CONTEST WILL BEGIN NOW.

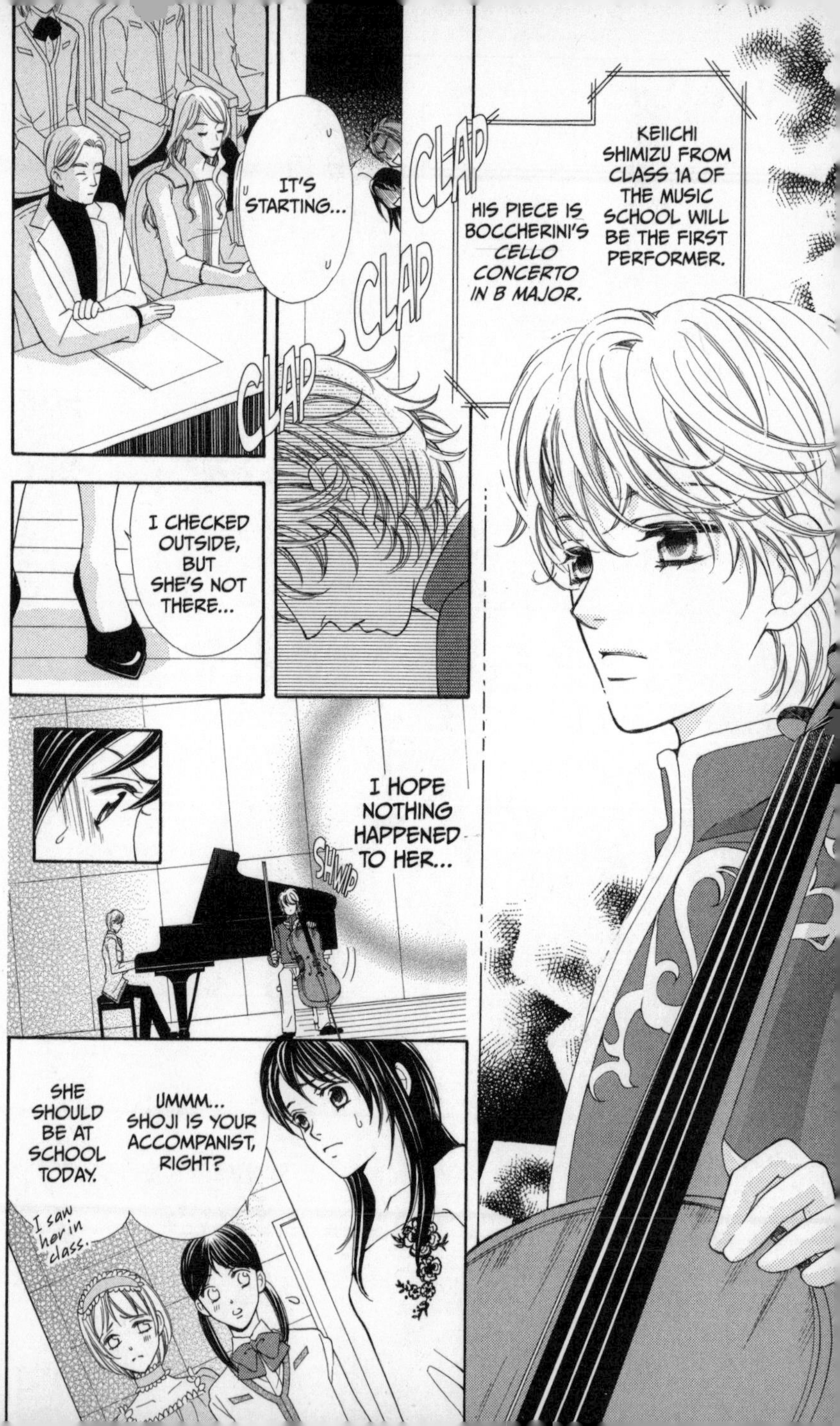
KEIICHI SHIMIZU FROM CLASS 1A OF THE MUSIC SCHOOL WILL BE THE FIRST PERFORMER.
HIS PIECE IS BOCCHERINI'S CELLO CONCERTO IN B MAJOR.
CLAP
CLAP
IT'S STARTING...
CLAP
I CHECKED OUTSIDE, BUT SHE'S NOT THERE...
I HOPE NOTHING HAPPENED TO HER...
SHWIP
UMMM... SHOJI IS YOUR ACCOMPANIST, RIGHT?
SHE SHOULD BE AT SCHOOL TODAY.
I saw her in class.

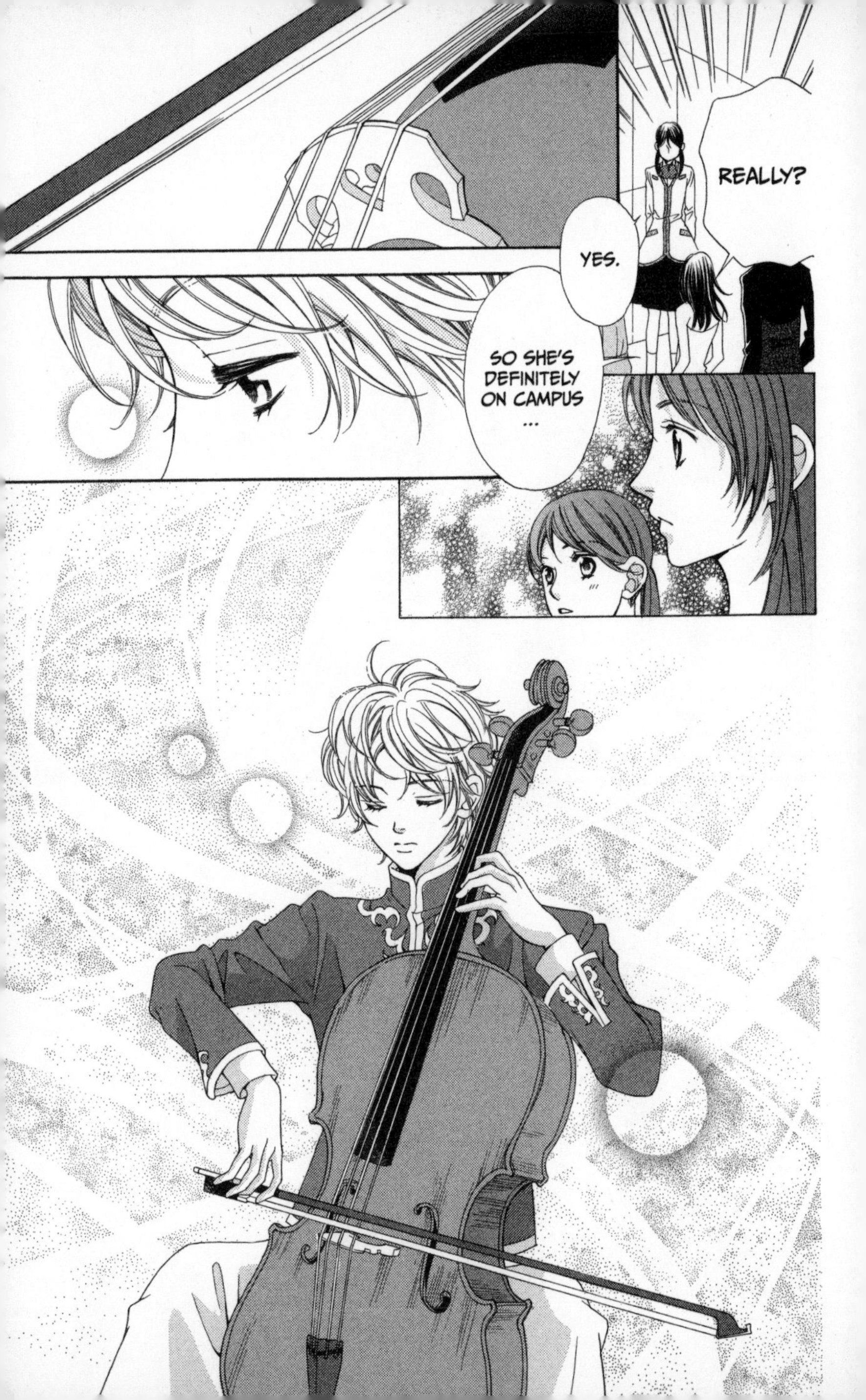
REALLY?
YES.
SO SHE'S DEFINITELY ON CAMPUS ...

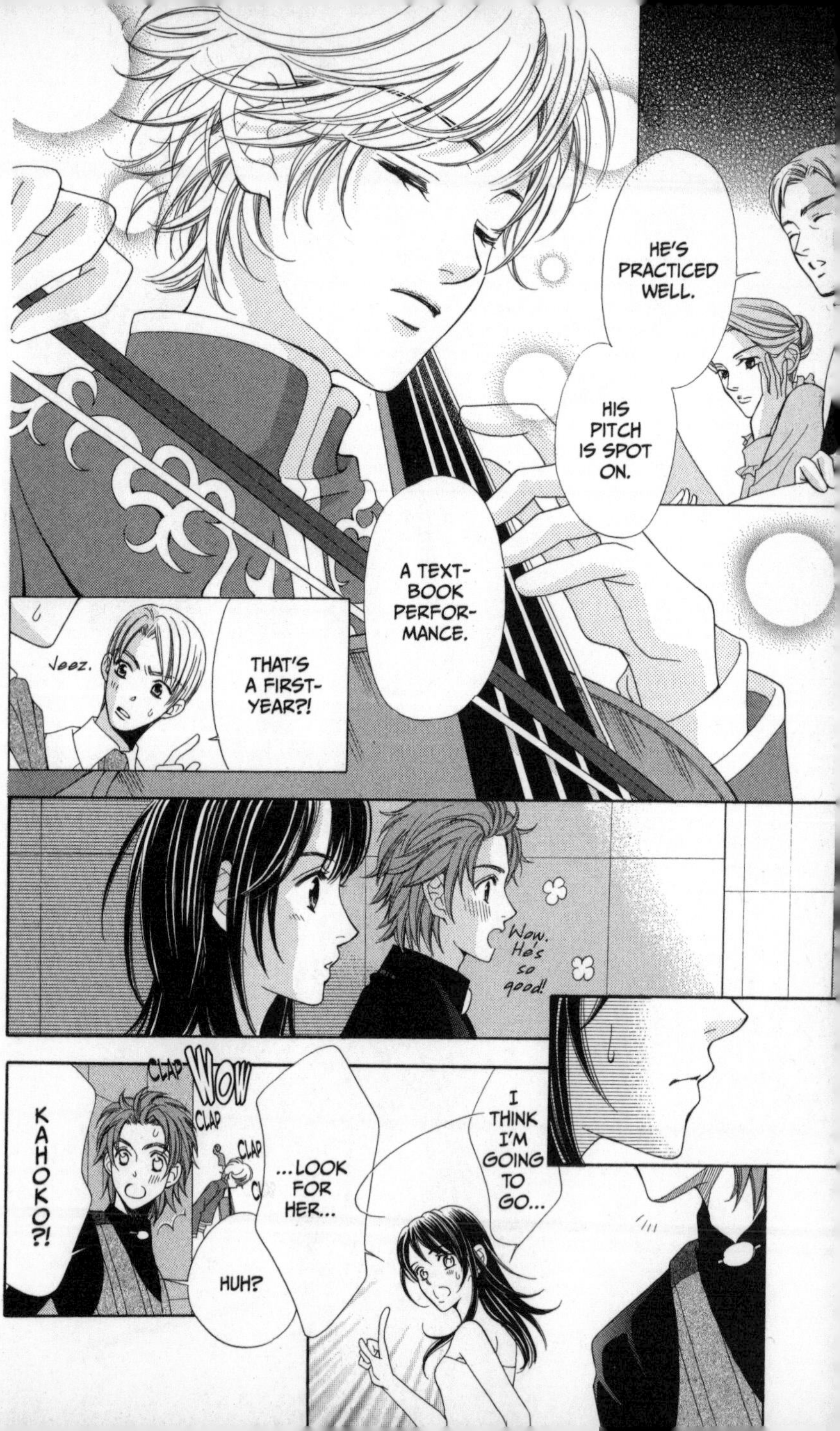
HE'S PRACTICED WELL.
HIS PITCH IS SPOT ON.
A TEXT-BOOK PERFORMANCE.
THAT'S A FIRST-YEAR?!
Jeez.
Wow. He's so good!
I THINK I'M GOING TO GO...
...LOOK FOR HER...
HUH?
CLAP
WOW
CLAP
CLAP
KAHOKO?!

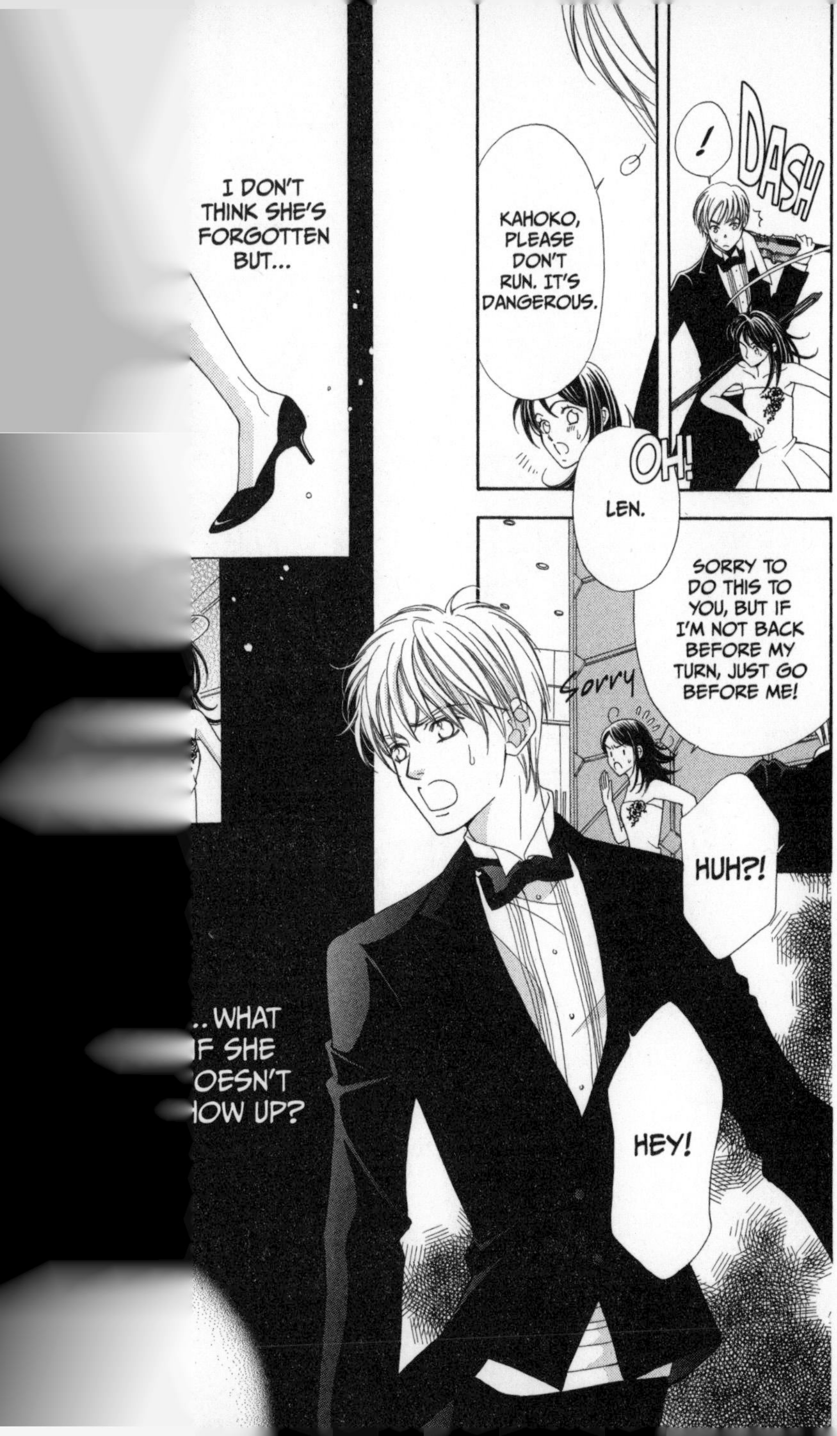
!
DASH
KAHOKO, PLEASE DON'T RUN. IT'S DANGEROUS.
OH!
LEN.
SORRY TO DO THIS TO YOU, BUT IF I'M NOT BACK BEFORE MY TURN, JUST GO BEFORE ME!
Sorry
HUH?!
HEY!
I DON'T THINK SHE'S FORGOTTEN BUT...
..WHAT F SHE OESN'T HOW UP?

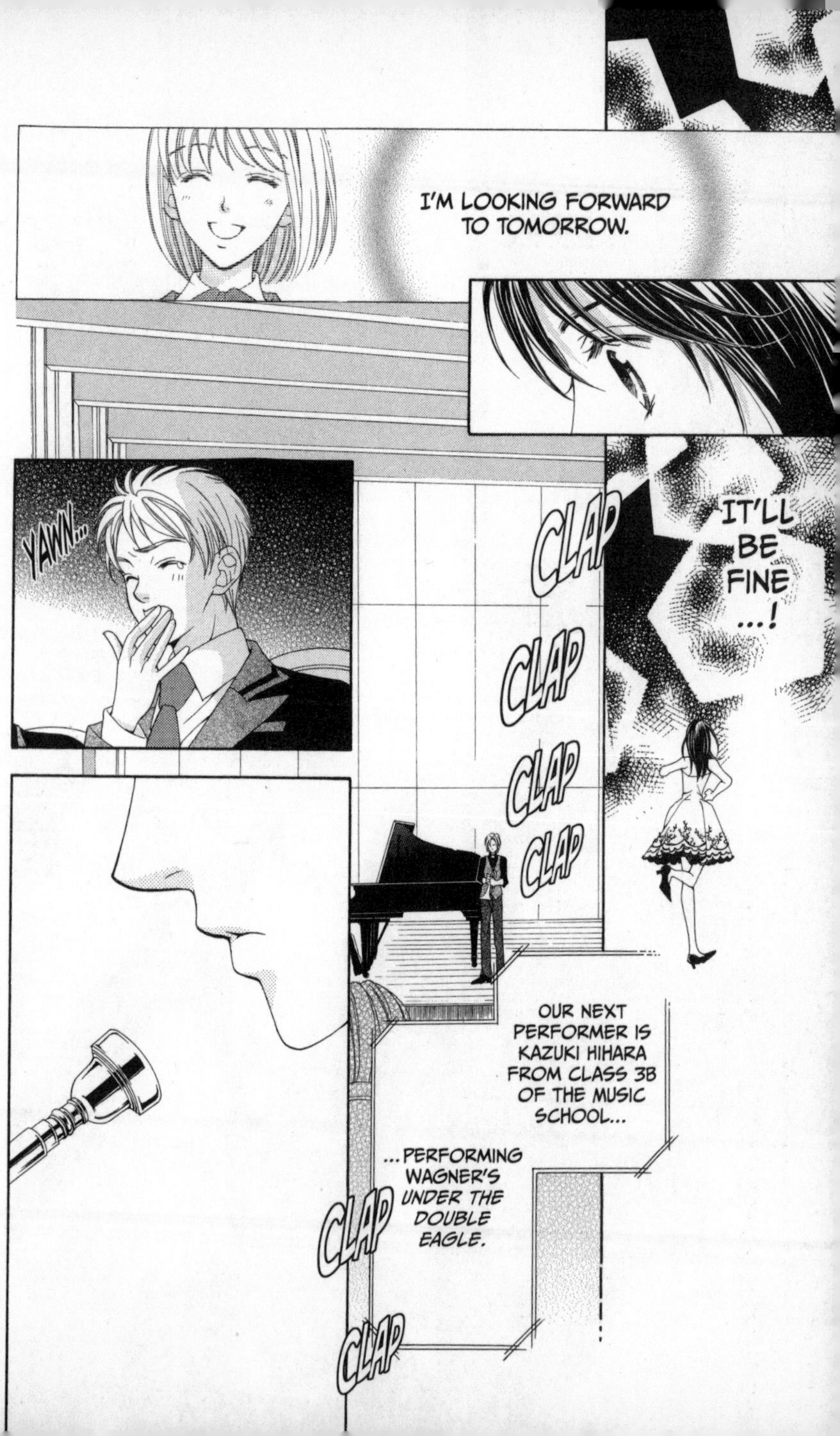
I'M LOOKING FORWARD TO TOMORROW.
IT'LL BE FINE ...!
CLAP
CLAP
CLAP
CLAP
YAWN...
OUR NEXT PERFORMER IS KAZUKI HIHARA FROM CLASS 3B OF THE MUSIC SCHOOL...
...PERFORMING WAGNER'S UNDER THE DOUBLE EAGLE.
CLAP
CLAP

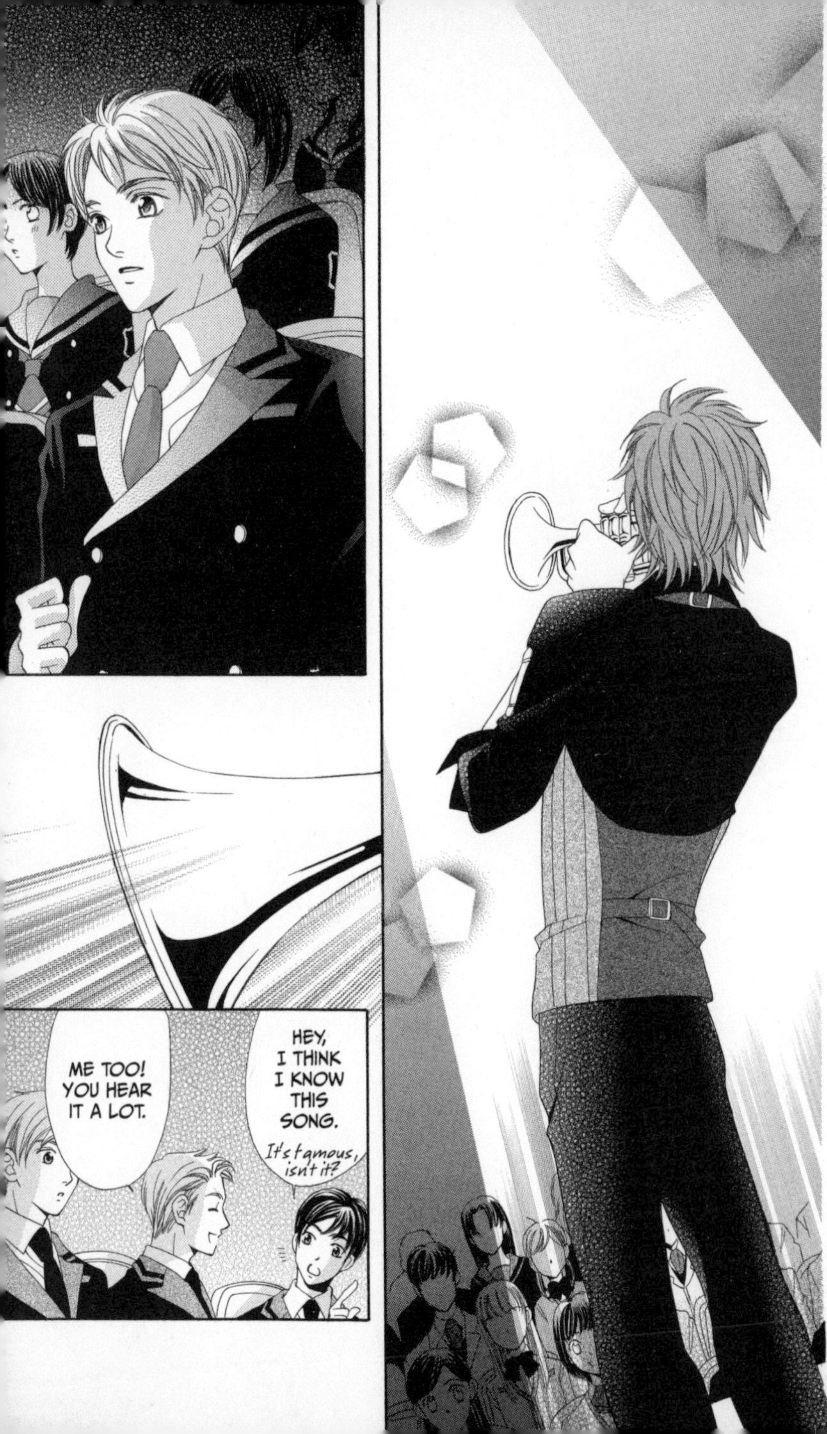
HEY, I THINK I KNOW THIS SONG.
It's famous, isn't it?
ME TOO! YOU HEAR IT A LOT.

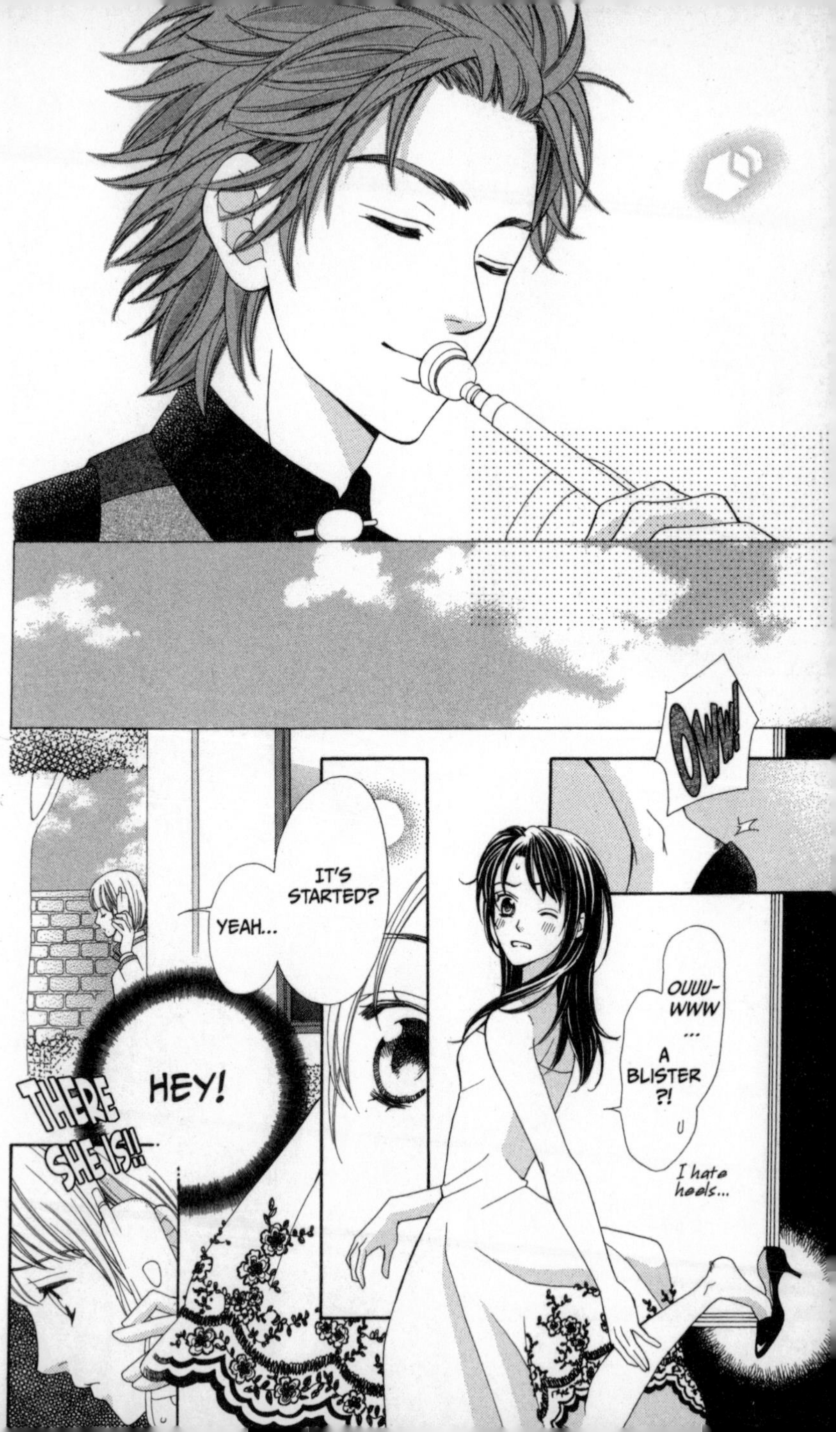
OWW!
OUUU-WWW... A BLISTER?!
I hate heels...
IT'S STARTED?
YEAH...
HEY!
THERE SHE IS!!

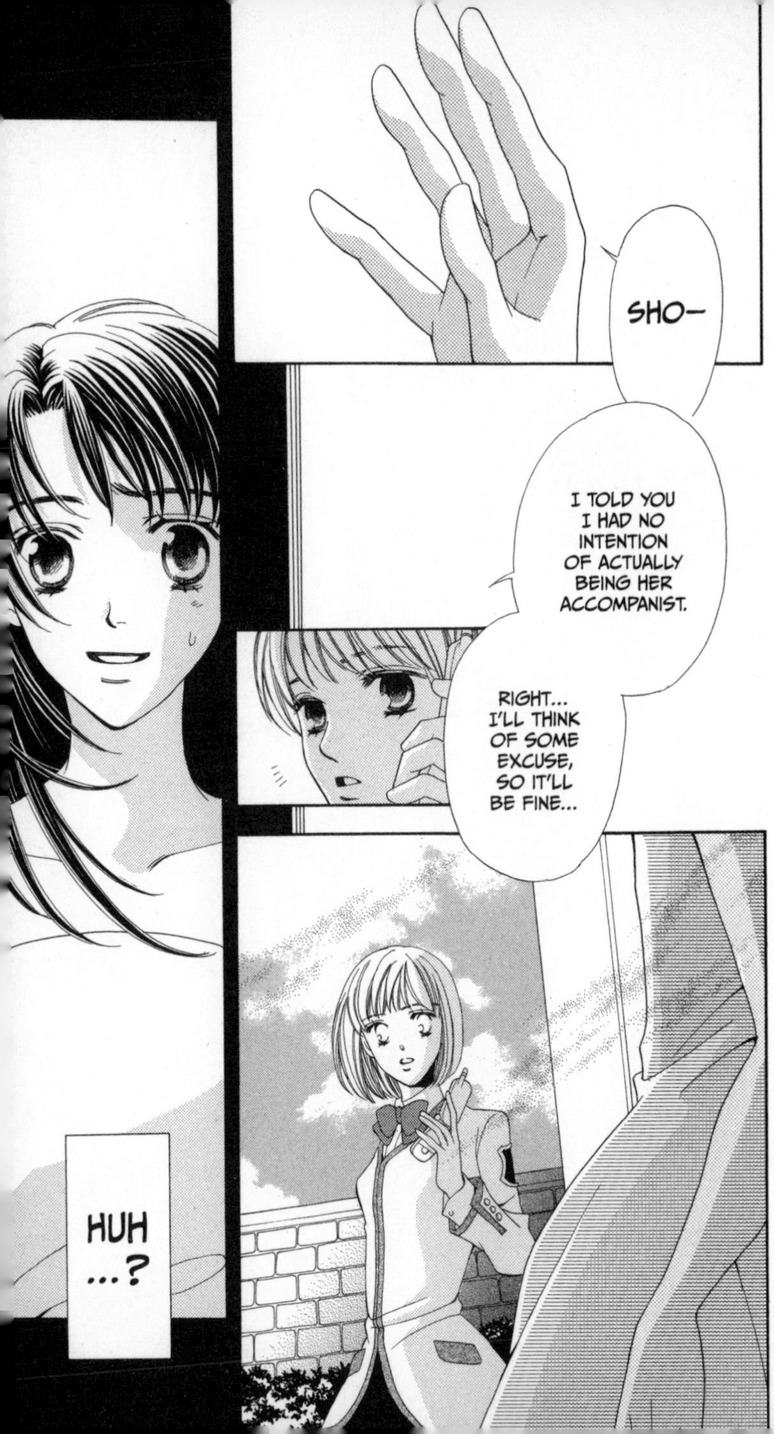
SHO—
I TOLD YOU I HAD NO INTENTION OF ACTUALLY BEING HER ACCOMPANIST.
RIGHT... I'LL THINK OF SOME EXCUSE, SO IT'LL BE FINE...
HUH ...?

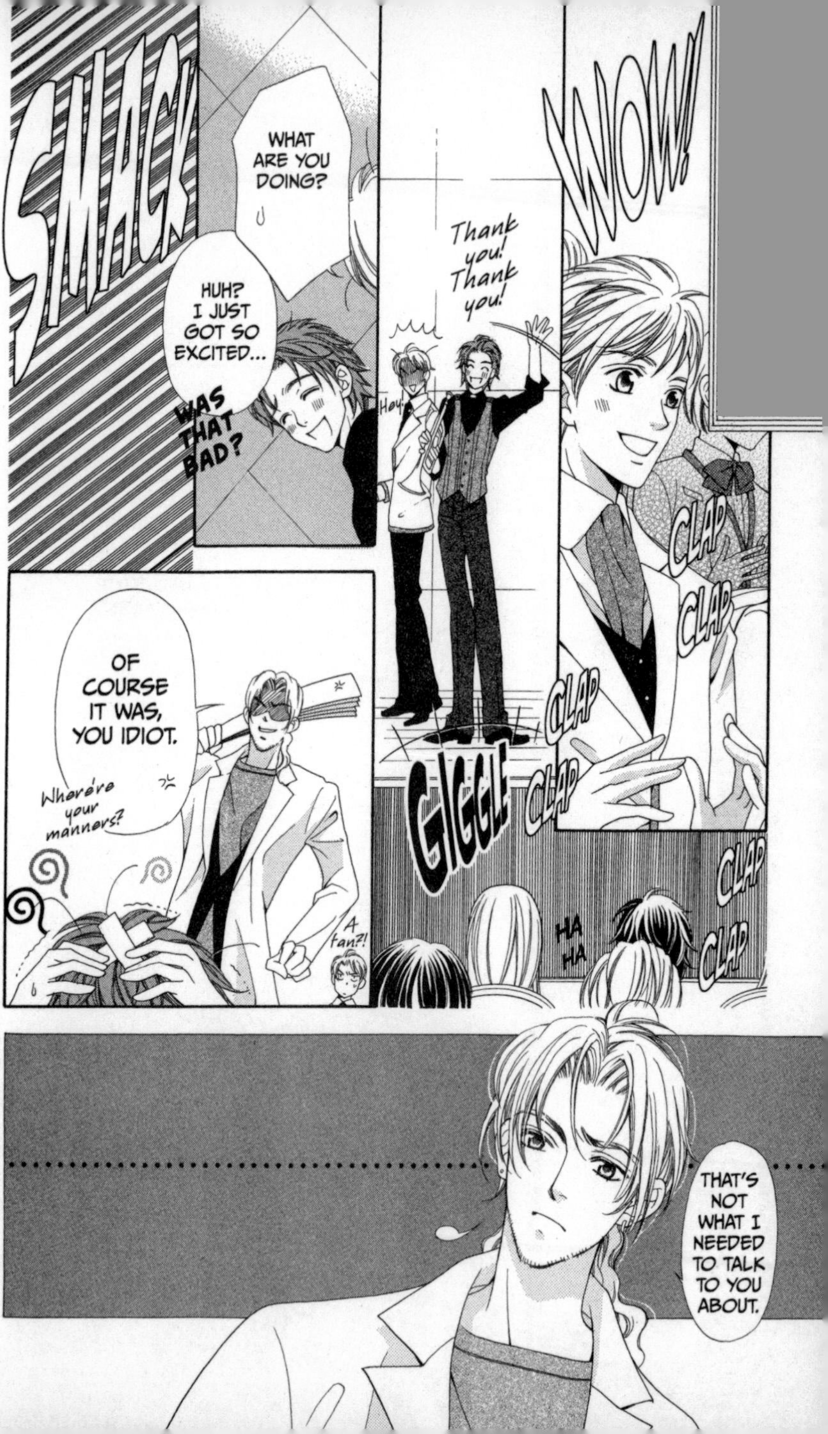
WOW!
CLAP
CLAP
CLAP
CLAP
CLAP
CLAP
Thank you! Thank you!
Hey!
GIGGLE
HA HA
SMACK
WHAT ARE YOU DOING?
HUH? I JUST GOT SO EXCITED...
WAS THAT BAD?
OF COURSE IT WAS, YOU IDIOT.
Where're your manners?
4 tan?!
THAT'S NOT WHAT I NEEDED TO TALK TO YOU ABOUT.

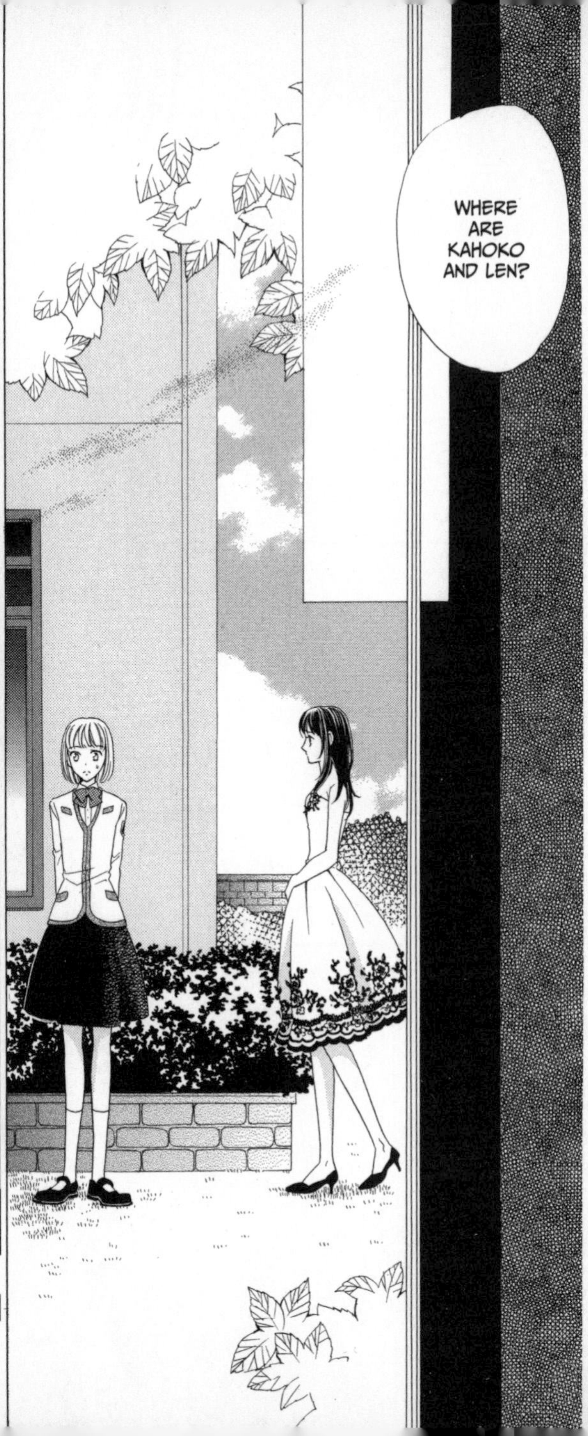
WHERE ARE KAHOKO AND LEN?

ONE

Hello.
I'm Yuki Kure.
Thank you for buying volume 3 of *La Corda d'Oro*.

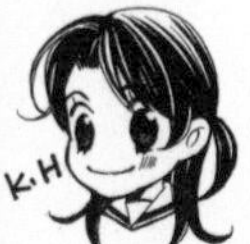
K.H

The third volume continues with the first round that started in volume 2.

Everyone except Kahoko is wearing their outfits from the game.
It's refreshing drawing them in something other than their uniforms.
It's been fun.

I hope you enjoy it.
Until next time...

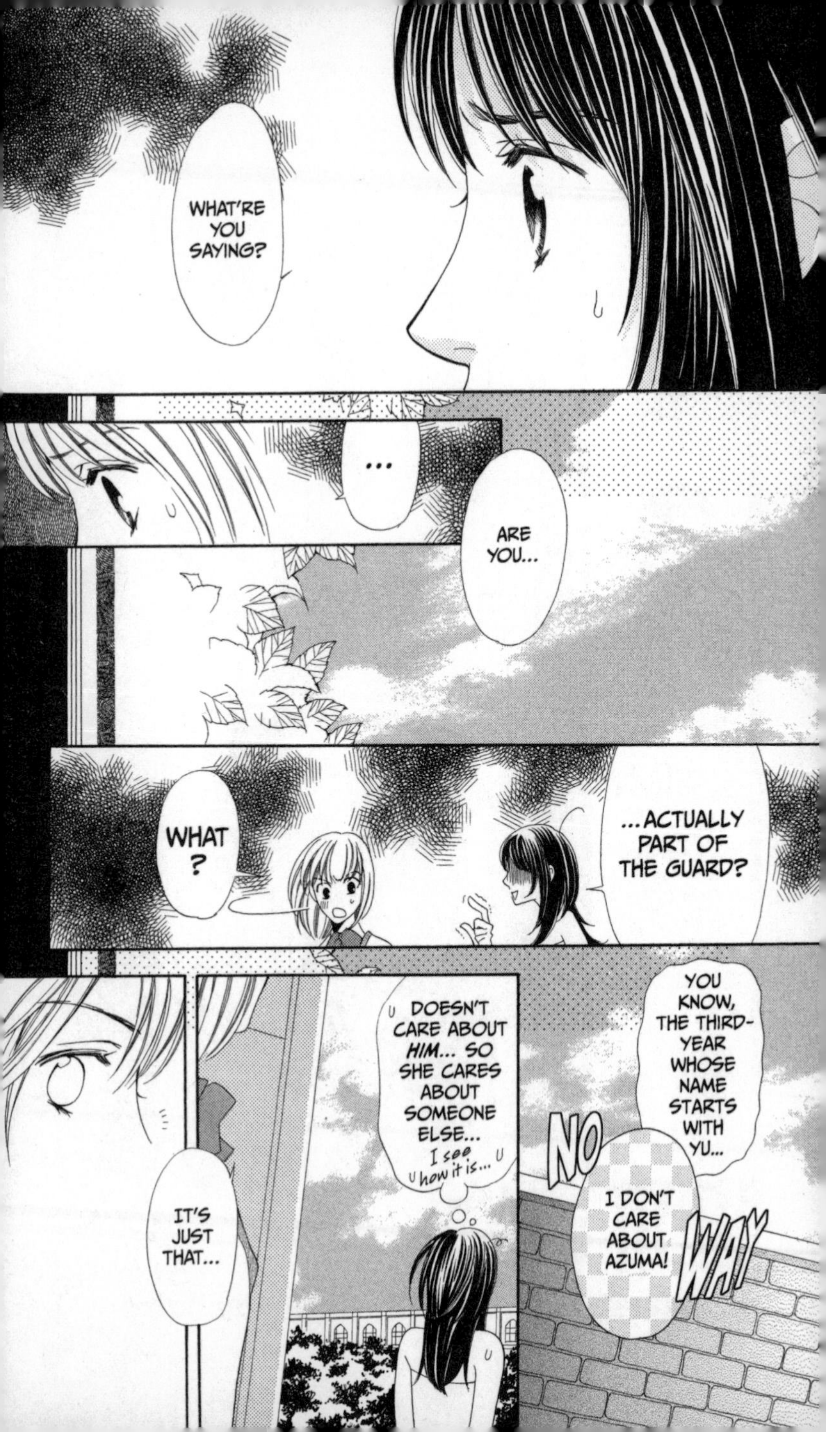

WHAT'RE YOU SAYING?
...
ARE YOU...
...ACTUALLY PART OF THE GUARD?
WHAT?
YOU KNOW, THE THIRD-YEAR WHOSE NAME STARTS WITH YU...
NO WAY
I DON'T CARE ABOUT AZUMA!
DOESN'T CARE ABOUT HIM... SO SHE CARES ABOUT SOMEONE ELSE...
I see how it is...
IT'S JUST THAT...

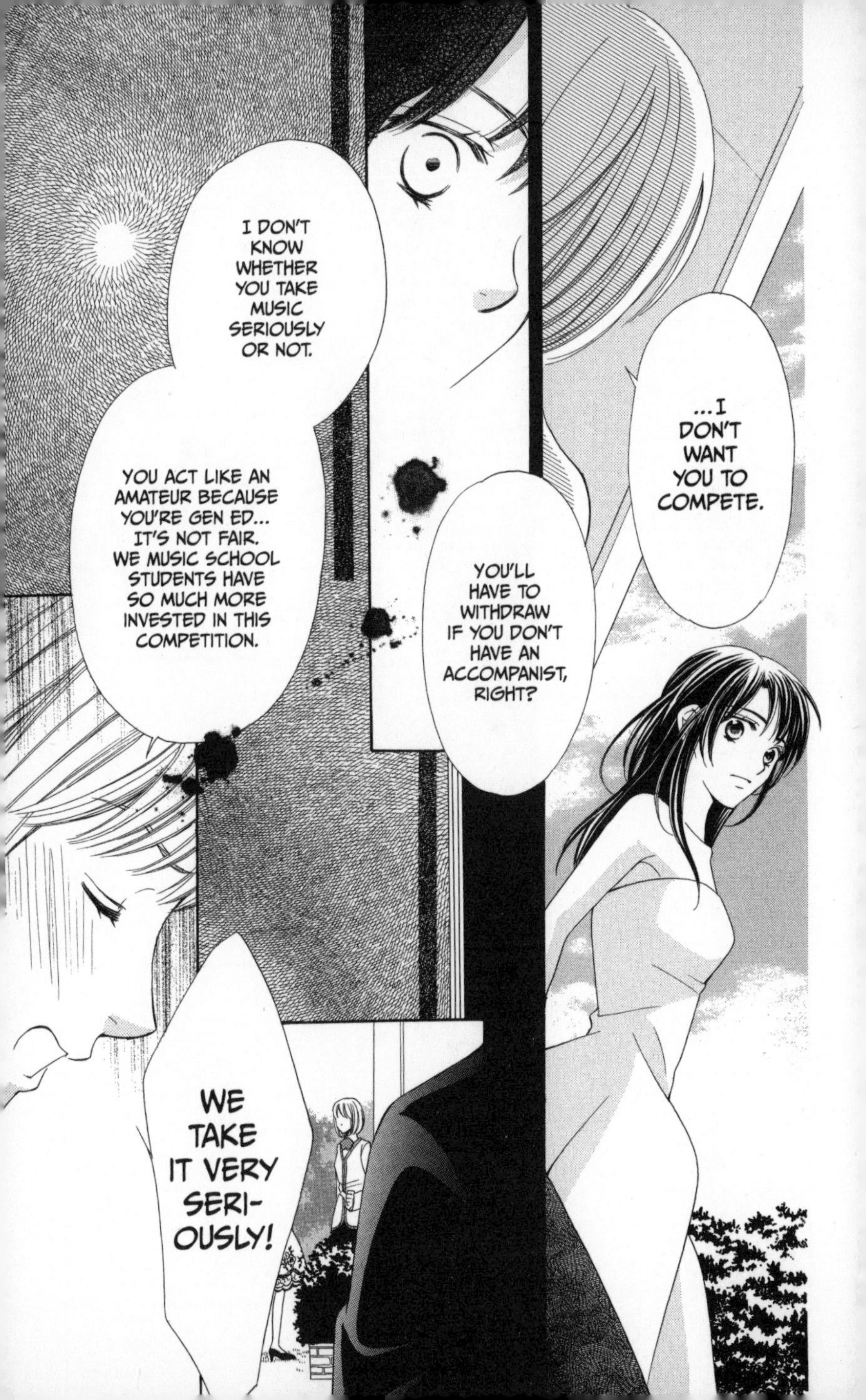
...I DON'T WANT YOU TO COMPETE.
YOU'LL HAVE TO WITHDRAW IF YOU DON'T HAVE AN ACCOMPANIST, RIGHT?
I DON'T KNOW WHETHER YOU TAKE MUSIC SERIOUSLY OR NOT.
YOU ACT LIKE AN AMATEUR BECAUSE YOU'RE GEN ED... IT'S NOT FAIR. WE MUSIC SCHOOL STUDENTS HAVE SO MUCH MORE INVESTED IN THIS COMPETITION.
WE TAKE IT VERY SERI-OUSLY!

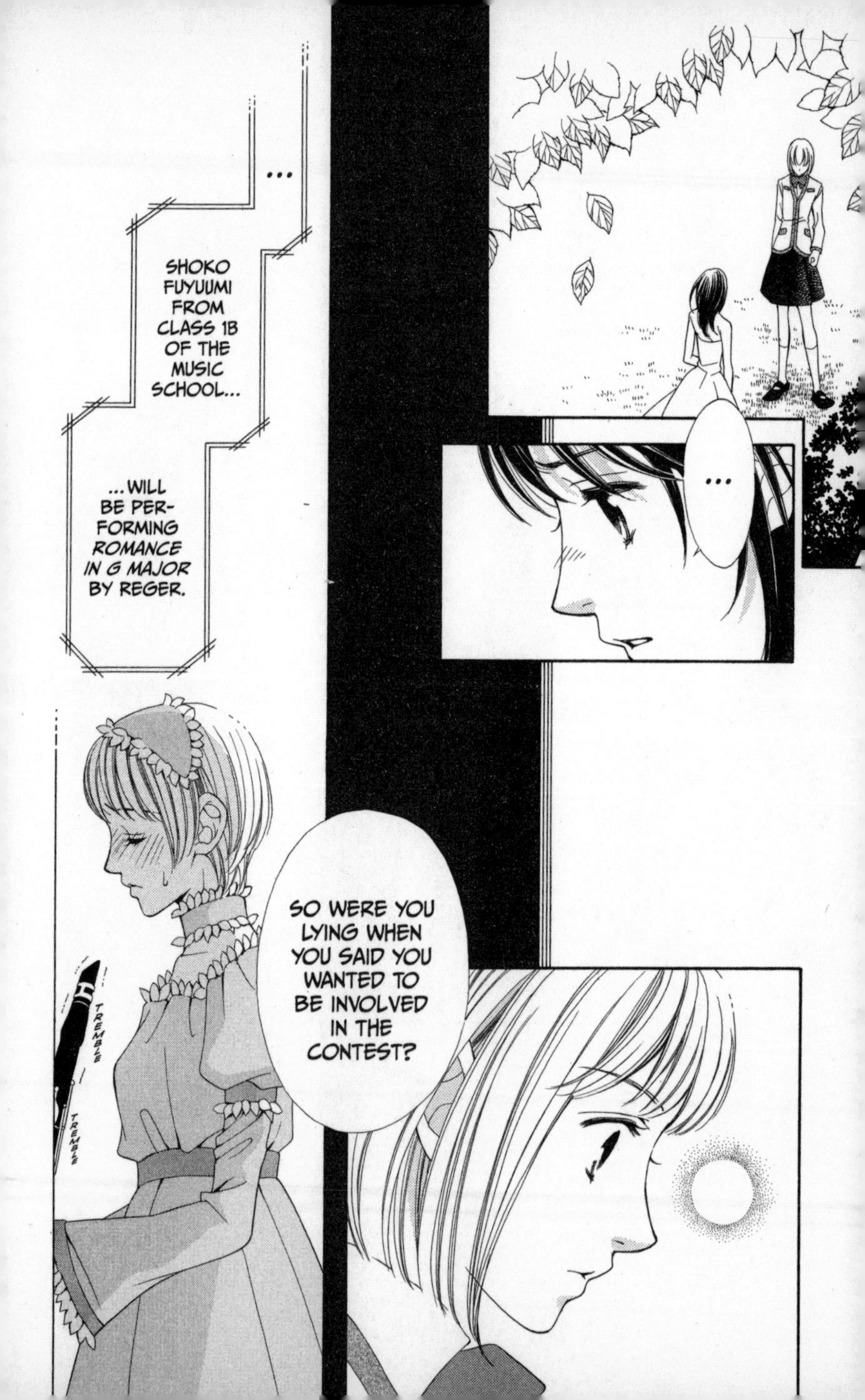

...
...
SHOKO FUYUUMI FROM CLASS 1B OF THE MUSIC SCHOOL...
...WILL BE PERFORMING ROMANCE IN G MAJOR BY REGER.
SO WERE YOU LYING WHEN YOU SAID YOU WANTED TO BE INVOLVED IN THE CONTEST?
TREMBLE
TREMBLE

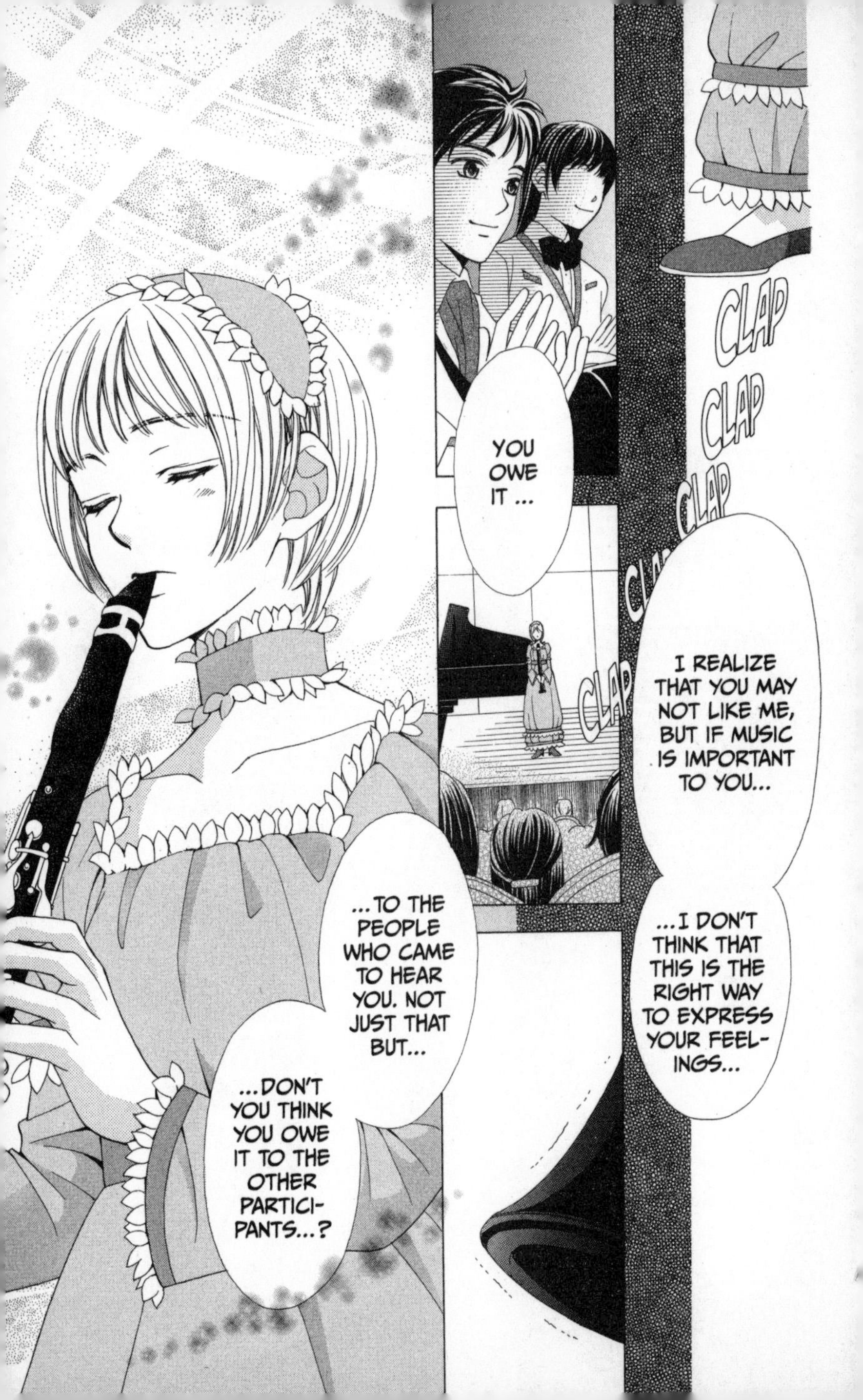
CLAP
CLAP
CLAP
CLAP
I REALIZE THAT YOU MAY NOT LIKE ME, BUT IF MUSIC IS IMPORTANT TO YOU...
...I DON'T THINK THAT THIS IS THE RIGHT WAY TO EXPRESS YOUR FEEL-INGS...
YOU OWE IT ...
...TO THE PEOPLE WHO CAME TO HEAR YOU. NOT JUST THAT BUT...
...DON'T YOU THINK YOU OWE IT TO THE OTHER PARTICI-PANTS...?

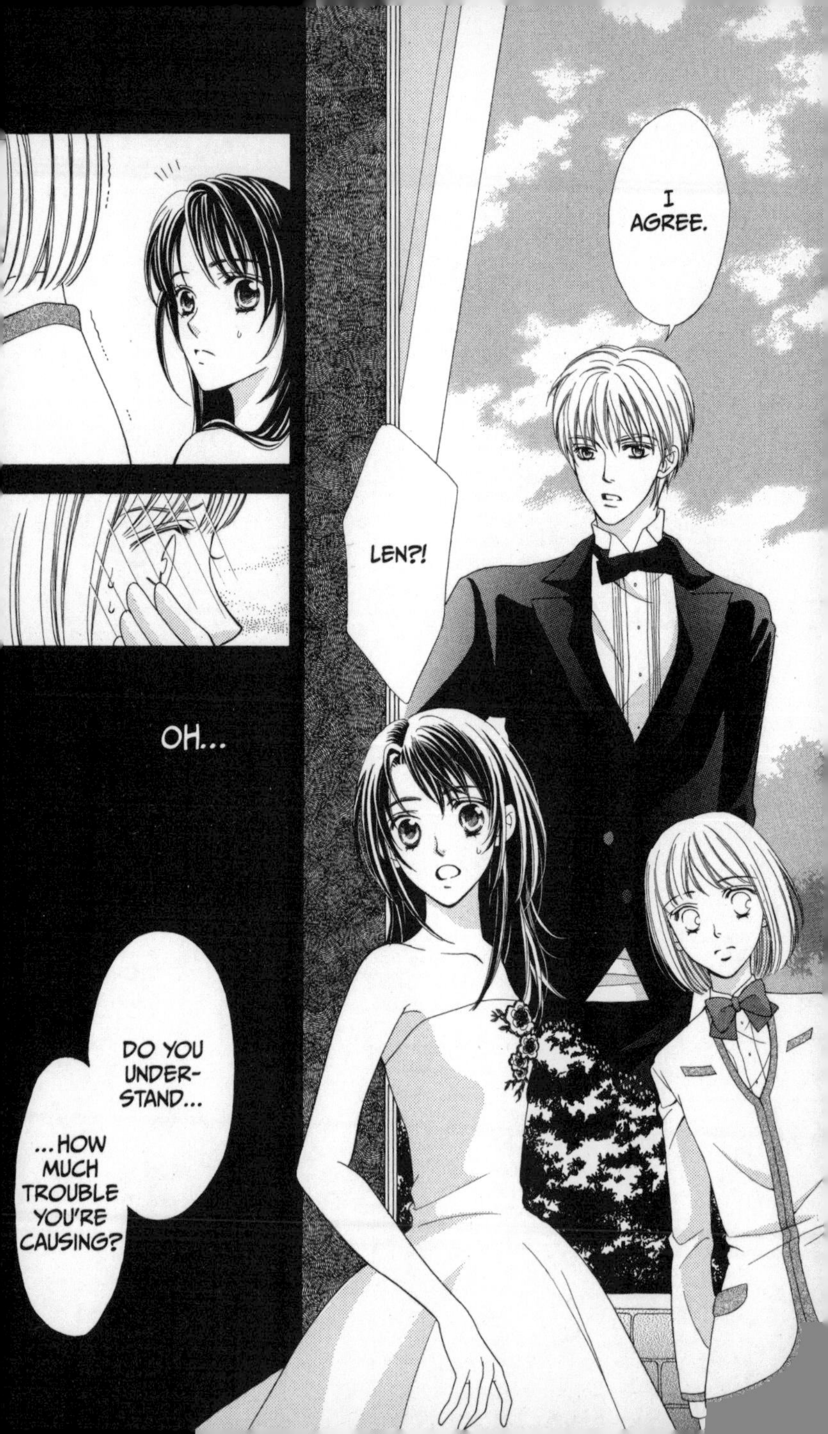
I AGREE.
LEN?!
OH...
DO YOU UNDER-STAND...
...HOW MUCH TROUBLE YOU'RE CAUSING?

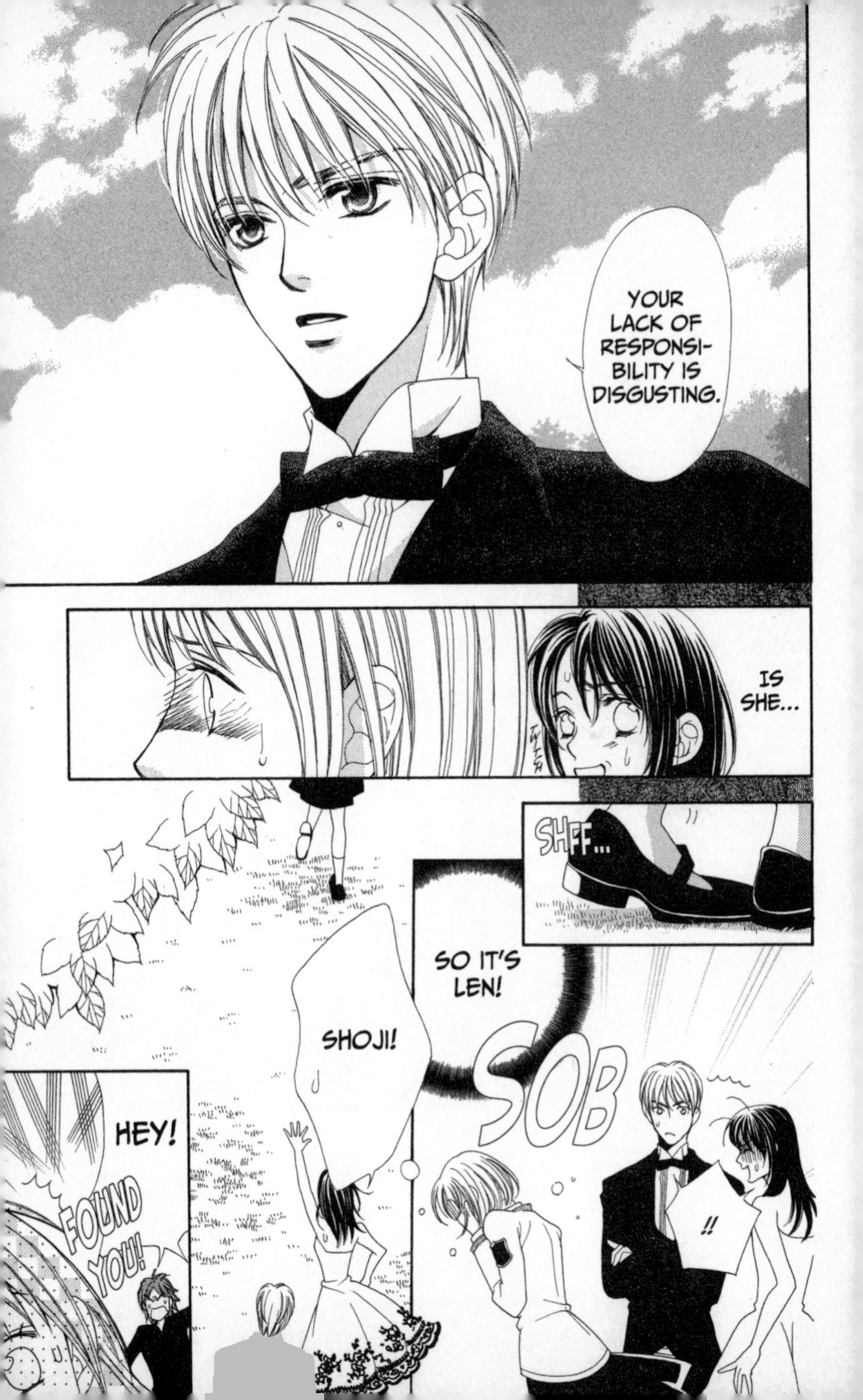
YOUR LACK OF RESPONSIBILITY IS DISGUSTING.
IS SHE...
TWITCH
SHFF...
SO IT'S LEN!
SOB
!!
SHOJI!
HEY!
FOUND YOU!

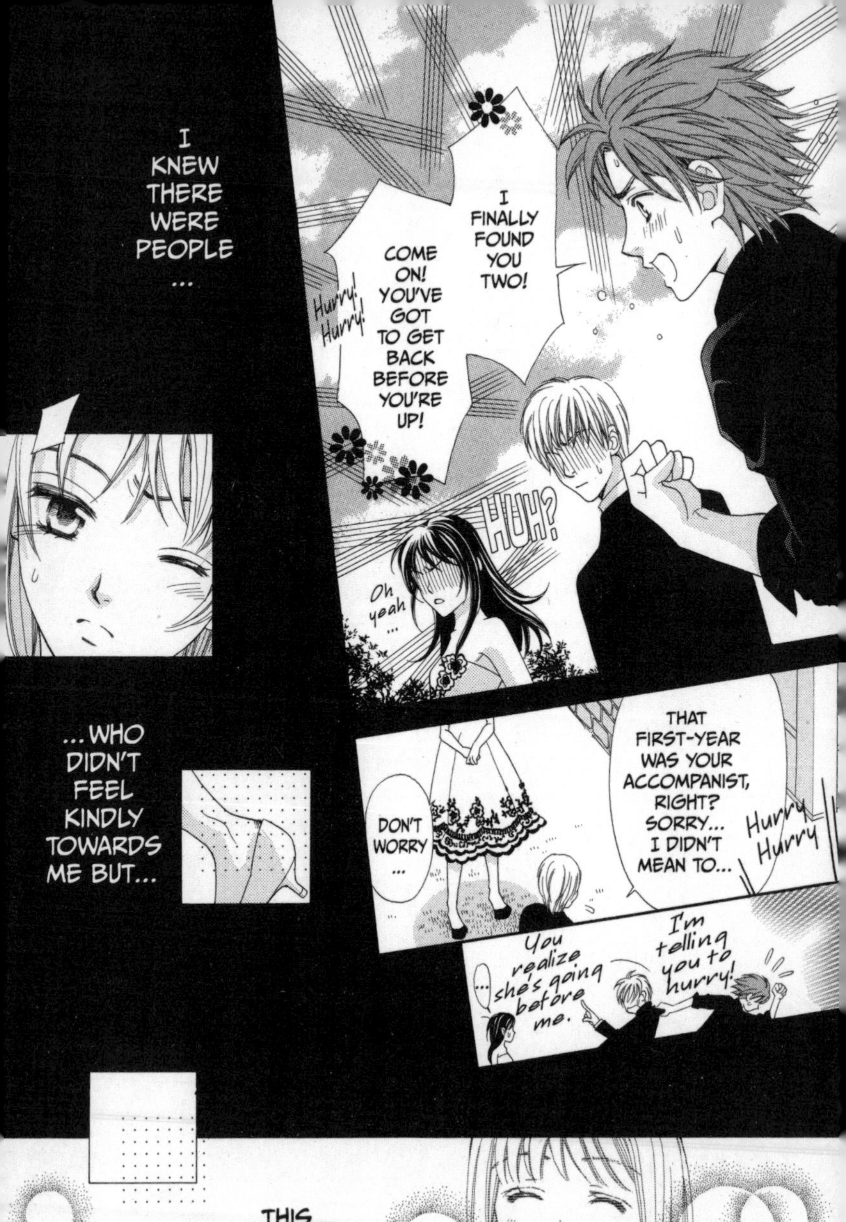
I FINALLY FOUND YOU TWO!
COME ON! YOU'VE GOT TO GET BACK BEFORE YOU'RE UP!
Hurry! Hurry!
HUH?
Oh yeah ...
I KNEW THERE WERE PEOPLE ...
THAT FIRST-YEAR WAS YOUR ACCOMPANIST, RIGHT? SORRY... I DIDN'T MEAN TO...
Hurry Hurry
DON'T WORRY ...
I'm telling you to hurry!
You realize she's going before me.
...
...WHO DIDN'T FEEL KINDLY TOWARDS ME BUT...
...THIS...

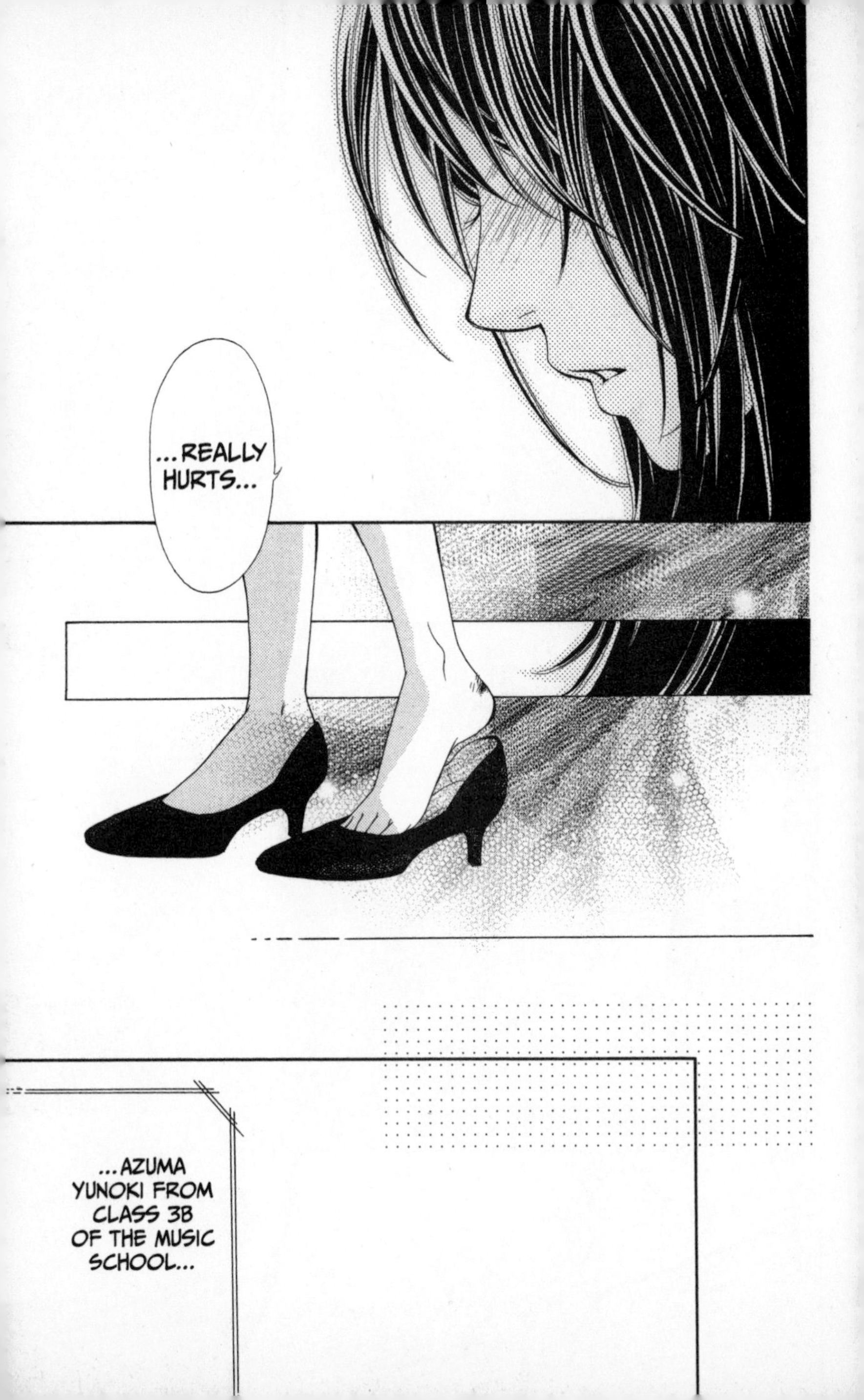
...REALLY HURTS...
...AZUMA YUNOKI FROM CLASS 3B OF THE MUSIC SCHOOL...

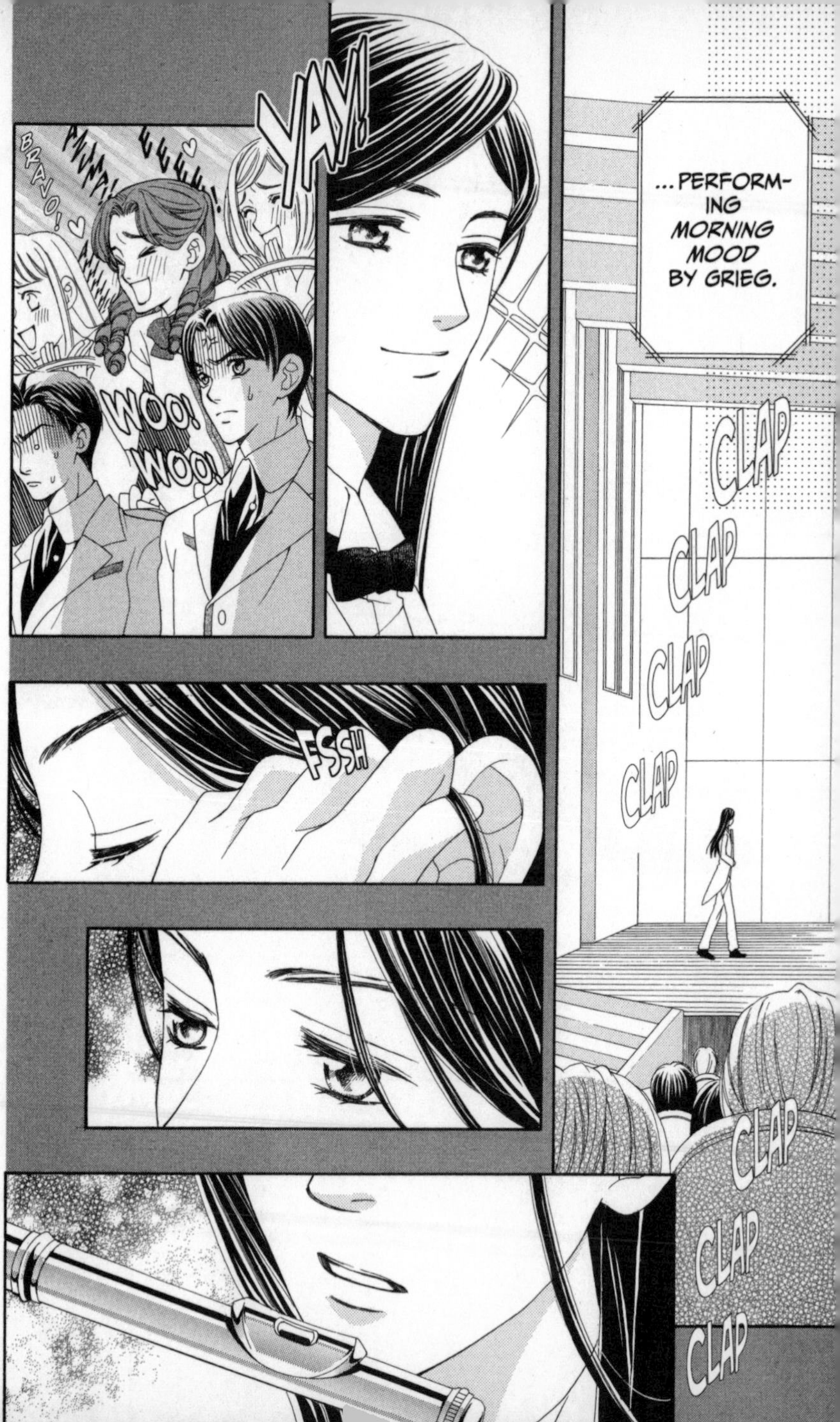
...PERFORM-
ING
MORNING
MOOD
BY GRIEG.
CLAP
CLAP
CLAP
CLAP
CLAP
CLAP
CLAP
YAY!
BRAVO!
WOO!
WOO!
FSSH

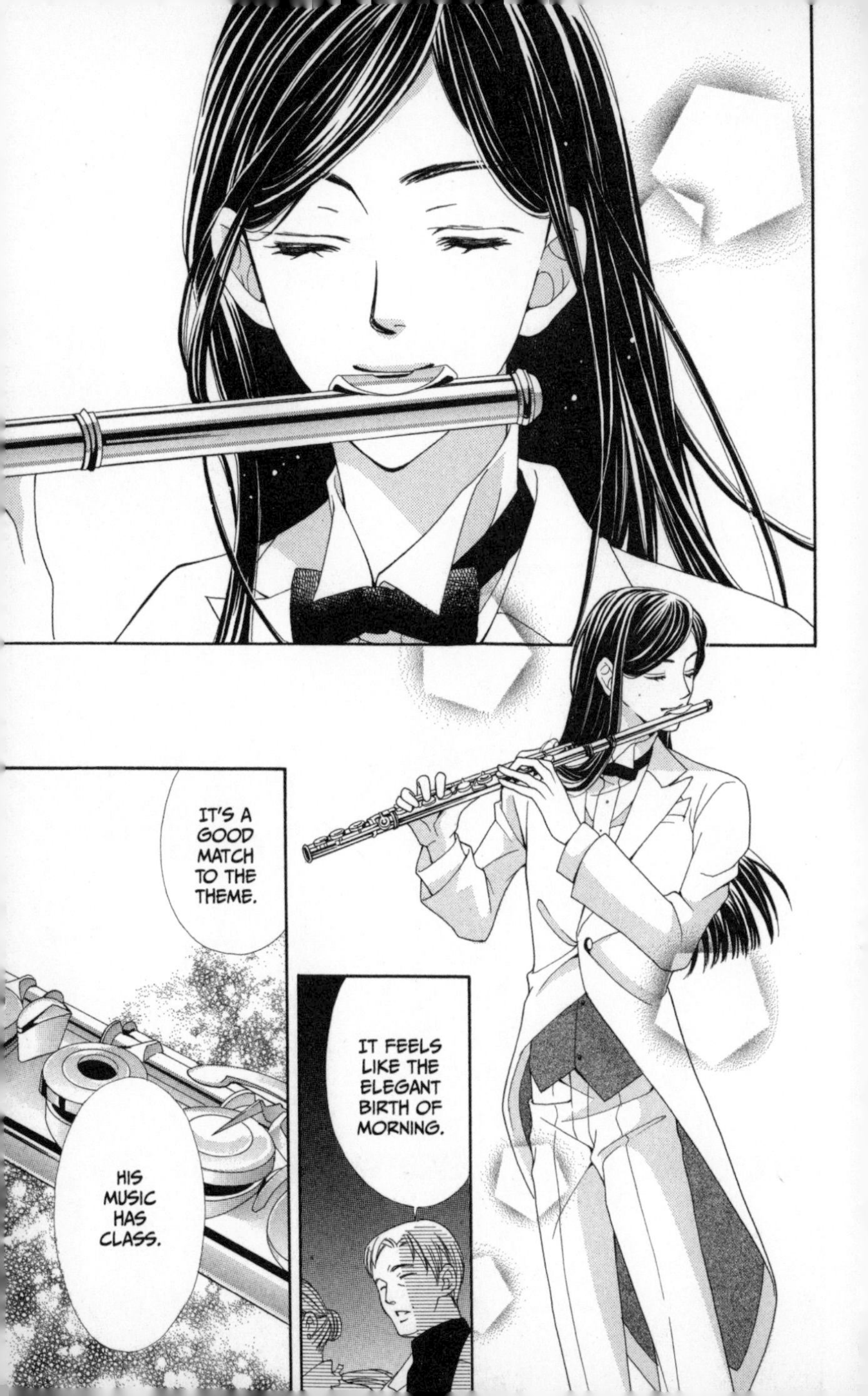
IT'S A GOOD MATCH TO THE THEME.
IT FEELS LIKE THE ELEGANT BIRTH OF MORNING.
HIS MUSIC HAS CLASS.

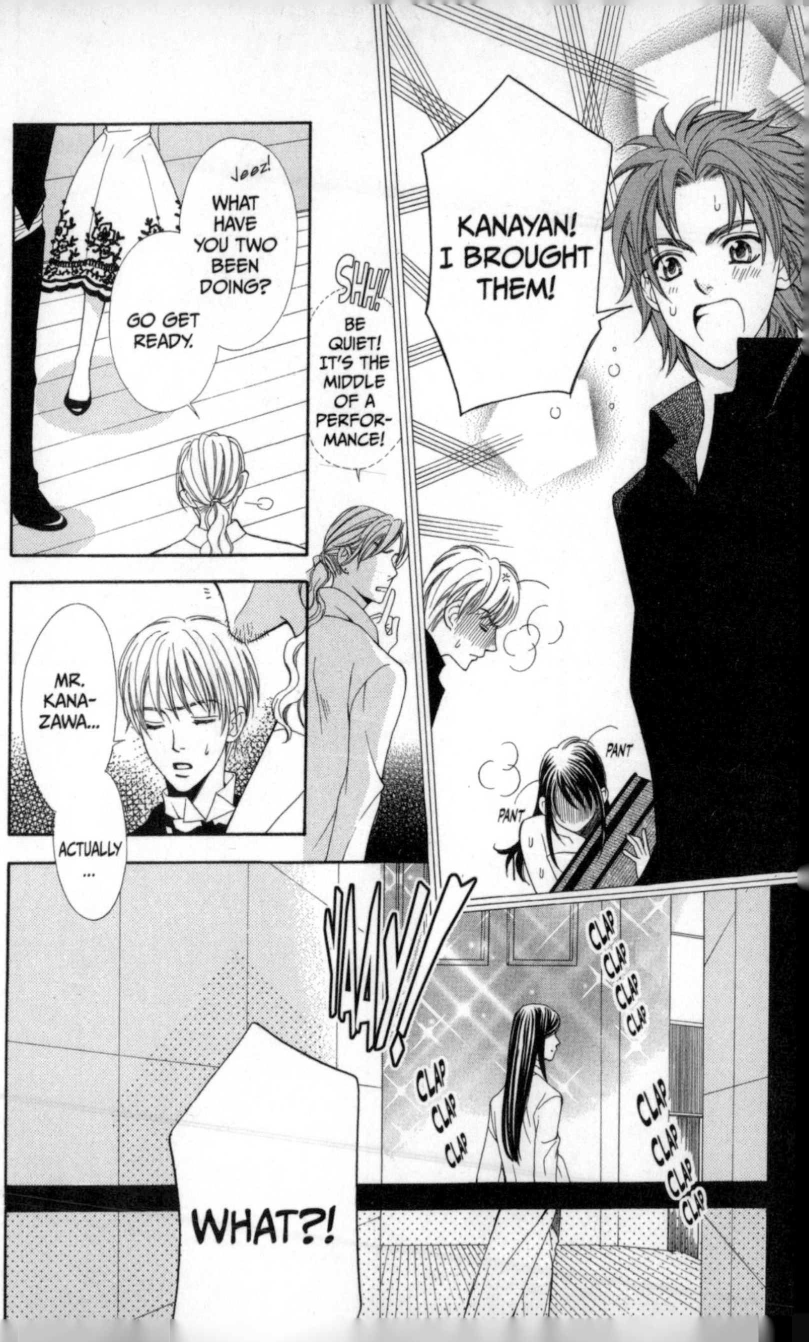
KANAYAN! I BROUGHT THEM!
PANT
PANT
SHH!
BE QUIET! IT'S THE MIDDLE OF A PERFORMANCE!
Jeez!
WHAT HAVE YOU TWO BEEN DOING?
GO GET READY.
MR. KANAZAWA...
ACTUALLY...
CLAP CLAP CLAP CLAP
CLAP CLAP CLAP CLAP CLAP
CLAP CLAP CLAP
WHAT?!

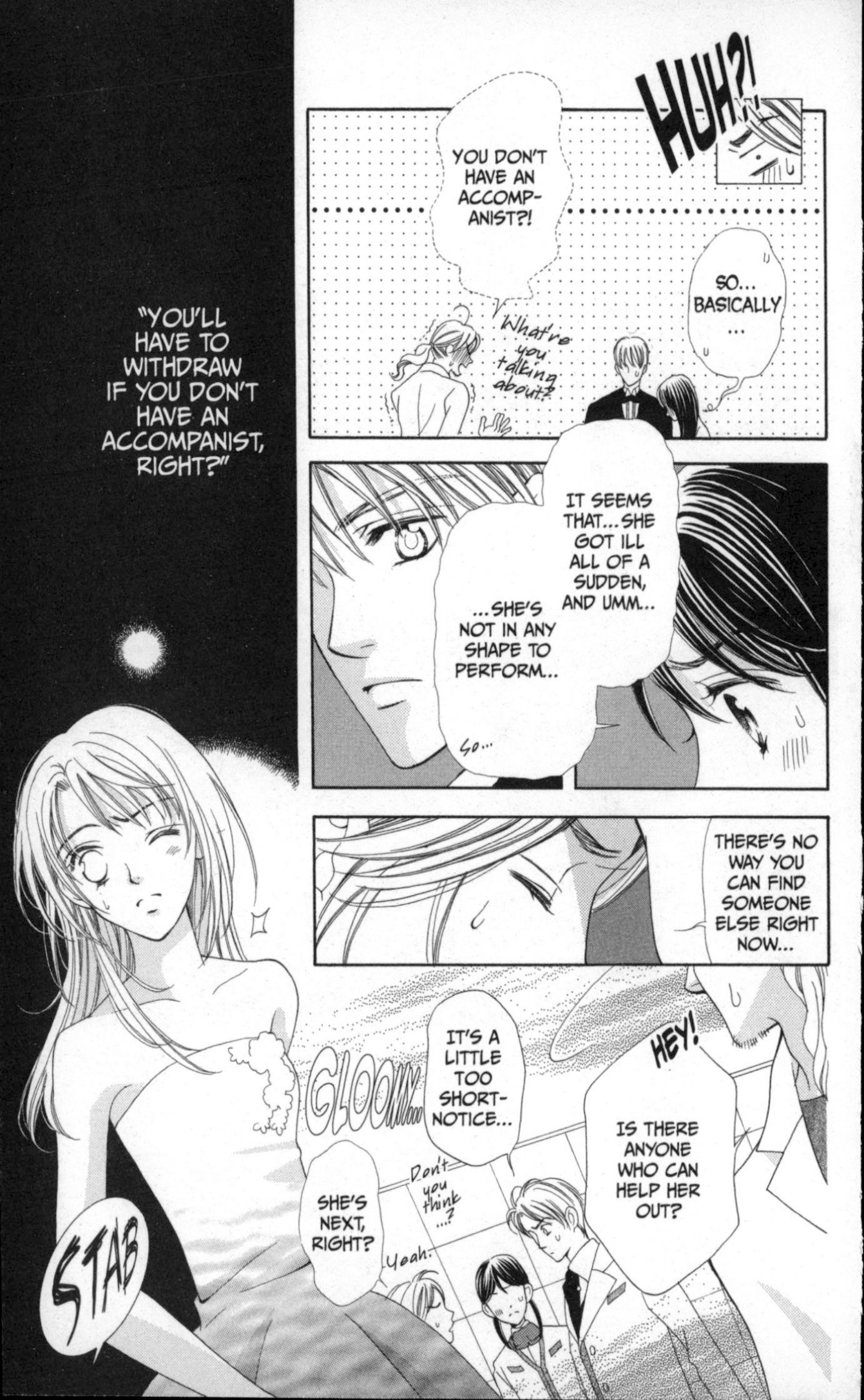
HUH?!
YOU DON'T HAVE AN ACCOMPANIST?!
SO... BASICALLY...
What're you talking about?!
IT SEEMS THAT... SHE GOT ILL ALL OF A SUDDEN, AND UMM...
...SHE'S NOT IN ANY SHAPE TO PERFORM...
So...
THERE'S NO WAY YOU CAN FIND SOMEONE ELSE RIGHT NOW...
HEY!
IS THERE ANYONE WHO CAN HELP HER OUT?
IT'S A LITTLE TOO SHORT-NOTICE...
Don't you think...?
SHE'S NEXT, RIGHT?
Yeah.
GLOOM...
STAB
"YOU'LL HAVE TO WITHDRAW IF YOU DON'T HAVE AN ACCOMPANIST, RIGHT?"

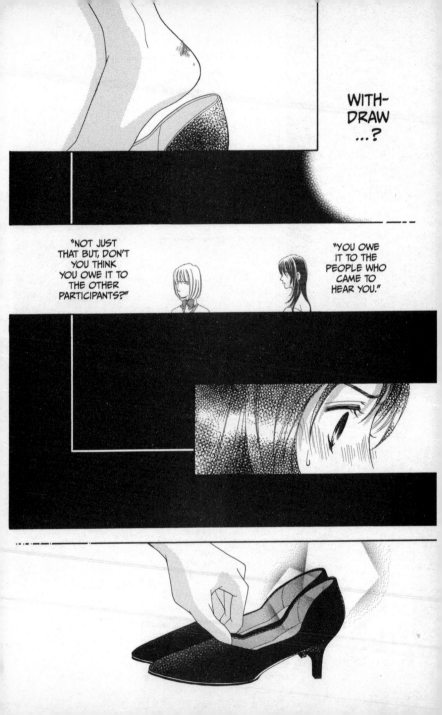

WITH-
DRAW
...?

"NOT JUST
THAT BUT, DON'T
YOU THINK
YOU OWE IT TO
THE OTHER
PARTICIPANTS?"

"YOU OWE
IT TO THE
PEOPLE WHO
CAME TO
HEAR YOU."

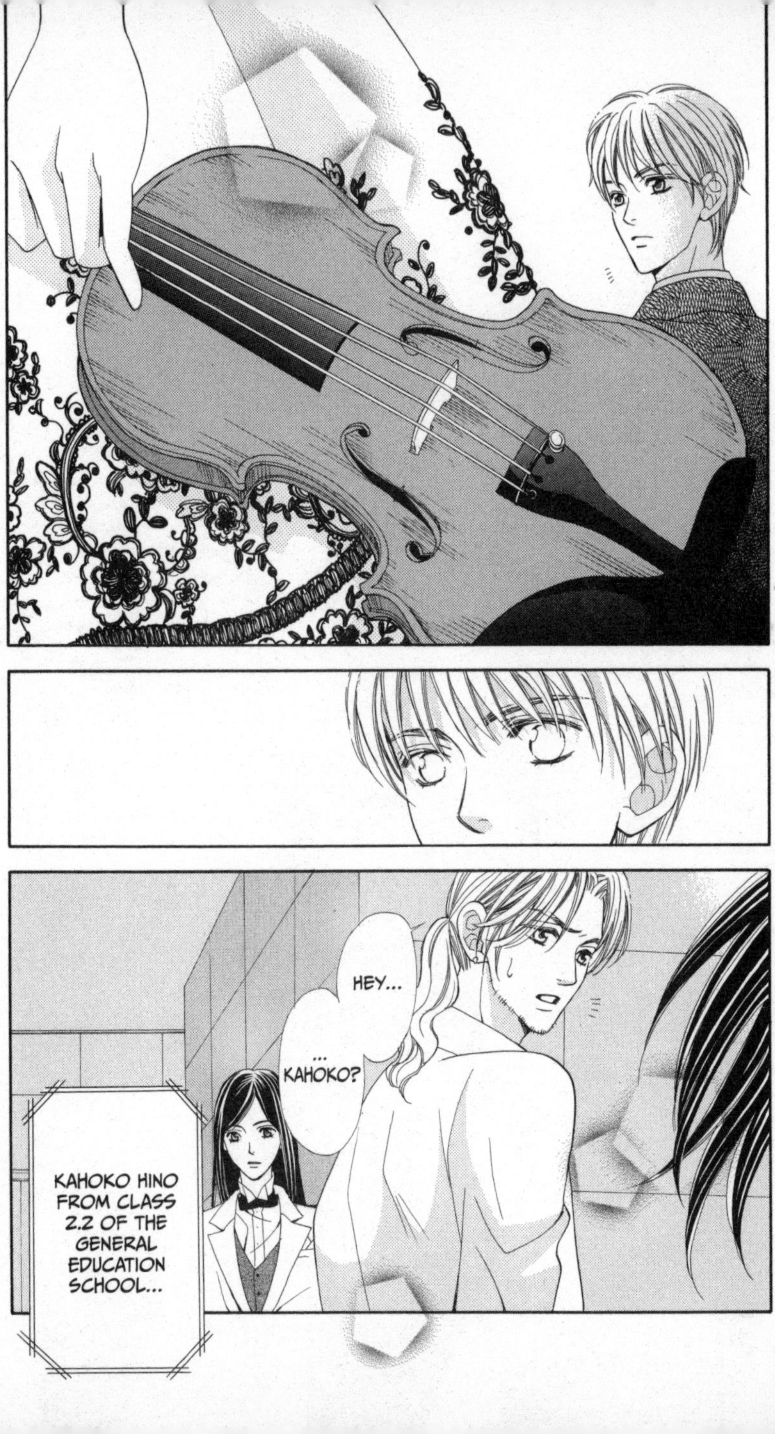
HEY...
... KAHOKO?
KAHOKO HINO FROM CLASS 2.2 OF THE GENERAL EDUCATION SCHOOL...

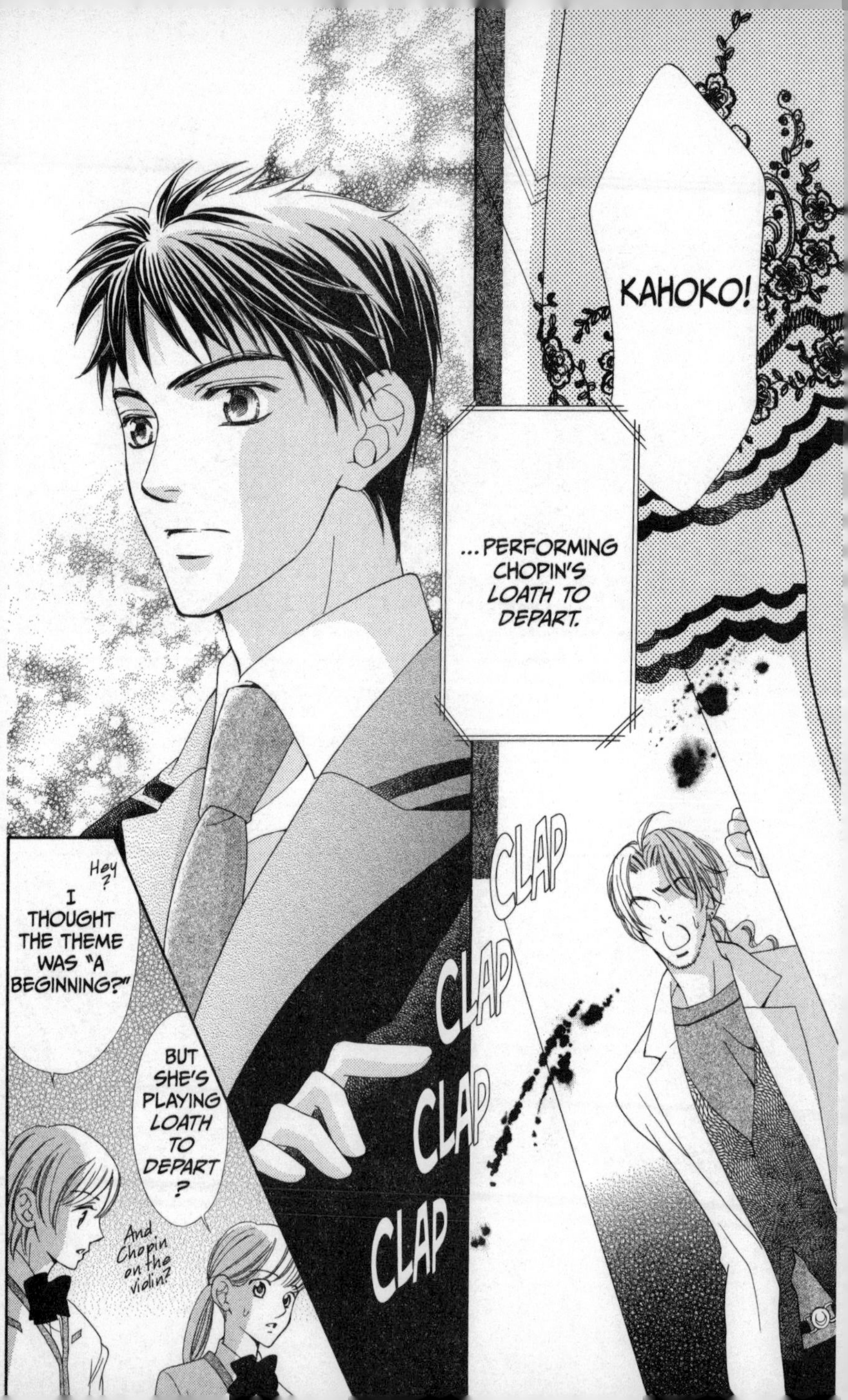
KAHOKO!
...PERFORMING CHOPIN'S LOATH TO DEPART.
CLAP
CLAP
CLAP
CLAP
CLAP
Hey?
I THOUGHT THE THEME WAS "A BEGINNING?"
BUT SHE'S PLAYING LOATH TO DEPART?
And Chopin on the violin?

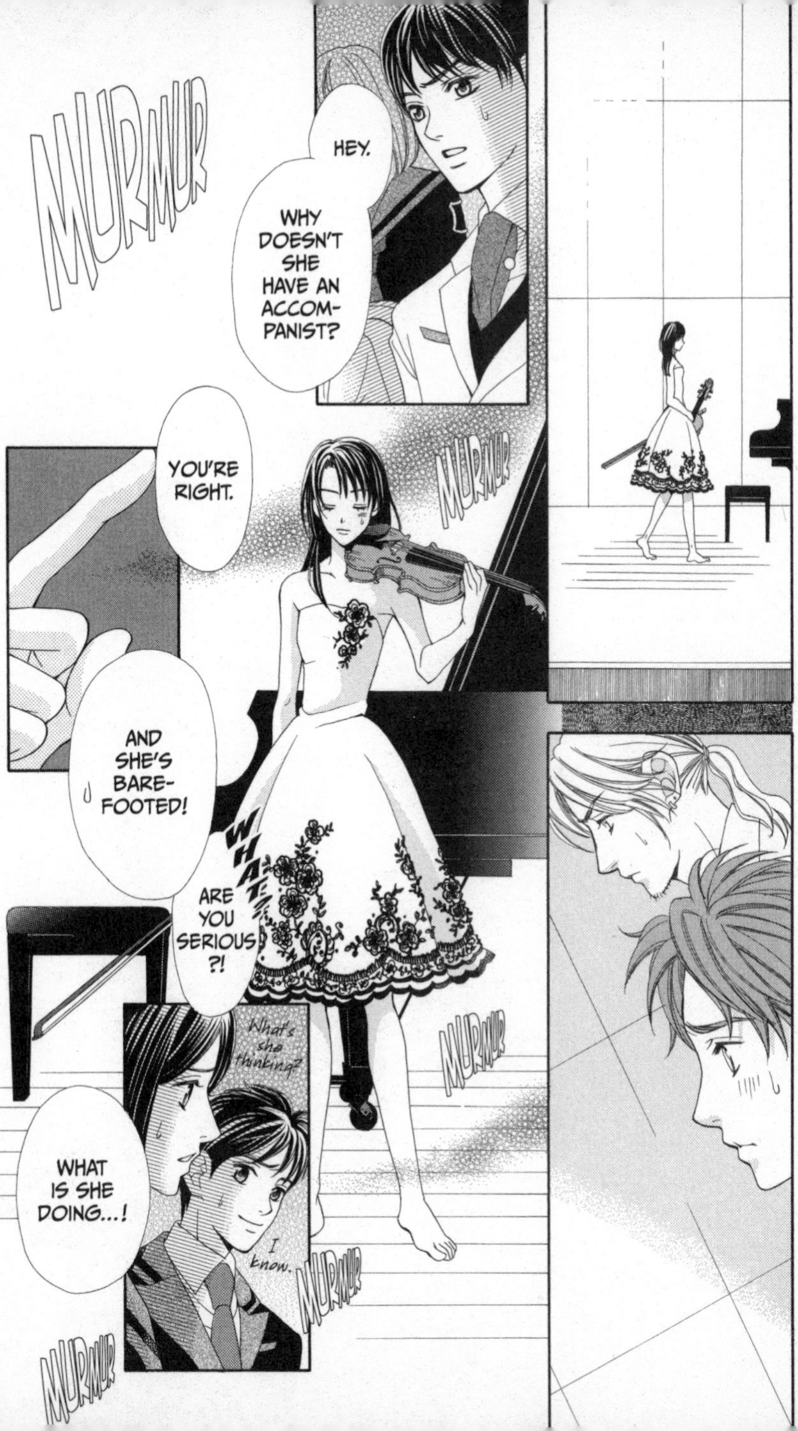
HEY.
WHY DOESN'T SHE HAVE AN ACCOMPANIST?
MURMUR
MURMUR
YOU'RE RIGHT.
AND SHE'S BAREFOOTED!
WHAT?!
ARE YOU SERIOUS?!
MURMUR
What's she thinking?
WHAT IS SHE DOING...!
I know.
MURMUR
MURMUR

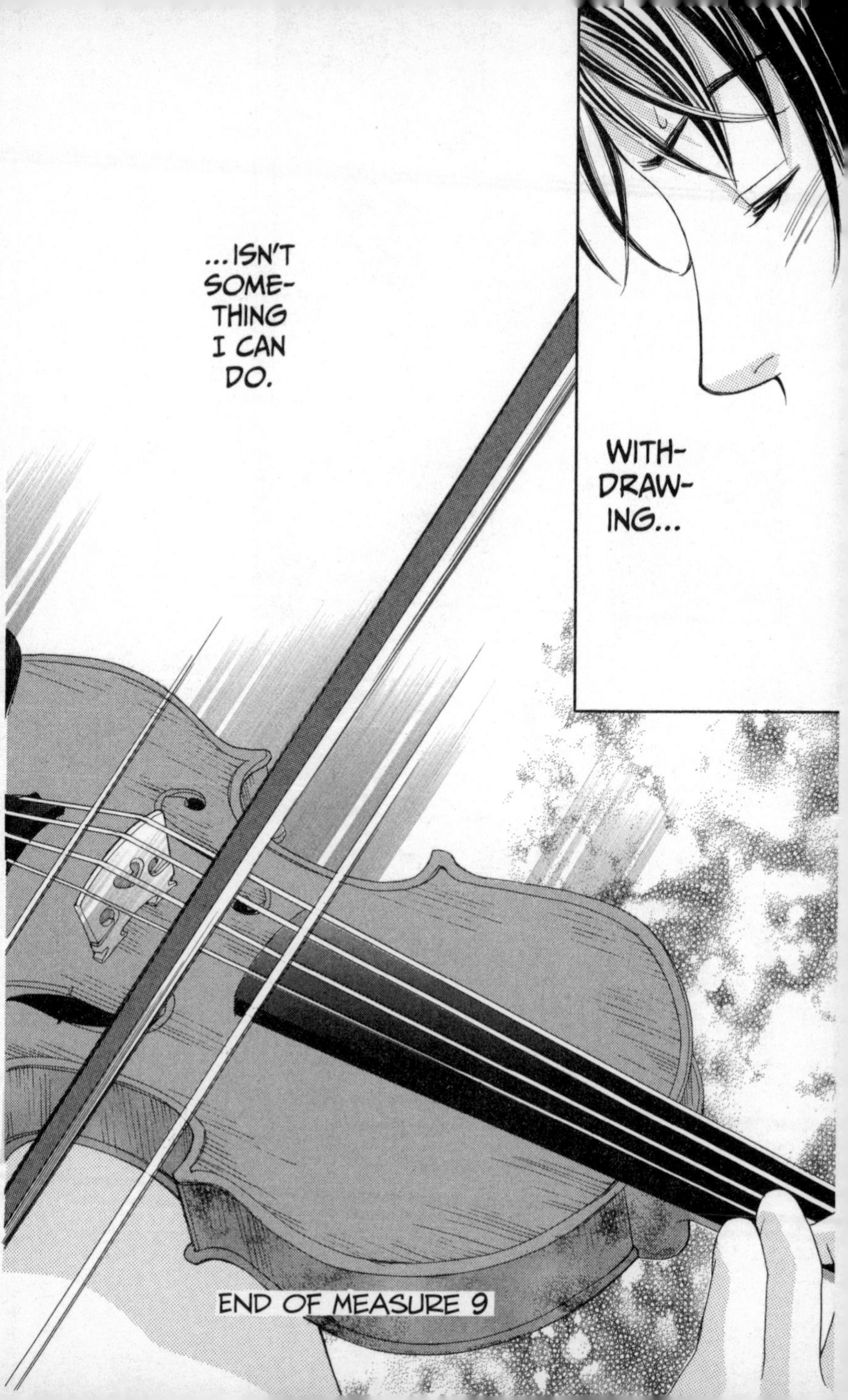
WITH-DRAWING...
...ISN'T SOMETHING I CAN DO.
END OF MEASURE 9

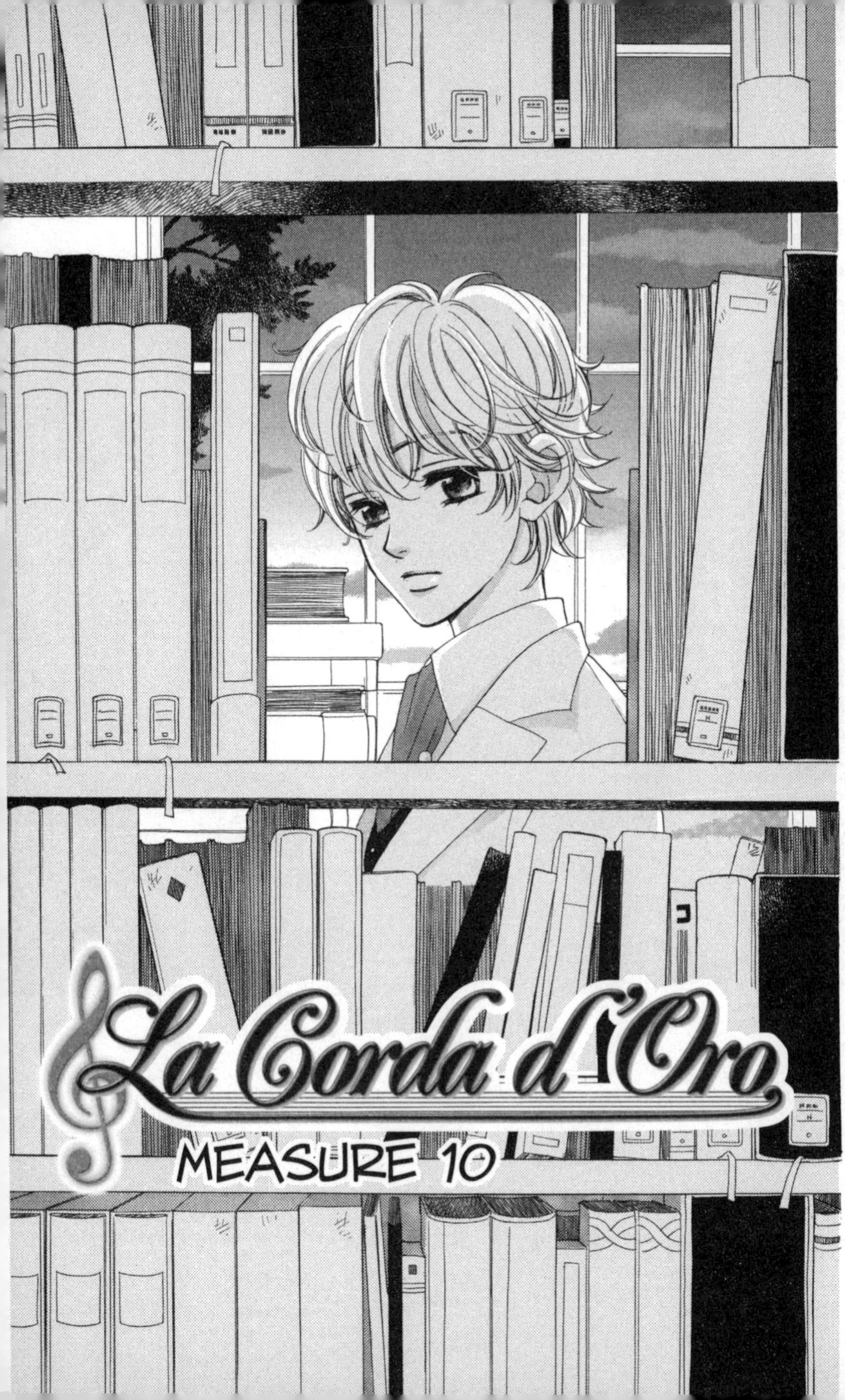
La Corda d'Oro
MEASURE 10

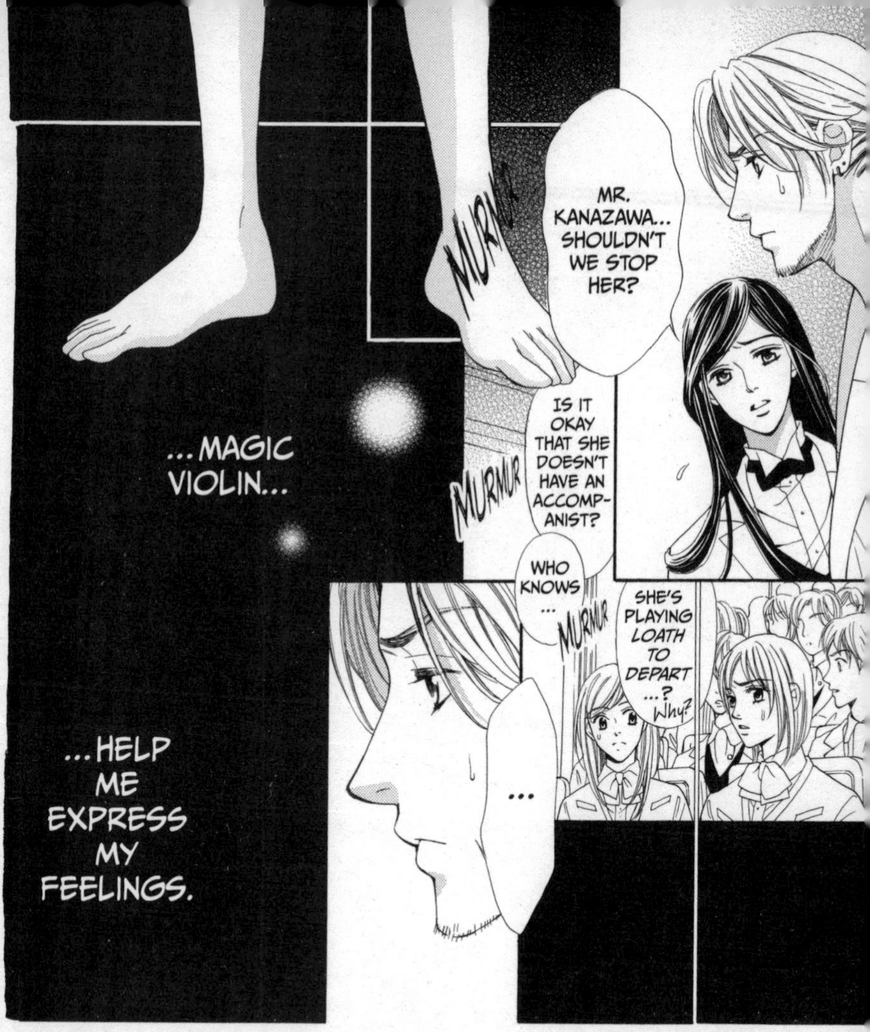
MR. KANAZAWA... SHOULDN'T WE STOP HER?
MURMUR
IS IT OKAY THAT SHE DOESN'T HAVE AN ACCOMPANIST?
MURMUR
WHO KNOWS ...
MURMUR
SHE'S PLAYING LOATH TO DEPART ...? Why?
...
...MAGIC VIOLIN...
...HELP ME EXPRESS MY FEELINGS.

DAILY HAPPENINGS
② The signing

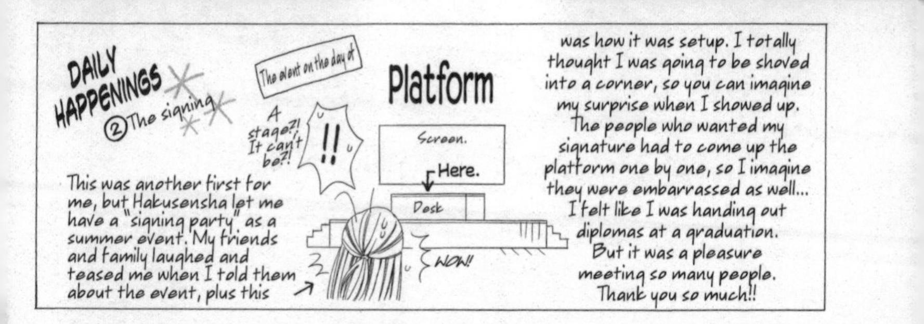
The event on the day of
Platform
A stage?! It can't be?!
!!
Screen.
Here.
Desk
WOW!

This was another first for me, but Hakusensha let me have a "signing party" as a summer event. My friends and family laughed and teased me when I told them about the event, plus this was how it was setup. I totally thought I was going to be shoved into a corner, so you can imagine my surprise when I showed up. The people who wanted my signature had to come up the platform one by one, so I imagine they were embarrassed as well... I felt like I was handing out diplomas at a graduation. But it was a pleasure meeting so many people. Thank you so much!!

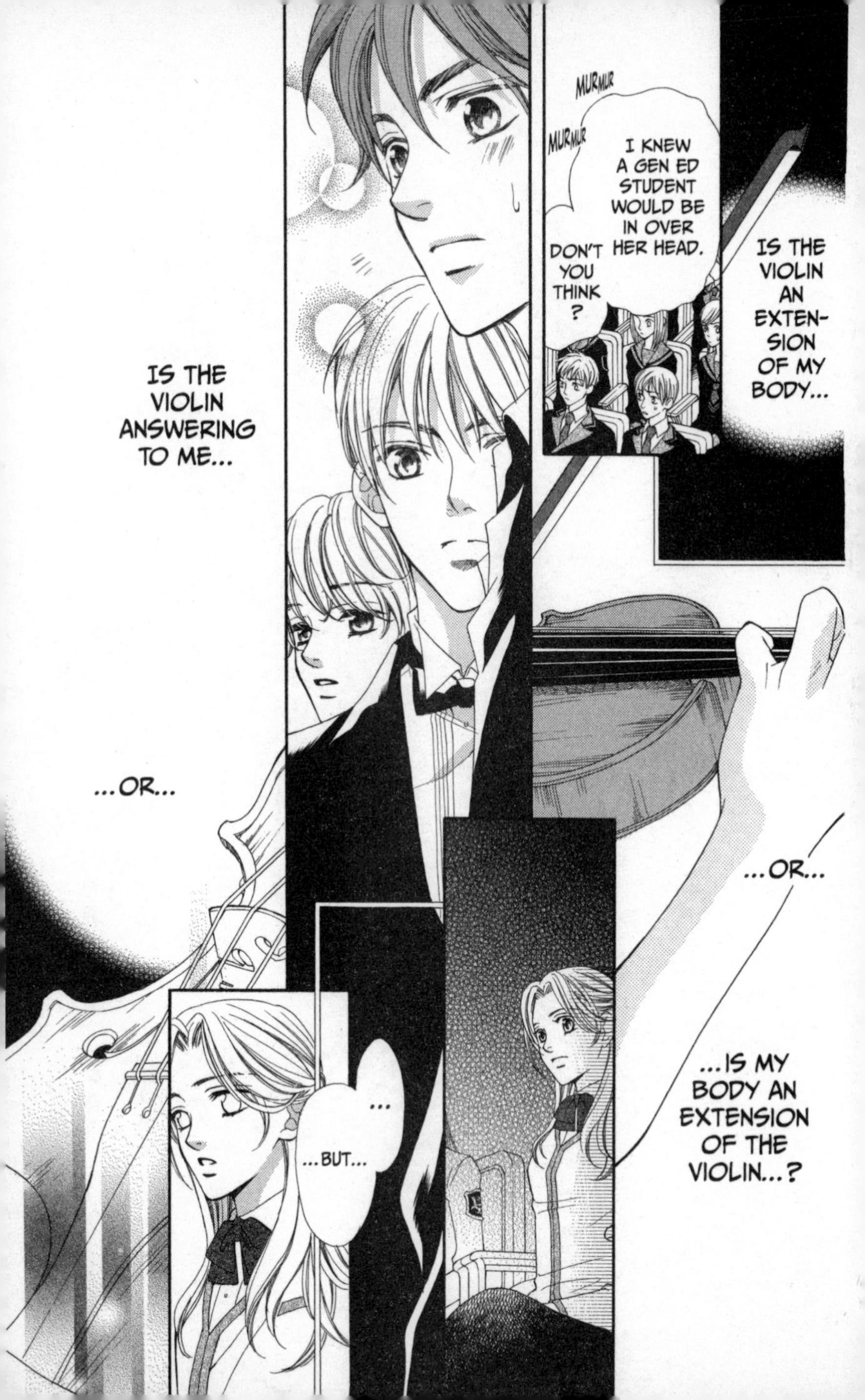
IS THE VIOLIN AN EXTENSION OF MY BODY...
MURMUR
MURMUR
I KNEW A GEN ED STUDENT WOULD BE IN OVER HER HEAD.
DON'T YOU THINK?
IS THE VIOLIN ANSWERING TO ME...
...OR...
...OR...
...IS MY BODY AN EXTENSION OF THE VIOLIN...?
...
...BUT...

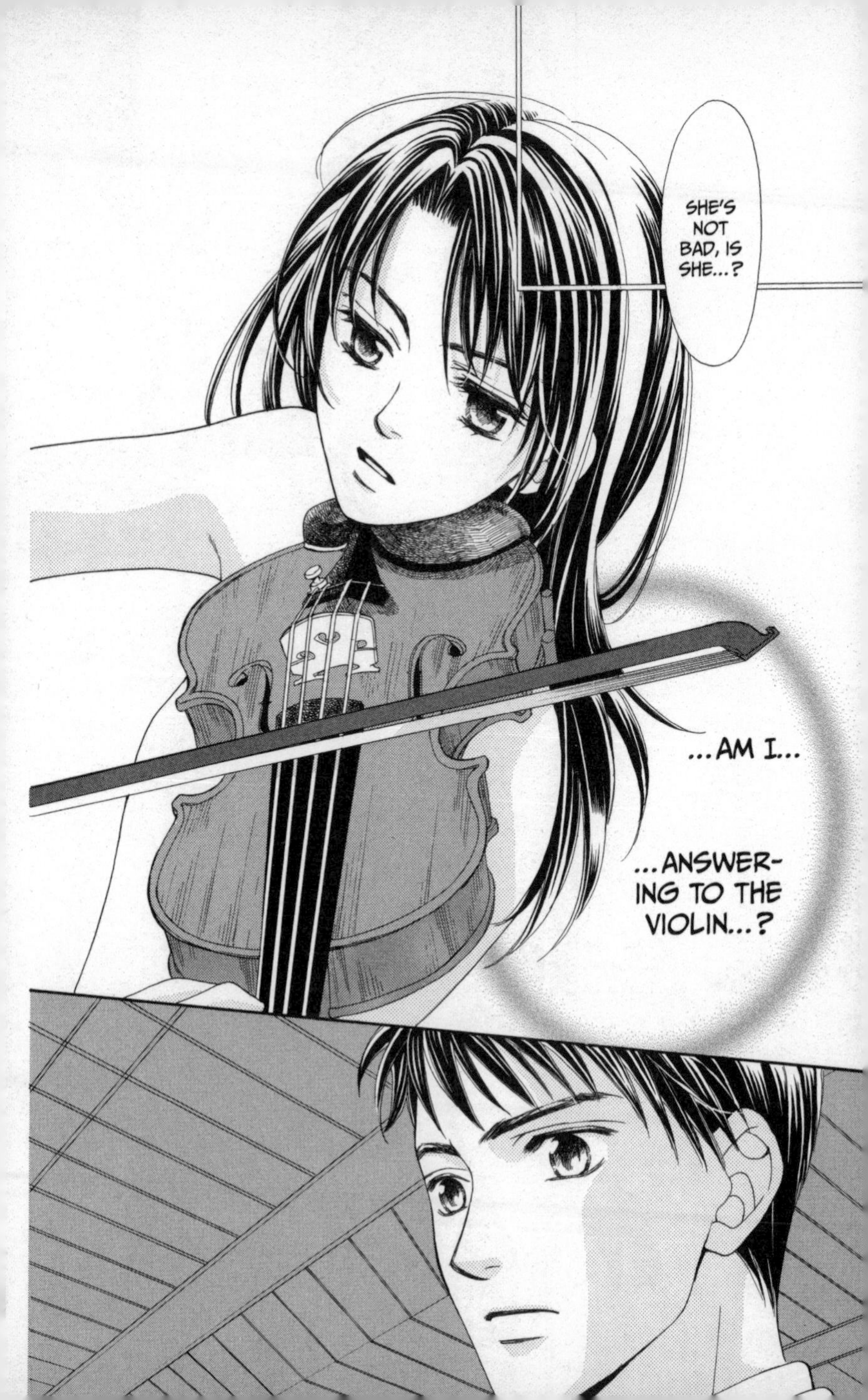
SHE'S NOT BAD, IS SHE...?
...AM I...
...ANSWER-ING TO THE VIOLIN...?

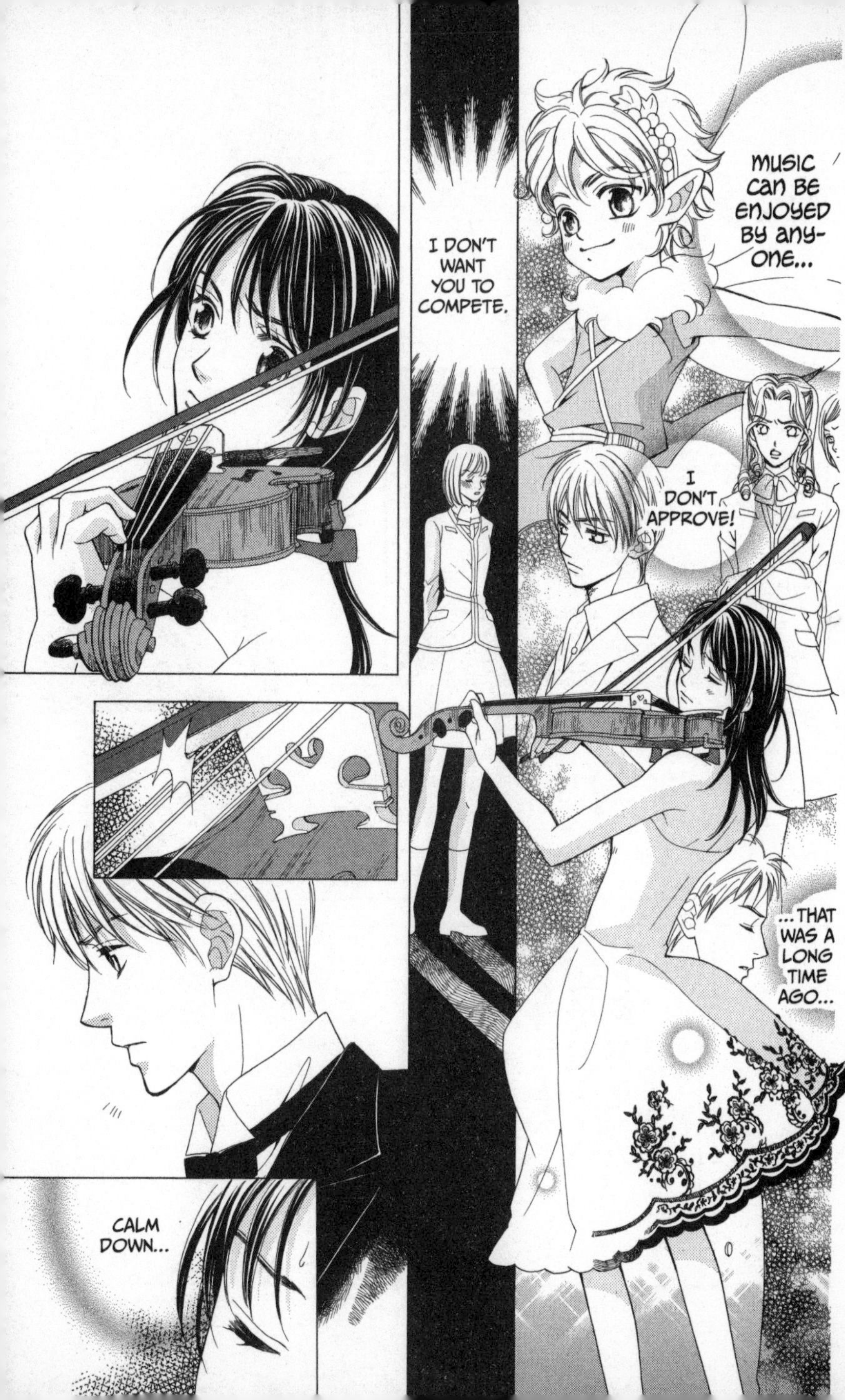
MUSIC CAN BE ENJOYED BY ANY-ONE...
I DON'T WANT YOU TO COMPETE.
I DON'T APPROVE!
...THAT WAS A LONG TIME AGO...
CALM DOWN...

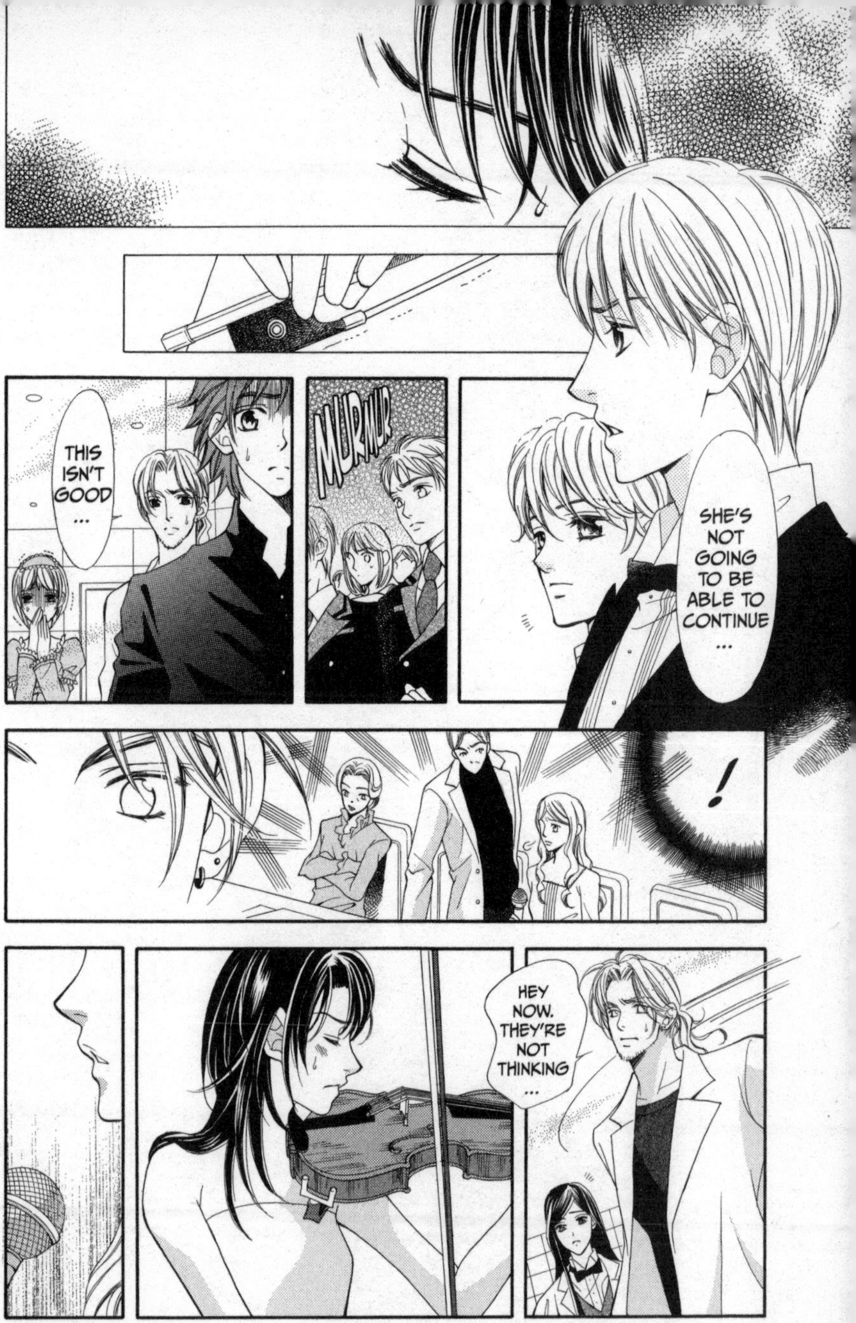
SHE'S NOT GOING TO BE ABLE TO CONTINUE ...
MURMUR
THIS ISN'T GOOD ...
!
HEY NOW. THEY'RE NOT THINKING ...

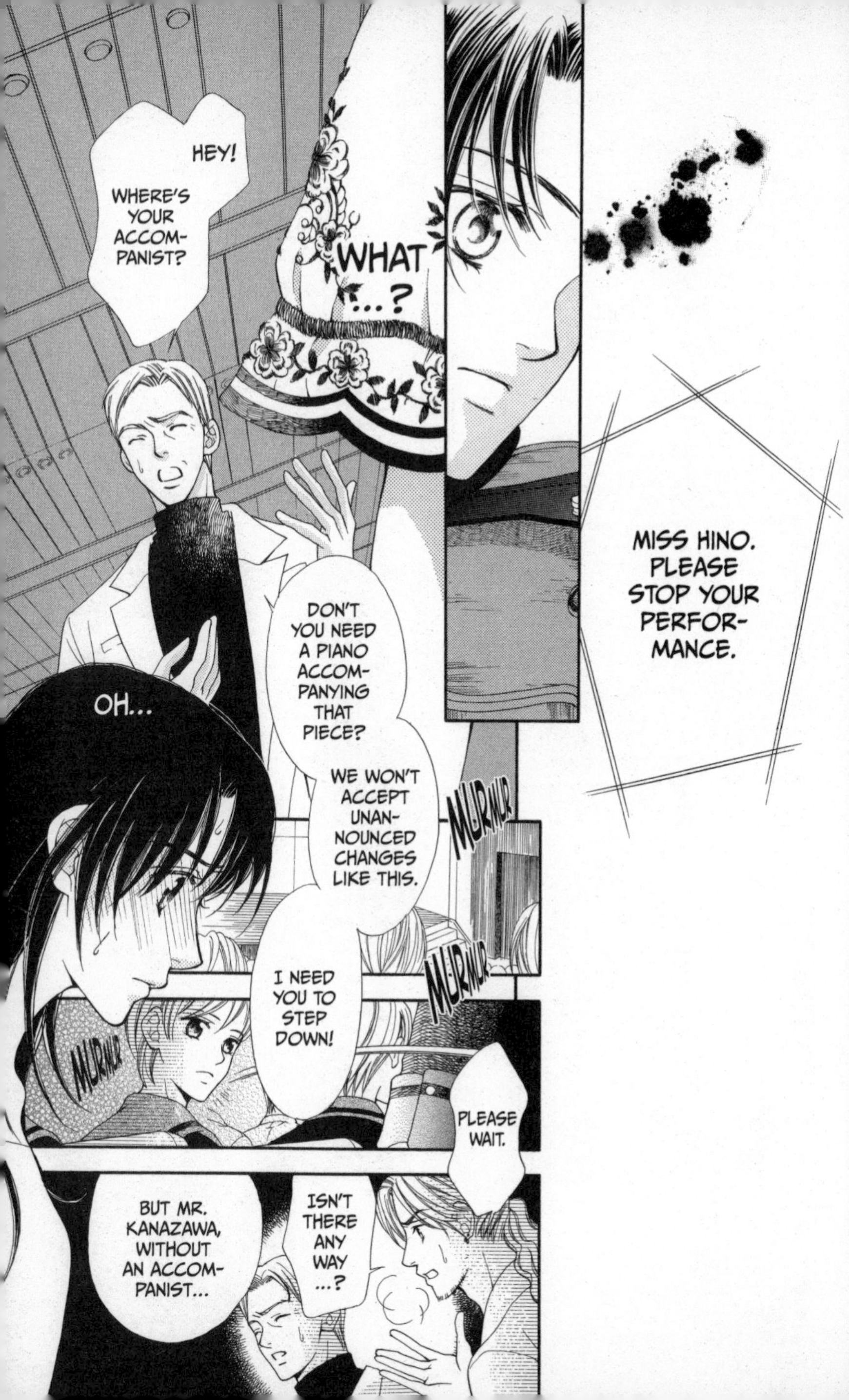
MISS HINO. PLEASE STOP YOUR PERFORMANCE.
WHAT ...?
HEY!
WHERE'S YOUR ACCOMPANIST?
DON'T YOU NEED A PIANO ACCOMPANYING THAT PIECE?
WE WON'T ACCEPT UNANNOUNCED CHANGES LIKE THIS.
MURMUR
I NEED YOU TO STEP DOWN!
MURMUR
OH...
MURMUR
PLEASE WAIT.
ISN'T THERE ANY WAY ...?
BUT MR. KANAZAWA, WITHOUT AN ACCOMPANIST...

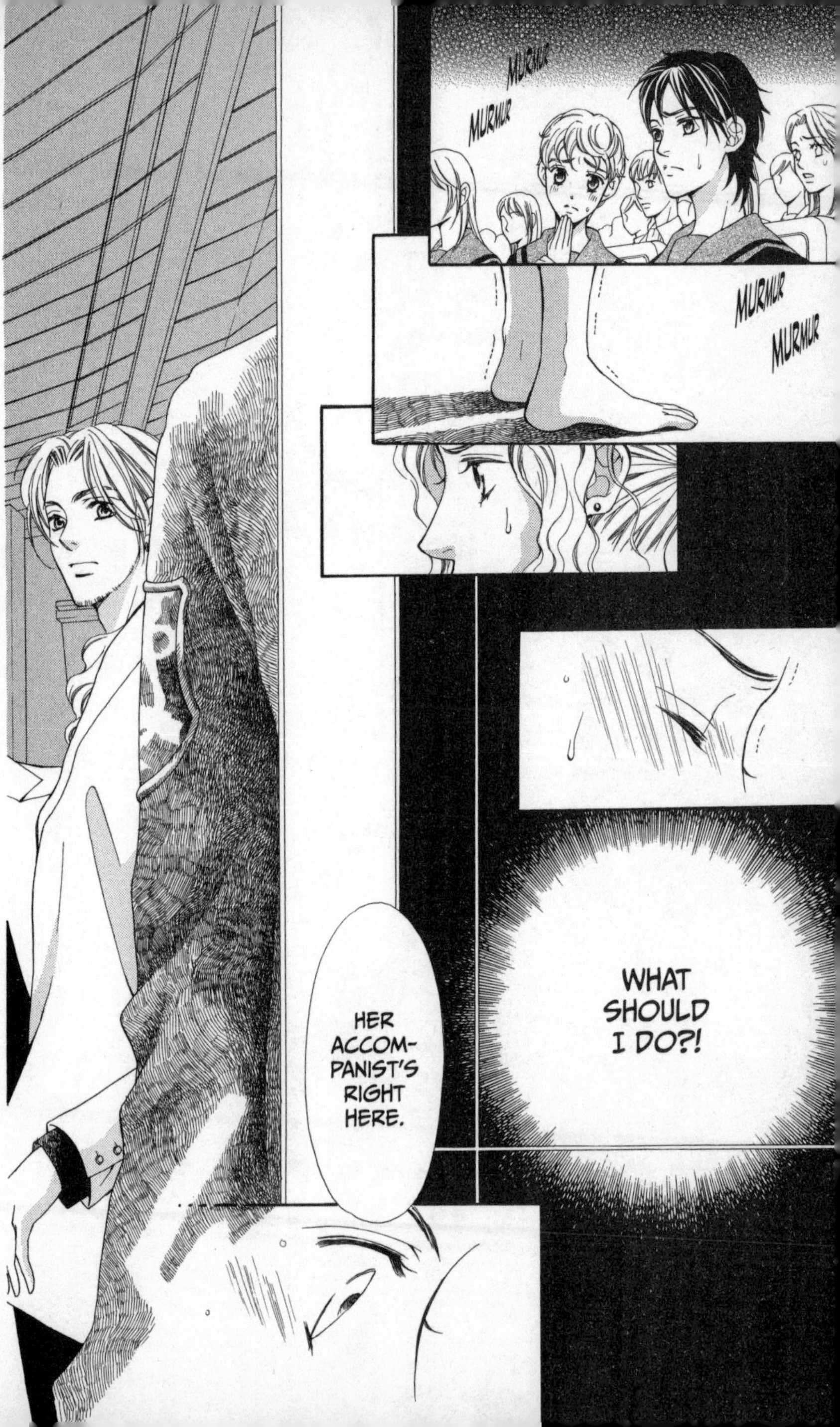
MURMUR
MURMUR
MURMUR
MURMUR
WHAT SHOULD I DO?!
HER ACCOMPANIST'S RIGHT HERE.

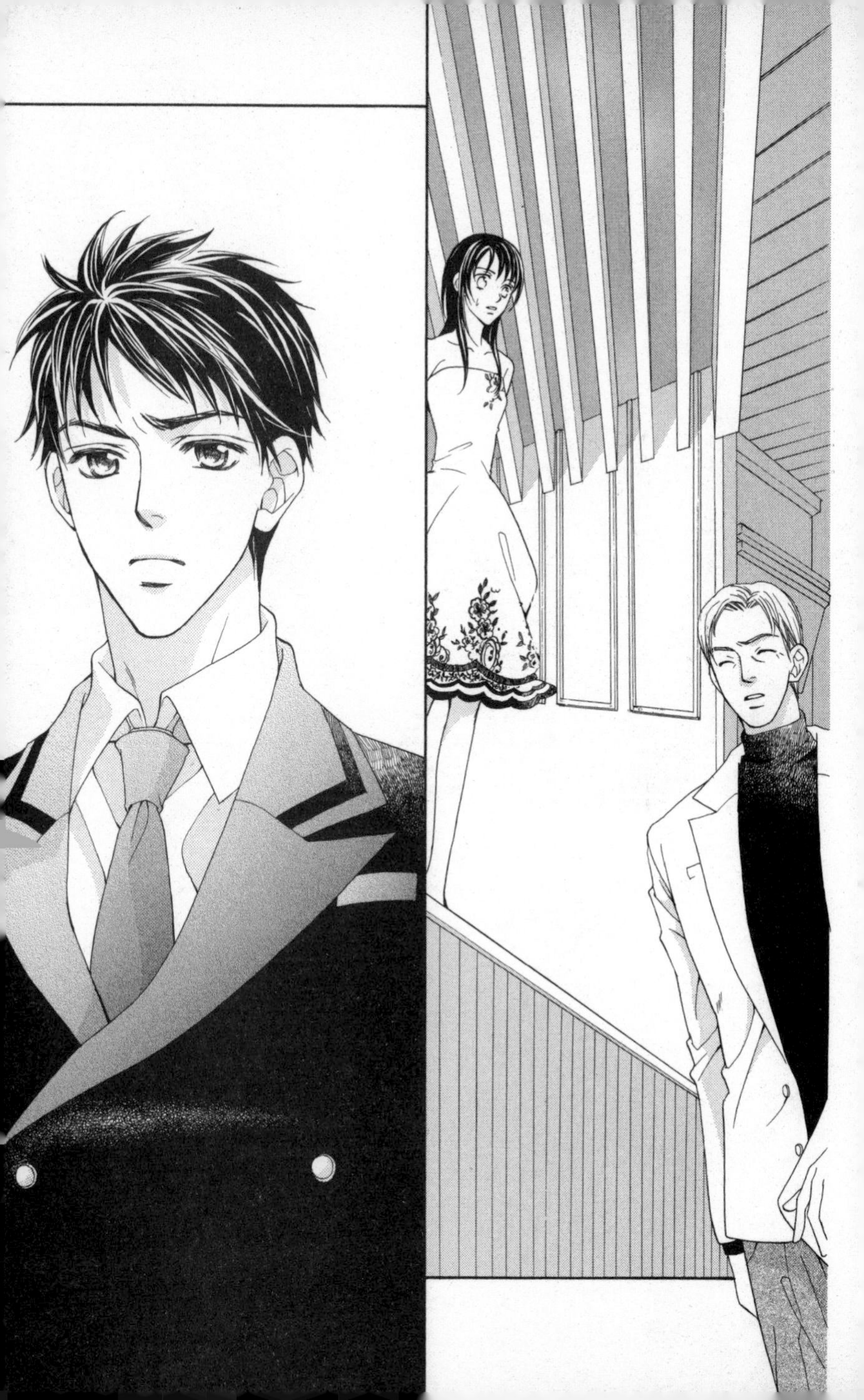

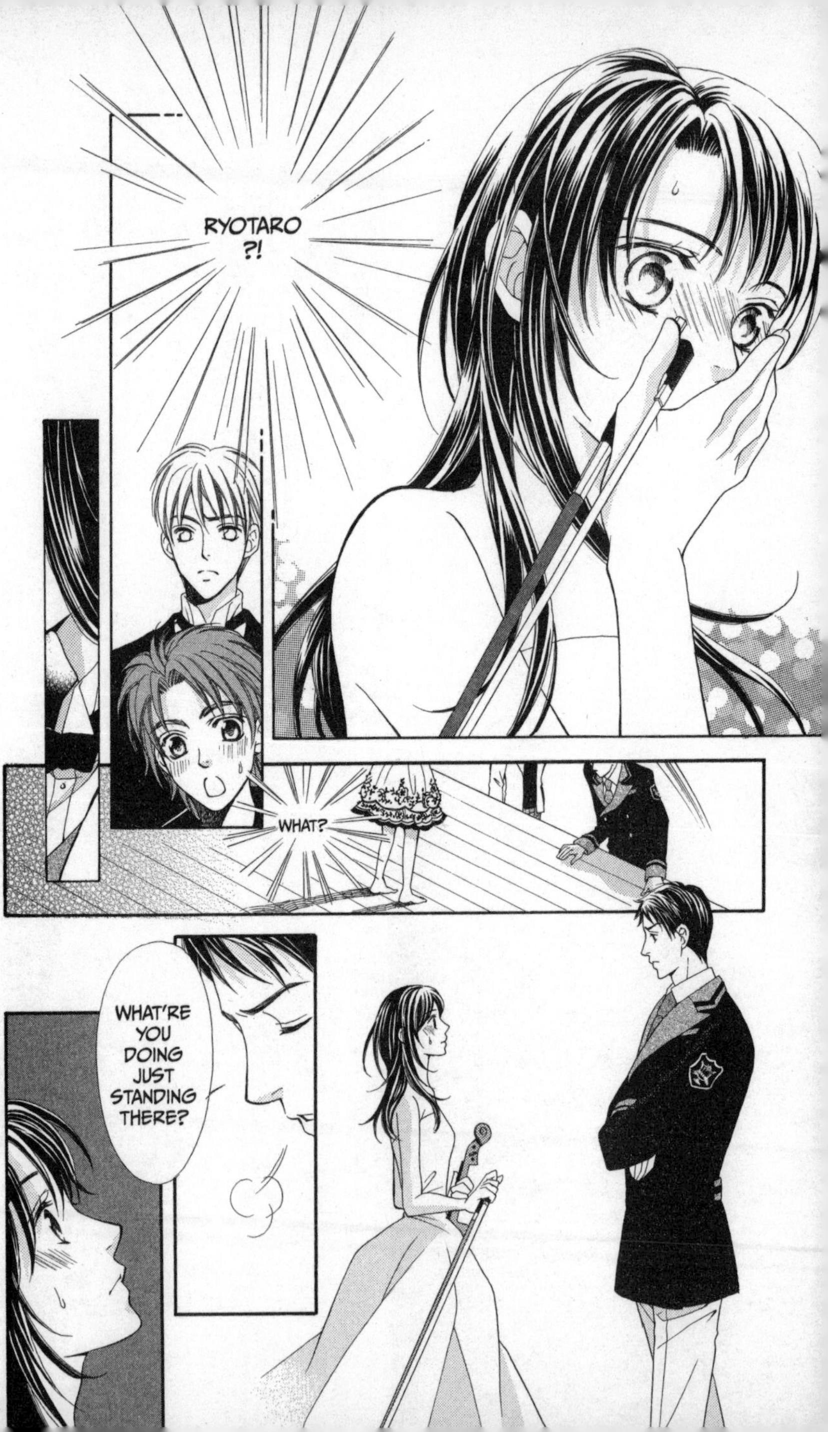
RYOTARO ?!
WHAT?
WHAT'RE YOU DOING JUST STANDING THERE?

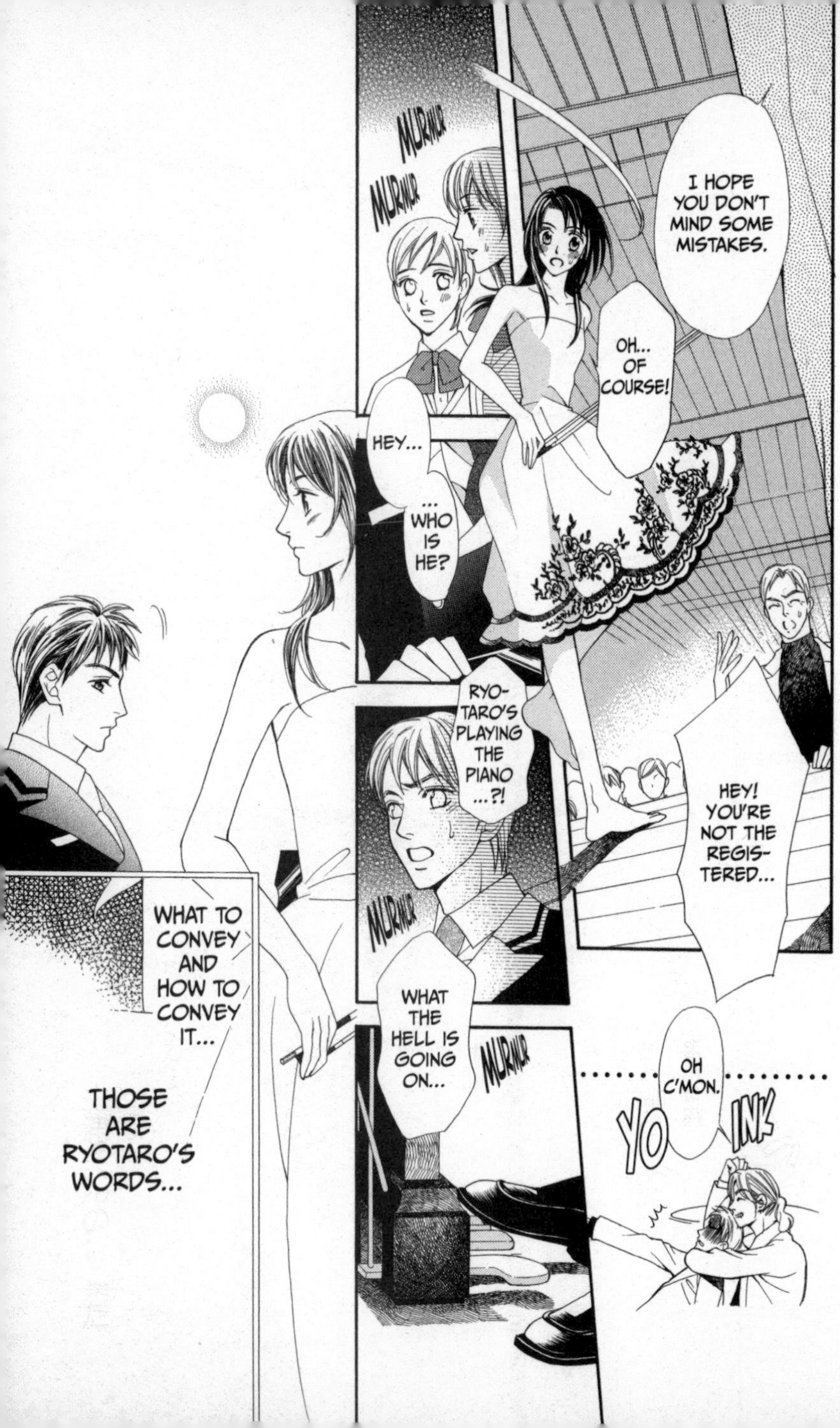

I HOPE YOU DON'T MIND SOME MISTAKES.
OH... OF COURSE!
MURMUR
MURMUR
HEY... ...WHO IS HE?
HEY! YOU'RE NOT THE REGIS-TERED...
RYO-TARO'S PLAYING THE PIANO ...?!
MURMUR
OH C'MON.
YOINK
WHAT THE HELL IS GOING ON...
MURMUR
WHAT TO CONVEY AND HOW TO CONVEY IT...
THOSE ARE RYOTARO'S WORDS...

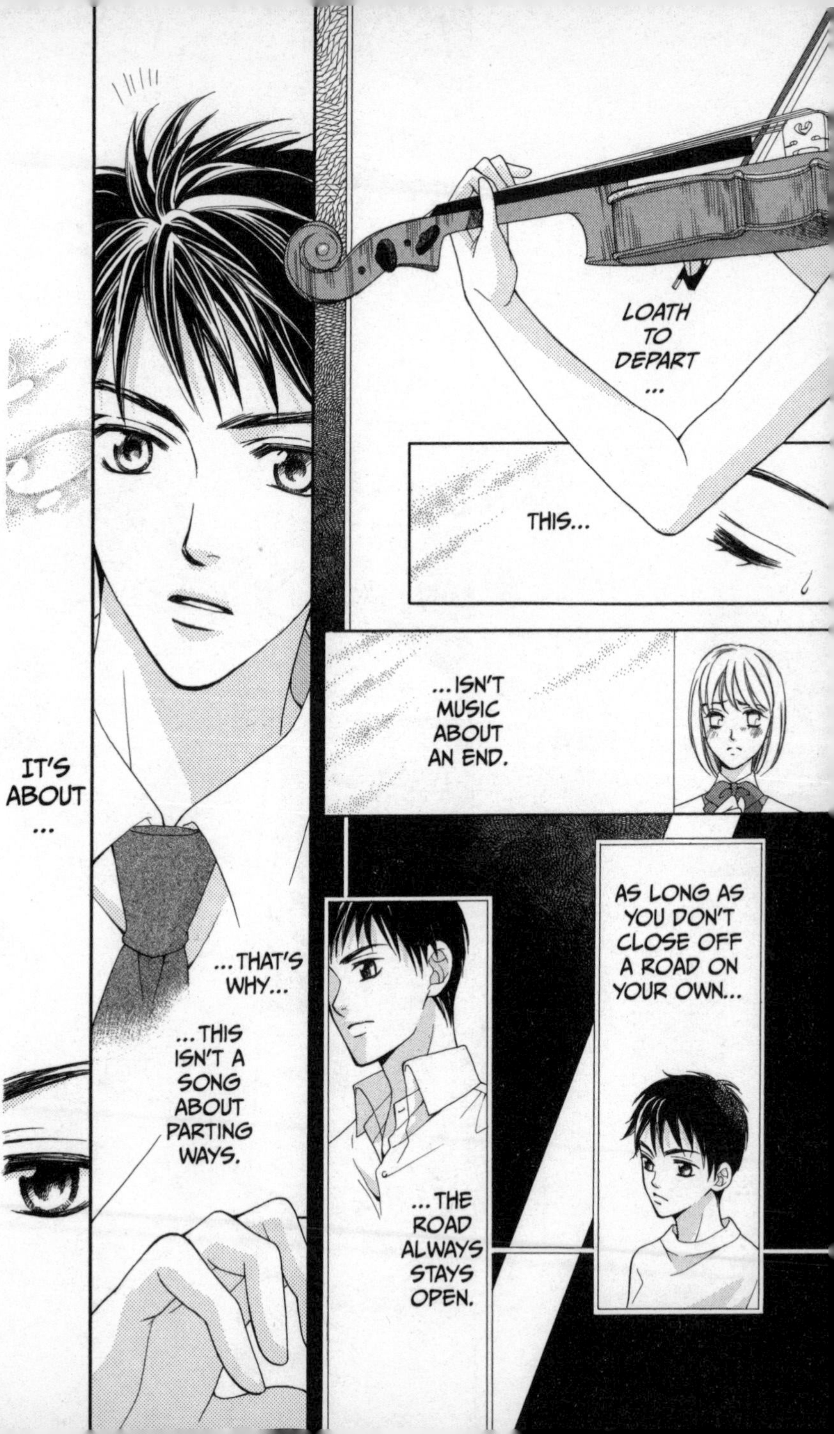
LOATH TO DEPART...
THIS...
...ISN'T MUSIC ABOUT AN END.
AS LONG AS YOU DON'T CLOSE OFF A ROAD ON YOUR OWN...
...THE ROAD ALWAYS STAYS OPEN.
...THAT'S WHY...
...THIS ISN'T A SONG ABOUT PARTING WAYS.
IT'S ABOUT...

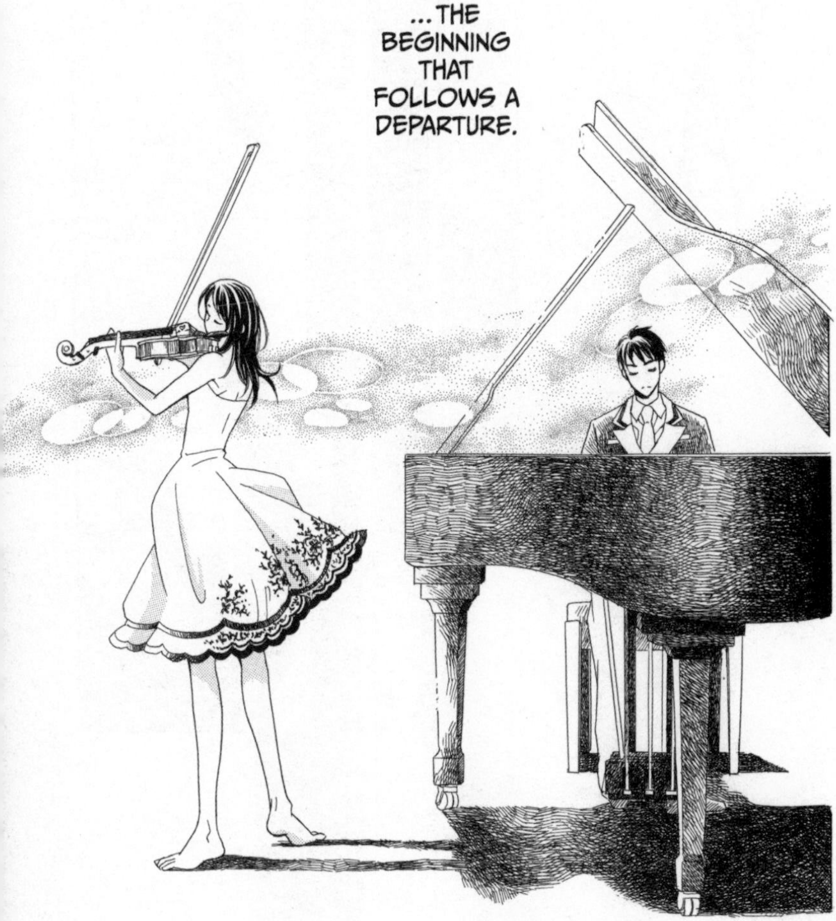
...THE BEGINNING THAT FOLLOWS A DEPARTURE.

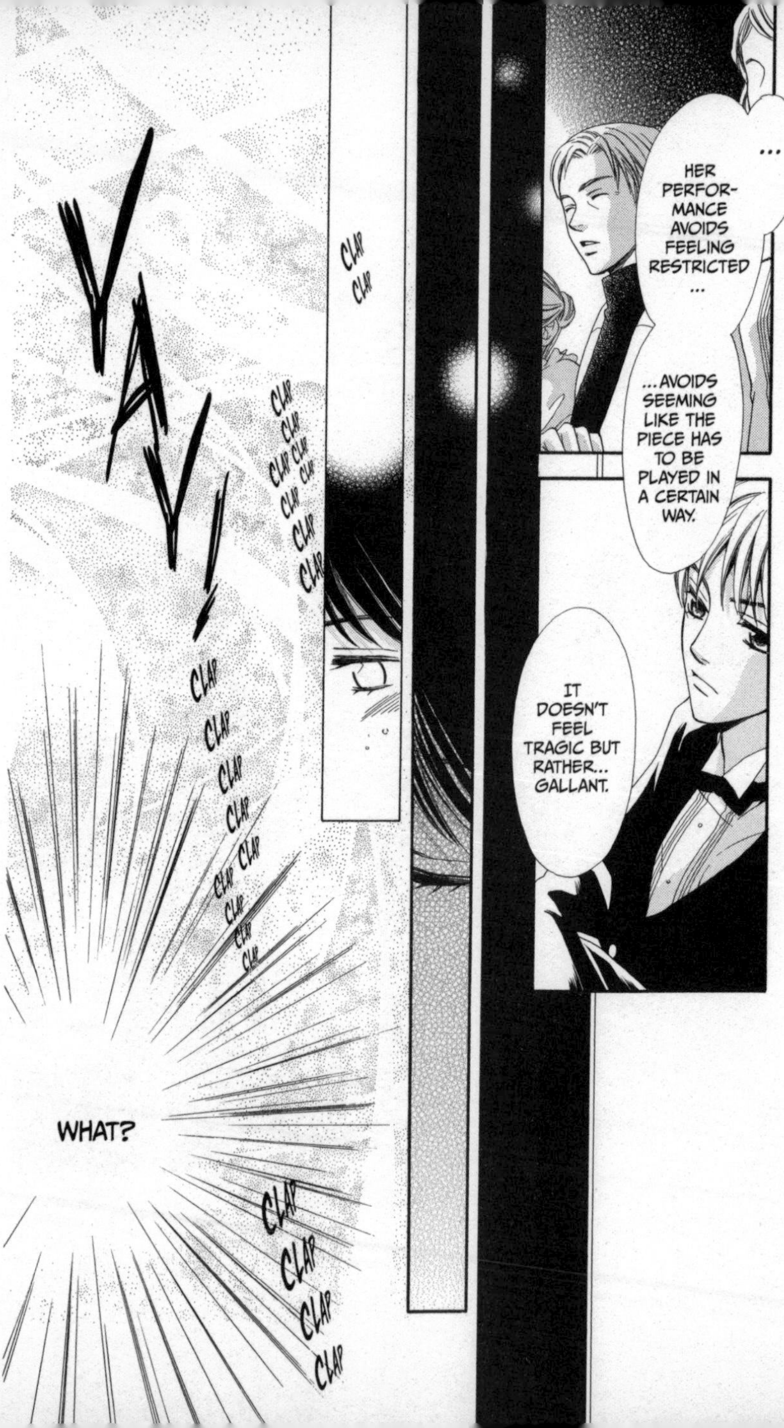
...
HER PERFORMANCE AVOIDS FEELING RESTRICTED ...
...AVOIDS SEEMING LIKE THE PIECE HAS TO BE PLAYED IN A CERTAIN WAY.
IT DOESN'T FEEL TRAGIC BUT RATHER... GALLANT.
CLAP CLAP
CLAP CLAP CLAP CLAP CLAP CLAP CLAP CLAP
YAY!
CLAP CLAP CLAP CLAP CLAP CLAP CLAP CLAP CLAP
WHAT?
CLAP CLAP CLAP CLAP

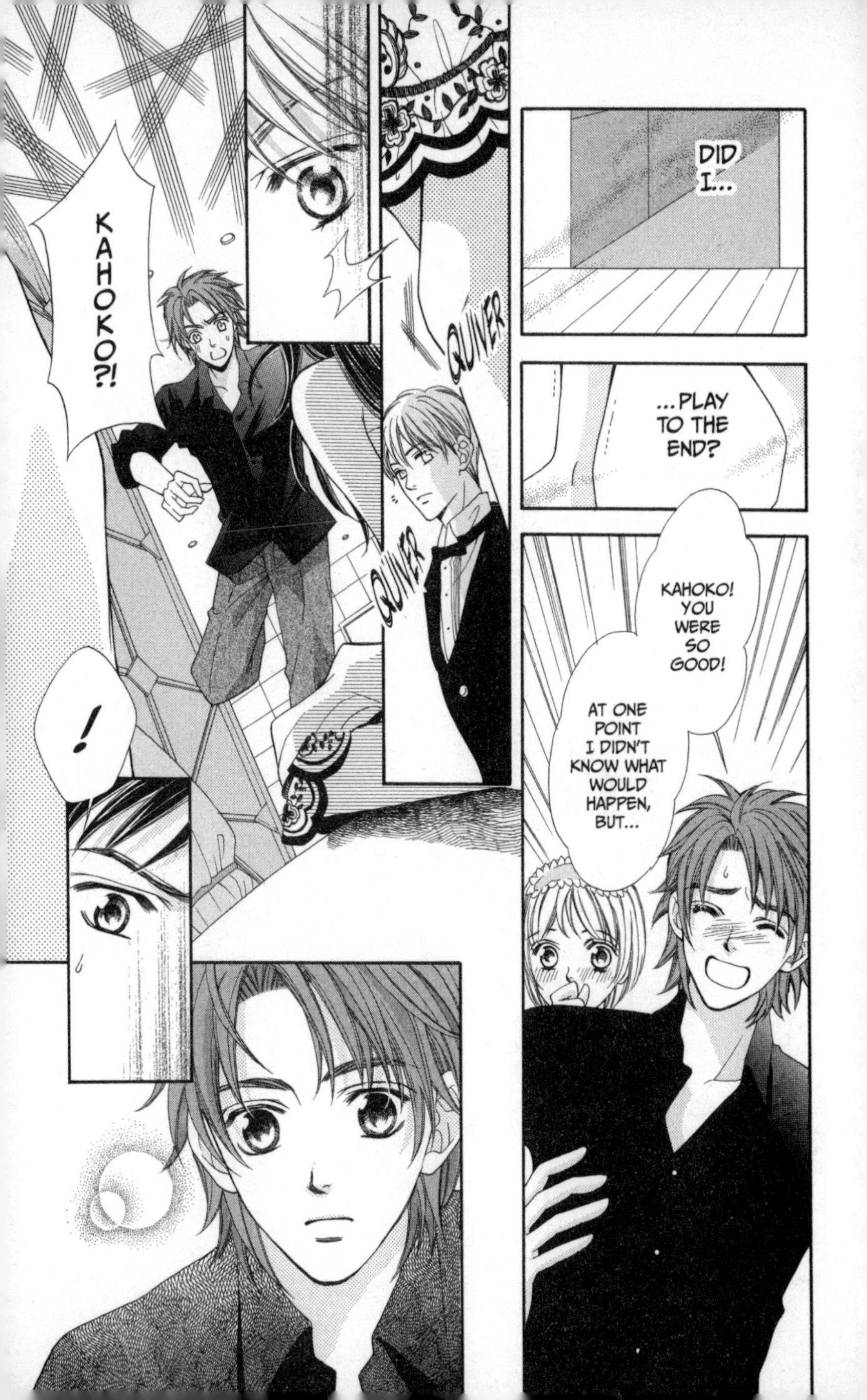
DID I...
...PLAY TO THE END?
KAHOKO! YOU WERE SO GOOD!
AT ONE POINT I DIDN'T KNOW WHAT WOULD HAPPEN, BUT...
QUIVER
QUIVER
KAHOKO?!
!

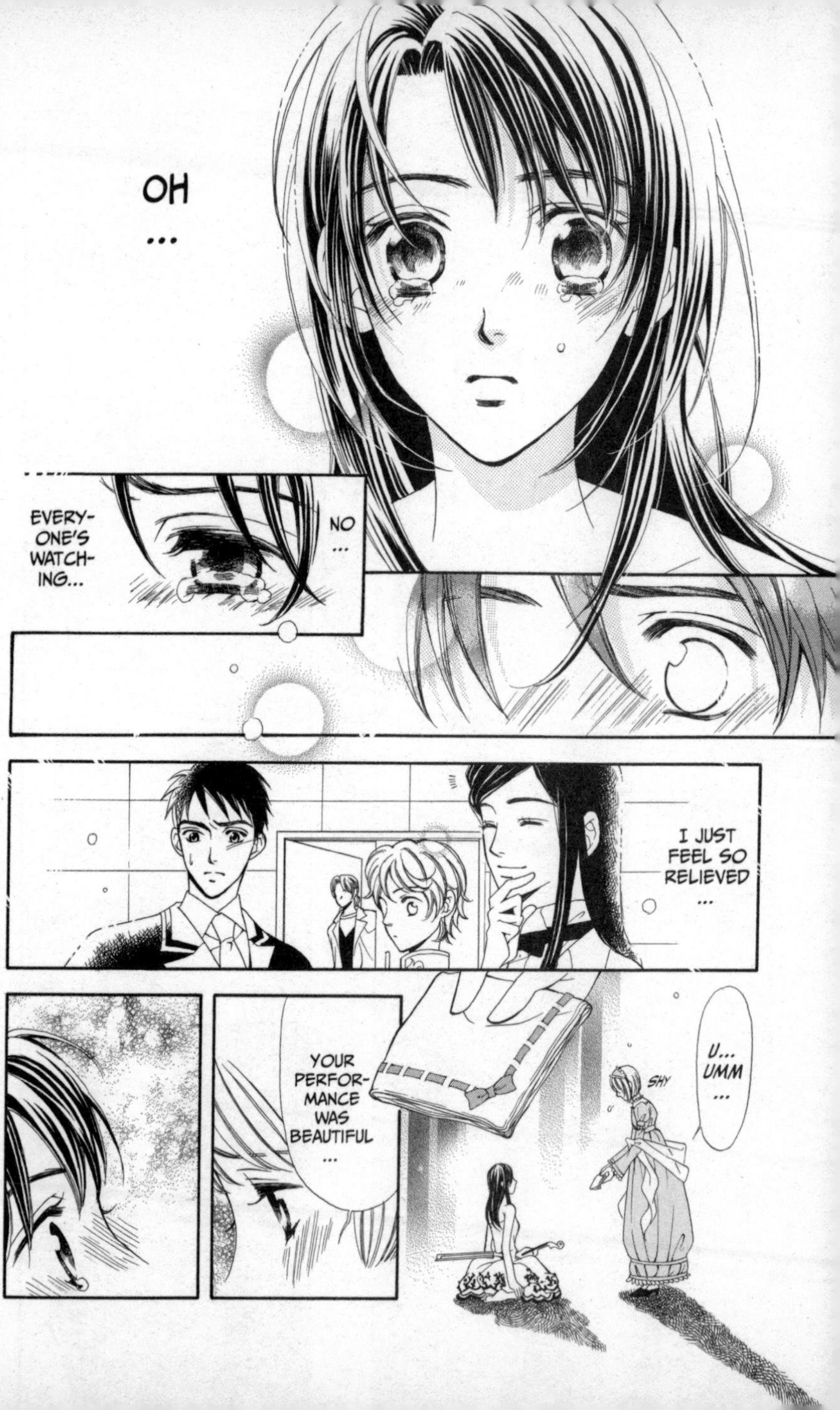
OH ...
NO ...
EVERY-ONE'S WATCH-ING...
I JUST FEEL SO RELIEVED ...
U... UMM ...
SHY
YOUR PERFOR-MANCE WAS BEAUTIFUL ...

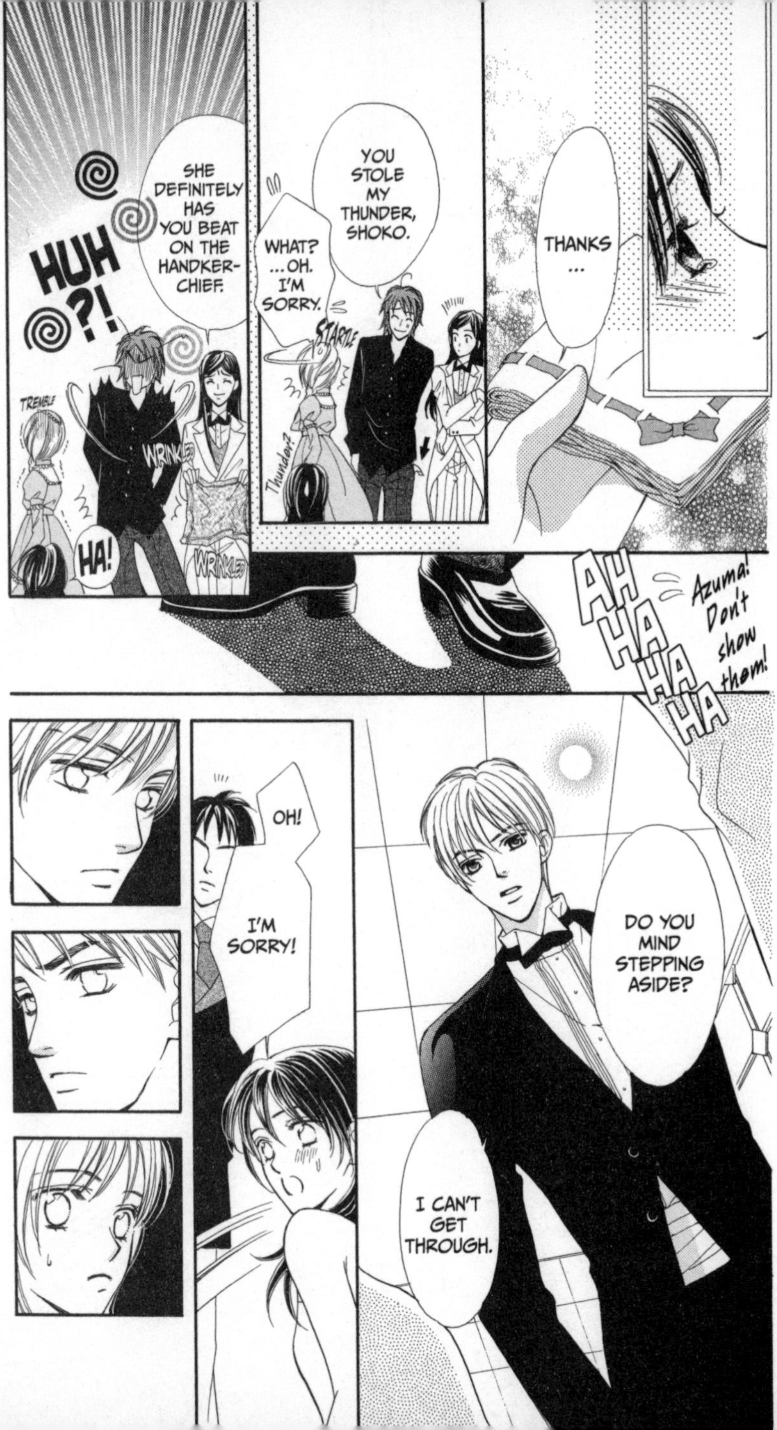
THANKS ...
YOU STOLE MY THUNDER, SHOKO.
WHAT? ...OH. I'M SORRY.
STARTLE
Thunder?
SHE DEFINITELY HAS YOU BEAT ON THE HANDKER-CHIEF.
HUH ?!
TREMBLE
WRINKLED
WRINKLED
HA!
AH HA HA HA HA
Azuma! Don't show them!
DO YOU MIND STEPPING ASIDE?
I CAN'T GET THROUGH.
OH!
I'M SORRY!

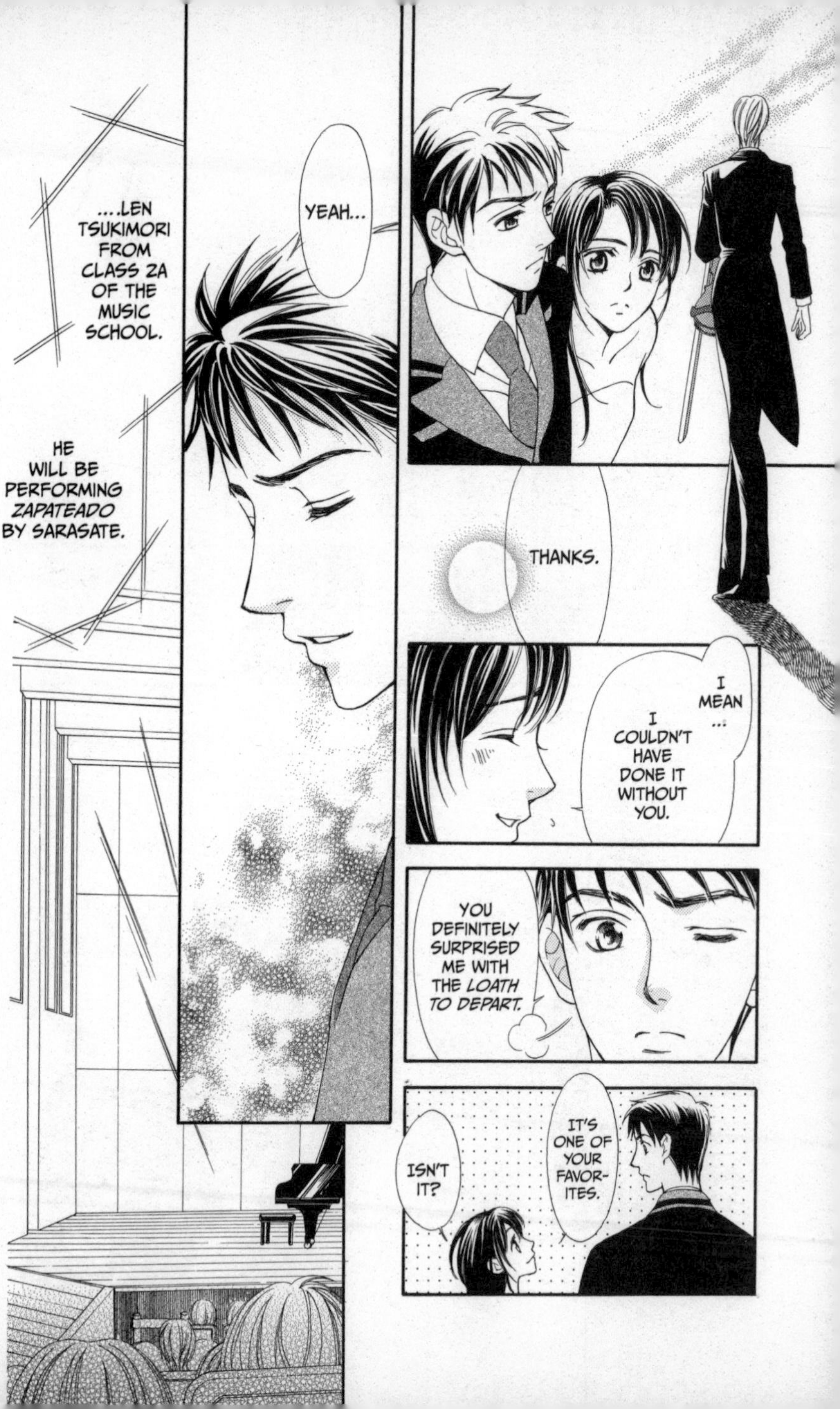
THANKS.
I MEAN...
I COULDN'T HAVE DONE IT WITHOUT YOU.
YOU DEFINITELY SURPRISED ME WITH THE *LOATH TO DEPART.*
IT'S ONE OF YOUR FAVORITES.
ISN'T IT?
YEAH...
....LEN TSUKIMORI FROM CLASS 2A OF THE MUSIC SCHOOL.
HE WILL BE PERFORMING *ZAPATEADO* BY SARASATE.

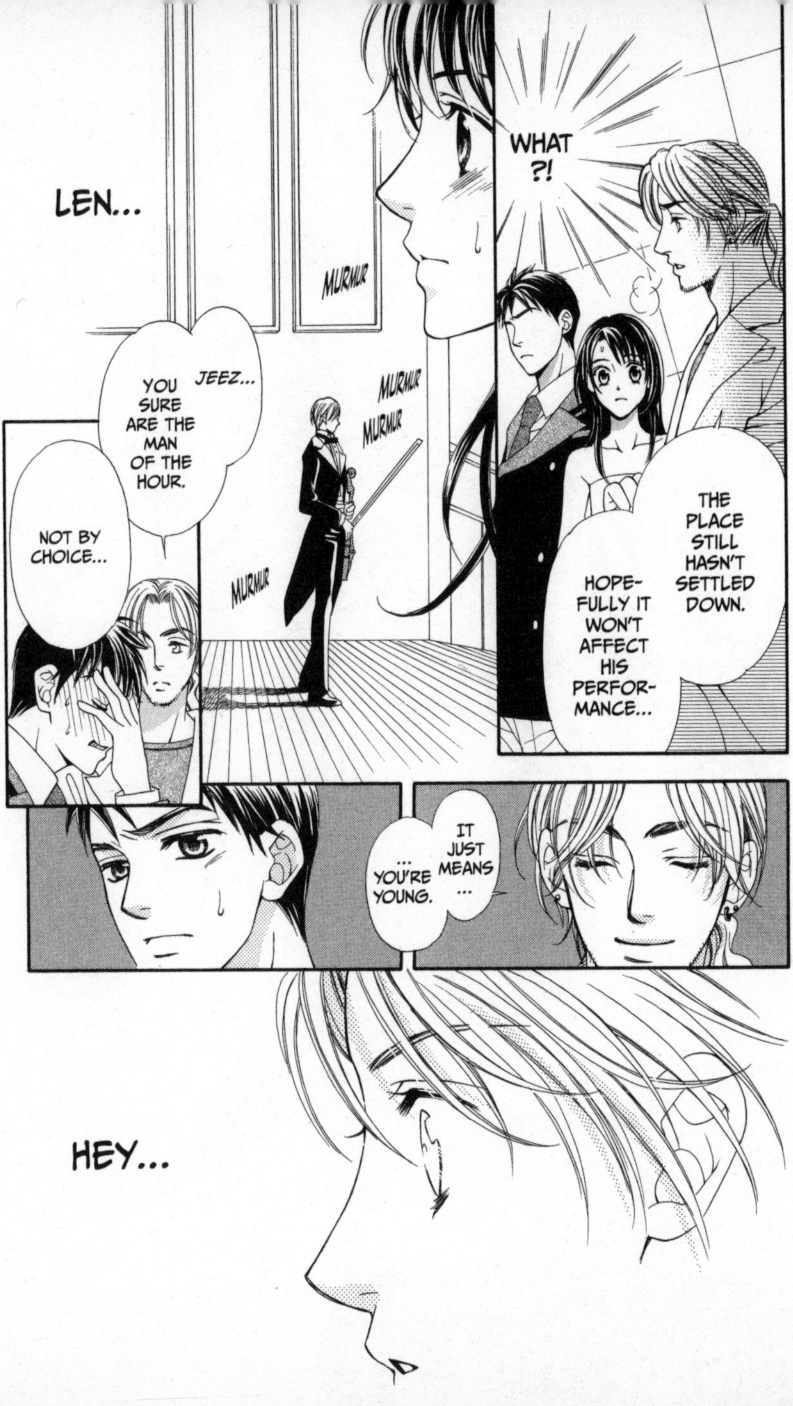
WHAT ?!
THE PLACE STILL HASN'T SETTLED DOWN.
HOPE-FULLY IT WON'T AFFECT HIS PERFORM-MANCE...
LEN...
MURMUR
MURMUR
MURMUR
MURMUR
JEEZ...
YOU SURE ARE THE MAN OF THE HOUR.
NOT BY CHOICE...
IT JUST MEANS ...
... YOU'RE YOUNG.
HEY...

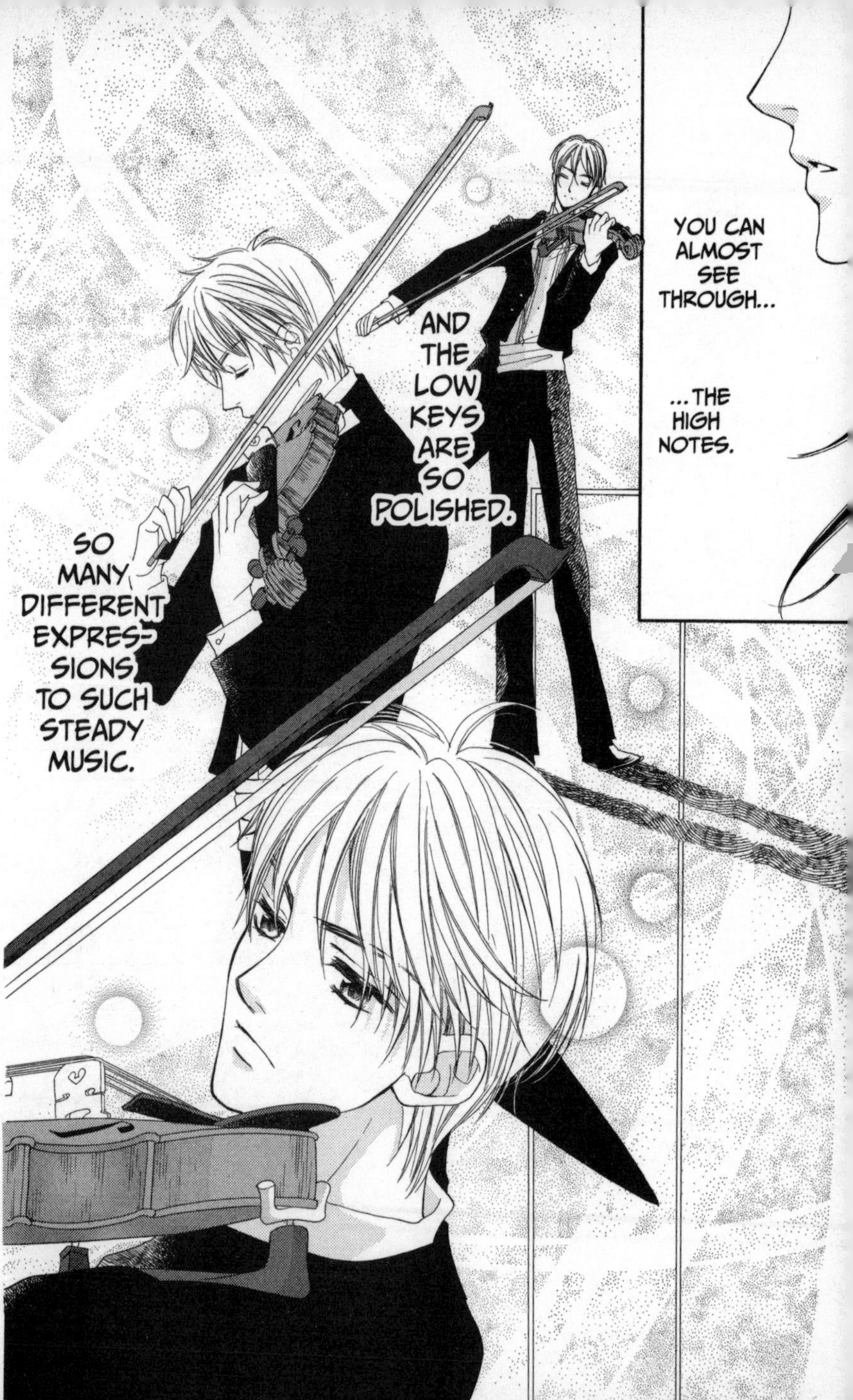
YOU CAN ALMOST SEE THROUGH...
...THE HIGH NOTES.
AND THE LOW KEYS ARE SO POLISHED.
SO MANY DIFFERENT EXPRES-SIONS TO SUCH STEADY MUSIC.

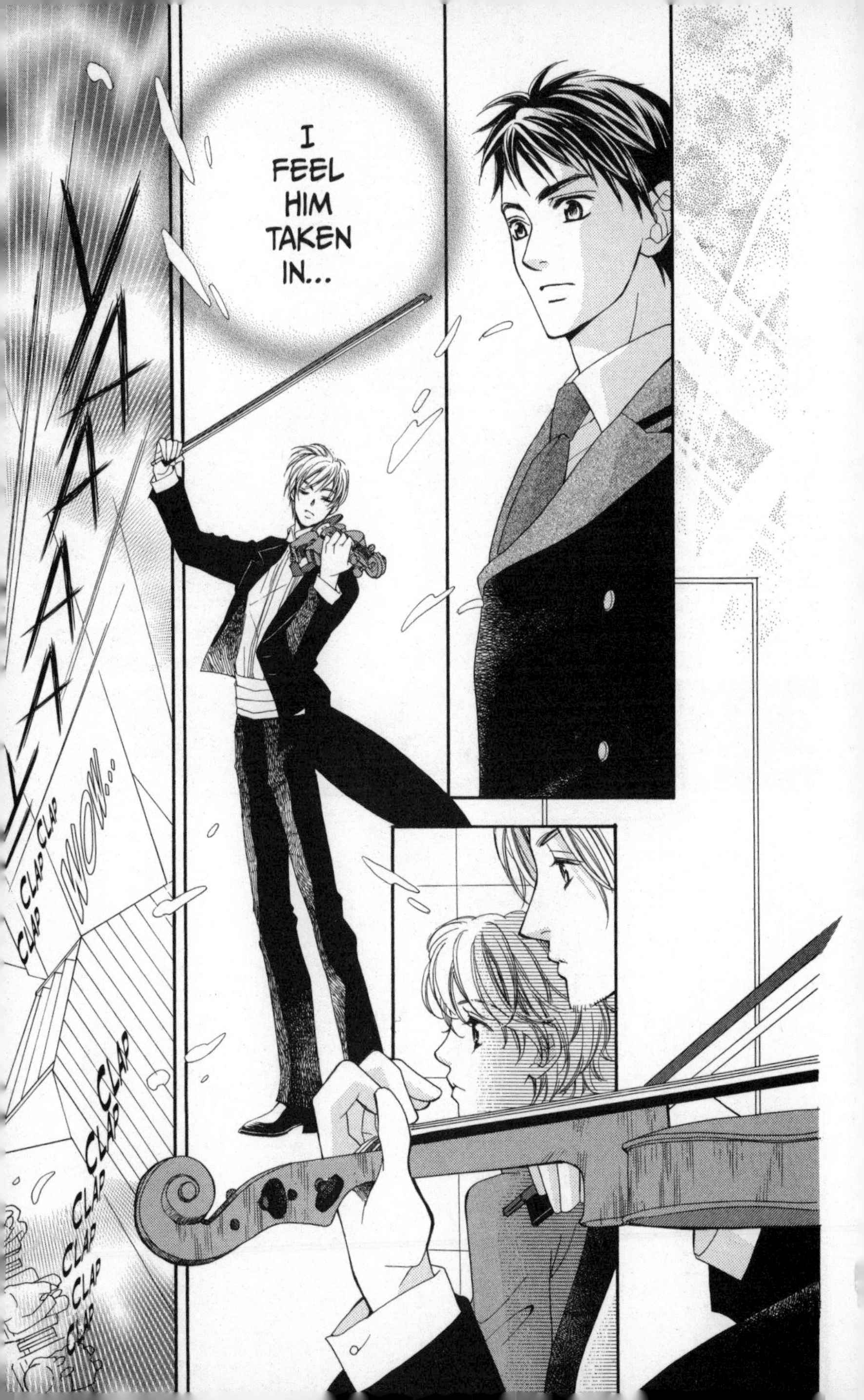
I FEEL HIM TAKEN IN...
YAAAAA
CLAP CLAP CLAP
WOW...
CLAP CLAP CLAP CLAP CLAP CLAP CLAP

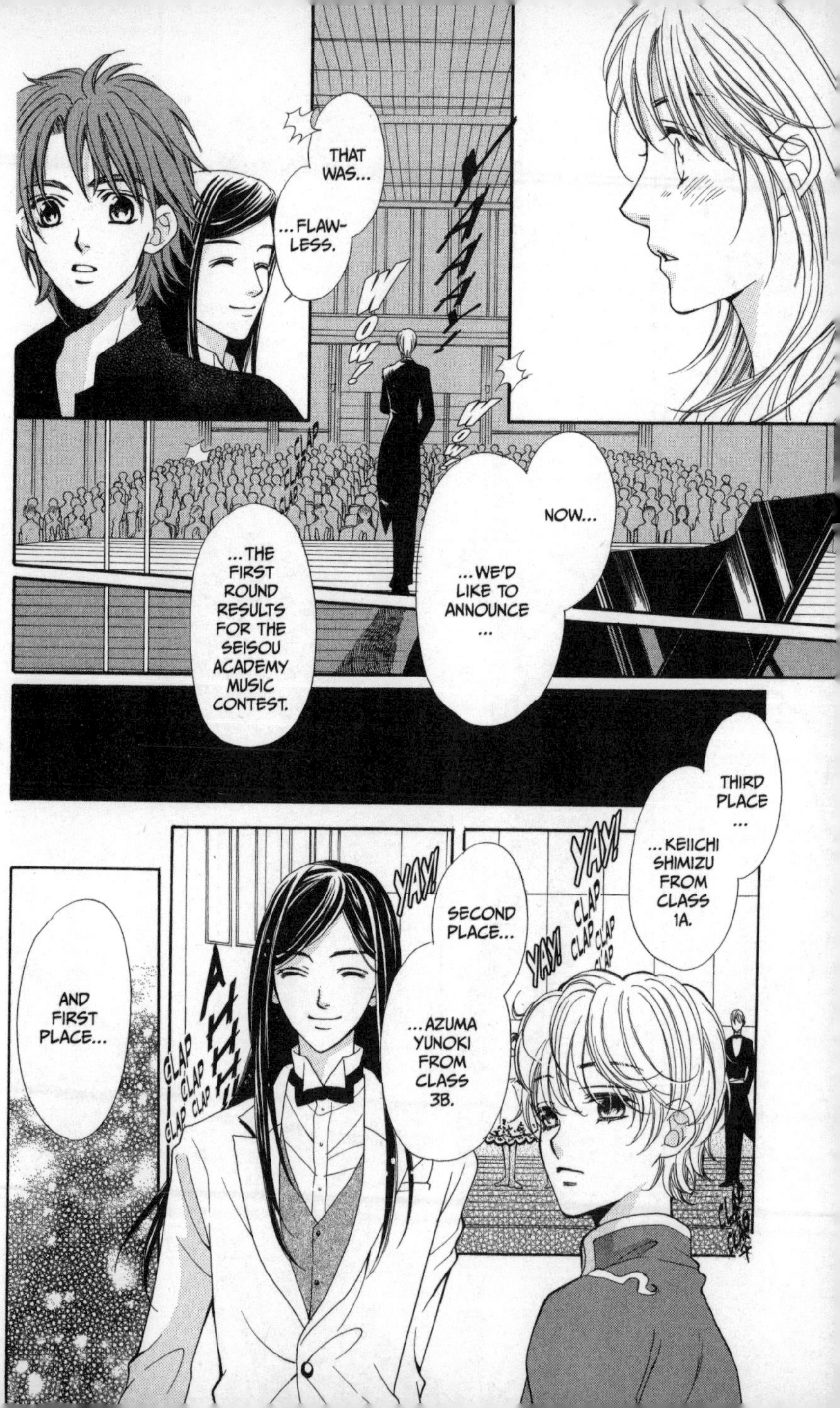
THAT WAS...
...FLAWLESS.
WOW!
WOW!
NOW...
...WE'D LIKE TO ANNOUNCE ...
...THE FIRST ROUND RESULTS FOR THE SEISOU ACADEMY MUSIC CONTEST.
CLAP CLAP CLAP
THIRD PLACE ...
...KEIICHI SHIMIZU FROM CLASS 1A.
YAY!
YAY!
CLAP CLAP CLAP CLAP
YAY!
SECOND PLACE...
...AZUMA YUNOKI FROM CLASS 3B.
CLAP CLAP CLAP CLAP
AND FIRST PLACE...

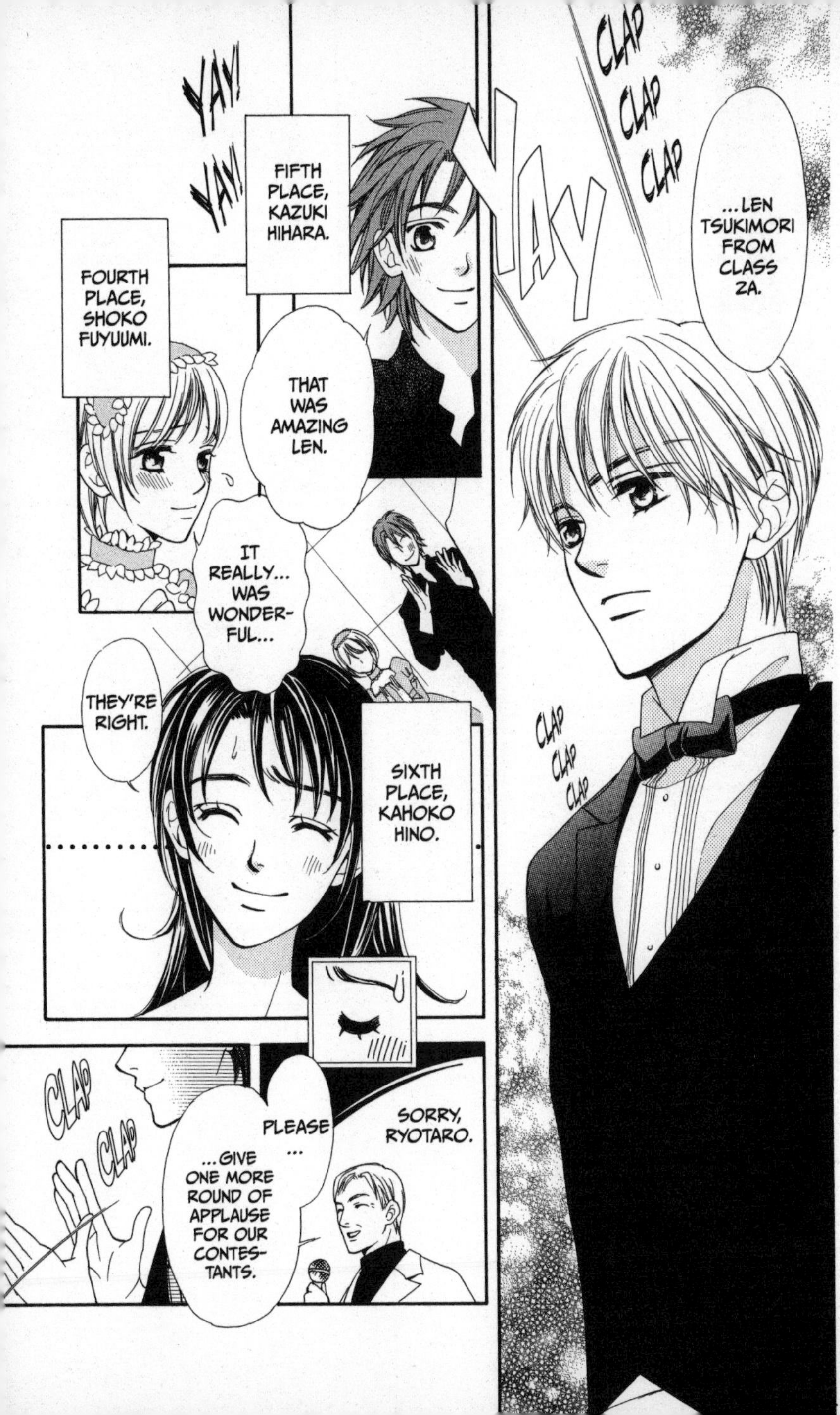

CLAP CLAP CLAP
...LEN TSUKIMORI FROM CLASS 2A.
CLAP CLAP CLAP
YAY
YAY! YAY!
FIFTH PLACE, KAZUKI HIHARA.
FOURTH PLACE, SHOKO FUYUUMI.
THAT WAS AMAZING LEN.
IT REALLY... WAS WONDERFUL...
SIXTH PLACE, KAHOKO HINO.
THEY'RE RIGHT.
....
SORRY, RYOTARO.
PLEASE ...
...GIVE ONE MORE ROUND OF APPLAUSE FOR OUR CONTESTANTS.
CLAP CLAP

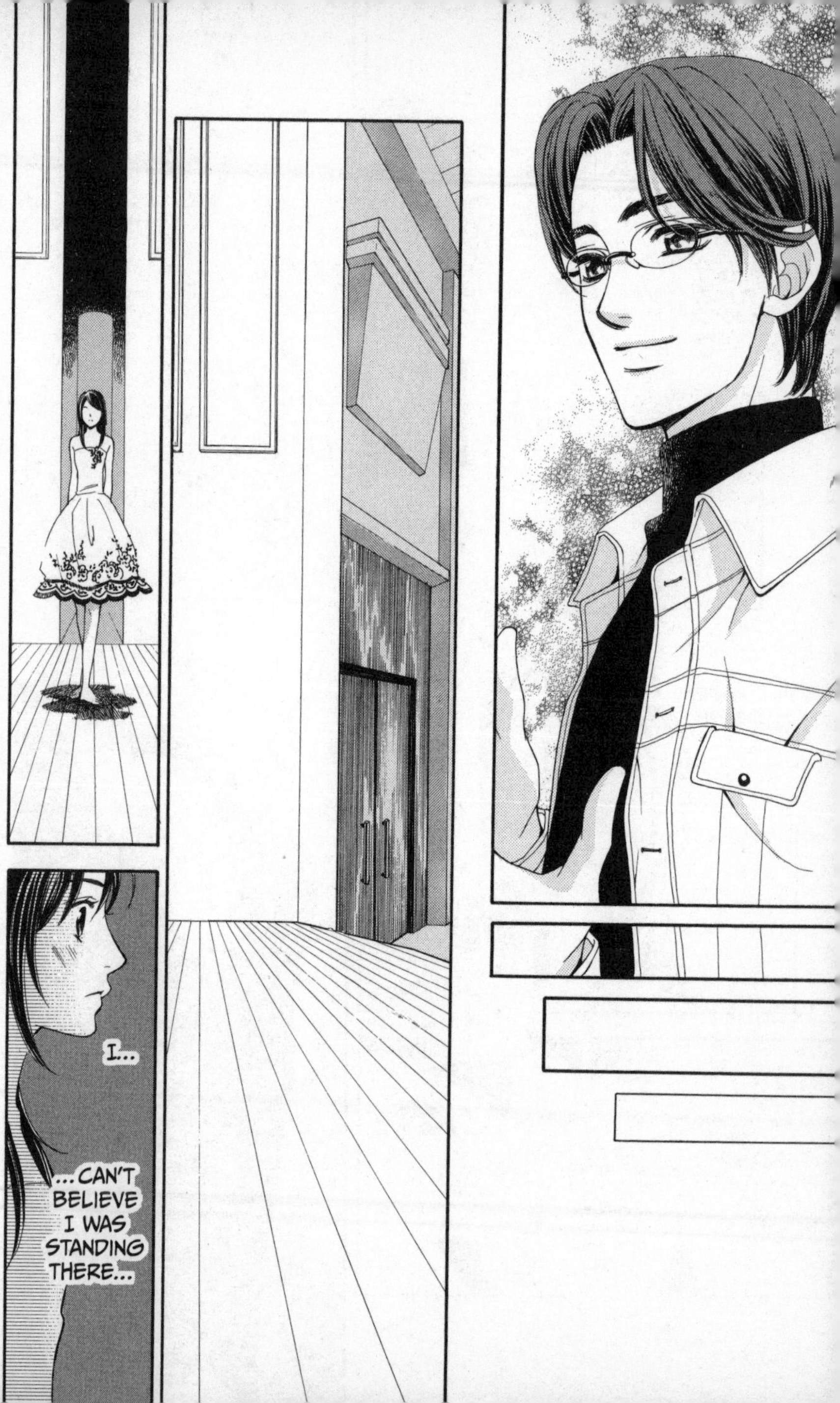
I...
...CAN'T BELIEVE I WAS STANDING THERE...

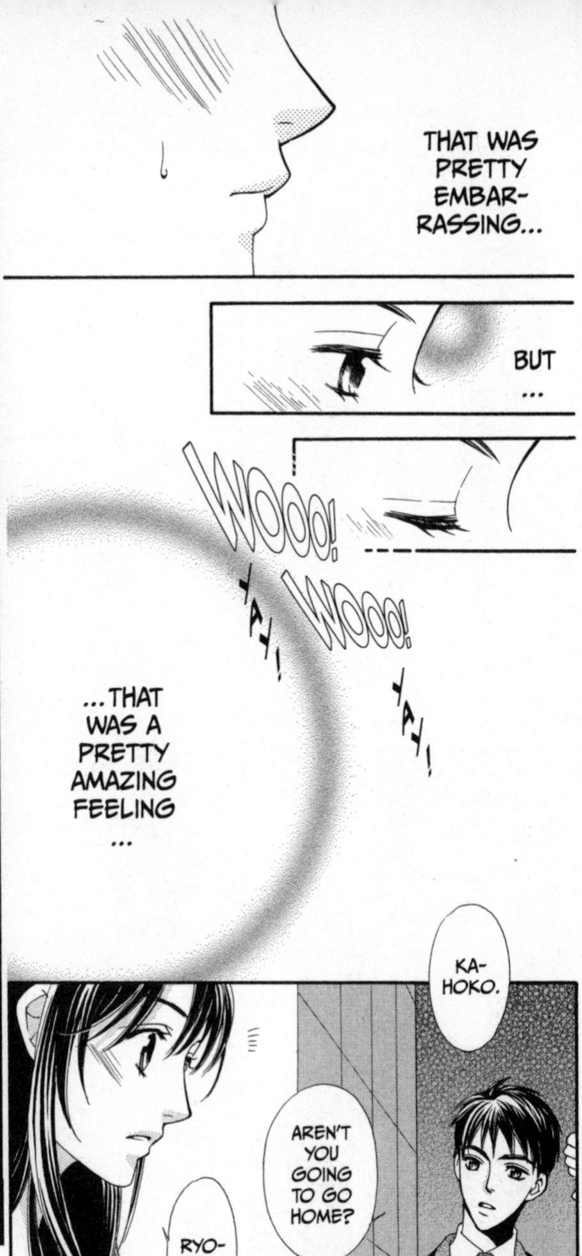
THAT WAS PRETTY EMBAR-RASSING...
BUT ...
WOOO!
YAY!
WOOO!
YAY!
...THAT WAS A PRETTY AMAZING FEELING ...
KA-HOKO.
AREN'T YOU GOING TO GO HOME?
RYO-TARO.

TWO

♥

The First Round Edition

This was where I tried to get Ryotaro to play the piano. Yep...

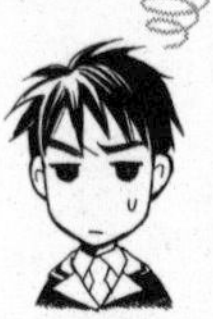

As with their outfits, I used the music that each character plays in the game, with the exception of Kahoko. I'm a huge fan of Len's Zapateado. It's a great piece of music. I thought that their ranking was pretty innocuous, but what do you think? There may be more variation in their placement for the Second Round... Probably... I hope to be able to draw the performance scenes better as well. I'll do my best.

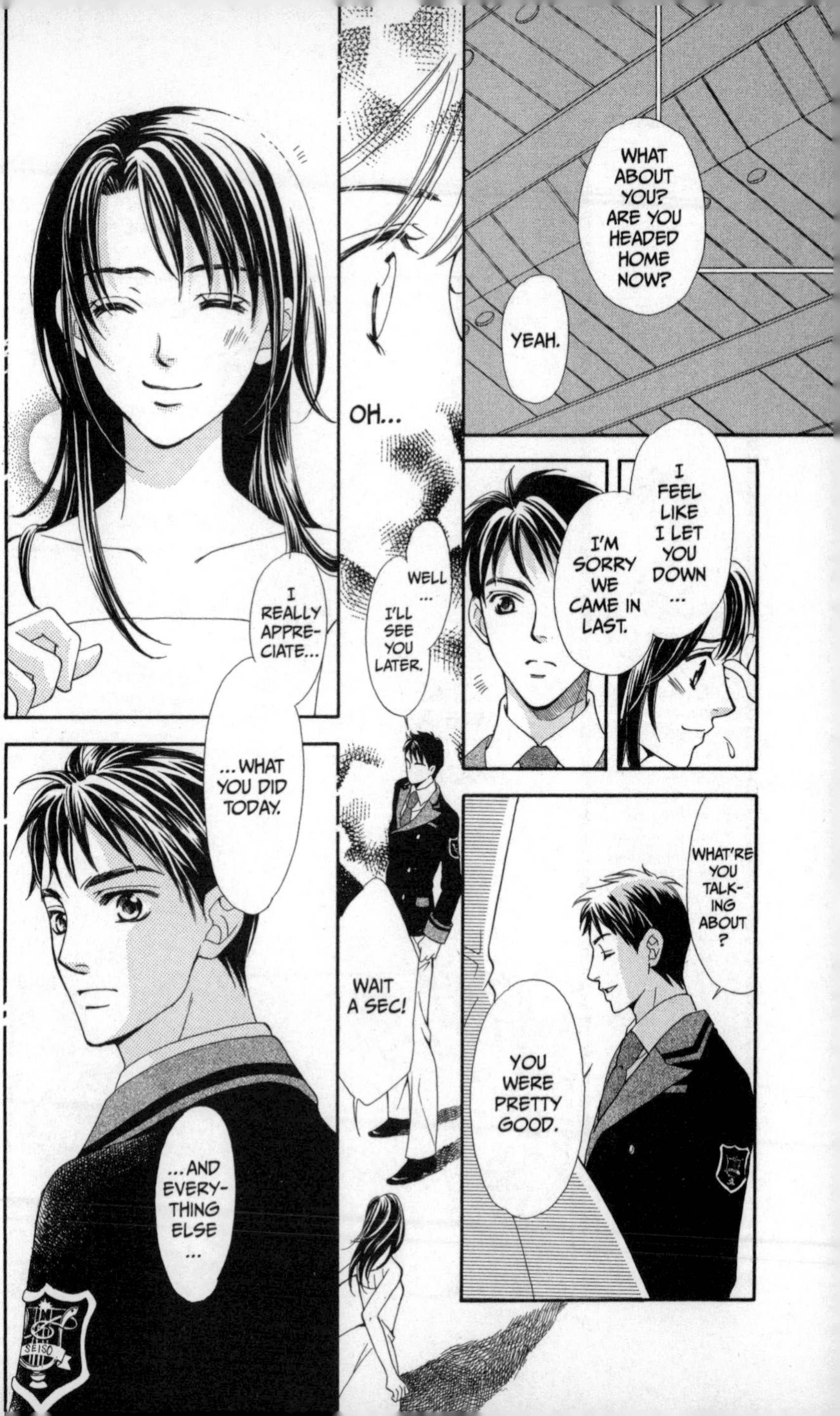
WHAT ABOUT YOU? ARE YOU HEADED HOME NOW?
YEAH.
I FEEL LIKE I LET YOU DOWN...
I'M SORRY WE CAME IN LAST.
WHAT'RE YOU TALKING ABOUT?
YOU WERE PRETTY GOOD.
OH...
WELL... I'LL SEE YOU LATER.
WAIT A SEC!
I REALLY APPRECIATE...
...WHAT YOU DID TODAY.
...AND EVERYTHING ELSE...
SEISO

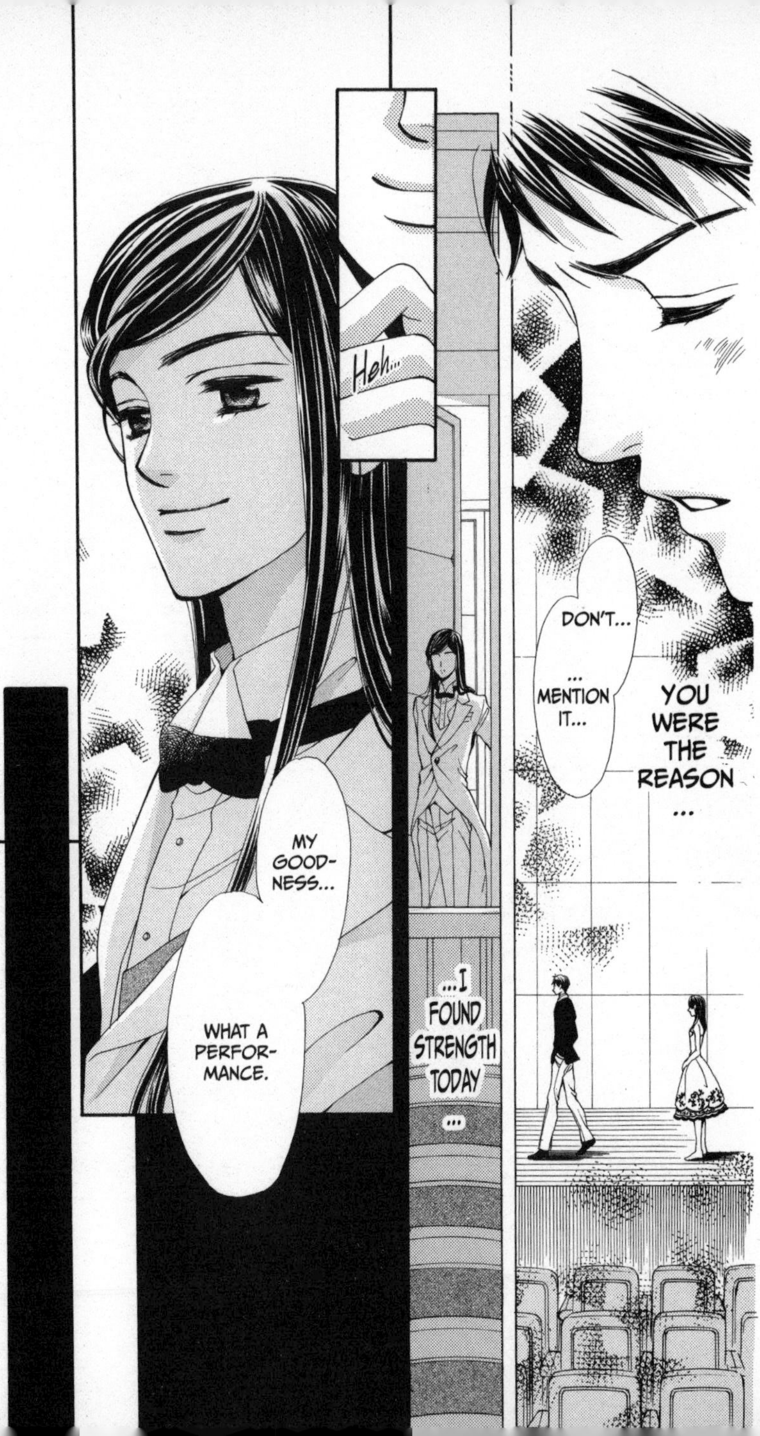
YOU WERE THE REASON ...
DON'T...
... MENTION IT...
...I FOUND STRENGTH TODAY ...
Heh...
MY GOODNESS...
WHAT A PERFORMANCE.

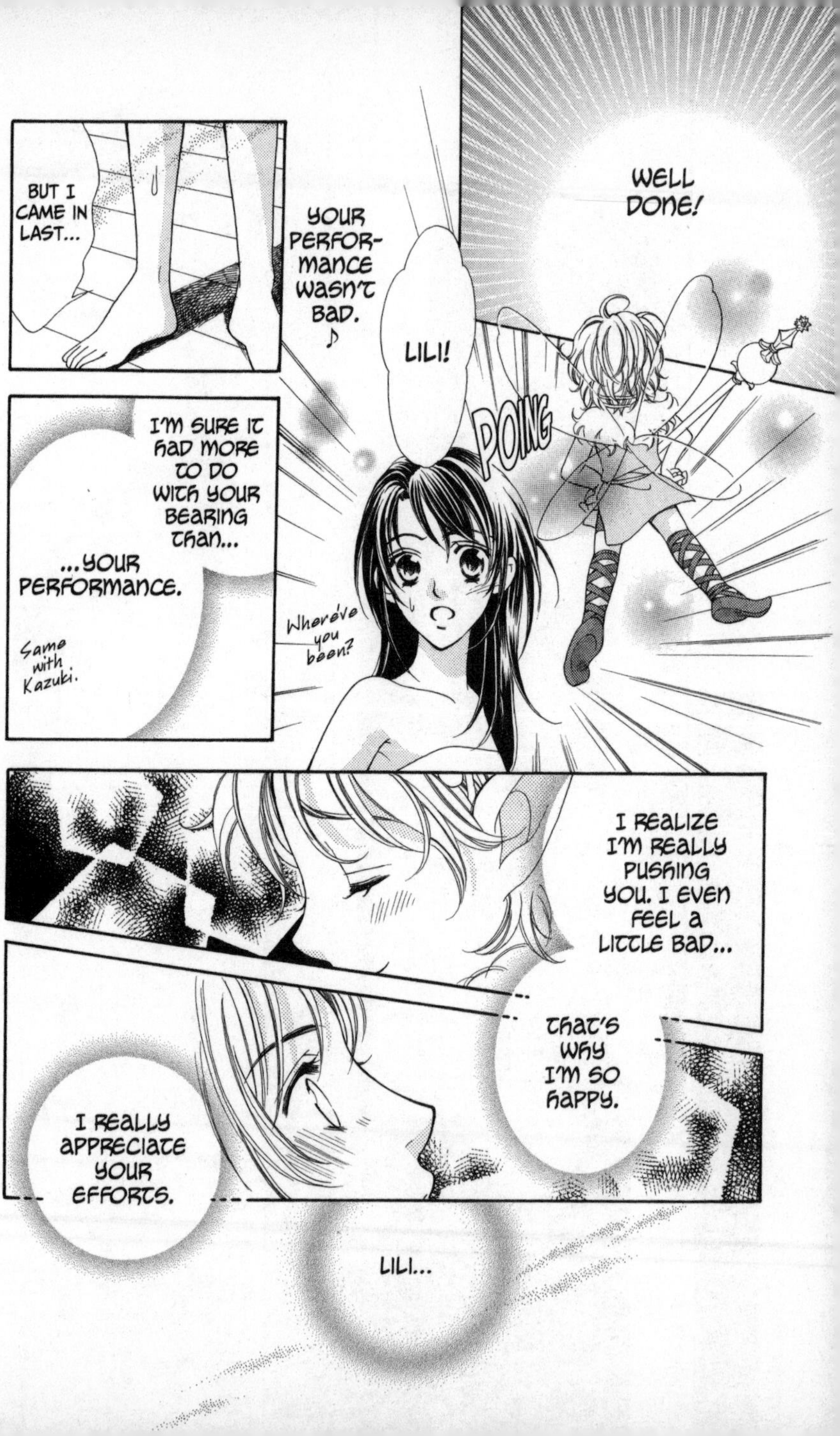
WELL DONE!
POING
LILI!
Where've you been?
YOUR PERFORMANCE WASN'T BAD. ♪
BUT I CAME IN LAST...
I'M SURE IT HAD MORE TO DO WITH YOUR BEARING THAN...
...YOUR PERFORMANCE.
Same with Kazuki.
I REALIZE I'M REALLY PUSHING YOU. I EVEN FEEL A LITTLE BAD...
THAT'S WHY I'M SO HAPPY.
I REALLY APPRECIATE YOUR EFFORTS.
LILI...

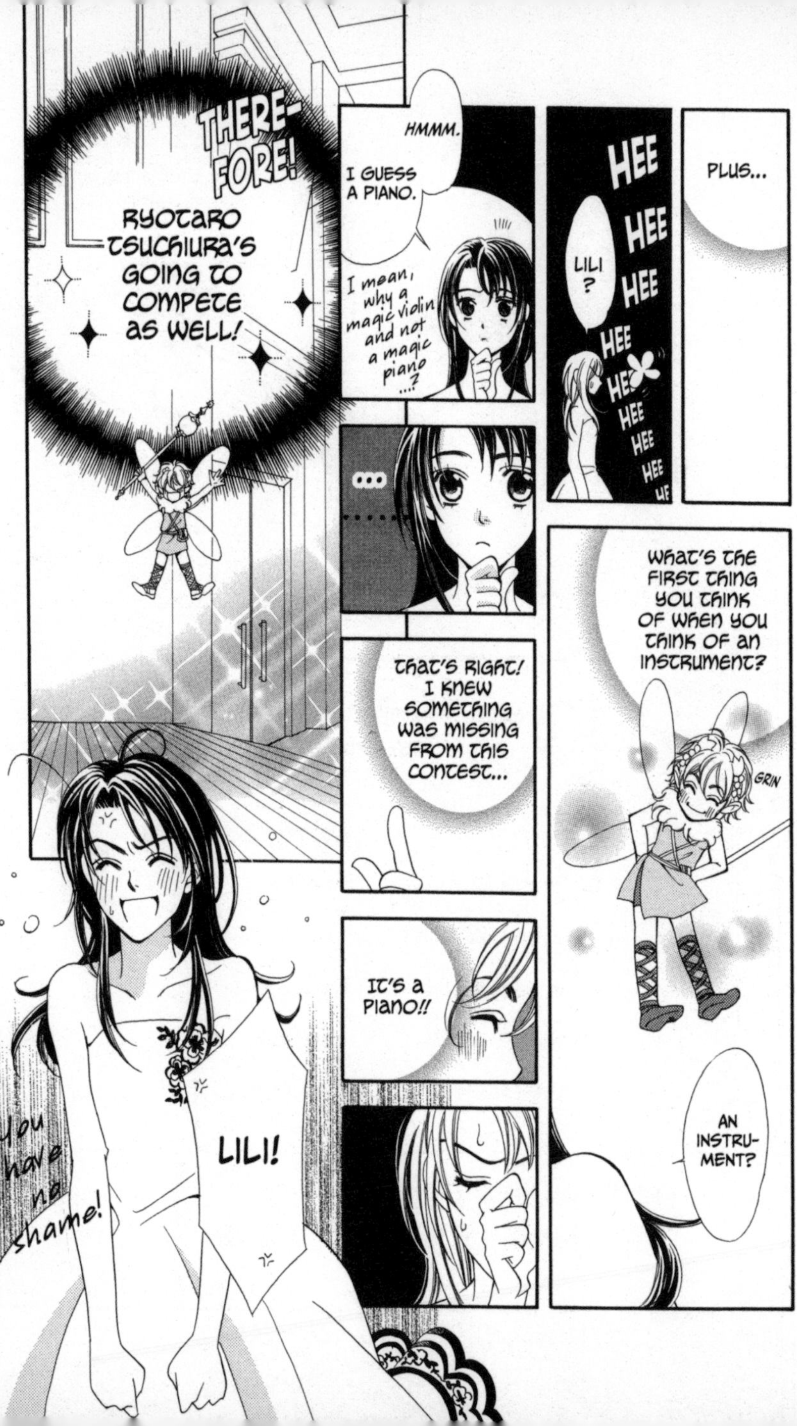
PLUS...
WHAT'S THE FIRST THING YOU THINK OF WHEN YOU THINK OF AN INSTRUMENT?
GRIN
AN INSTRUMENT?
HMMM.
I GUESS A PIANO.
I mean, why a magic violin and not a magic piano...?
...
THAT'S RIGHT! I KNEW SOMETHING WAS MISSING FROM THIS CONTEST...
IT'S A PIANO!!
LILI?
HEE HEE HEE HEE HEE HEE HEE HEE HE
THERE-FORE!
RYOTARO TSUCHIURA'S GOING TO COMPETE AS WELL!
LILI!
You have no shame!

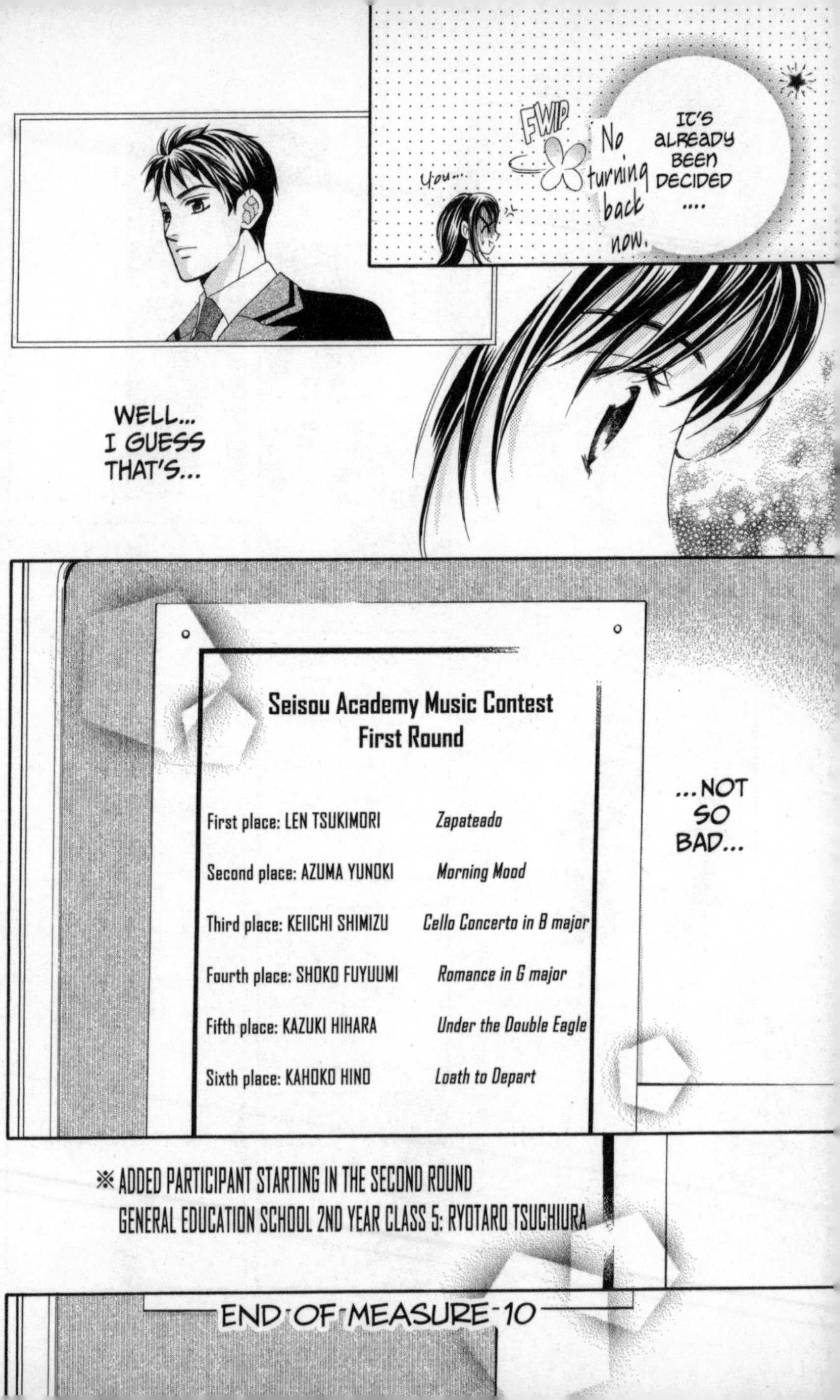
IT'S ALREADY BEEN DECIDED....
No turning back now.
FWIP
You...
WELL... I GUESS THAT'S...
...NOT SO BAD...
Seisou Academy Music Contest
First Round
First place: LEN TSUKIMORI	Zapateado
Second place: AZUMA YUNOKI	Morning Mood
Third place: KEIICHI SHIMIZU	Cello Concerto in B major
Fourth place: SHOKO FUYUUMI	Romance in G major
Fifth place: KAZUKI HIHARA	Under the Double Eagle
Sixth place: KAHOKO HINO	Loath to Depart
※ ADDED PARTICIPANT STARTING IN THE SECOND ROUND
GENERAL EDUCATION SCHOOL 2ND YEAR CLASS 5: RYOTARO TSUCHIURA
END OF MEASURE 10

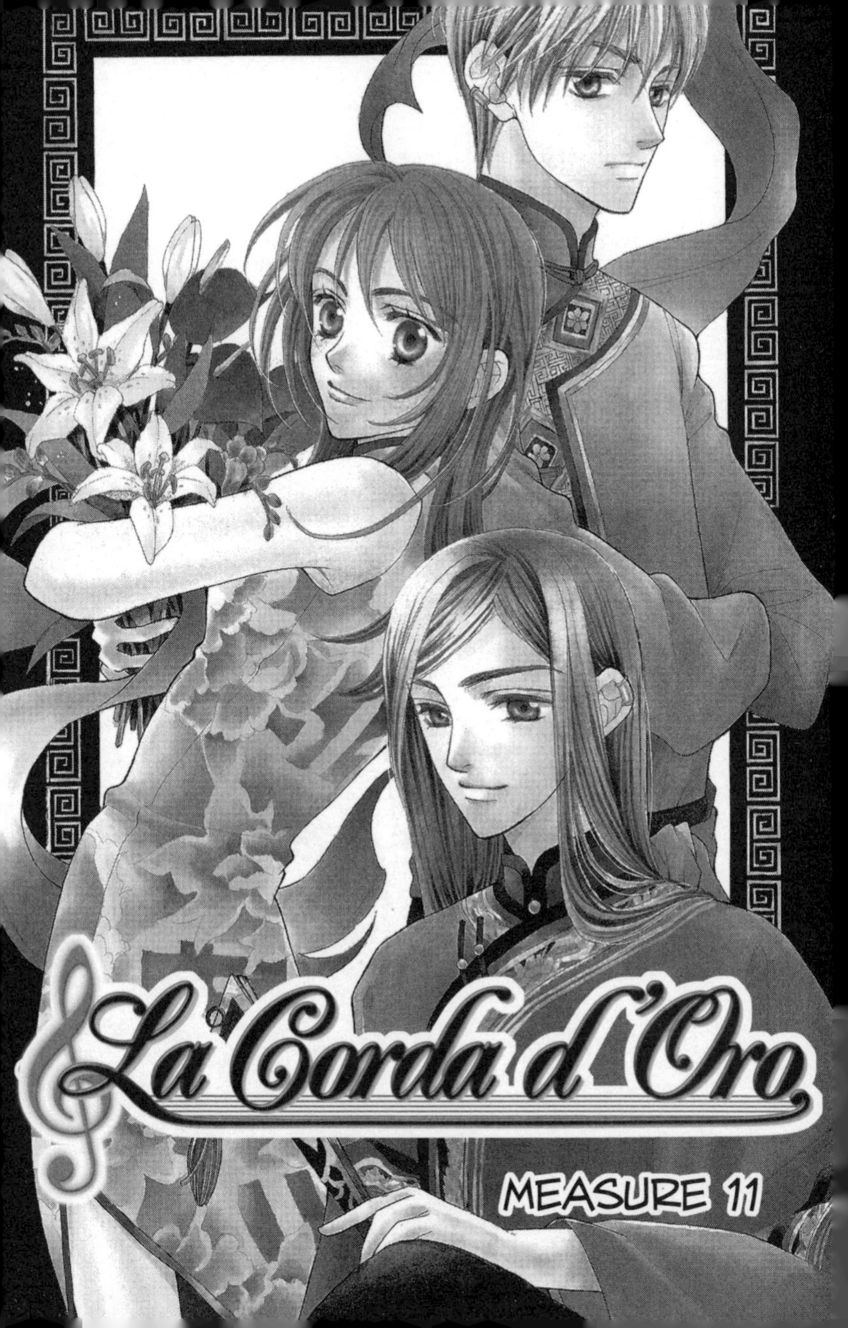
La Corda d'Oro
MEASURE 11

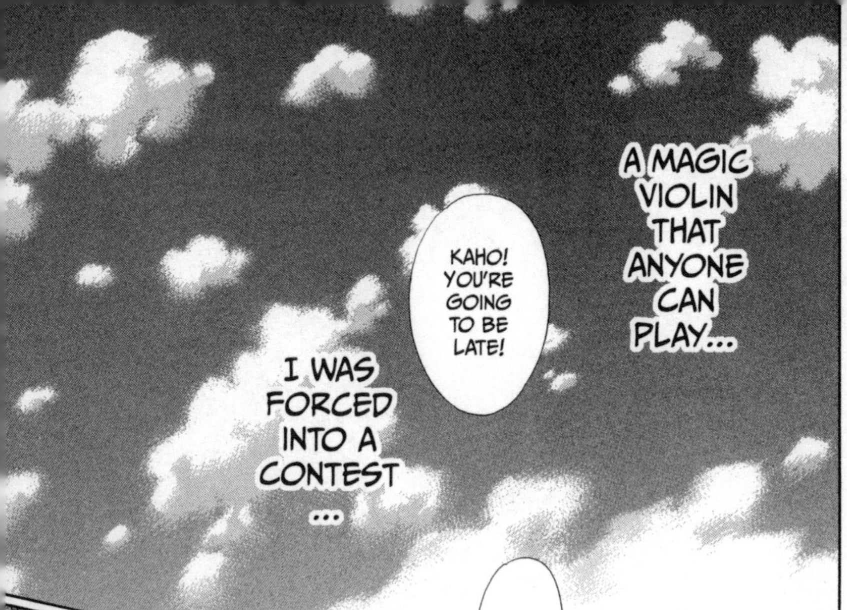
A MAGIC VIOLIN THAT ANYONE CAN PLAY...
KAHO! YOU'RE GOING TO BE LATE!
I WAS FORCED INTO A CONTEST...
I SOMEHOW SURVIVED THE FIRST ROUND. (THOUGH I CAME IN LAST...)
I KNOW!
SEE YOU LATER!

DAILY HAPPENINGS

③ Autograph boards

I've actually never gone to a signing party, but I do have two autographed boards. And they've got original illustrations! How did I come across them, you ask? I was at a bookstore one day, mindlessly looking up at the signed boards above the cashier. ↗

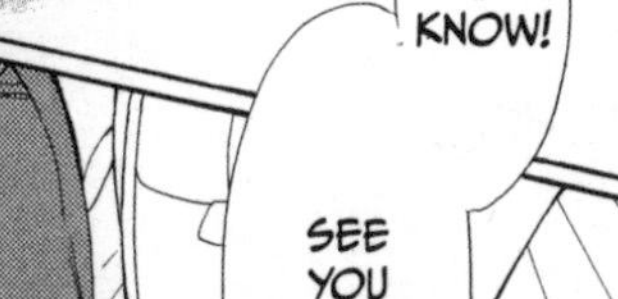
auto-graphed boards →
HUH ?!
Are you seri-ous?!
We've got a board that's not up there. Would you like it?

I was actually buying fashion magazines and not manga at the time, so why I don't know... I guess I looked pretty desperate... How embarrassing, but still a very happy day for me... It's by an author who's published through Kado[redacted]. Hee hee hee... The other one is signed by Mr. Takashi Yanase. My boss at my old job got it for me because I'm such a huge fan!

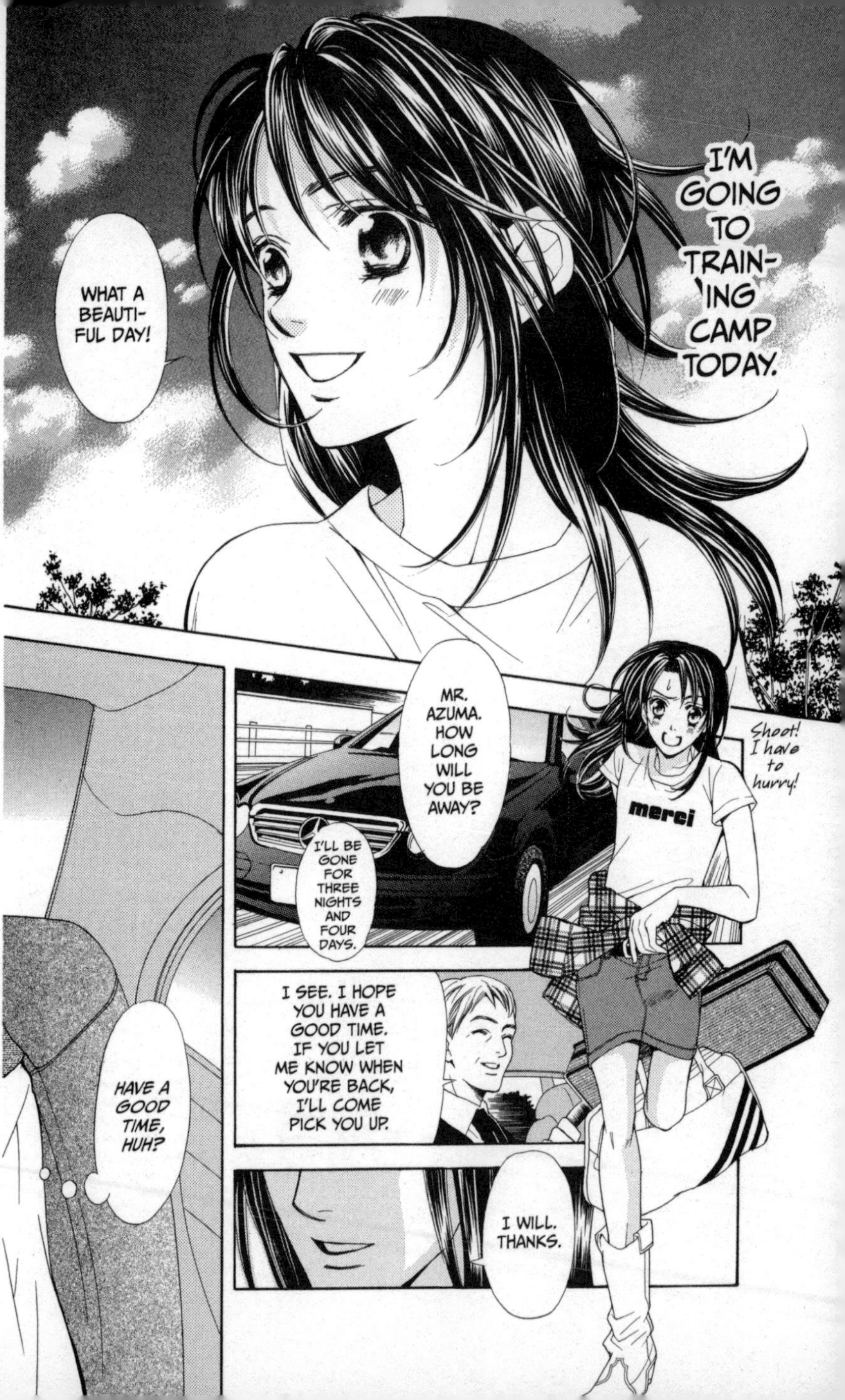
I'M GOING TO TRAIN-ING CAMP TODAY.
WHAT A BEAUTI-FUL DAY!
Shoot! I have to hurry!
merci
MR. AZUMA. HOW LONG WILL YOU BE AWAY?
I'LL BE GONE FOR THREE NIGHTS AND FOUR DAYS.
I SEE. I HOPE YOU HAVE A GOOD TIME. IF YOU LET ME KNOW WHEN YOU'RE BACK, I'LL COME PICK YOU UP.
I WILL. THANKS.
HAVE A GOOD TIME, HUH?

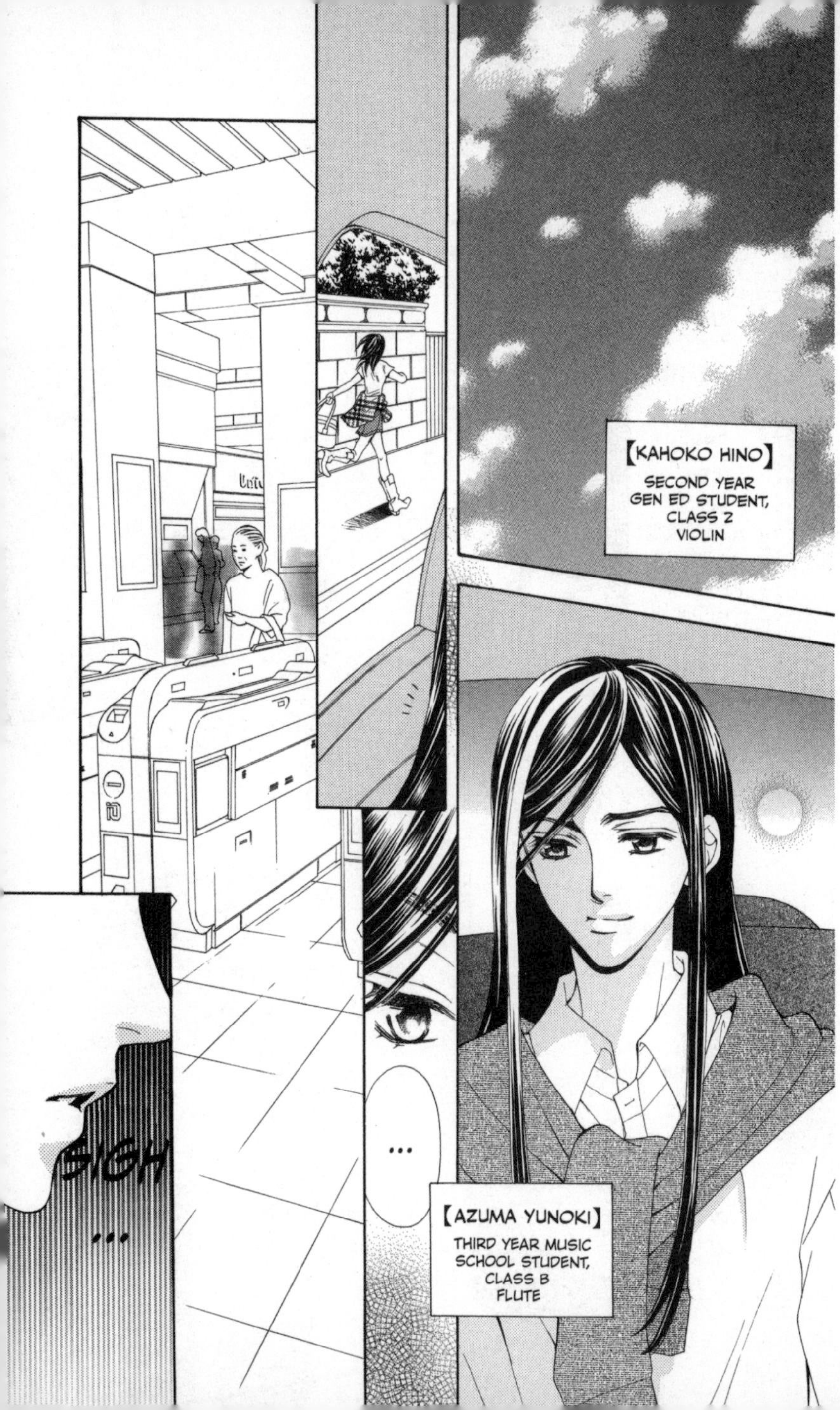
【KAHOKO HINO】
SECOND YEAR GEN ED STUDENT, CLASS 2 VIOLIN
【AZUMA YUNOKI】
THIRD YEAR MUSIC SCHOOL STUDENT, CLASS B FLUTE
...
SIGH
...

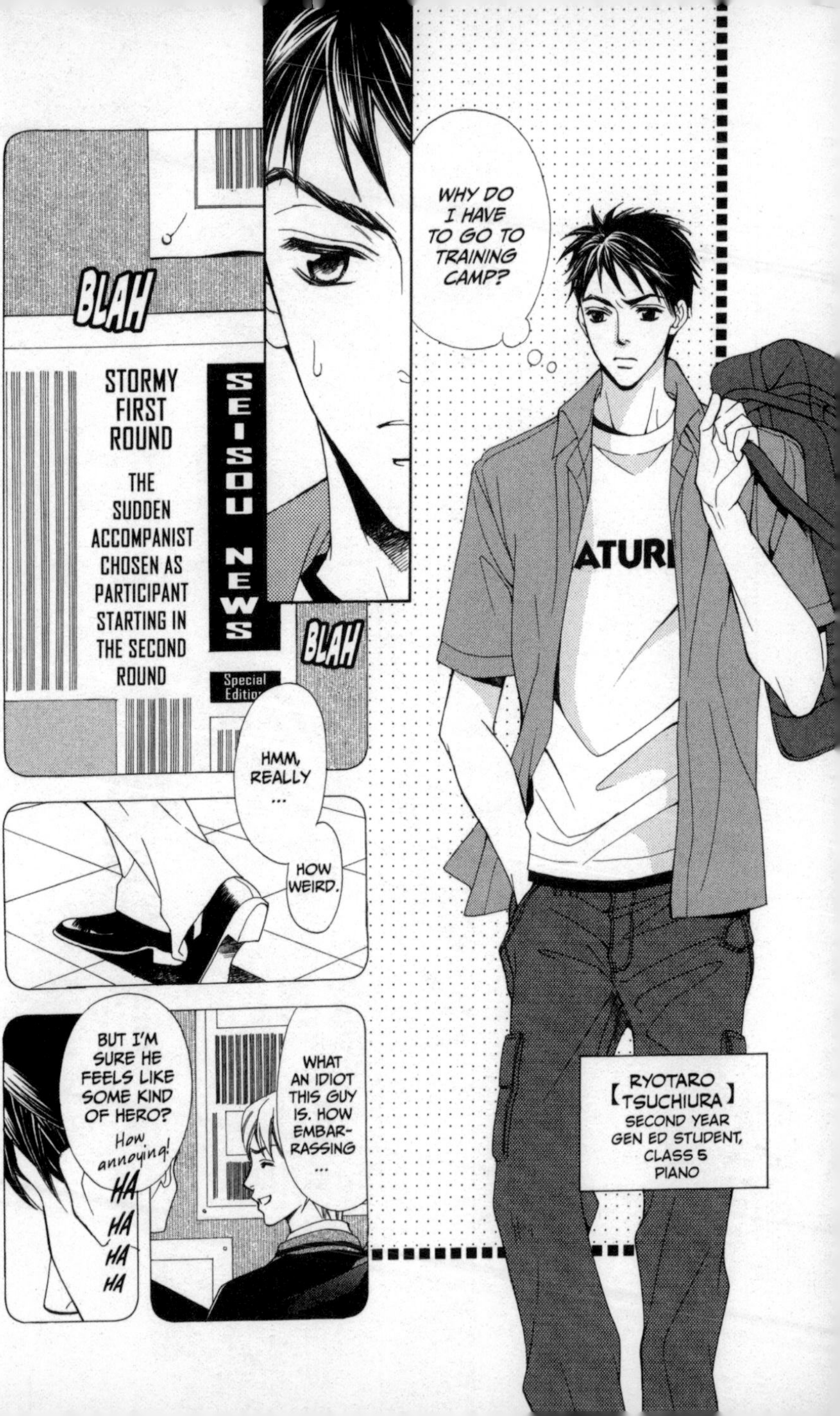
WHY DO I HAVE TO GO TO TRAINING CAMP?
【RYOTARO TSUCHIURA】 SECOND YEAR GEN ED STUDENT, CLASS 5 PIANO
SEISOU NEWS
Special Edition
STORMY FIRST ROUND
THE SUDDEN ACCOMPANIST CHOSEN AS PARTICIPANT STARTING IN THE SECOND ROUND
BLAH
BLAH
HMM, REALLY ...
HOW WEIRD.
WHAT AN IDIOT THIS GUY IS. HOW EMBARRASSING ...
BUT I'M SURE HE FEELS LIKE SOME KIND OF HERO?
How annoying!
HA HA HA HA HA

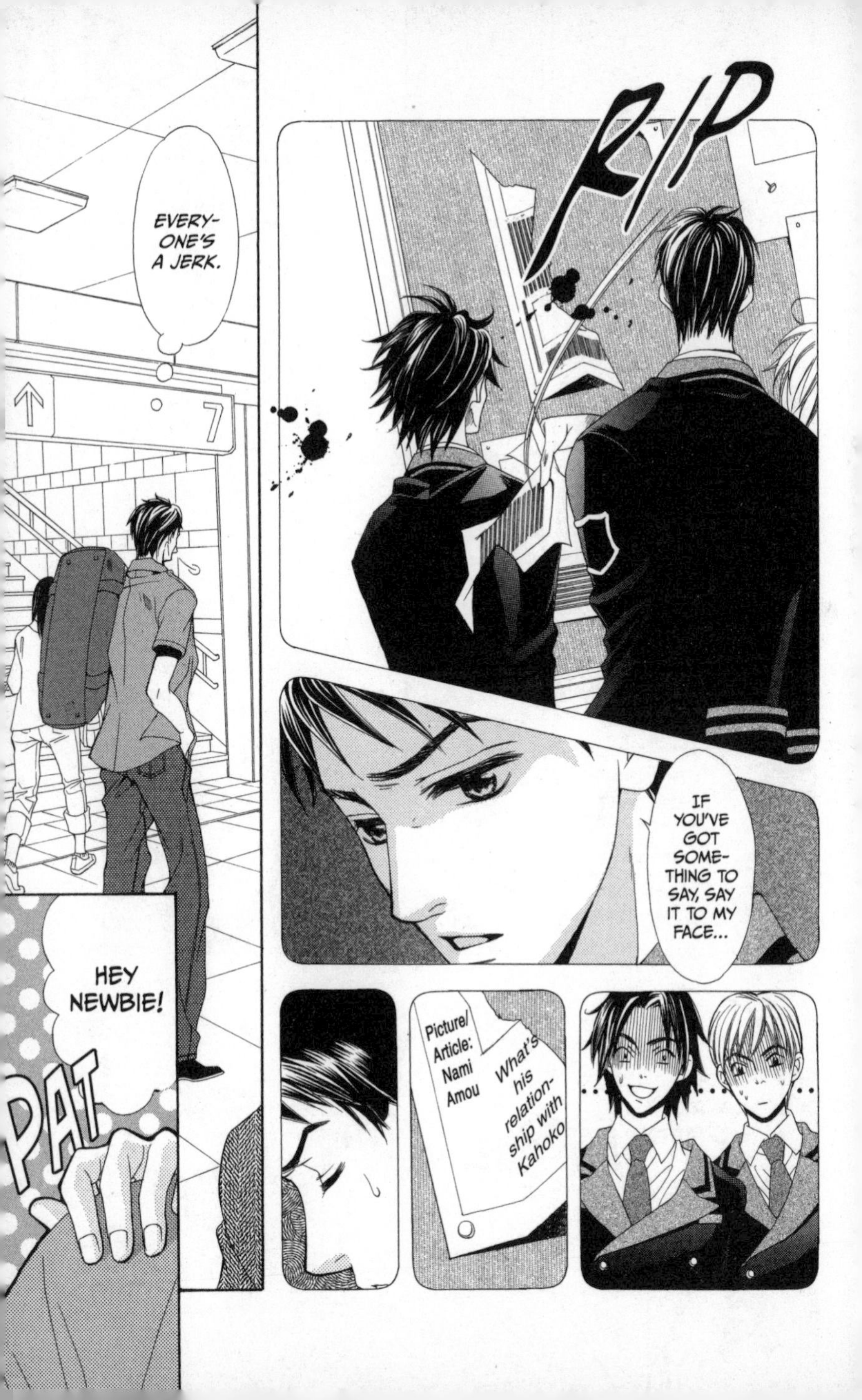
RIP
IF YOU'VE GOT SOMETHING TO SAY, SAY IT TO MY FACE...
Picture/ Article: Nami Amou
What's his relationship with Kahoko
EVERYONE'S A JERK.
HEY NEWBIE!
PAT

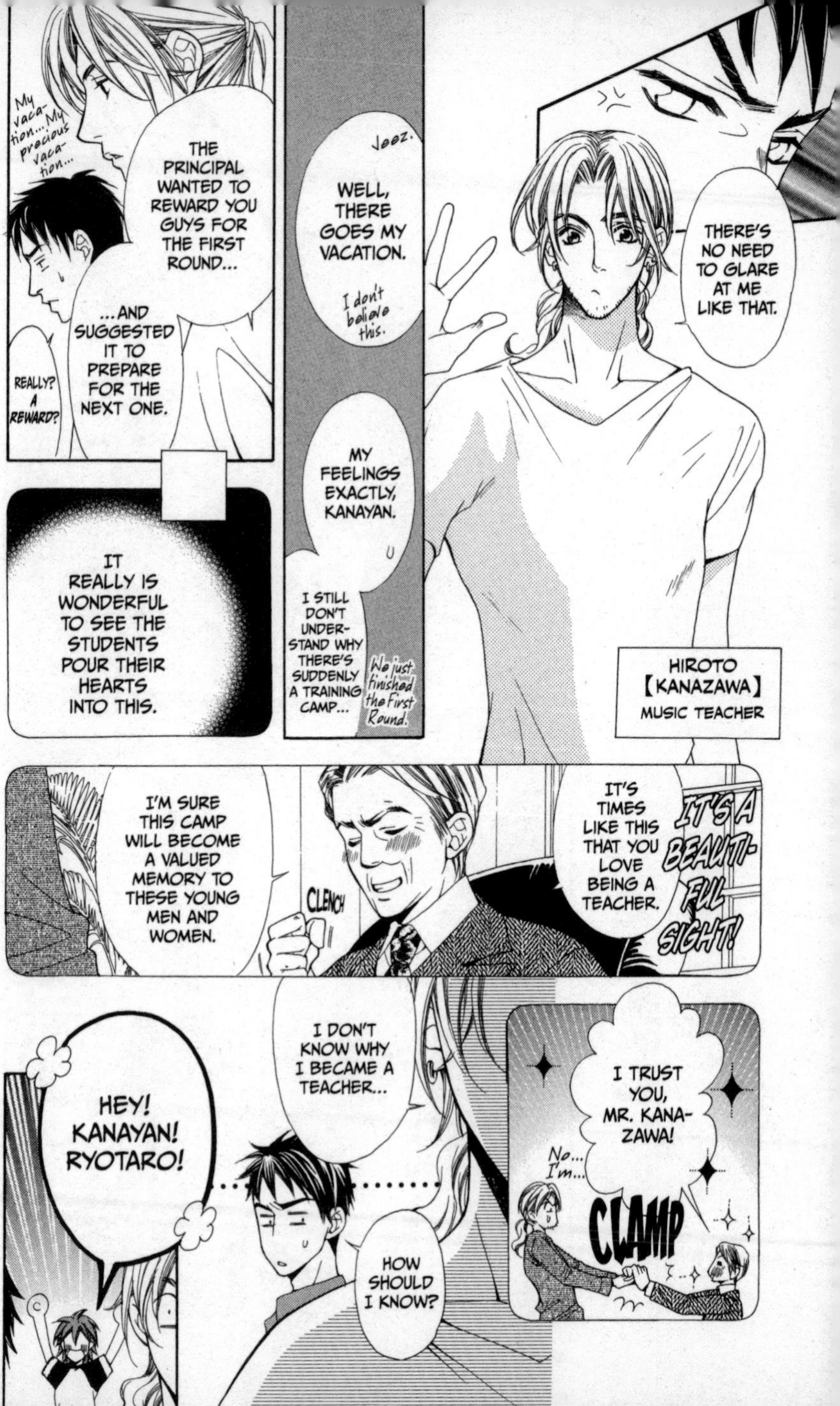
THERE'S NO NEED TO GLARE AT ME LIKE THAT.
HIROTO 【KANAZAWA】 MUSIC TEACHER
Jeez.
WELL, THERE GOES MY VACATION.
I don't believe this.
MY FEELINGS EXACTLY, KANAYAN.
I STILL DON'T UNDERSTAND WHY THERE'S SUDDENLY A TRAINING CAMP...
We just finished the First Round.
My vacation... My precious vacation...
THE PRINCIPAL WANTED TO REWARD YOU GUYS FOR THE FIRST ROUND...
...AND SUGGESTED IT TO PREPARE FOR THE NEXT ONE.
REALLY? A REWARD?
IT REALLY IS WONDERFUL TO SEE THE STUDENTS POUR THEIR HEARTS INTO THIS.
IT'S A BEAUTIFUL SIGHT!
IT'S TIMES LIKE THIS THAT YOU LOVE BEING A TEACHER.
CLENCH
I'M SURE THIS CAMP WILL BECOME A VALUED MEMORY TO THESE YOUNG MEN AND WOMEN.
I TRUST YOU, MR. KANAZAWA!
No... I'm...
CLAMP
I DON'T KNOW WHY I BECAME A TEACHER...
HOW SHOULD I KNOW?
HEY! KANAYAN! RYOTARO!

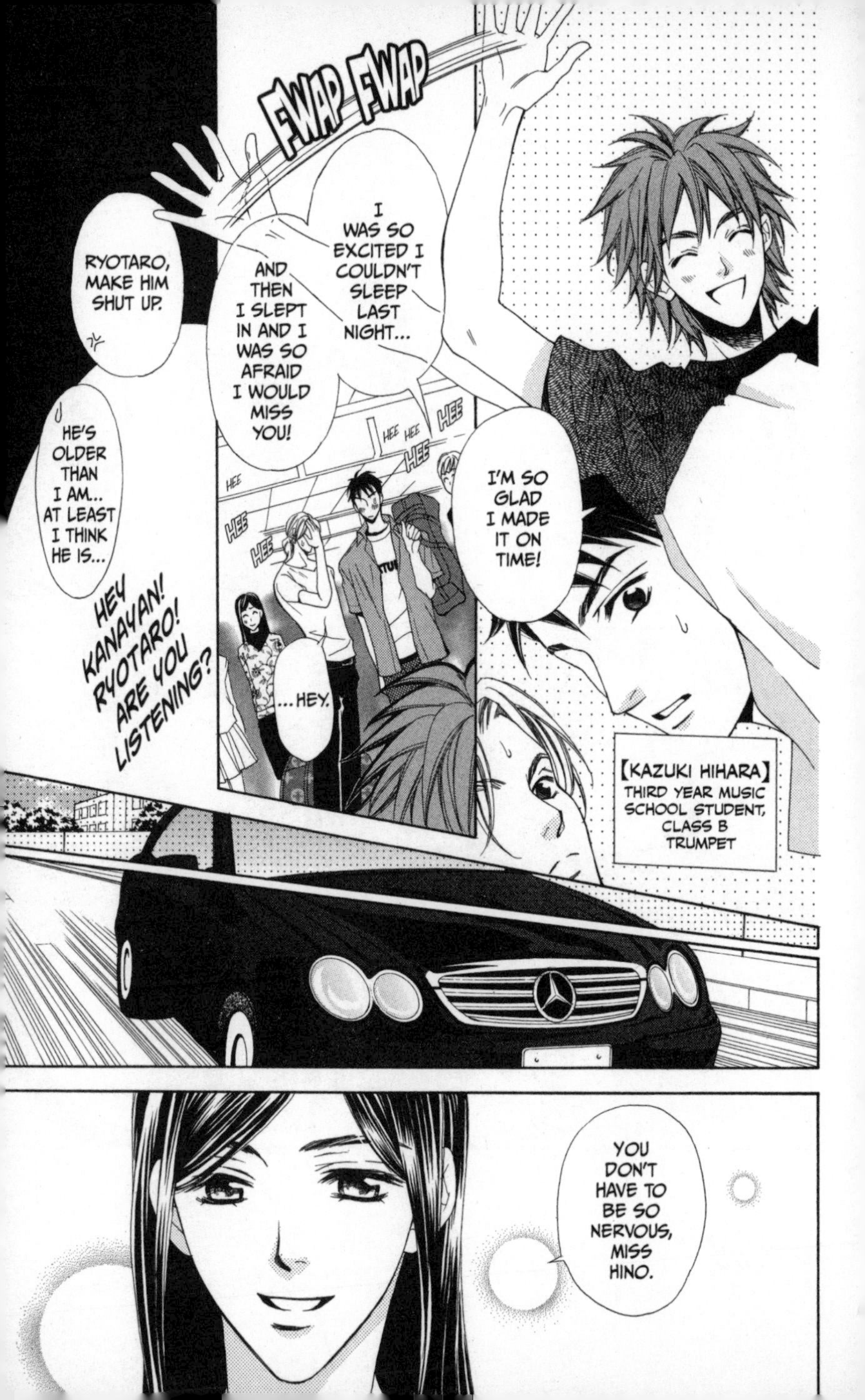
FWAP FWAP
I WAS SO EXCITED I COULDN'T SLEEP LAST NIGHT...
AND THEN I SLEPT IN AND I WAS SO AFRAID I WOULD MISS YOU!
I'M SO GLAD I MADE IT ON TIME!
【KAZUKI HIHARA】 THIRD YEAR MUSIC SCHOOL STUDENT, CLASS B TRUMPET
HEE HEE HEE HEE HEE HEE HEE
...HEY.
RYOTARO, MAKE HIM SHUT UP.
HE'S OLDER THAN I AM... AT LEAST I THINK HE IS...
HEY KANAYAN! RYOTARO! ARE YOU LISTENING?
YOU DON'T HAVE TO BE SO NERVOUS, MISS HINO.

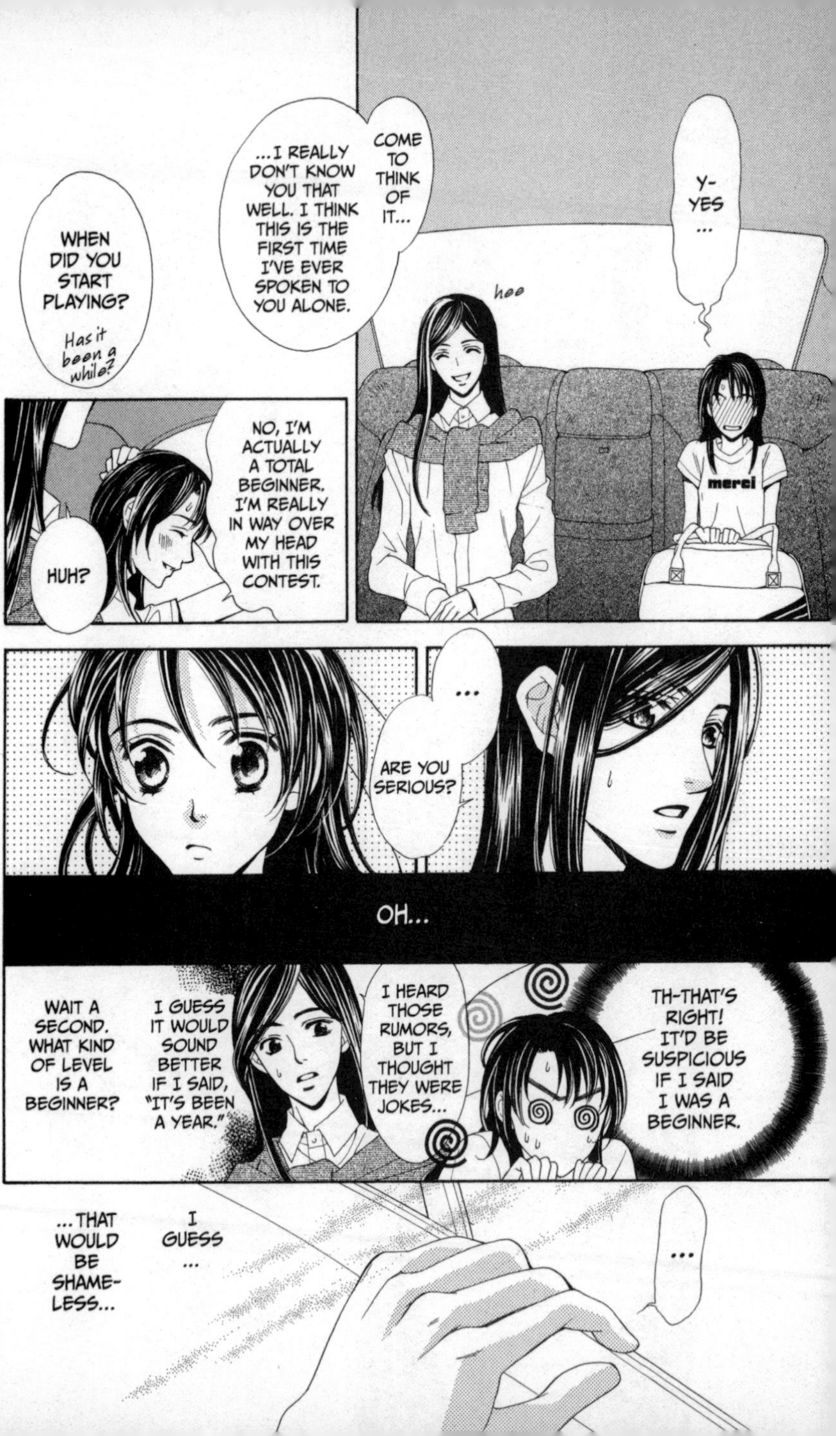
Y-YES...
hee
COME TO THINK OF IT...
...I REALLY DON'T KNOW YOU THAT WELL. I THINK THIS IS THE FIRST TIME I'VE EVER SPOKEN TO YOU ALONE.
WHEN DID YOU START PLAYING?
Has it been a while?
NO, I'M ACTUALLY A TOTAL BEGINNER. I'M REALLY IN WAY OVER MY HEAD WITH THIS CONTEST.
HUH?
...
ARE YOU SERIOUS?
OH...
TH-THAT'S RIGHT! IT'D BE SUSPICIOUS IF I SAID I WAS A BEGINNER.
I HEARD THOSE RUMORS, BUT I THOUGHT THEY WERE JOKES...
I GUESS IT WOULD SOUND BETTER IF I SAID, "IT'S BEEN A YEAR."
WAIT A SECOND. WHAT KIND OF LEVEL IS A BEGINNER?
...
I GUESS...
...THAT WOULD BE SHAME-LESS...

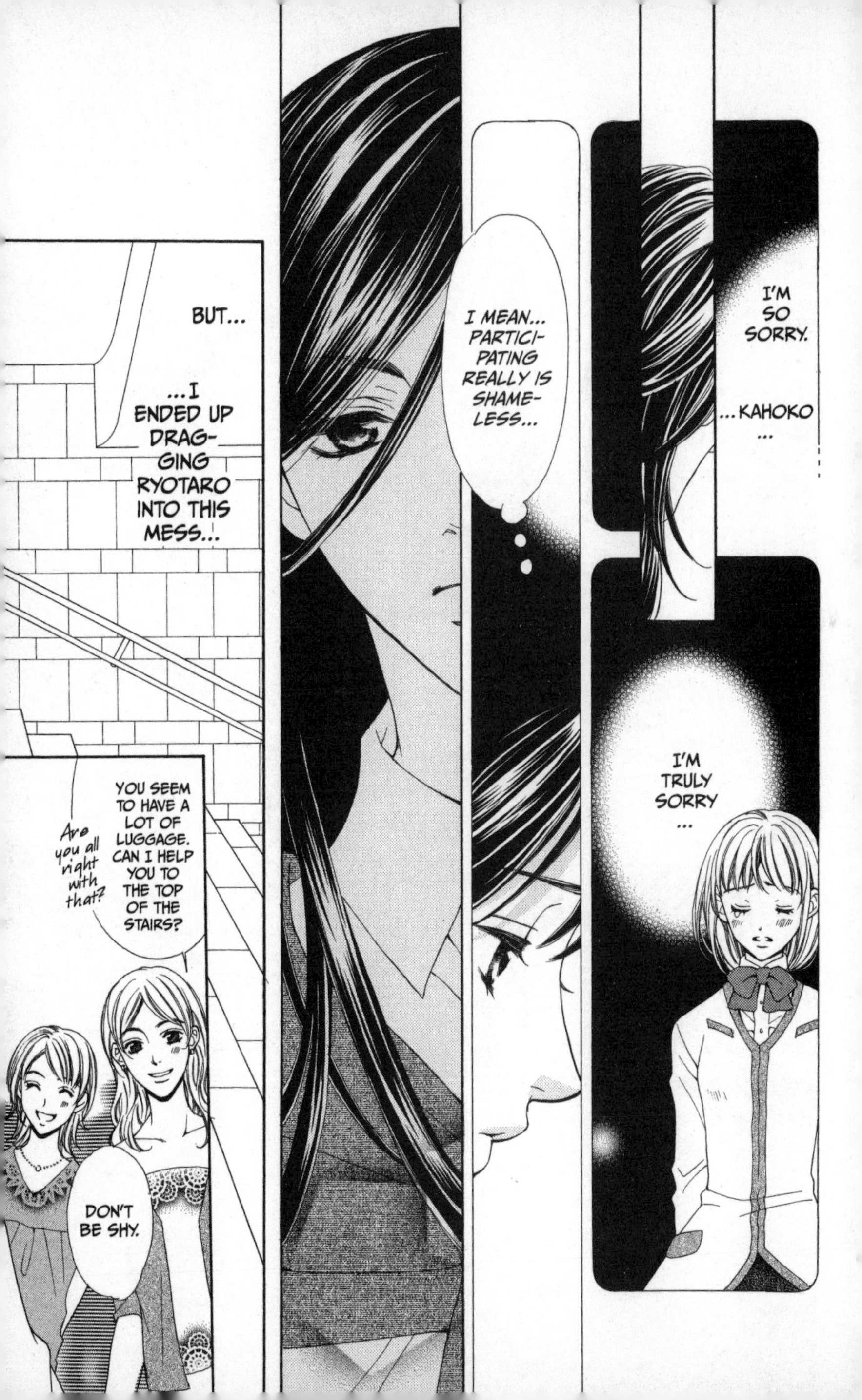
I'M SO SORRY.
...KAHOKO...
I'M TRULY SORRY...
I MEAN... PARTICIPATING REALLY IS SHAMELESS...
BUT...
...I ENDED UP DRAGGING RYOTARO INTO THIS MESS...
YOU SEEM TO HAVE A LOT OF LUGGAGE. CAN I HELP YOU TO THE TOP OF THE STAIRS?
Are you all right with that?
DON'T BE SHY.

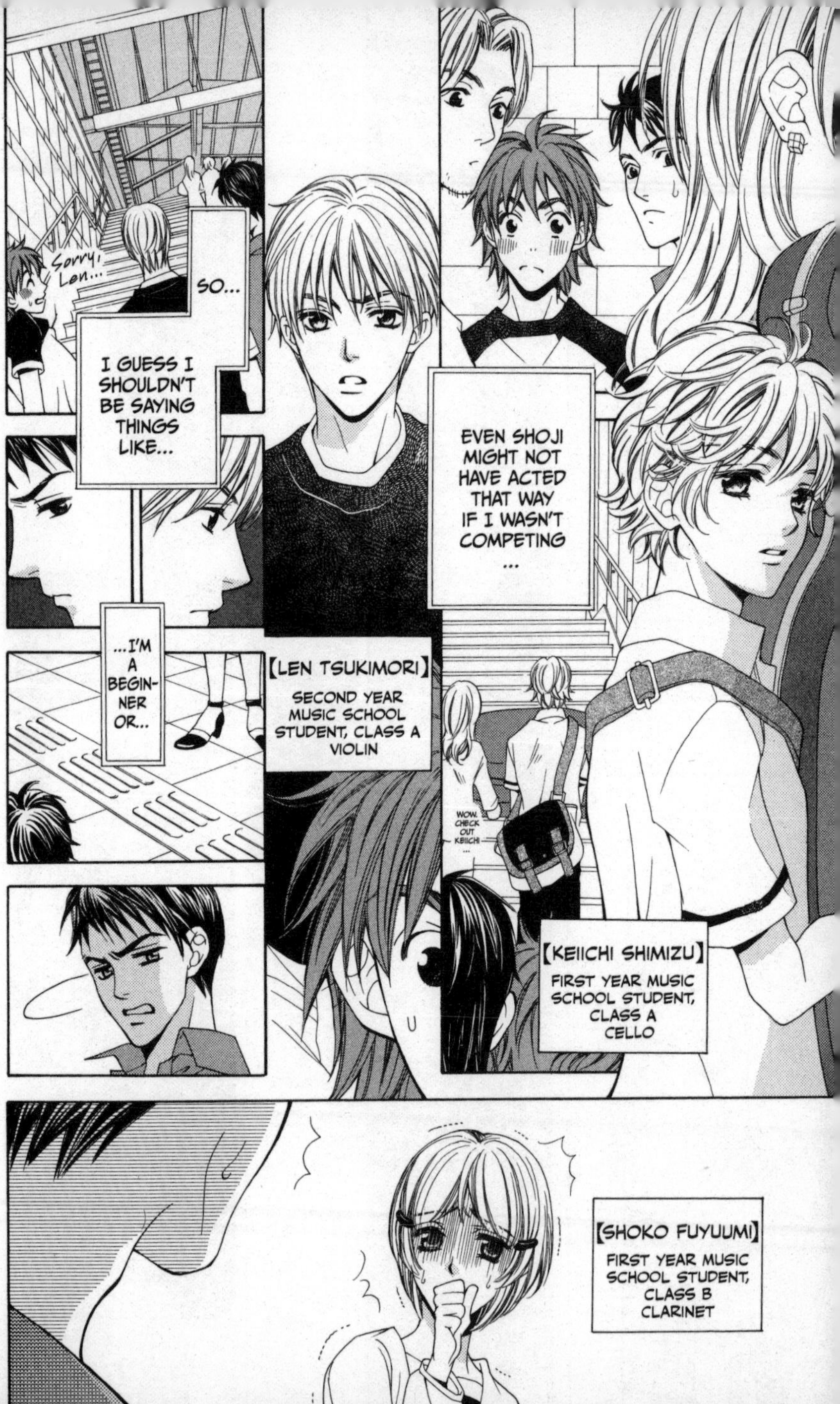
EVEN SHOJI MIGHT NOT HAVE ACTED THAT WAY IF I WASN'T COMPETING ...
WOW. CHECK OUT KEIICHI ...
【KEIICHI SHIMIZU】 FIRST YEAR MUSIC SCHOOL STUDENT, CLASS A CELLO
【LEN TSUKIMORI】 SECOND YEAR MUSIC SCHOOL STUDENT, CLASS A VIOLIN
Sorry! Len...
SO...
I GUESS I SHOULDN'T BE SAYING THINGS LIKE...
...I'M A BEGIN-NER OR...
【SHOKO FUYUUMI】 FIRST YEAR MUSIC SCHOOL STUDENT, CLASS B CLARINET

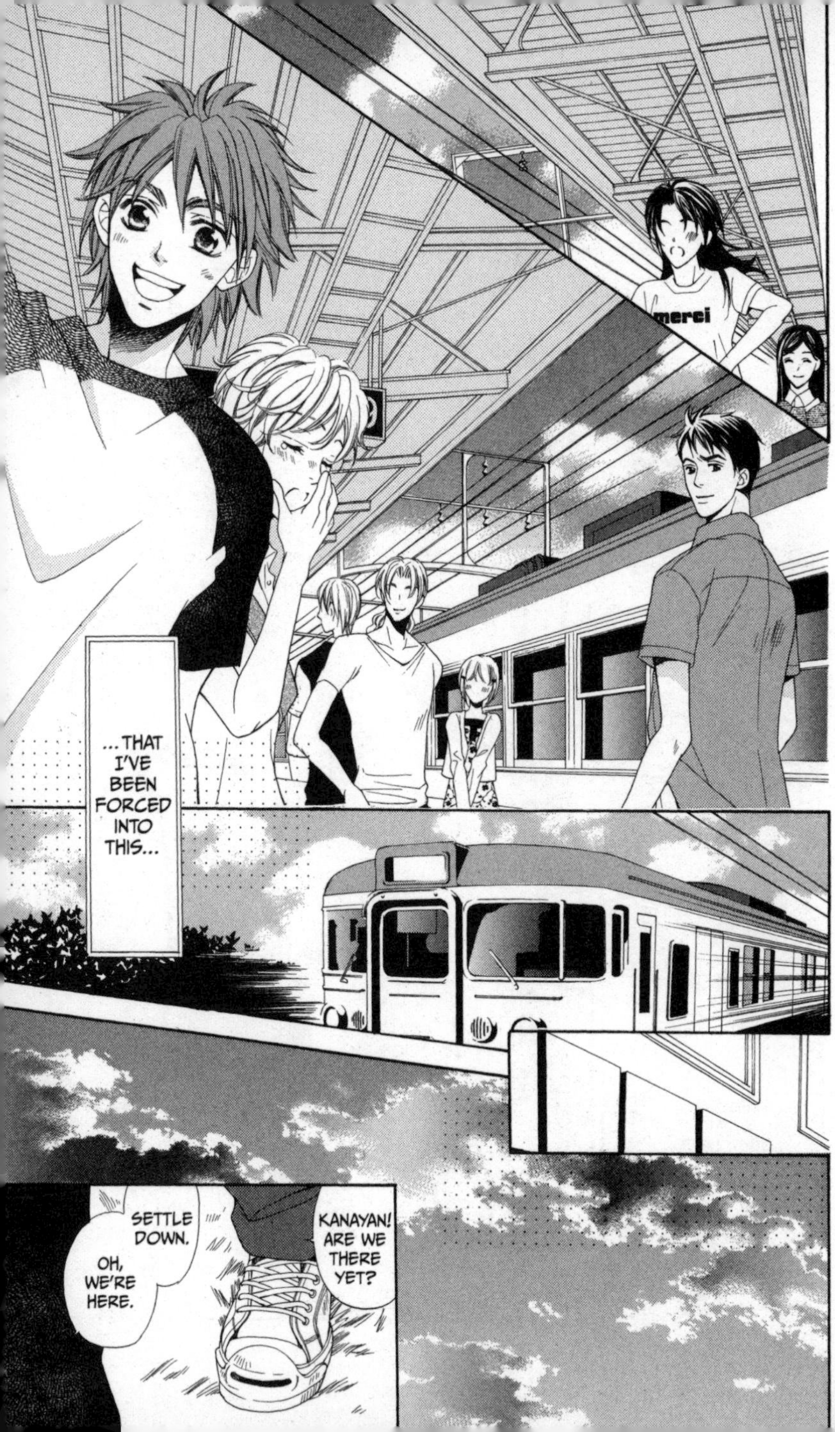
merci
...THAT I'VE BEEN FORCED INTO THIS...
KANAYAN! ARE WE THERE YET?
SETTLE DOWN.
OH, WE'RE HERE.

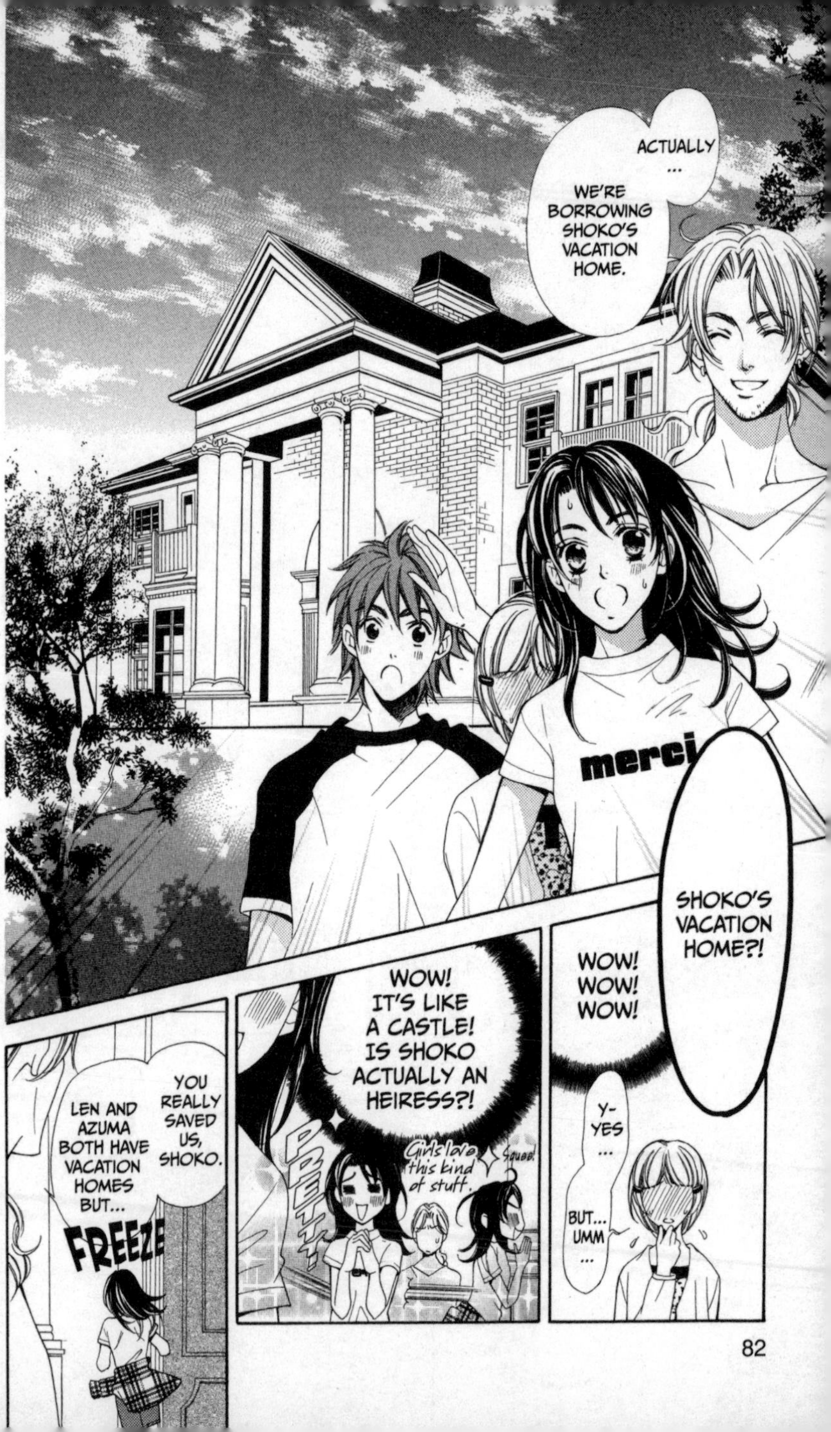
ACTUALLY ...
WE'RE BORROWING SHOKO'S VACATION HOME.
SHOKO'S VACATION HOME?!
WOW! WOW! WOW!
Y-YES ...
BUT... UMM ...
WOW! IT'S LIKE A CASTLE! IS SHOKO ACTUALLY AN HEIRESS?!
Girls love this kind of stuff.
Squee!
YOU REALLY SAVED US, SHOKO.
LEN AND AZUMA BOTH HAVE VACATION HOMES BUT...
FREEZE

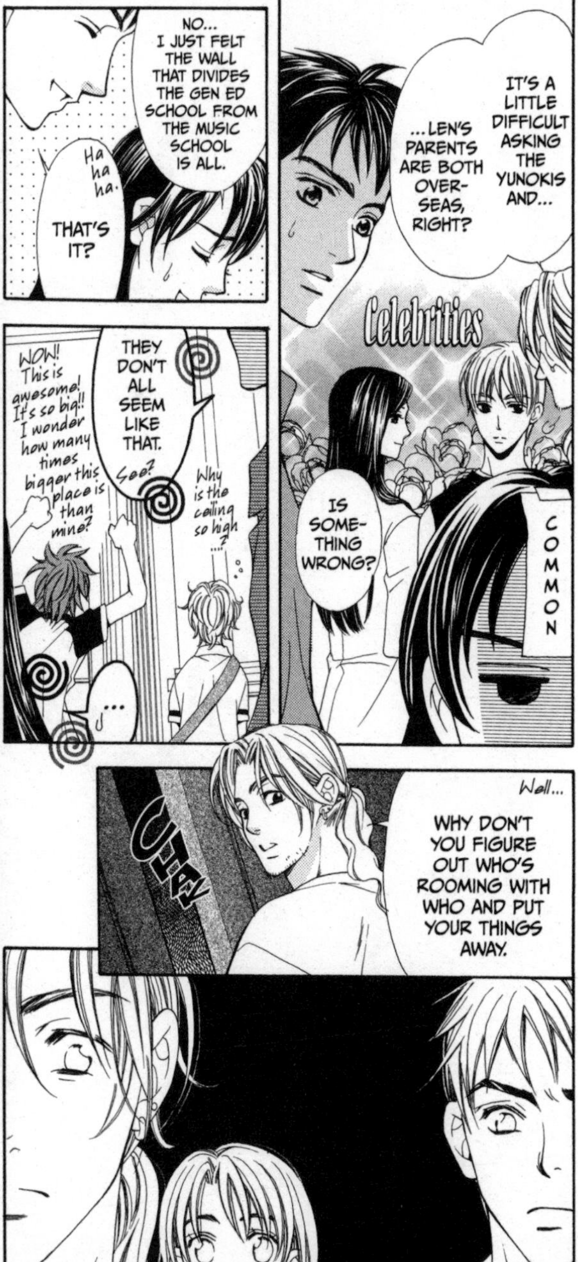
IT'S A LITTLE DIFFICULT ASKING THE YUNOKIS AND...
...LEN'S PARENTS ARE BOTH OVER-SEAS, RIGHT?
Celebrities
COMMON
IS SOME-THING WRONG?
NO... I JUST FELT THE WALL THAT DIVIDES THE GEN ED SCHOOL FROM THE MUSIC SCHOOL IS ALL.
Ha ha ha.
THAT'S IT?
THEY DON'T ALL SEEM LIKE THAT.
Why is the ceiling so high...?
See?
WOW! This is awesome! It's so big!! I wonder how many times bigger this place is than mine?
...
Well...
WHY DON'T YOU FIGURE OUT WHO'S ROOMING WITH WHO AND PUT YOUR THINGS AWAY.

THREE

♥

The Training Camp Edition

The 11th-13th Measures are part of the Training Camp Edition. I mentioned in Part One that it's refreshing to draw them not dressed in uniform, but I guess none of them wear their uniforms in this volume.

S.F.

The hardest person to come up with non-uniform clothes for is Azuma. Because his hair is unique... At least for a high school student. Len doesn't seem the type who would wear anything patterned.

I feel like I can dress the other characters in whatever I want. For whatever reason the cover for the first story in the Training Camp Edition is a Chinese theme. I felt like those two were the best fit, as far as the boys go.

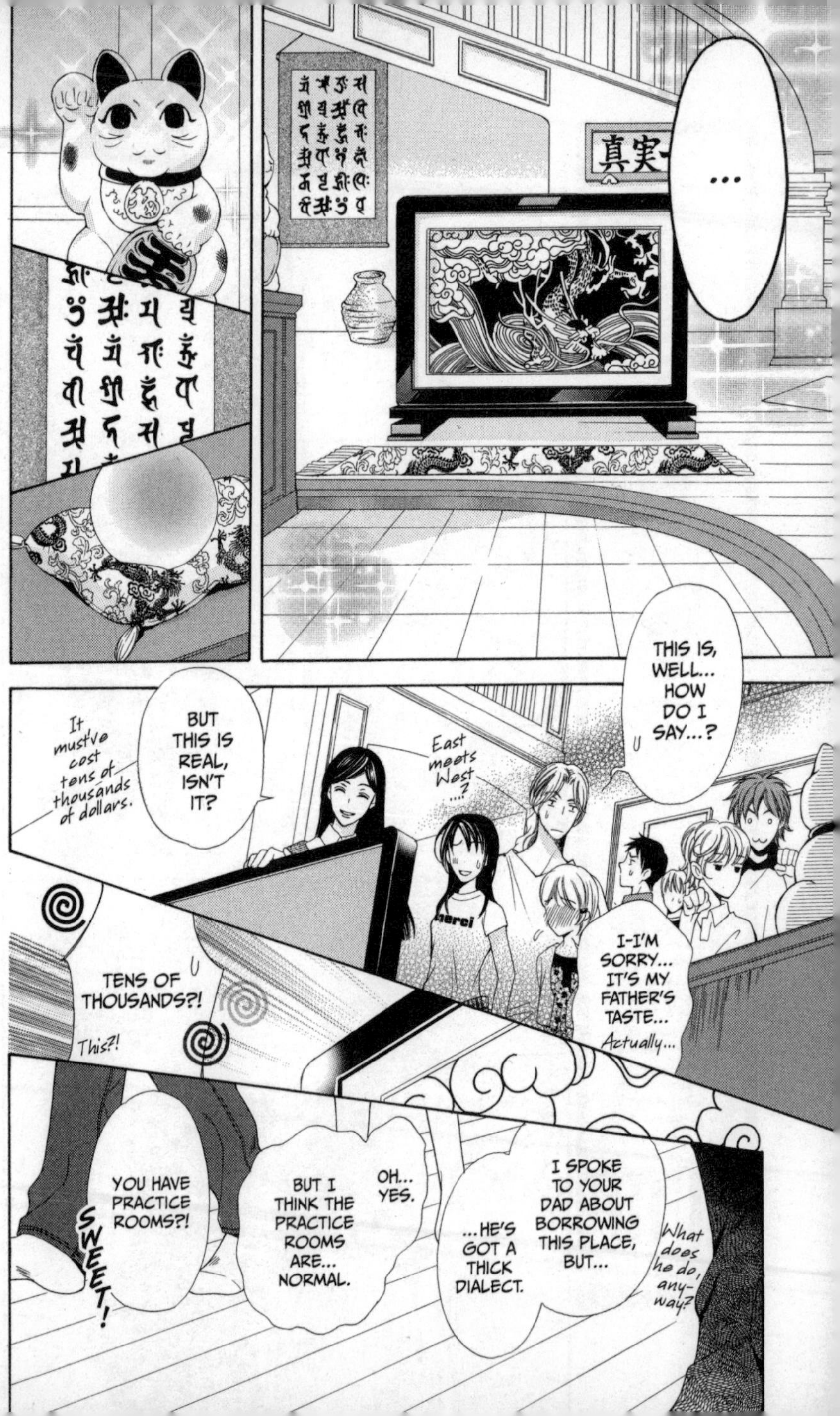
真実
...
THIS IS, WELL... HOW DO I SAY...?
East meets West...?
BUT THIS IS REAL, ISN'T IT?
It must've cost tens of thousands of dollars.
I-I'M SORRY... IT'S MY FATHER'S TASTE...
Actually...
TENS OF THOUSANDS?!
This?!
What does he do, anyway?
I SPOKE TO YOUR DAD ABOUT BORROWING THIS PLACE, BUT...
...HE'S GOT A THICK DIALECT.
OH... YES.
BUT I THINK THE PRACTICE ROOMS ARE... NORMAL.
YOU HAVE PRACTICE ROOMS?!
SWEET!

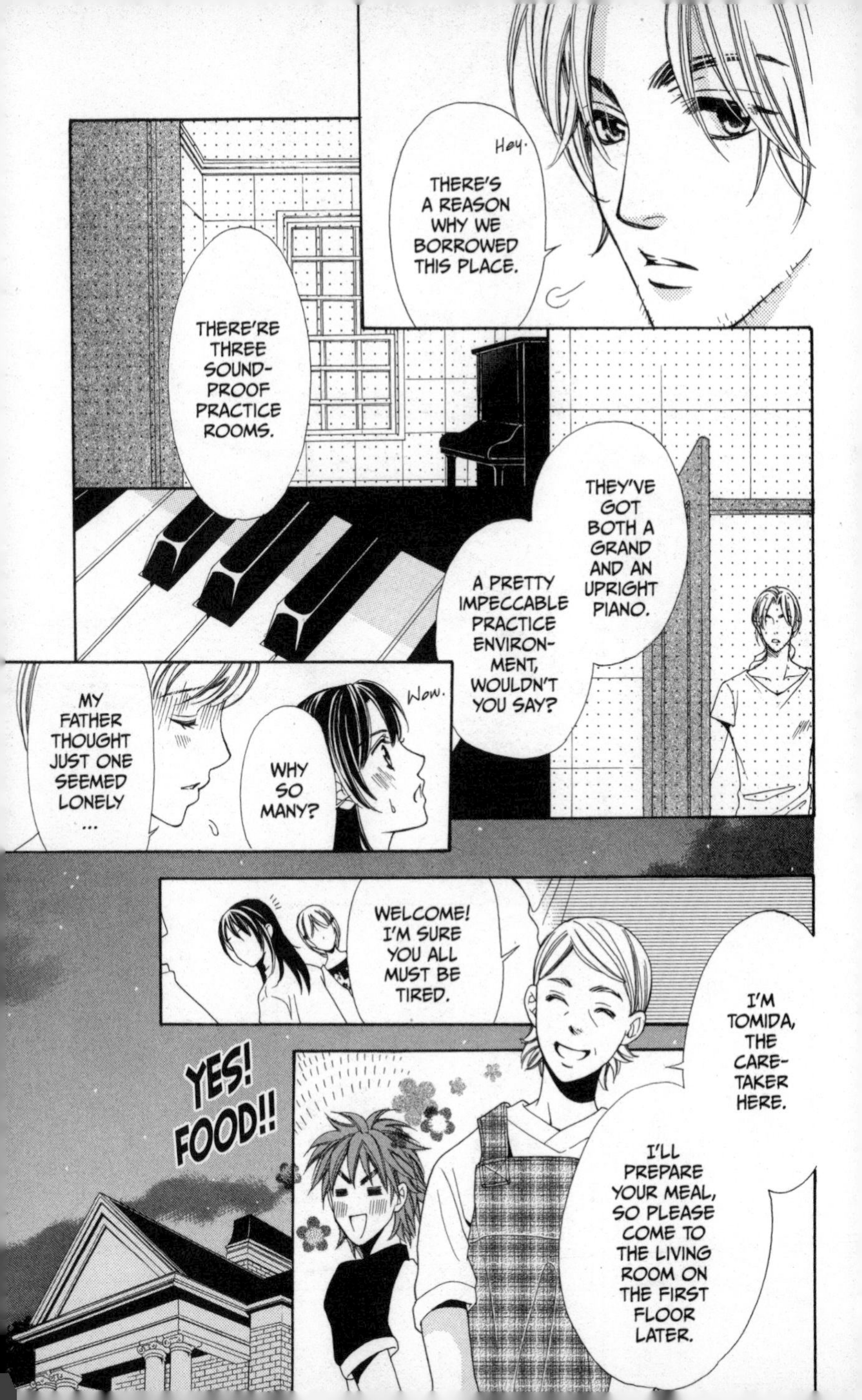
Hey.
THERE'S A REASON WHY WE BORROWED THIS PLACE.
THERE'RE THREE SOUND-PROOF PRACTICE ROOMS.
THEY'VE GOT BOTH A GRAND AND AN UPRIGHT PIANO.
A PRETTY IMPECCABLE PRACTICE ENVIRON-MENT, WOULDN'T YOU SAY?
Wow.
WHY SO MANY?
MY FATHER THOUGHT JUST ONE SEEMED LONELY ...
WELCOME! I'M SURE YOU ALL MUST BE TIRED.
I'M TOMIDA, THE CARE-TAKER HERE.
I'LL PREPARE YOUR MEAL, SO PLEASE COME TO THE LIVING ROOM ON THE FIRST FLOOR LATER.
YES! FOOD!!

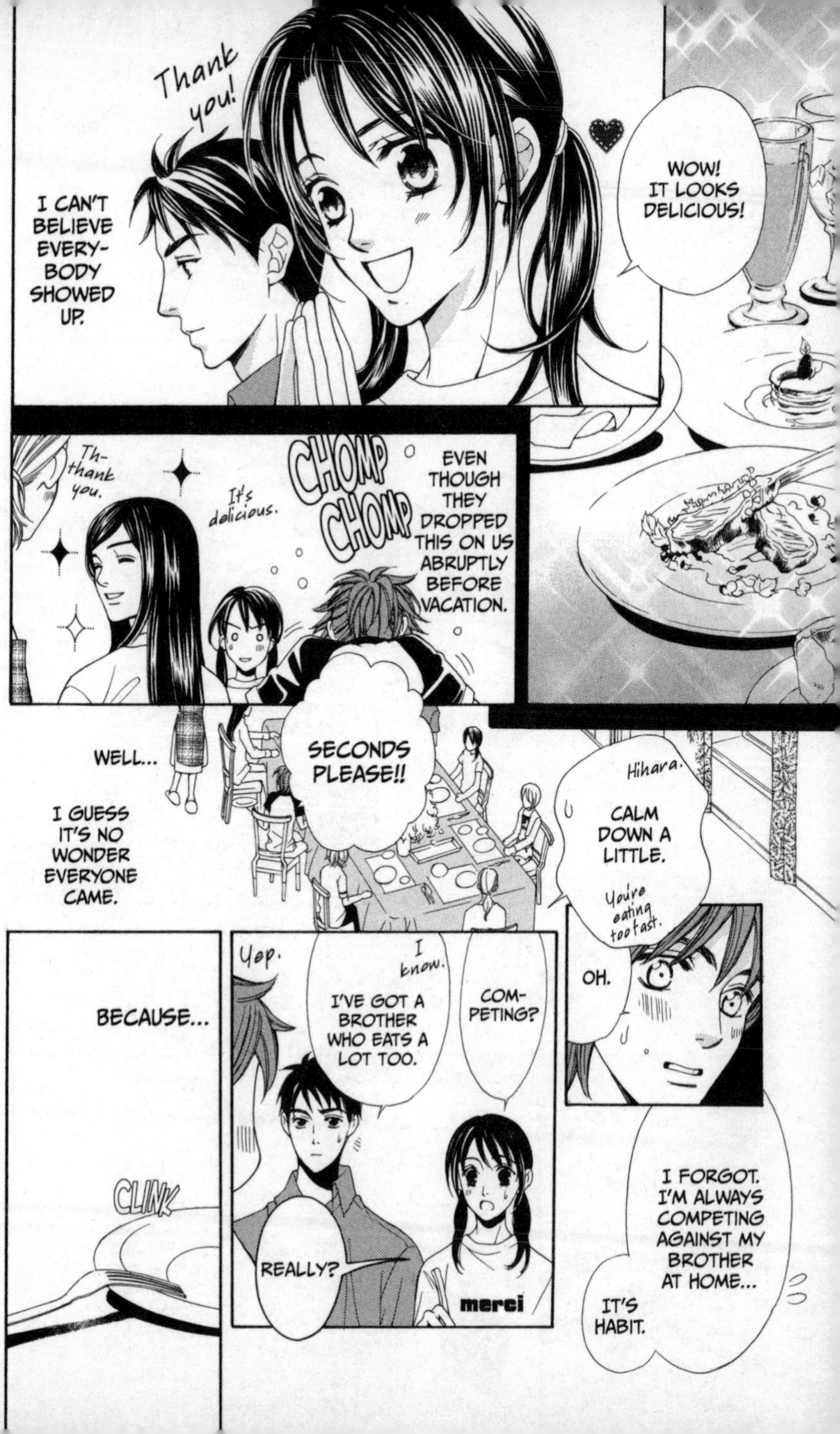
WOW! IT LOOKS DELICIOUS!
Thank you!
I CAN'T BELIEVE EVERY-BODY SHOWED UP.
EVEN THOUGH THEY DROPPED THIS ON US ABRUPTLY BEFORE VACATION.
CHOMP CHOMP
It's delicious.
Th-thank you.
Hihara.
CALM DOWN A LITTLE.
You're eating too fast.
SECONDS PLEASE!!
WELL...
I GUESS IT'S NO WONDER EVERYONE CAME.
OH.
I FORGOT. I'M ALWAYS COMPETING AGAINST MY BROTHER AT HOME...
IT'S HABIT.
COM-PETING?
I know.
I'VE GOT A BROTHER WHO EATS A LOT TOO.
Yep.
REALLY?
merci
BECAUSE...
CLINK

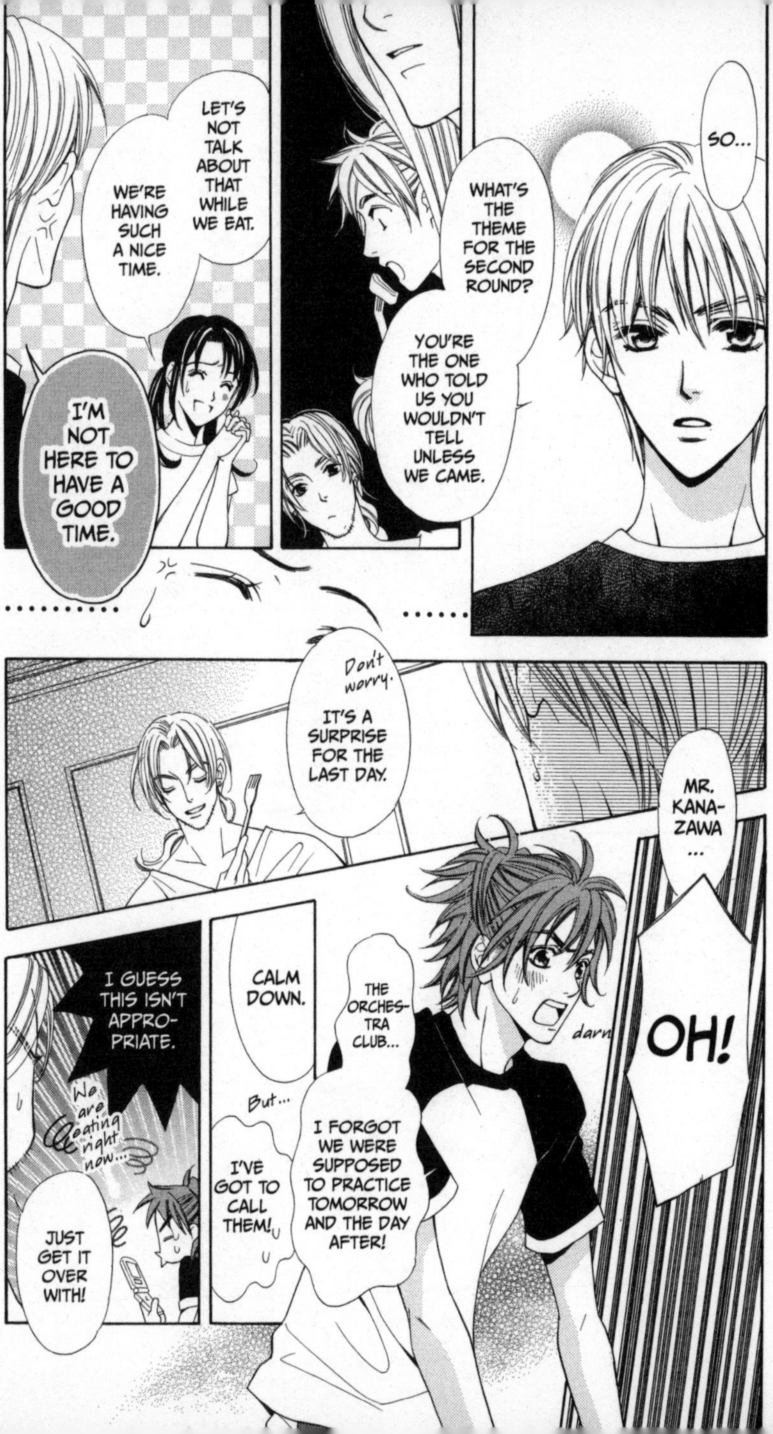
SO...
WHAT'S THE THEME FOR THE SECOND ROUND?
YOU'RE THE ONE WHO TOLD US YOU WOULDN'T TELL UNLESS WE CAME.
LET'S NOT TALK ABOUT THAT WHILE WE EAT.
WE'RE HAVING SUCH A NICE TIME.
I'M NOT HERE TO HAVE A GOOD TIME.
Don't worry.
IT'S A SURPRISE FOR THE LAST DAY.
MR. KANAZAWA...
OH!
darn
THE ORCHESTRA CLUB...
I FORGOT WE WERE SUPPOSED TO PRACTICE TOMORROW AND THE DAY AFTER!
CALM DOWN.
But...
I'VE GOT TO CALL THEM!
I GUESS THIS ISN'T APPROPRIATE.
We are eating right now...
JUST GET IT OVER WITH!

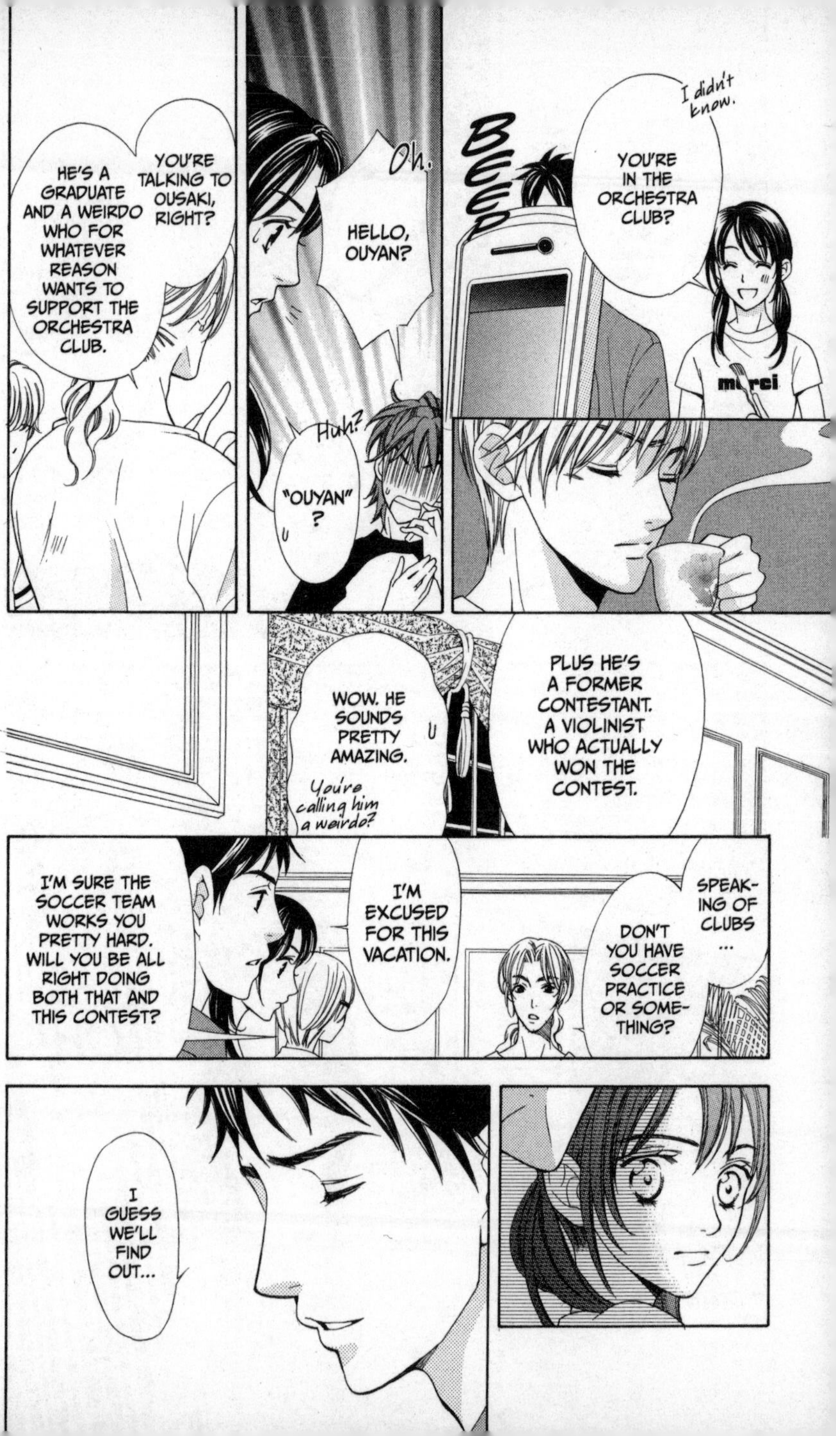
I didn't know.
YOU'RE IN THE ORCHESTRA CLUB?
BEEP
Oh.
HELLO, OUYAN?
Huh?
"OUYAN" ?
YOU'RE TALKING TO OUSAKI, RIGHT?
HE'S A GRADUATE AND A WEIRDO WHO FOR WHATEVER REASON WANTS TO SUPPORT THE ORCHESTRA CLUB.
PLUS HE'S A FORMER CONTESTANT. A VIOLINIST WHO ACTUALLY WON THE CONTEST.
WOW. HE SOUNDS PRETTY AMAZING.
You're calling him a weirdo?
SPEAKING OF CLUBS...
DON'T YOU HAVE SOCCER PRACTICE OR SOMETHING?
I'M EXCUSED FOR THIS VACATION.
I'M SURE THE SOCCER TEAM WORKS YOU PRETTY HARD. WILL YOU BE ALL RIGHT DOING BOTH THAT AND THIS CONTEST?
I GUESS WE'LL FIND OUT...

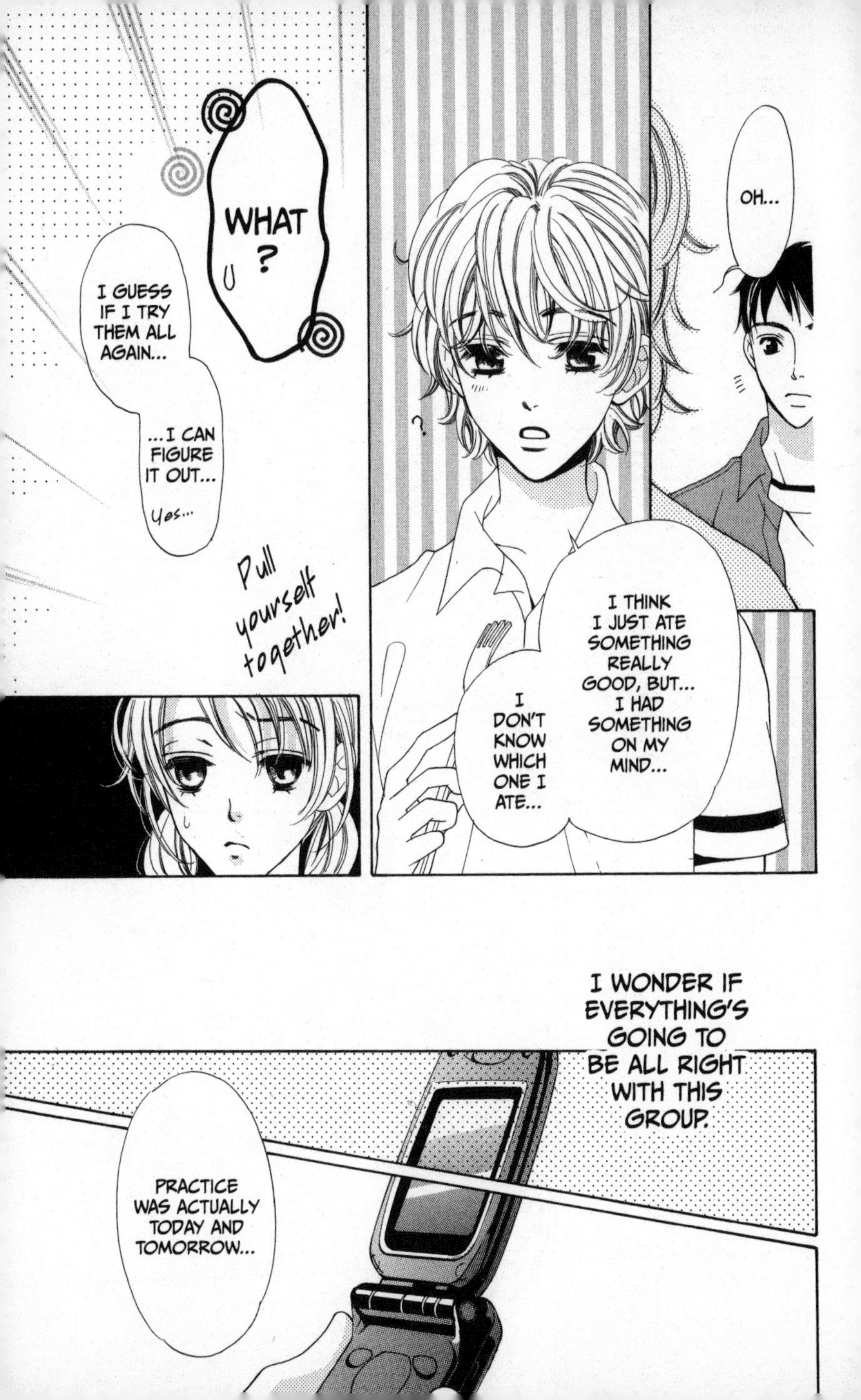
OH...
I THINK I JUST ATE SOMETHING REALLY GOOD, BUT... I HAD SOMETHING ON MY MIND...
I DON'T KNOW WHICH ONE I ATE...
WHAT ?
I GUESS IF I TRY THEM ALL AGAIN...
...I CAN FIGURE IT OUT...
Yes...
Pull yourself together!
I WONDER IF EVERYTHING'S GOING TO BE ALL RIGHT WITH THIS GROUP.
PRACTICE WAS ACTUALLY TODAY AND TOMORROW...

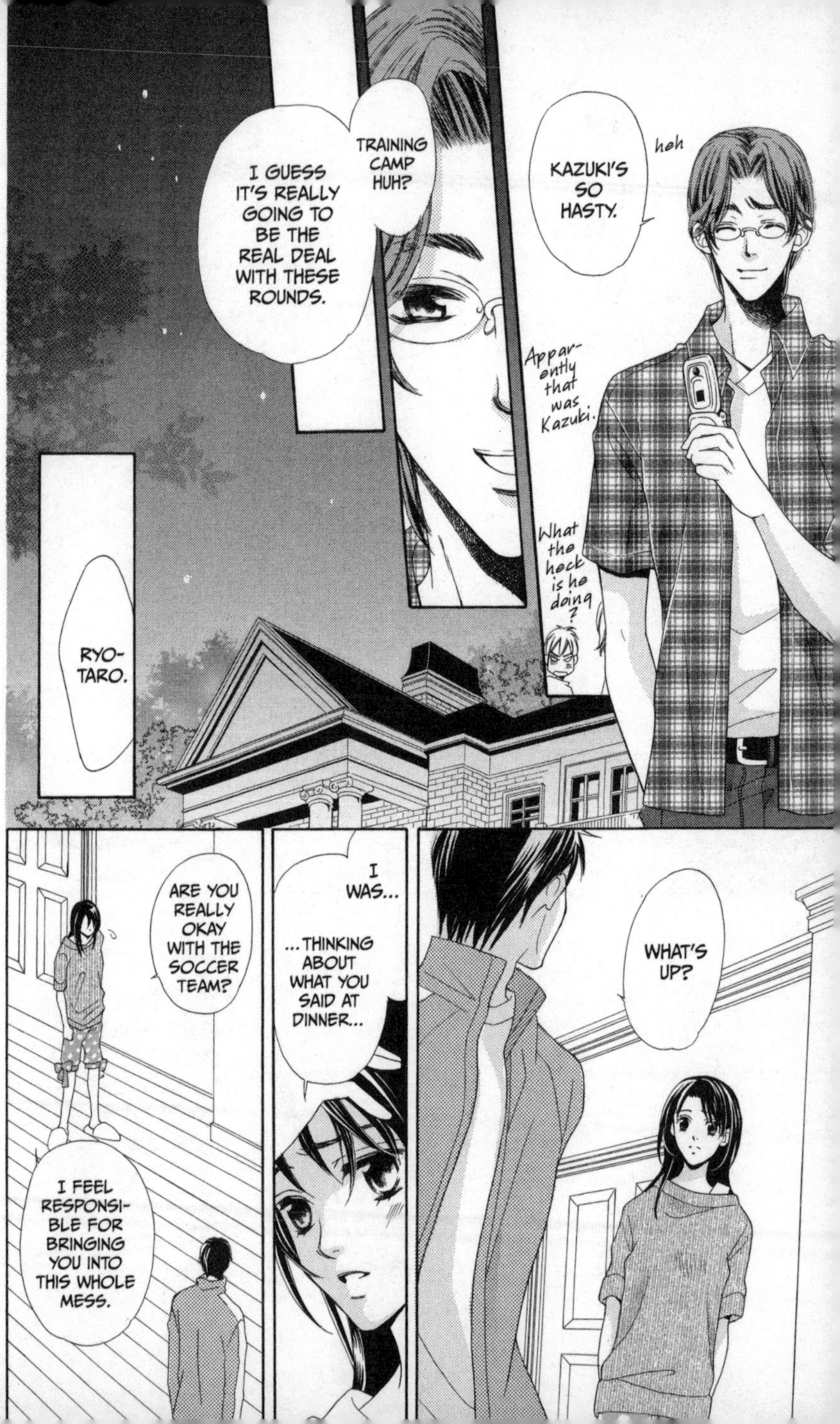
heh
KAZUKI'S SO HASTY.
Apparently that was Kazuki.
What the heck is he doing?
TRAINING CAMP HUH?
I GUESS IT'S REALLY GOING TO BE THE REAL DEAL WITH THESE ROUNDS.
RYO-TARO.
WHAT'S UP?
I WAS...
...THINKING ABOUT WHAT YOU SAID AT DINNER...
ARE YOU REALLY OKAY WITH THE SOCCER TEAM?
I FEEL RESPONSI-BLE FOR BRINGING YOU INTO THIS WHOLE MESS.

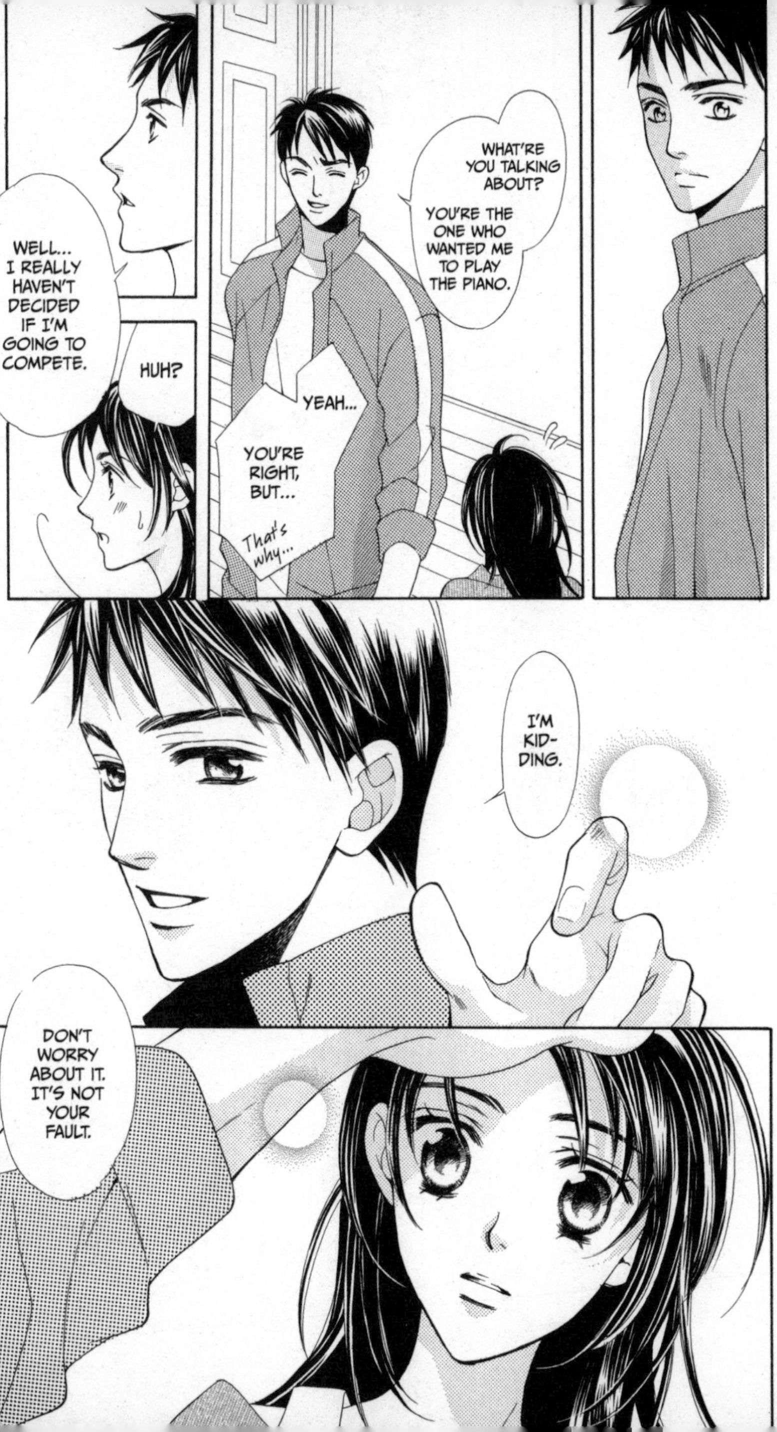
WHAT'RE YOU TALKING ABOUT?
YOU'RE THE ONE WHO WANTED ME TO PLAY THE PIANO.
YEAH...
YOU'RE RIGHT, BUT...
That's why...
WELL... I REALLY HAVEN'T DECIDED IF I'M GOING TO COMPETE.
HUH?
I'M KID-DING.
DON'T WORRY ABOUT IT. IT'S NOT YOUR FAULT.

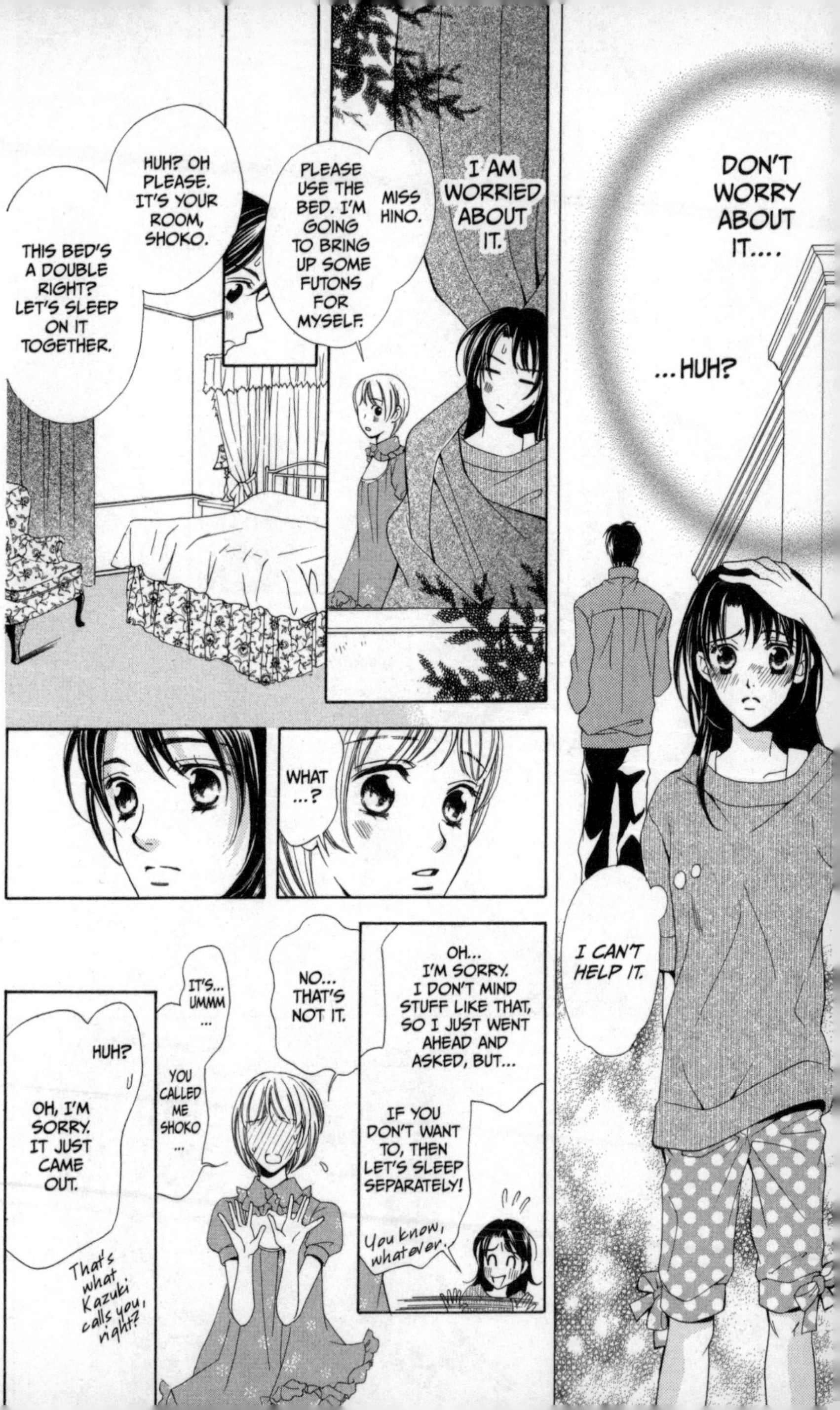
DON'T WORRY ABOUT IT....
...HUH?
I CAN'T HELP IT.
I AM WORRIED ABOUT IT.
MISS HINO.
PLEASE USE THE BED. I'M GOING TO BRING UP SOME FUTONS FOR MYSELF.
HUH? OH PLEASE. IT'S YOUR ROOM, SHOKO.
THIS BED'S A DOUBLE RIGHT? LET'S SLEEP ON IT TOGETHER.
WHAT ...?
OH... I'M SORRY. I DON'T MIND STUFF LIKE THAT, SO I JUST WENT AHEAD AND ASKED, BUT...
IF YOU DON'T WANT TO, THEN LET'S SLEEP SEPARATELY!
You know, whatever.
NO... THAT'S NOT IT.
IT'S... UMMM ...
YOU CALLED ME SHOKO ...
HUH?
OH, I'M SORRY. IT JUST CAME OUT.
That's what Kazuki calls you, right?

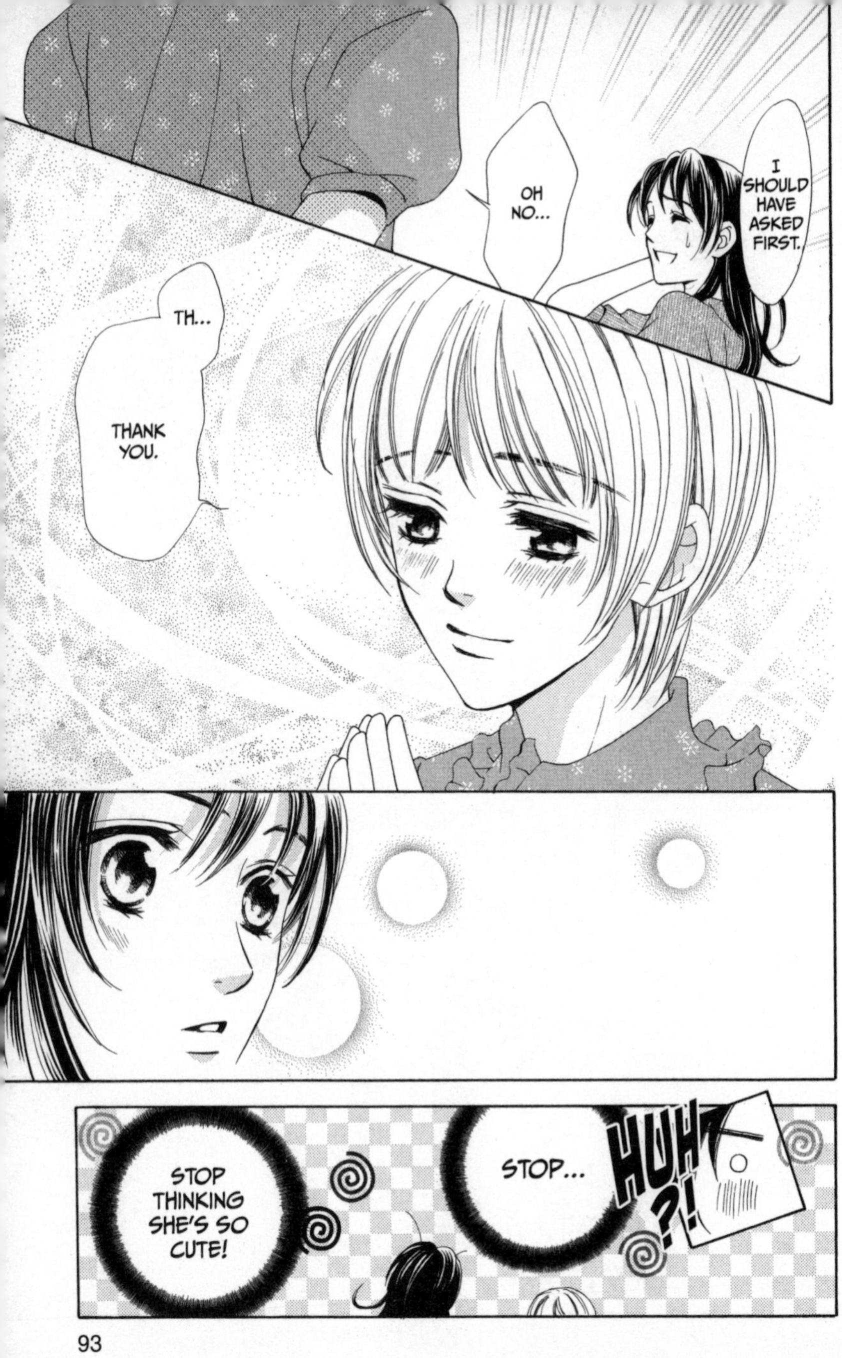
I SHOULD HAVE ASKED FIRST.
OH NO...
TH...
THANK YOU.
HUH?!
STOP...
STOP THINKING SHE'S SO CUTE!

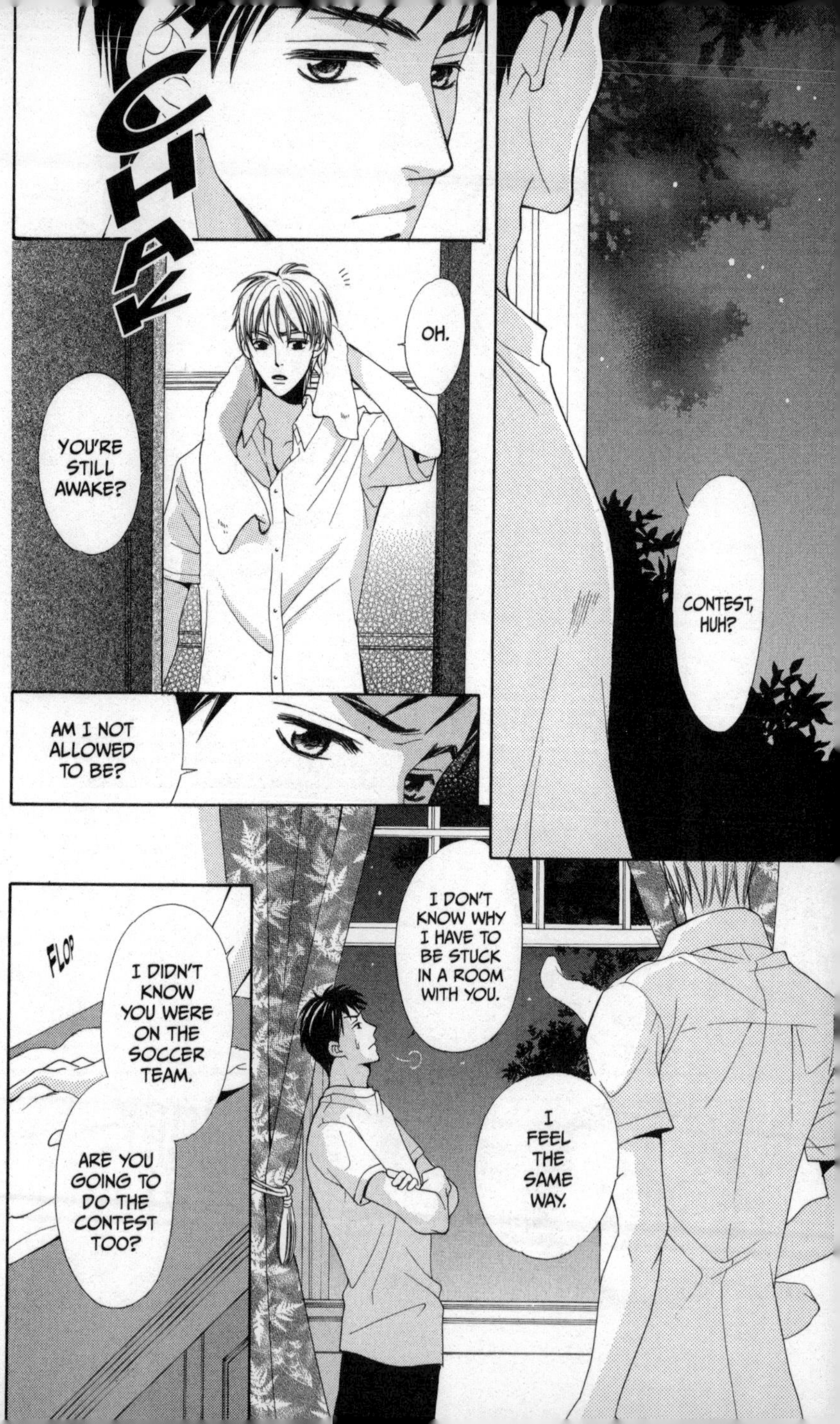
CONTEST, HUH?
CHAK
OH.
YOU'RE STILL AWAKE?
AM I NOT ALLOWED TO BE?
I DON'T KNOW WHY I HAVE TO BE STUCK IN A ROOM WITH YOU.
I FEEL THE SAME WAY.
FLOP
I DIDN'T KNOW YOU WERE ON THE SOCCER TEAM.
ARE YOU GOING TO DO THE CONTEST TOO?

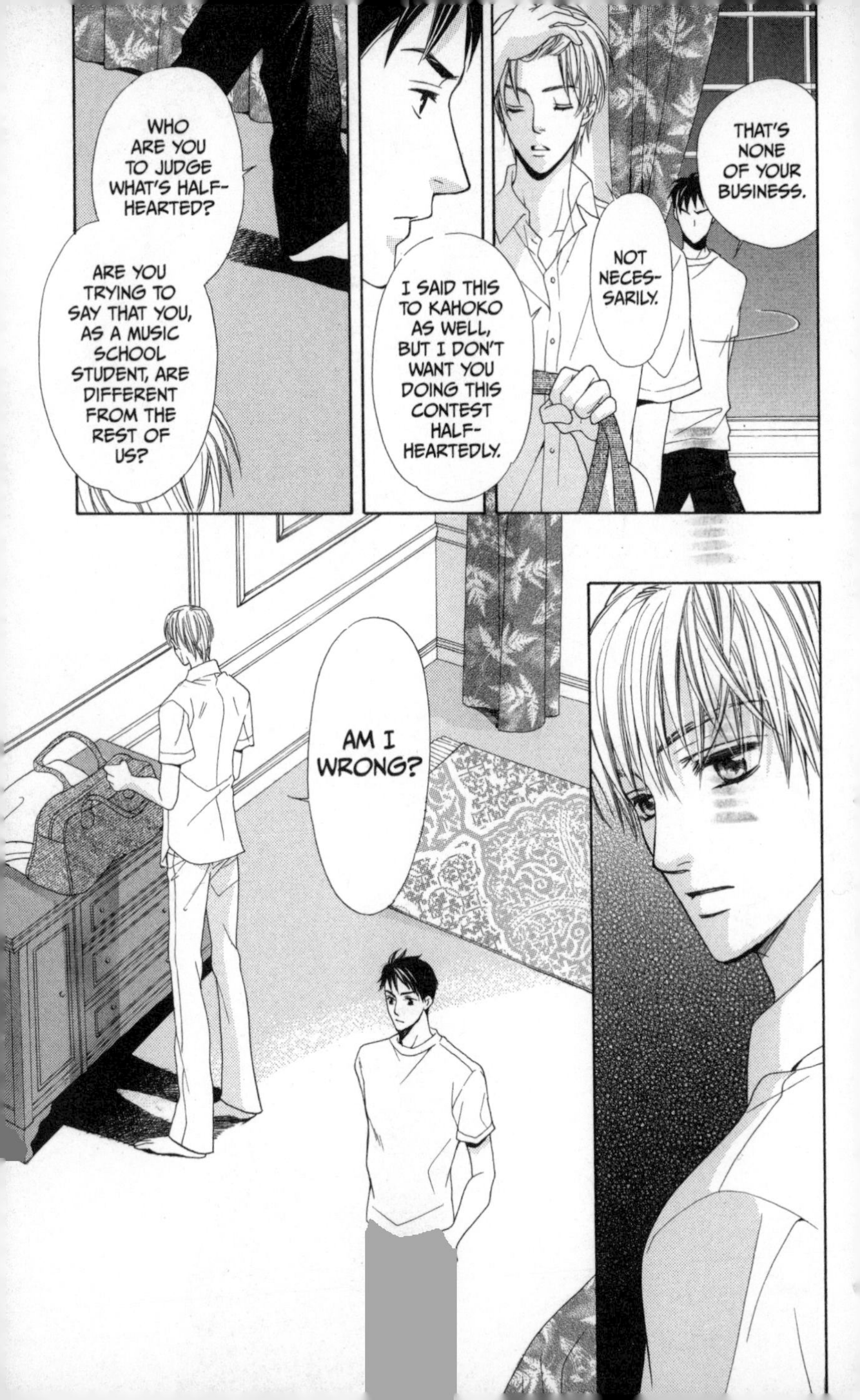
THAT'S NONE OF YOUR BUSINESS.
NOT NECES-SARILY.
I SAID THIS TO KAHOKO AS WELL, BUT I DON'T WANT YOU DOING THIS CONTEST HALF-HEARTEDLY.
WHO ARE YOU TO JUDGE WHAT'S HALF-HEARTED?
ARE YOU TRYING TO SAY THAT YOU, AS A MUSIC SCHOOL STUDENT, ARE DIFFERENT FROM THE REST OF US?
AM I WRONG?

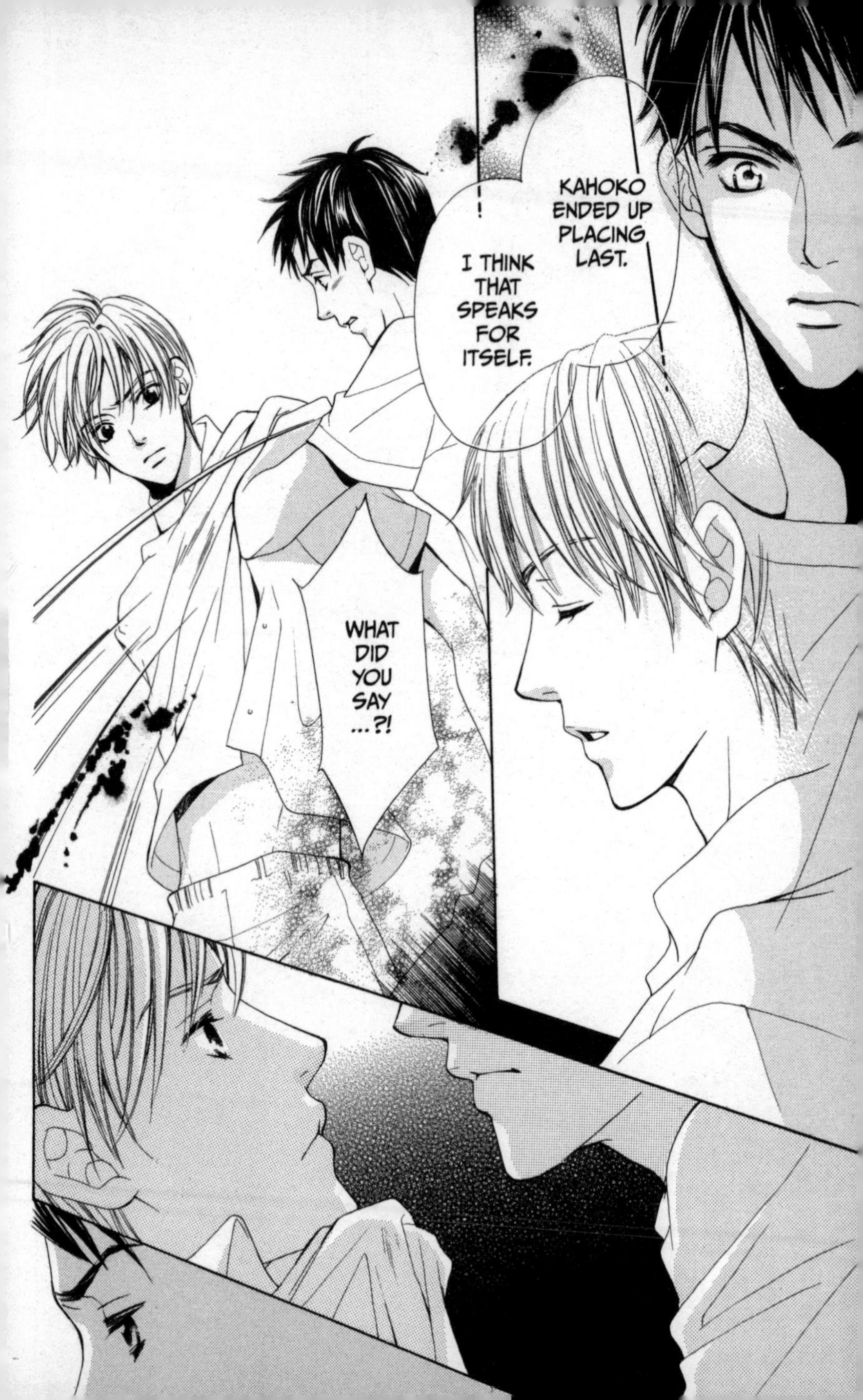
KAHOKO ENDED UP PLACING LAST.
I THINK THAT SPEAKS FOR ITSELF.
!
WHAT DID YOU SAY ...?!

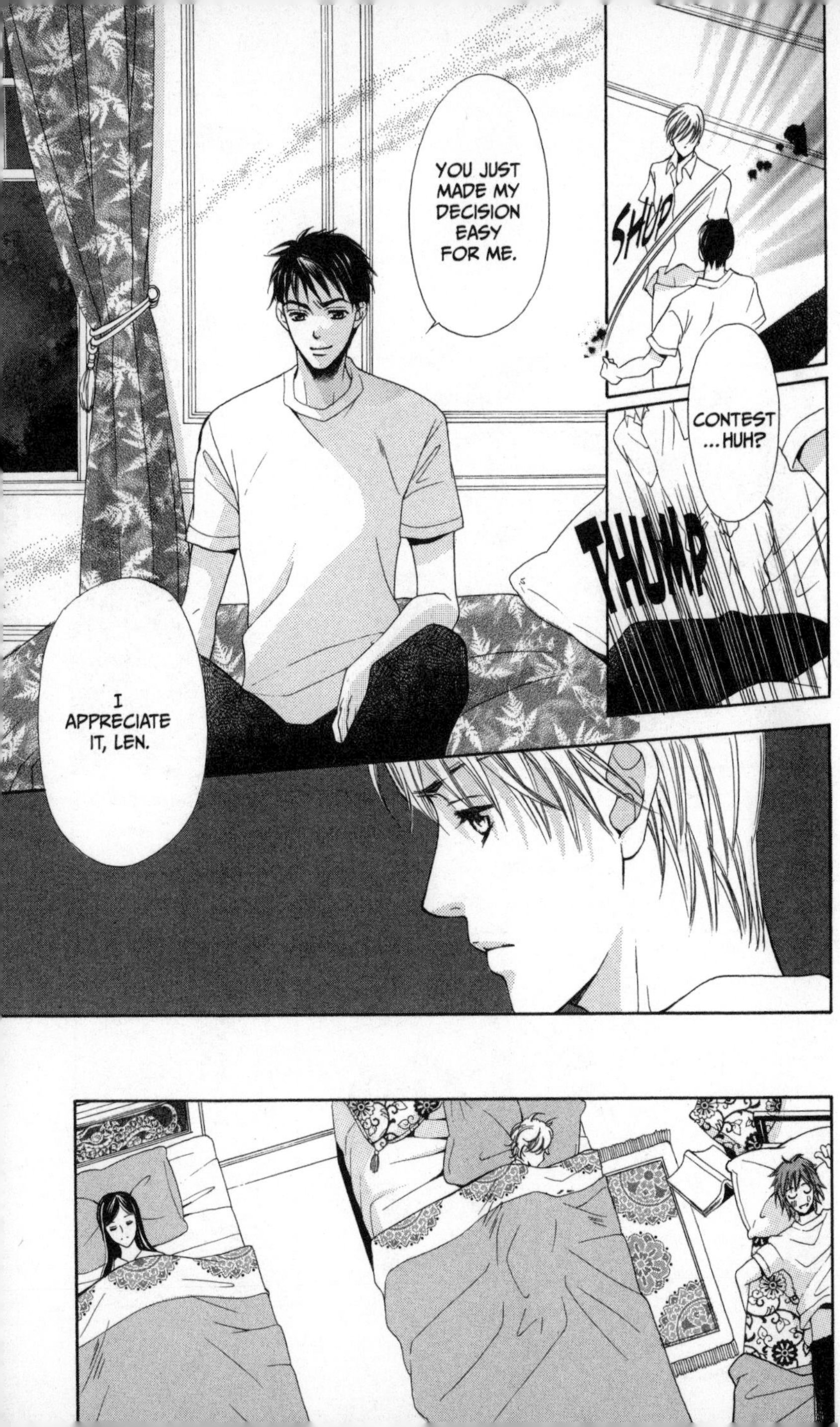
SHUP
CONTEST ...HUH?
THUMP
YOU JUST MADE MY DECISION EASY FOR ME.
I APPRECIATE IT, LEN.

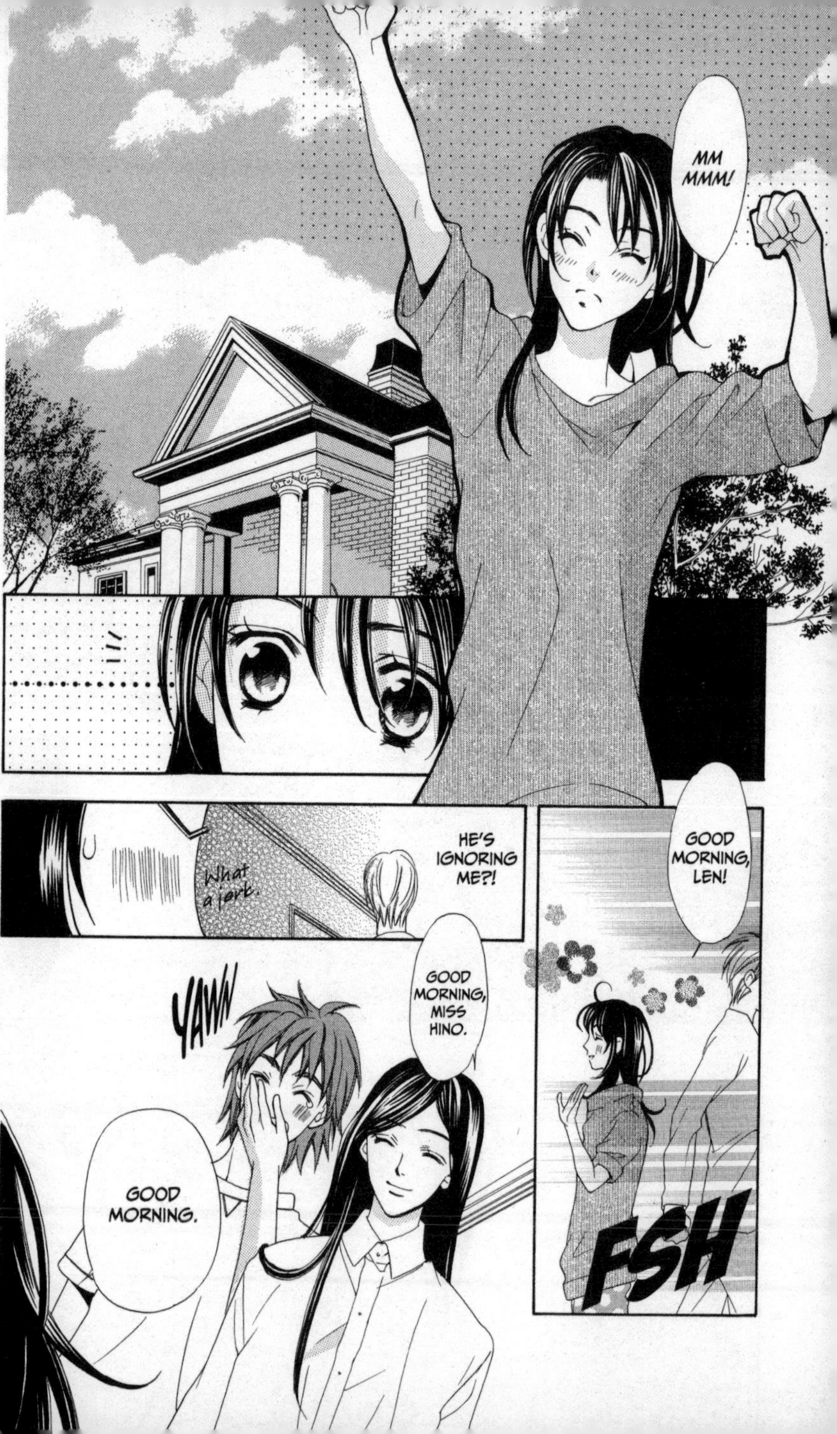
MM MMM!
GOOD MORNING, LEN!
FSH
HE'S IGNORING ME?!
What a jerk.
GOOD MORNING, MISS HINO.
YAWN
GOOD MORNING.

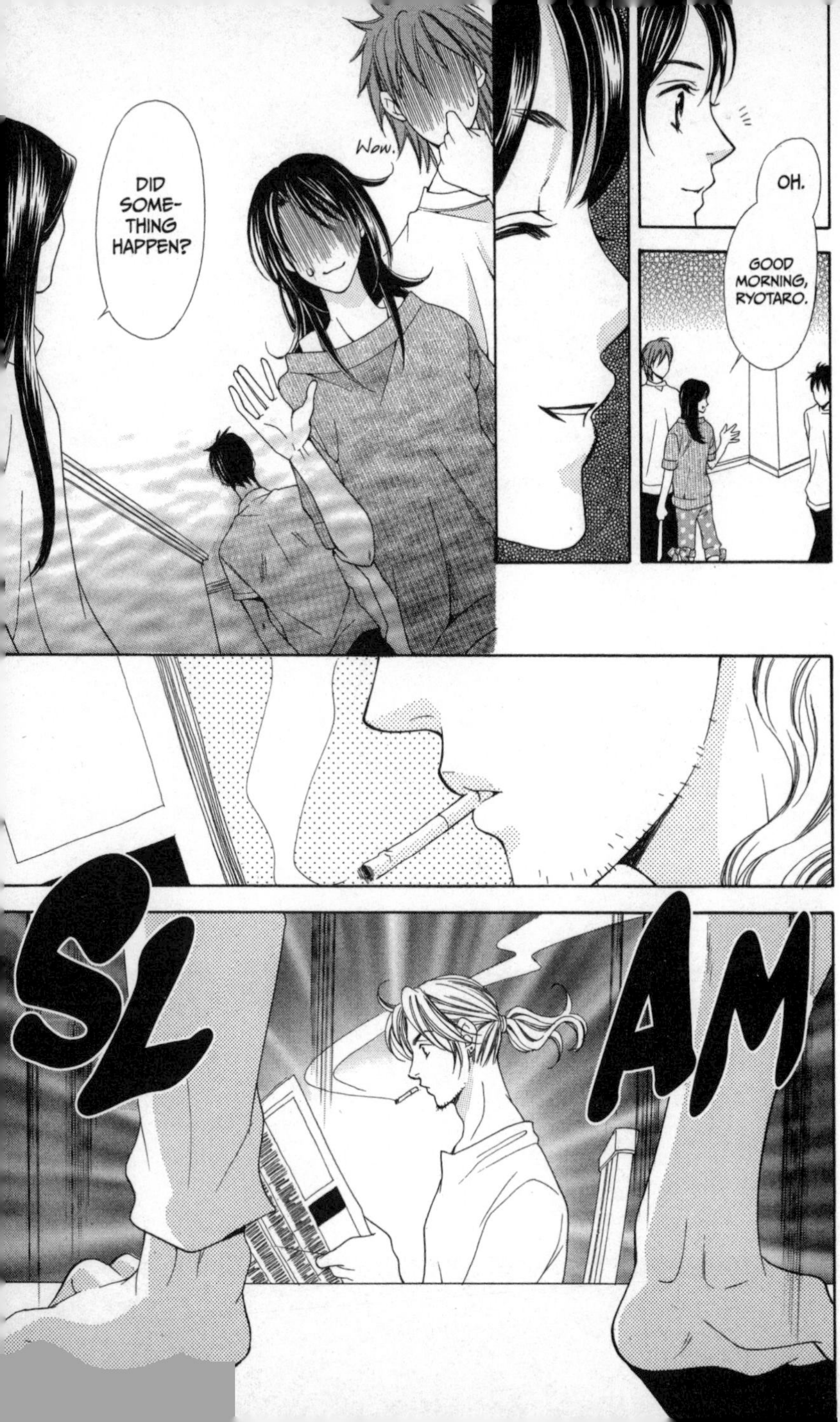
OH.
GOOD MORNING, RYOTARO.
Wow.
DID SOME-THING HAPPEN?
SLAM

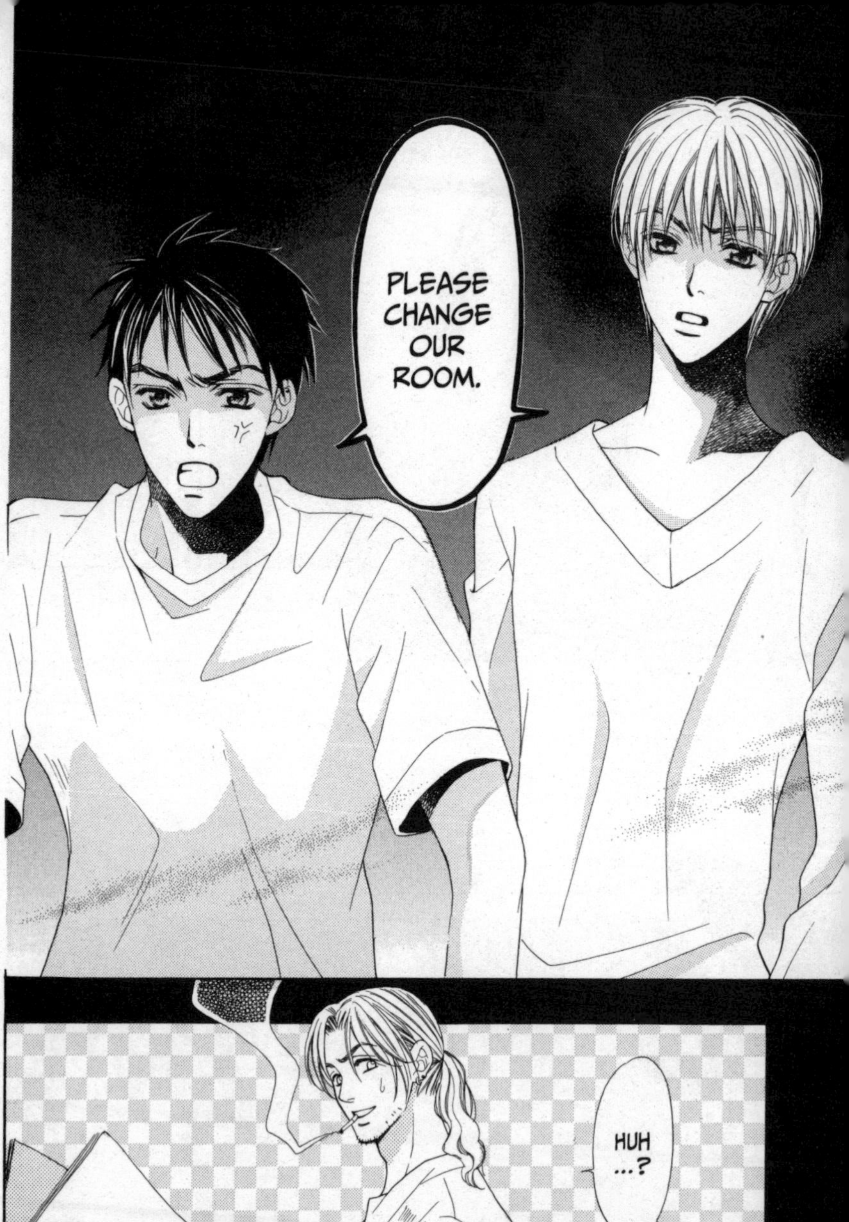
PLEASE CHANGE OUR ROOM.
HUH ...?

THE SECOND DAY OF TRAINING CAMP IS ABOUT TO START...(?)

END OF MEASURE 11

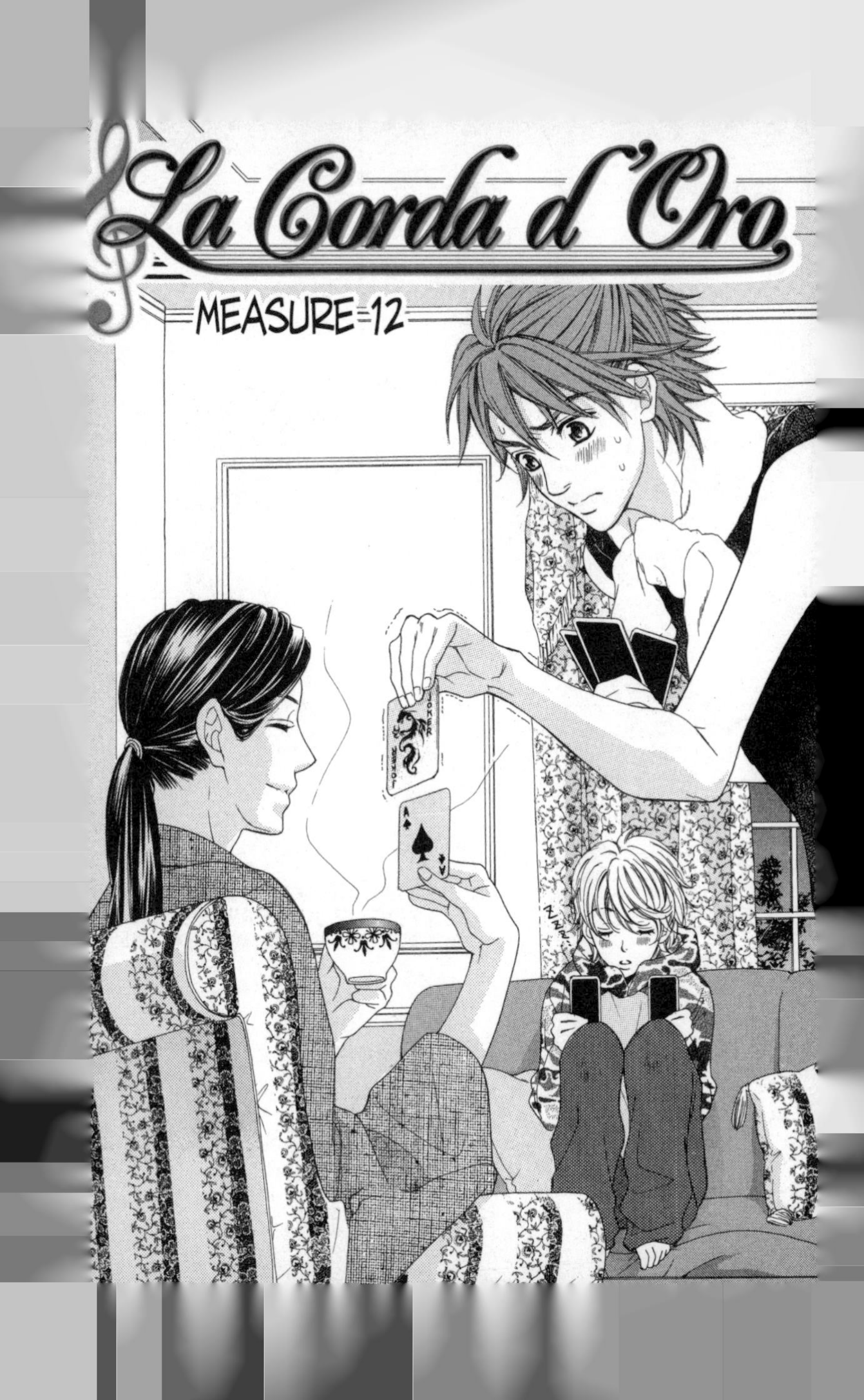
La Corda d'Oro
MEASURE 12

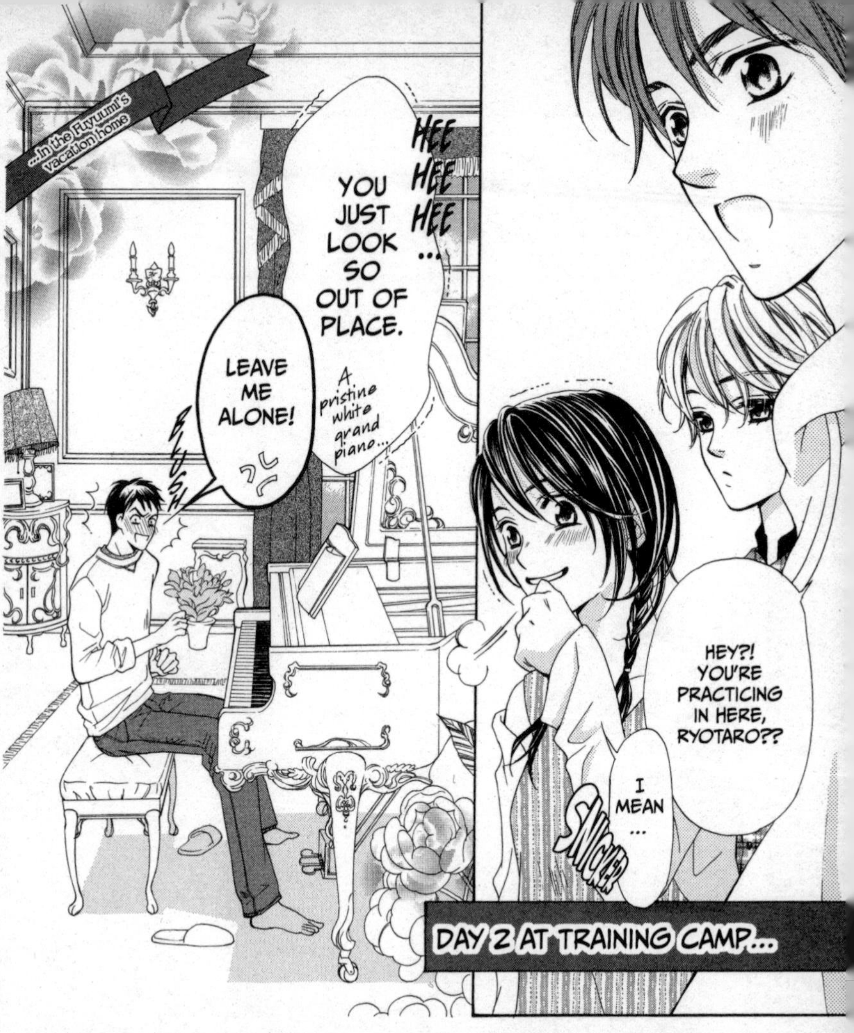
DAY 2 AT TRAINING CAMP...
HEY?! YOU'RE PRACTICING IN HERE, RYOTARO??
I MEAN ...
SNICKER
...In the Fuyuumi's vacation home
HEE HEE HEE ...
YOU JUST LOOK SO OUT OF PLACE.
A pristine white grand piano...
LEAVE ME ALONE!
BLUSH

DAILY HAPPENINGS

④ Things I'm scared of

That would be cicadas (although I would like to stay away from any member of the bug family). My mother often says, "They have such an ephemeral lifespan. How can you not like them?" but simply put, I don't. I was taking in my laundry one day and one of those creeps was hiding in my clothes and

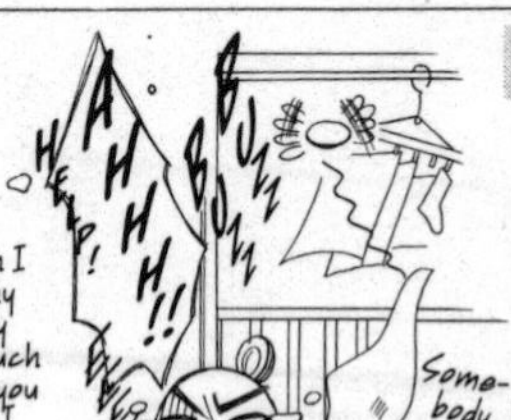
AHHHH!!
BZZZ
BZZZ
HELP!
Somebody save me!

Tried to invade my house!!

It flew around the room and ended up crying perched on my wall...And of course it was a day when everyone in my family was out and wasn't coming home that night... If I remember correctly...

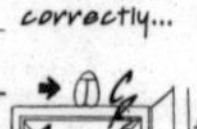
FRONT DOOR

Plus it decided to rest in the hallway leading to the front door...

Continued on ⑤ ⟷

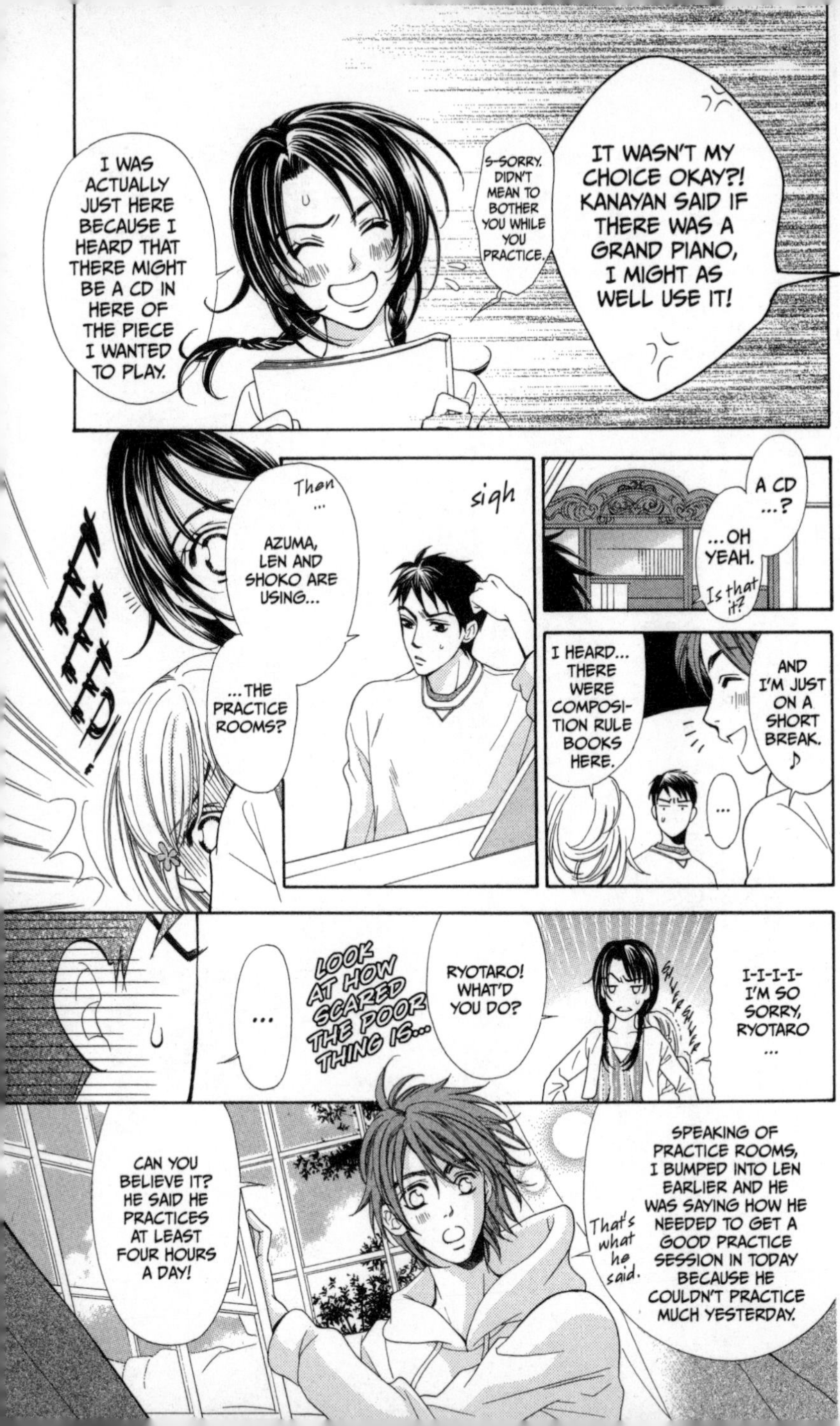
IT WASN'T MY CHOICE OKAY?! KANAYAN SAID IF THERE WAS A GRAND PIANO, I MIGHT AS WELL USE IT!
S-SORRY. DIDN'T MEAN TO BOTHER YOU WHILE YOU PRACTICE.
I WAS ACTUALLY JUST HERE BECAUSE I HEARD THAT THERE MIGHT BE A CD IN HERE OF THE PIECE I WANTED TO PLAY.
A CD ...?
...OH YEAH.
Is that it?
AND I'M JUST ON A SHORT BREAK. ♪
I HEARD... THERE WERE COMPOSITION RULE BOOKS HERE.
...
sigh
Then ...
AZUMA, LEN AND SHOKO ARE USING...
...THE PRACTICE ROOMS?
I-I-I-I- I'M SO SORRY, RYOTARO ...
RYOTARO! WHAT'D YOU DO?
LOOK AT HOW SCARED THE POOR THING IS...
...
SPEAKING OF PRACTICE ROOMS, I BUMPED INTO LEN EARLIER AND HE WAS SAYING HOW HE NEEDED TO GET A GOOD PRACTICE SESSION IN TODAY BECAUSE HE COULDN'T PRACTICE MUCH YESTERDAY.
That's what he said.
CAN YOU BELIEVE IT? HE SAID HE PRACTICES AT LEAST FOUR HOURS A DAY!

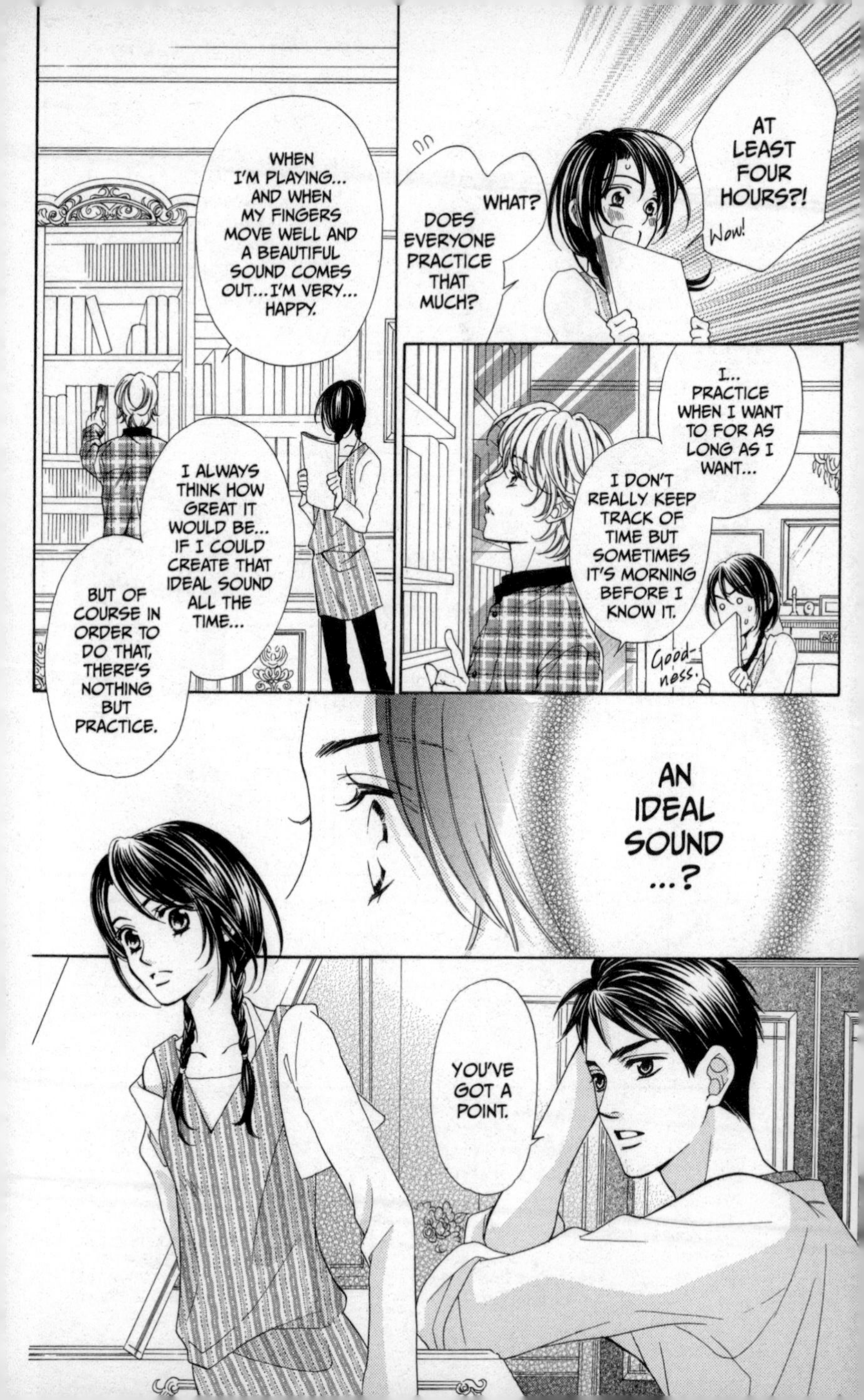
AT LEAST FOUR HOURS?!
Wow!
WHAT? DOES EVERYONE PRACTICE THAT MUCH?
I... PRACTICE WHEN I WANT TO FOR AS LONG AS I WANT...
I DON'T REALLY KEEP TRACK OF TIME BUT SOMETIMES IT'S MORNING BEFORE I KNOW IT.
Goodness.
WHEN I'M PLAYING... AND WHEN MY FINGERS MOVE WELL AND A BEAUTIFUL SOUND COMES OUT... I'M VERY... HAPPY.
I ALWAYS THINK HOW GREAT IT WOULD BE... IF I COULD CREATE THAT IDEAL SOUND ALL THE TIME...
BUT OF COURSE IN ORDER TO DO THAT, THERE'S NOTHING BUT PRACTICE.
AN IDEAL SOUND ...?
YOU'VE GOT A POINT.

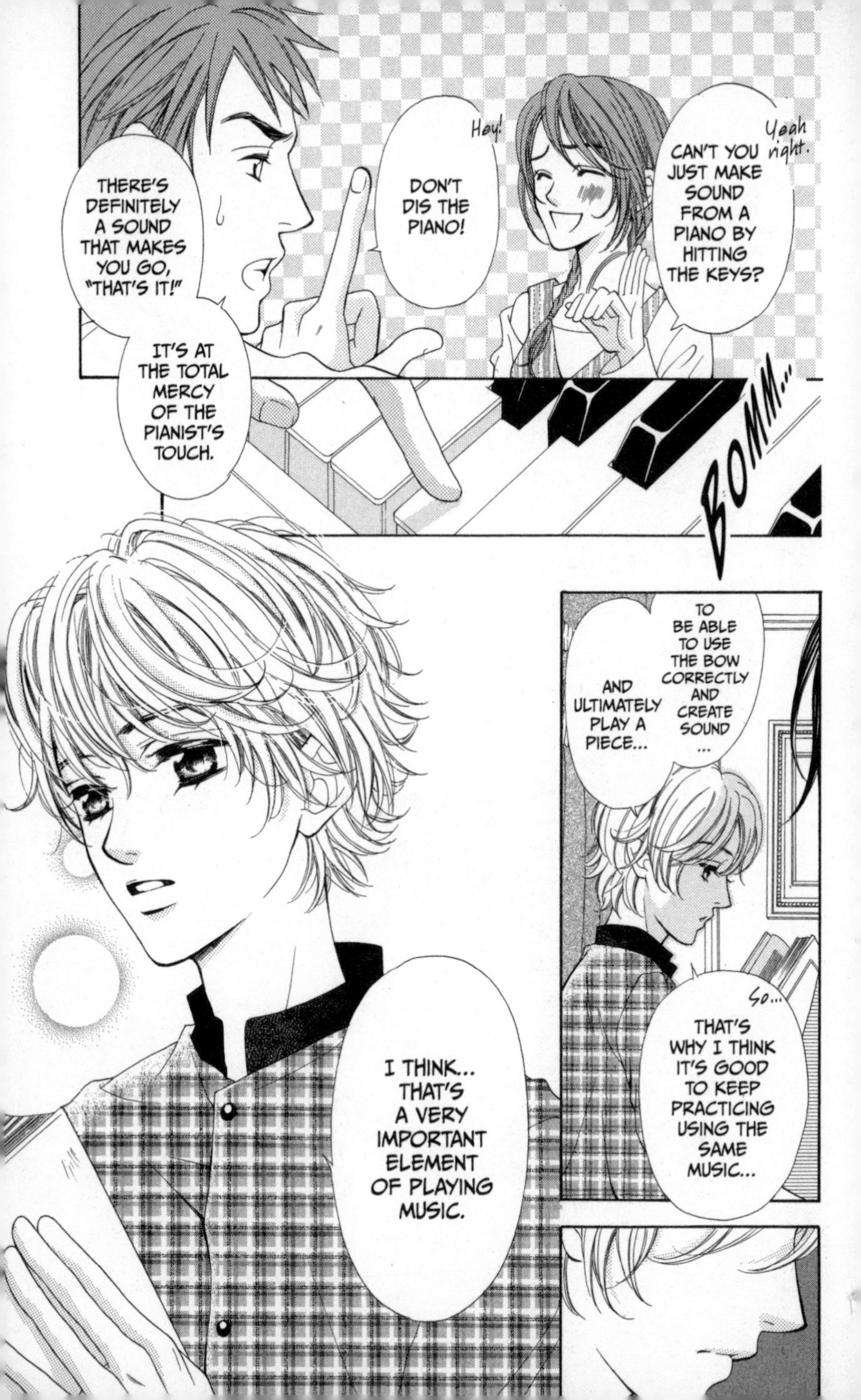
Yeah right.
CAN'T YOU JUST MAKE SOUND FROM A PIANO BY HITTING THE KEYS?
Hey!
DON'T DIS THE PIANO!
THERE'S DEFINITELY A SOUND THAT MAKES YOU GO, "THAT'S IT!"
IT'S AT THE TOTAL MERCY OF THE PIANIST'S TOUCH.
BOMM...
TO BE ABLE TO USE THE BOW CORRECTLY AND CREATE SOUND ...
AND ULTIMATELY PLAY A PIECE...
So...
THAT'S WHY I THINK IT'S GOOD TO KEEP PRACTICING USING THE SAME MUSIC...
I THINK... THAT'S A VERY IMPORTANT ELEMENT OF PLAYING MUSIC.

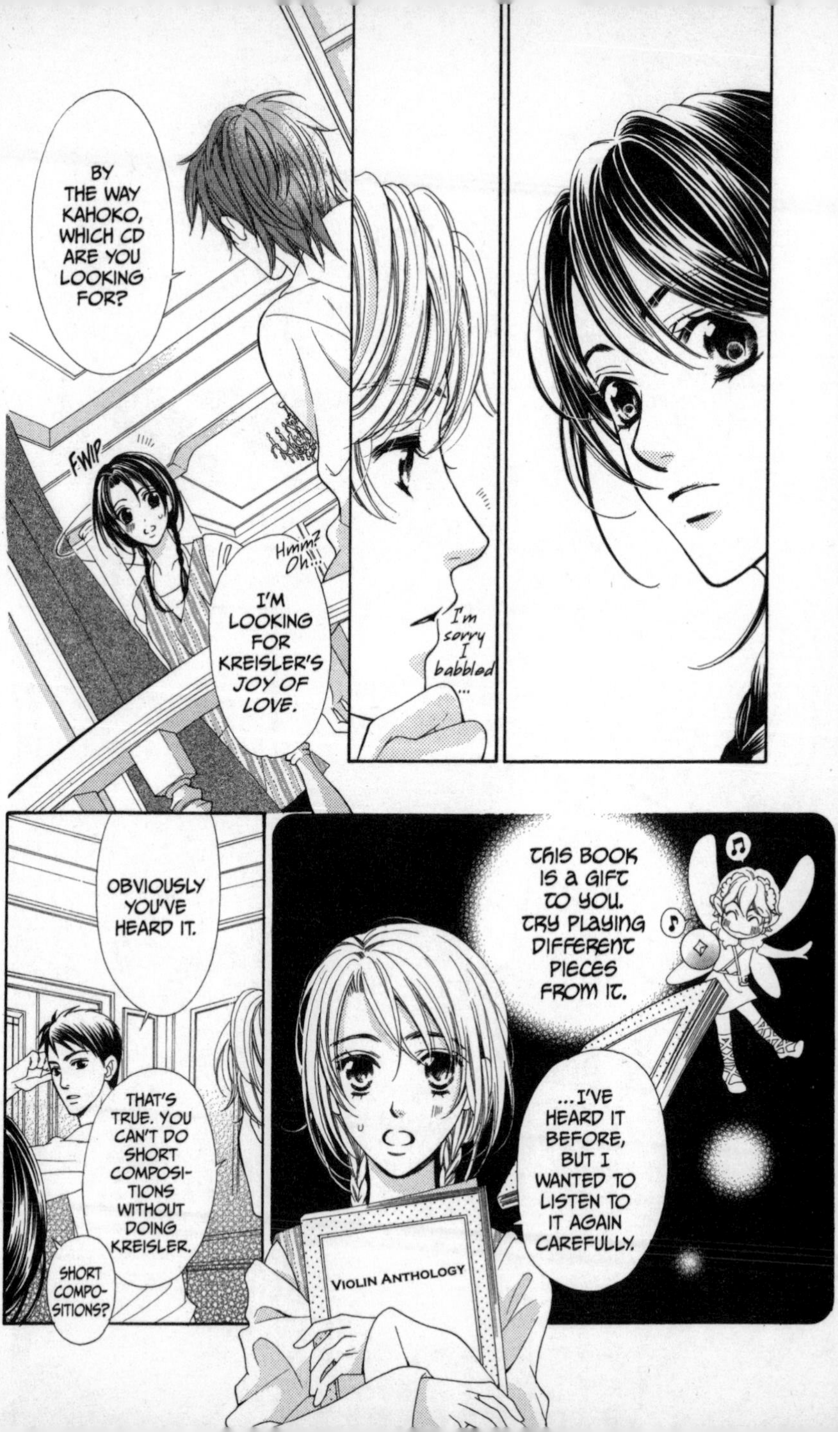
I'm sorry I babbled...
BY THE WAY KAHOKO, WHICH CD ARE YOU LOOKING FOR?
F-WIP
Hmm? Oh...
I'M LOOKING FOR KREISLER'S JOY OF LOVE.
THIS BOOK IS A GIFT TO YOU. TRY PLAYING DIFFERENT PIECES FROM IT.
...I'VE HEARD IT BEFORE, BUT I WANTED TO LISTEN TO IT AGAIN CAREFULLY.
VIOLIN ANTHOLOGY
OBVIOUSLY YOU'VE HEARD IT.
THAT'S TRUE. YOU CAN'T DO SHORT COMPOSITIONS WITHOUT DOING KREISLER.
SHORT COMPOSITIONS?

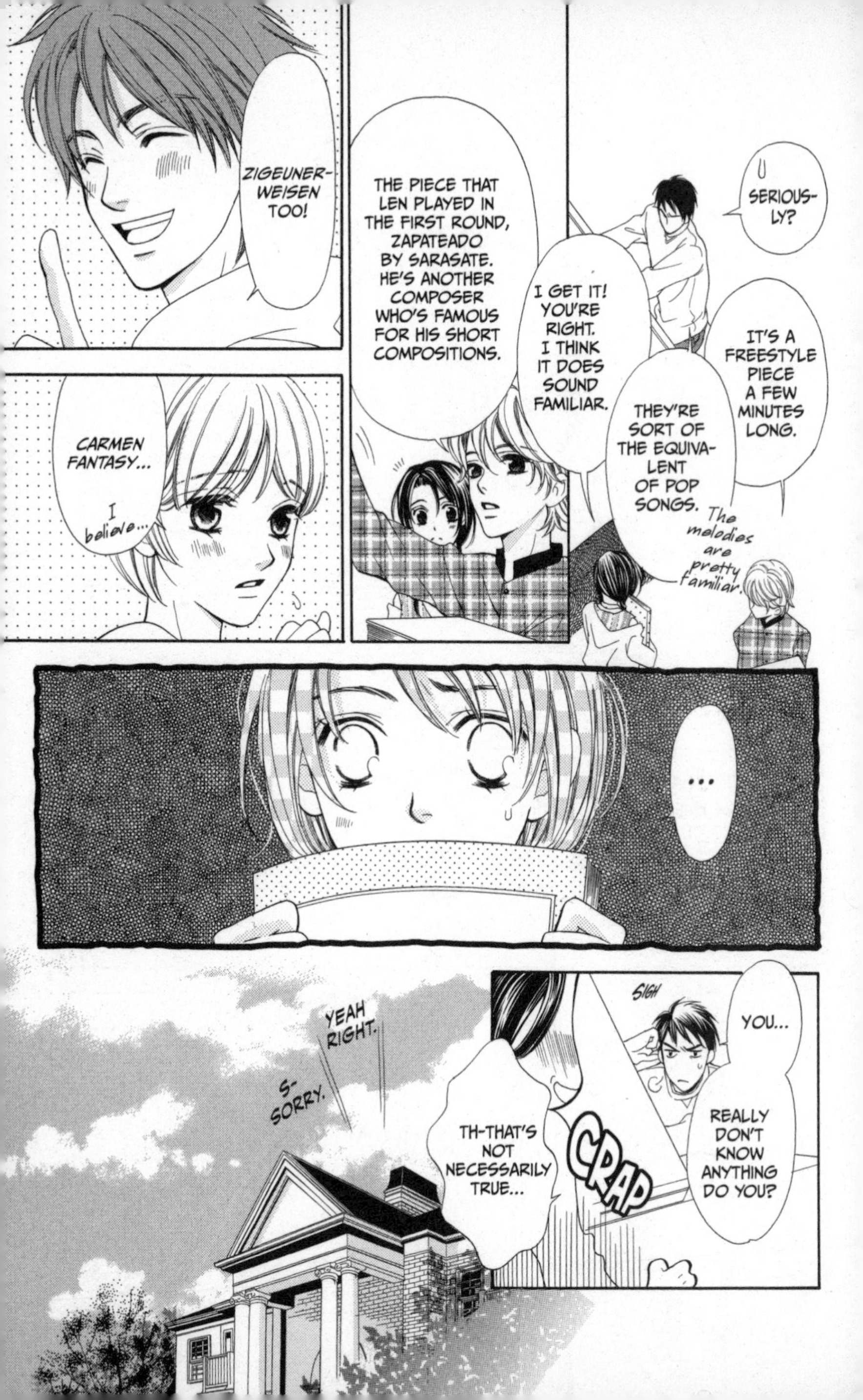
SERIOUS-LY?
IT'S A FREESTYLE PIECE A FEW MINUTES LONG.
THEY'RE SORT OF THE EQUIVALENT OF POP SONGS.
The melodies are pretty familiar.
THE PIECE THAT LEN PLAYED IN THE FIRST ROUND, ZAPATEADO BY SARASATE. HE'S ANOTHER COMPOSER WHO'S FAMOUS FOR HIS SHORT COMPOSITIONS.
I GET IT! YOU'RE RIGHT. I THINK IT DOES SOUND FAMILIAR.
ZIGEUNER-WEISEN TOO!
CARMEN FANTASY...
I believe...
...
SIGH
YOU...
REALLY DON'T KNOW ANYTHING DO YOU?
CRAP
TH-THAT'S NOT NECESSARILY TRUE...
YEAH RIGHT.
S-SORRY.

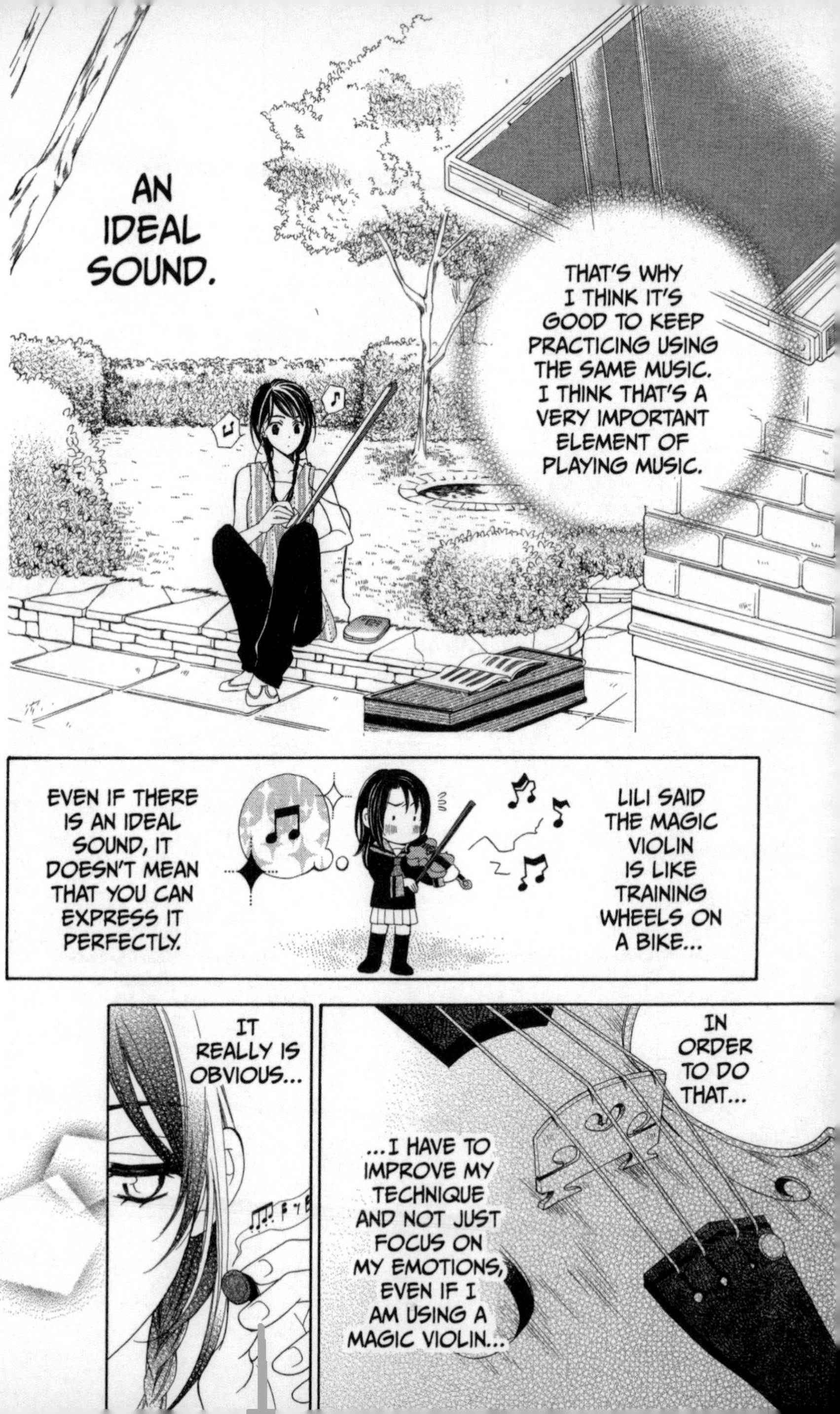
THAT'S WHY I THINK IT'S GOOD TO KEEP PRACTICING USING THE SAME MUSIC. I THINK THAT'S A VERY IMPORTANT ELEMENT OF PLAYING MUSIC.
AN IDEAL SOUND.
LILI SAID THE MAGIC VIOLIN IS LIKE TRAINING WHEELS ON A BIKE...
EVEN IF THERE IS AN IDEAL SOUND, IT DOESN'T MEAN THAT YOU CAN EXPRESS IT PERFECTLY.
IN ORDER TO DO THAT...
...I HAVE TO IMPROVE MY TECHNIQUE AND NOT JUST FOCUS ON MY EMOTIONS, EVEN IF I AM USING A MAGIC VIOLIN...
IT REALLY IS OBVIOUS...

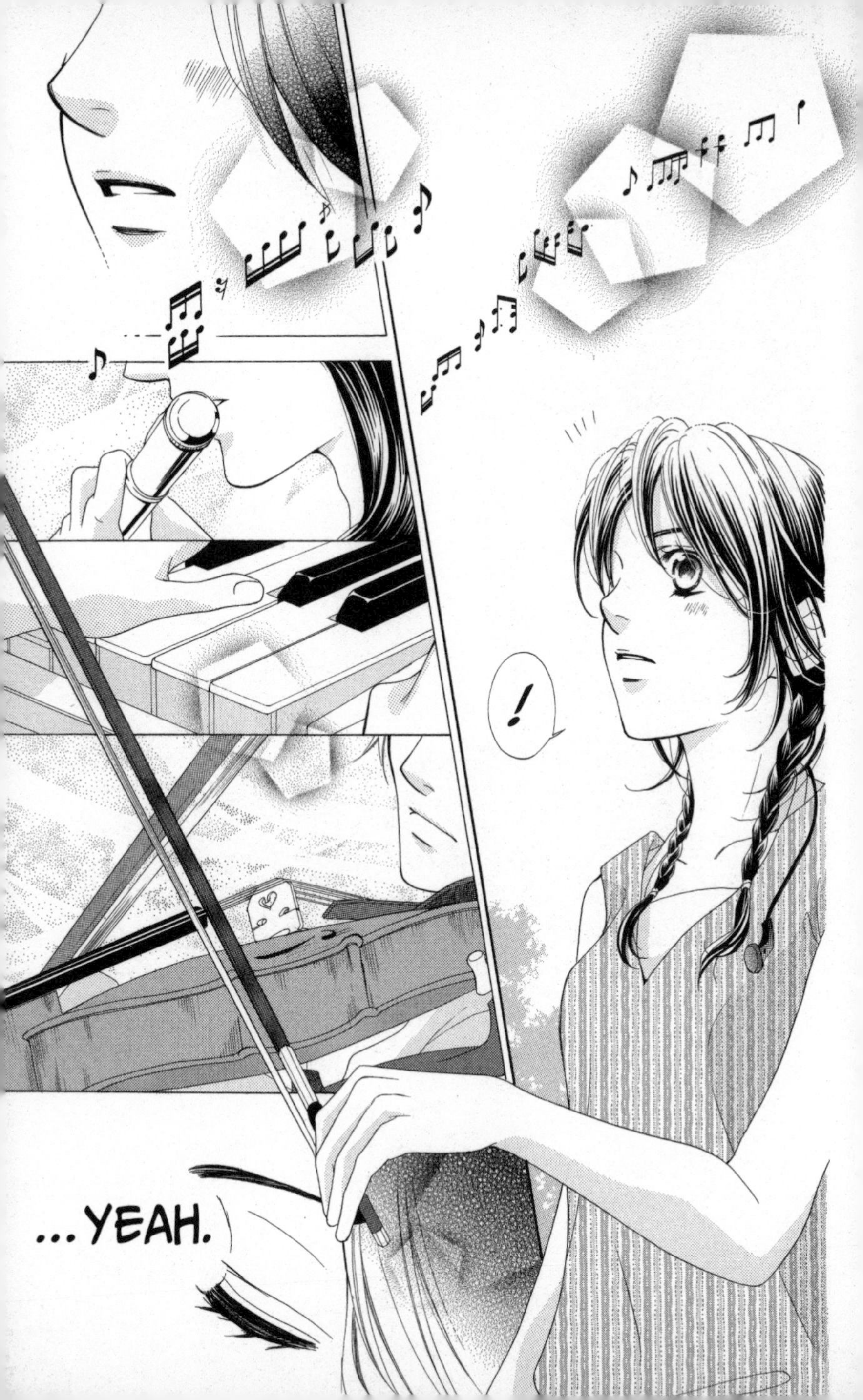
!
...YEAH.

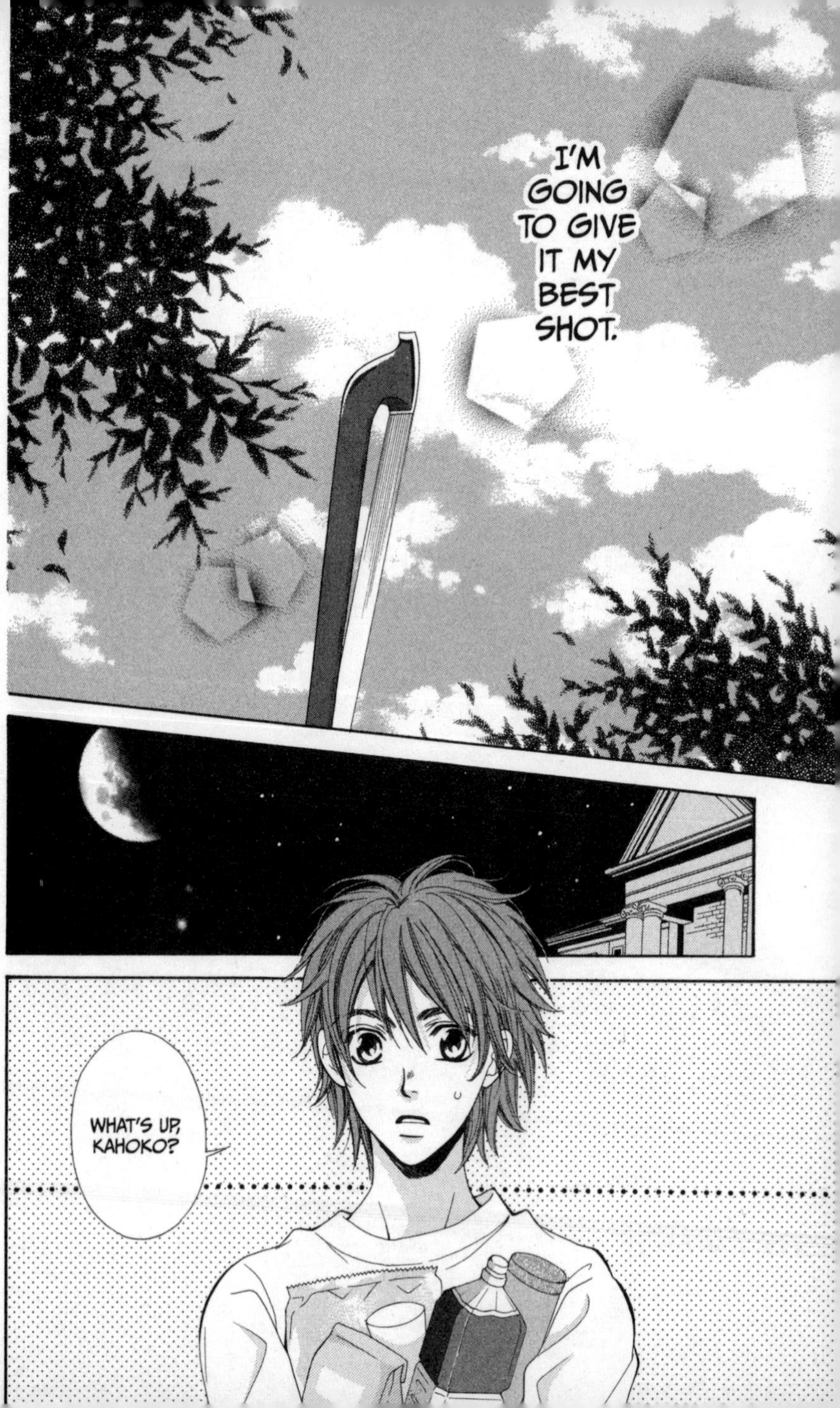
I'M GOING TO GIVE IT MY BEST SHOT.
WHAT'S UP, KAHOKO?

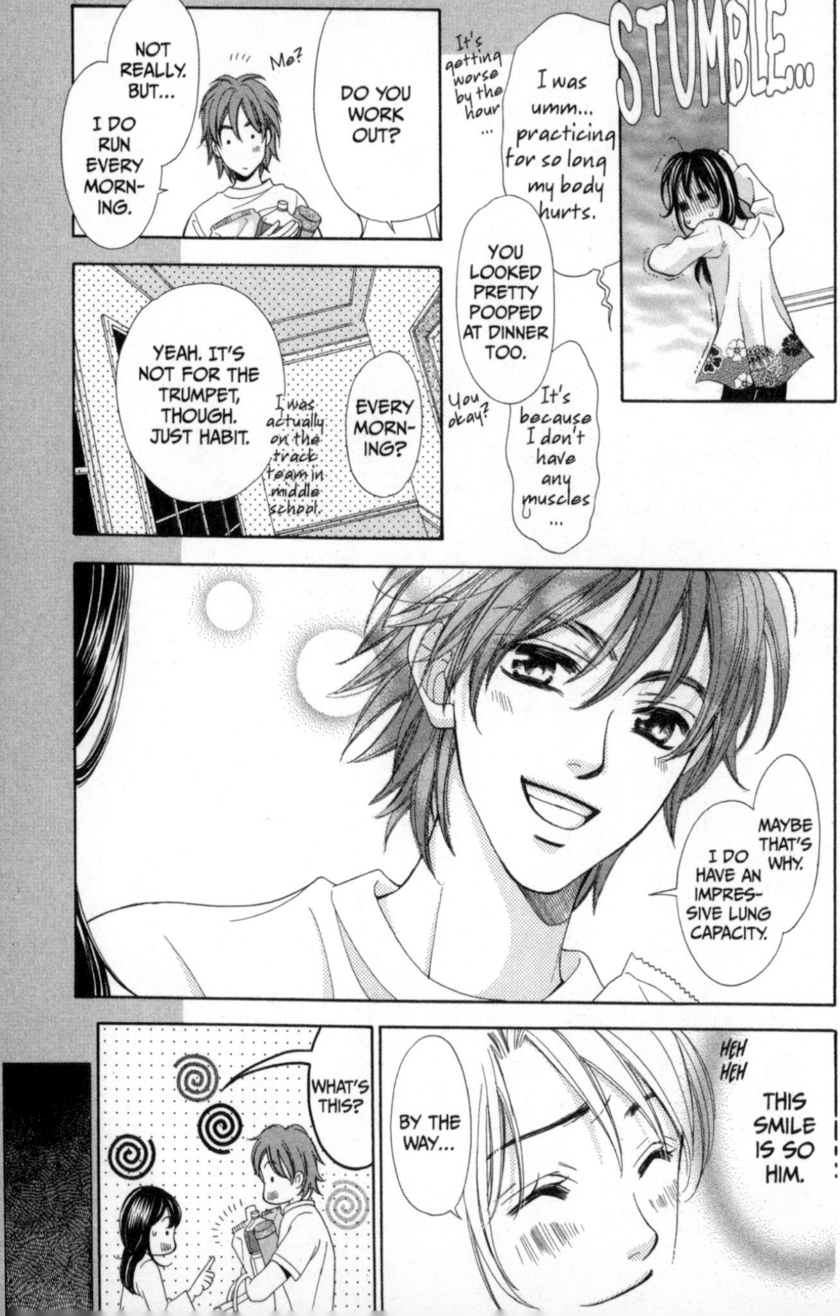
STUMBLE...
I was umm... practicing for so long my body hurts.
It's getting worse by the hour...
YOU LOOKED PRETTY POOPED AT DINNER TOO.
You okay?
It's because I don't have any muscles...
DO YOU WORK OUT?
Me?
NOT REALLY. BUT...
I DO RUN EVERY MORNING.
EVERY MORNING?
I was actually on the track team in middle school.
YEAH. IT'S NOT FOR THE TRUMPET, THOUGH. JUST HABIT.
MAYBE THAT'S WHY.
I DO HAVE AN IMPRESSIVE LUNG CAPACITY.
HEH HEH
THIS SMILE IS SO HIM.
BY THE WAY...
WHAT'S THIS?

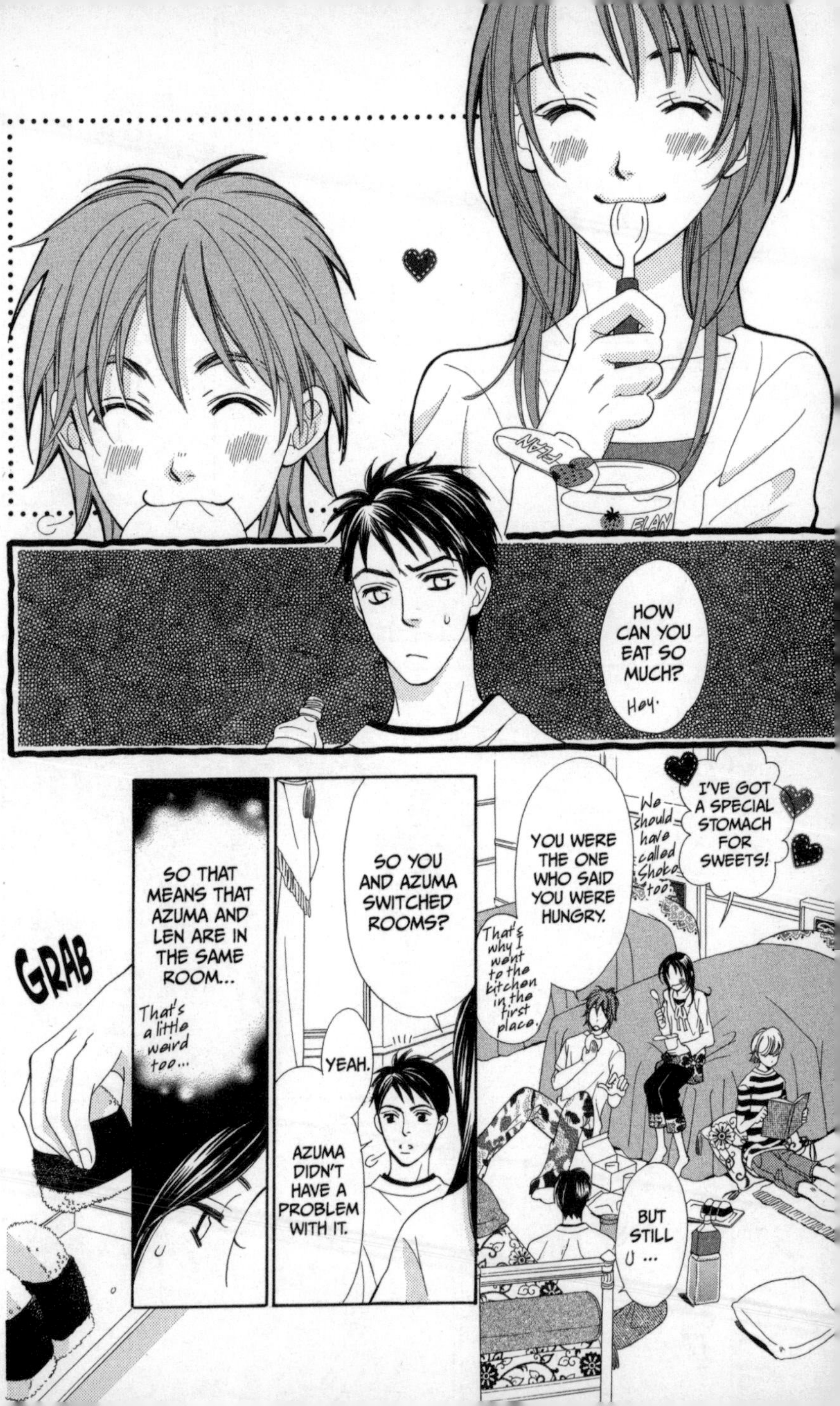
FLAN
FLAN
HOW CAN YOU EAT SO MUCH?
Hey.
I'VE GOT A SPECIAL STOMACH FOR SWEETS!
We should have called Shoko too.
YOU WERE THE ONE WHO SAID YOU WERE HUNGRY.
That's why I went to the kitchen in the first place.
BUT STILL...
SO YOU AND AZUMA SWITCHED ROOMS?
YEAH.
AZUMA DIDN'T HAVE A PROBLEM WITH IT.
SO THAT MEANS THAT AZUMA AND LEN ARE IN THE SAME ROOM...
That's a little weird too...
GRAB

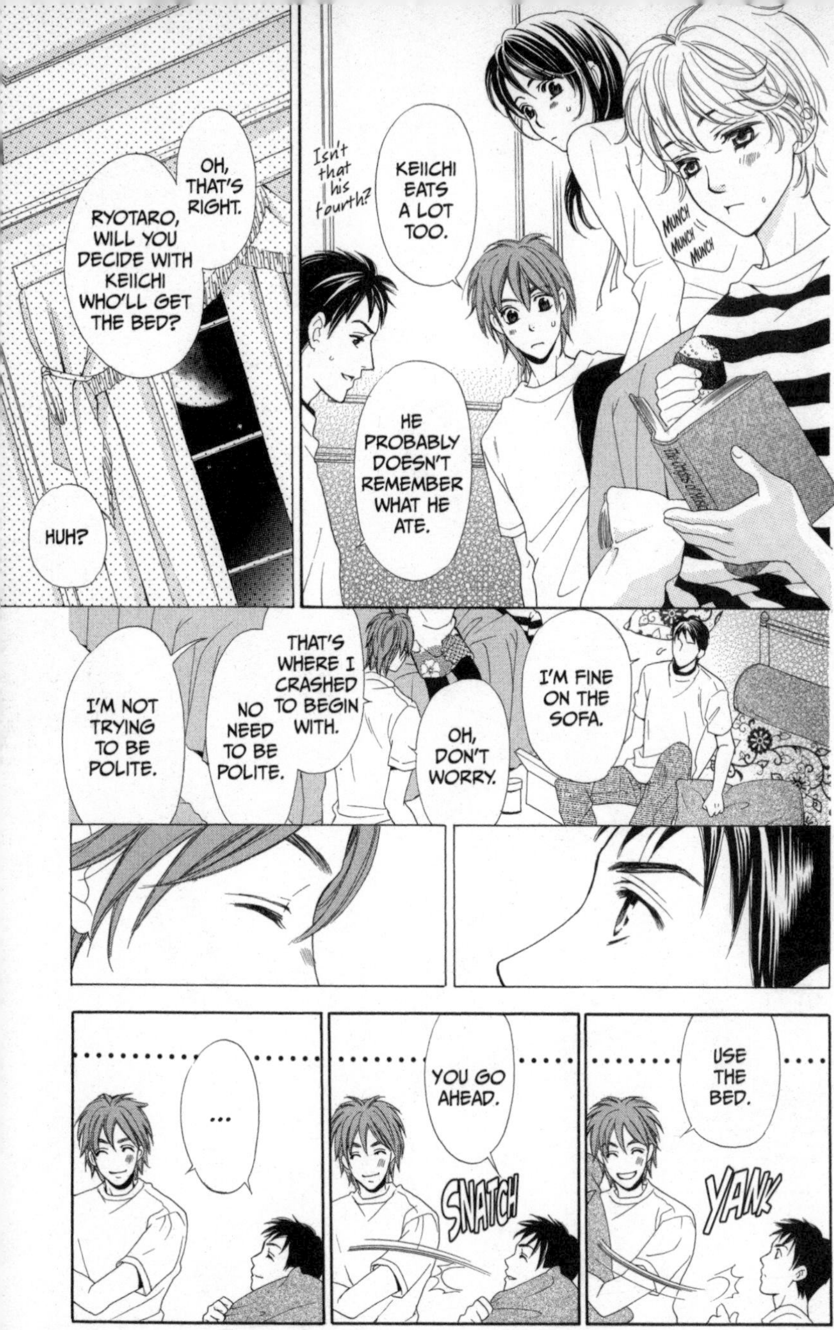
KEIICHI EATS A LOT TOO.
Isn't that his fourth?
MUNCH MUNCH MUNCH
HE PROBABLY DOESN'T REMEMBER WHAT HE ATE.
OH, THAT'S RIGHT.
RYOTARO, WILL YOU DECIDE WITH KEIICHI WHO'LL GET THE BED?
HUH?
I'M FINE ON THE SOFA.
OH, DON'T WORRY.
THAT'S WHERE I CRASHED TO BEGIN WITH.
NO NEED TO BE POLITE.
I'M NOT TRYING TO BE POLITE.
USE THE BED.
YANK
YOU GO AHEAD.
SNATCH
...

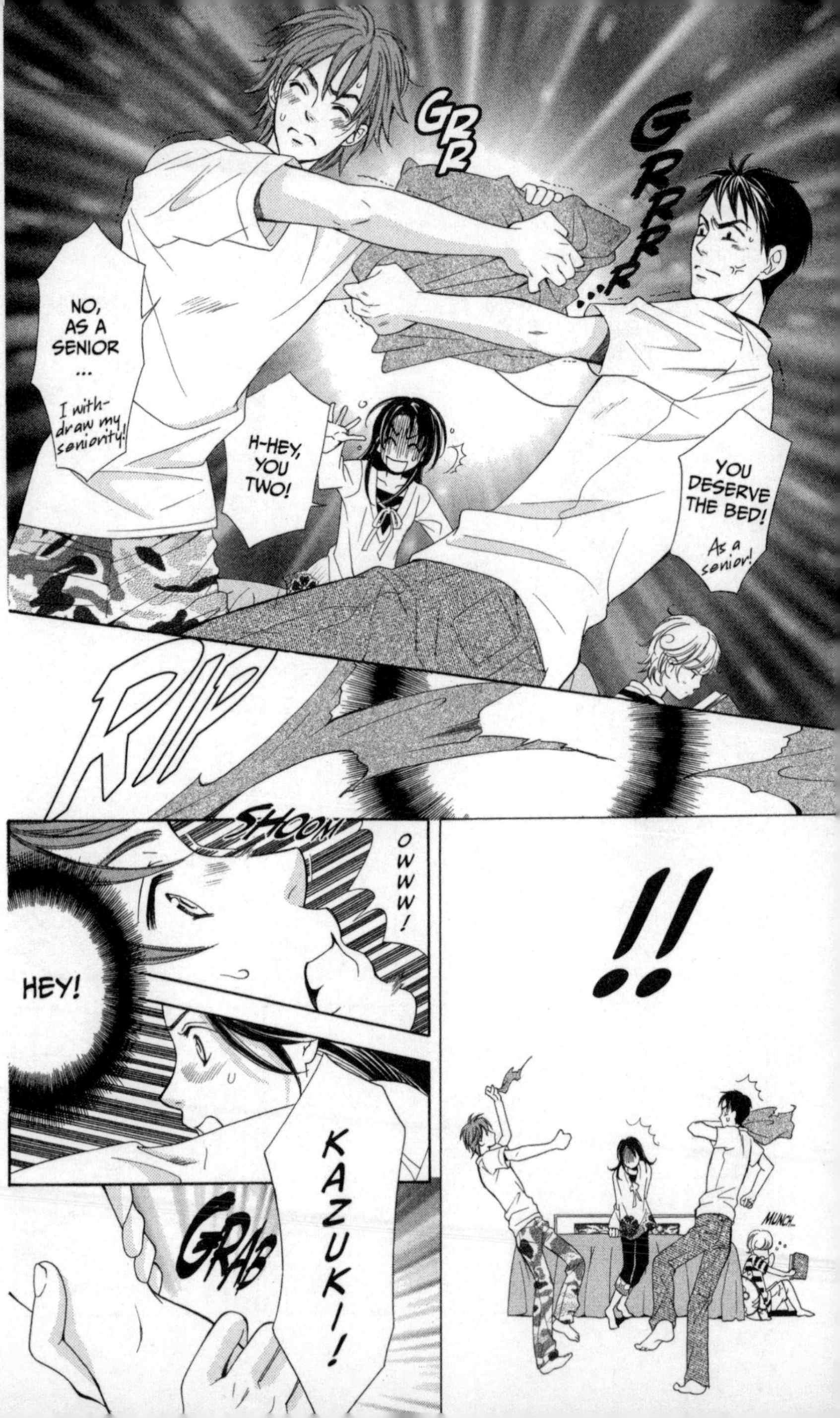
GRRRR...
GRR
YOU DESERVE THE BED!
As a senior!
H-HEY, YOU TWO!
NO, AS A SENIOR...
I with-draw my seniority!
RIP
!!
MUNCH...
SHOOM
OWWW!
HEY!
KAZUKI!
GRAB

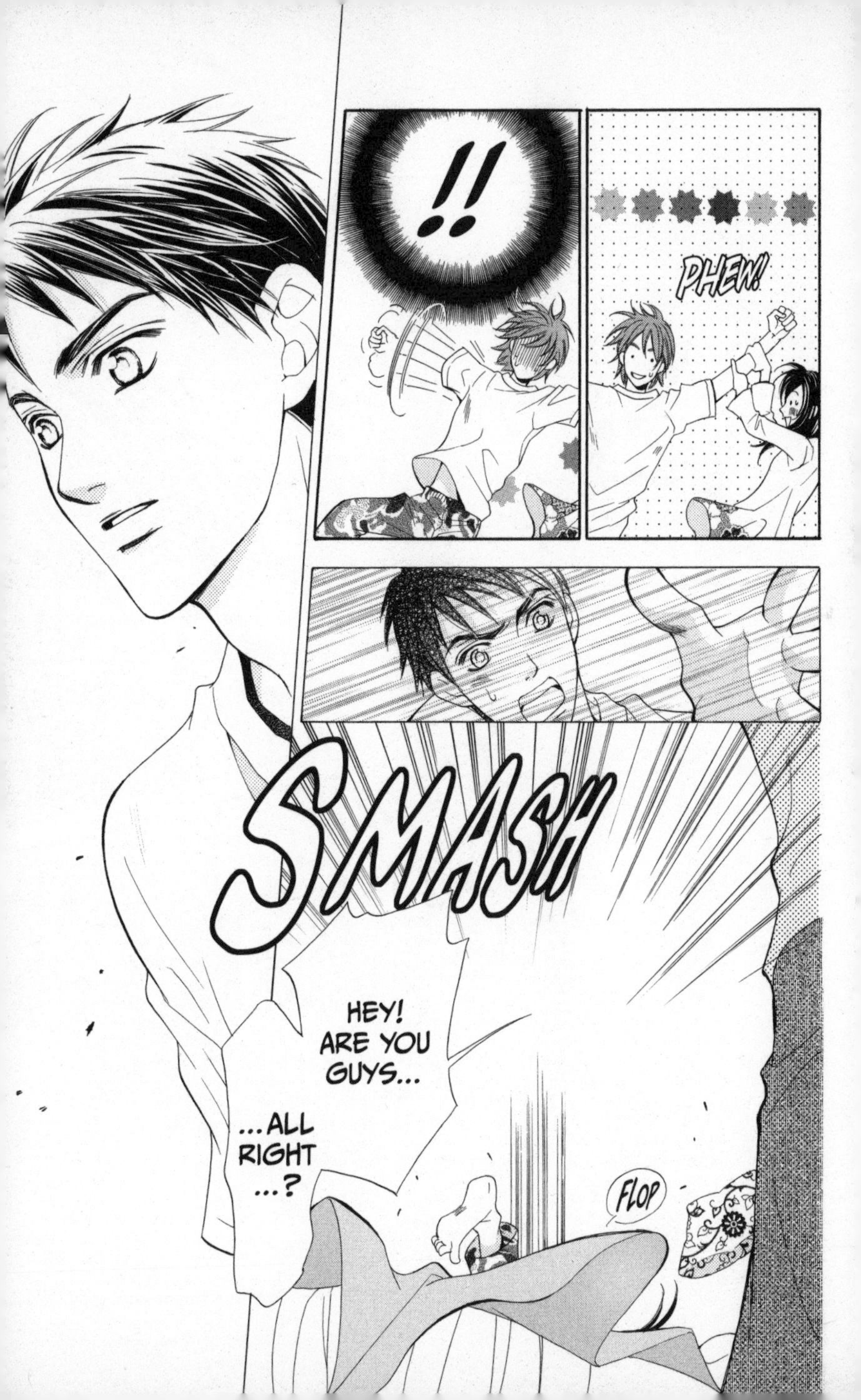
!!
PHEW!
SMASH
HEY! ARE YOU GUYS...
...ALL RIGHT ...?
FLOP

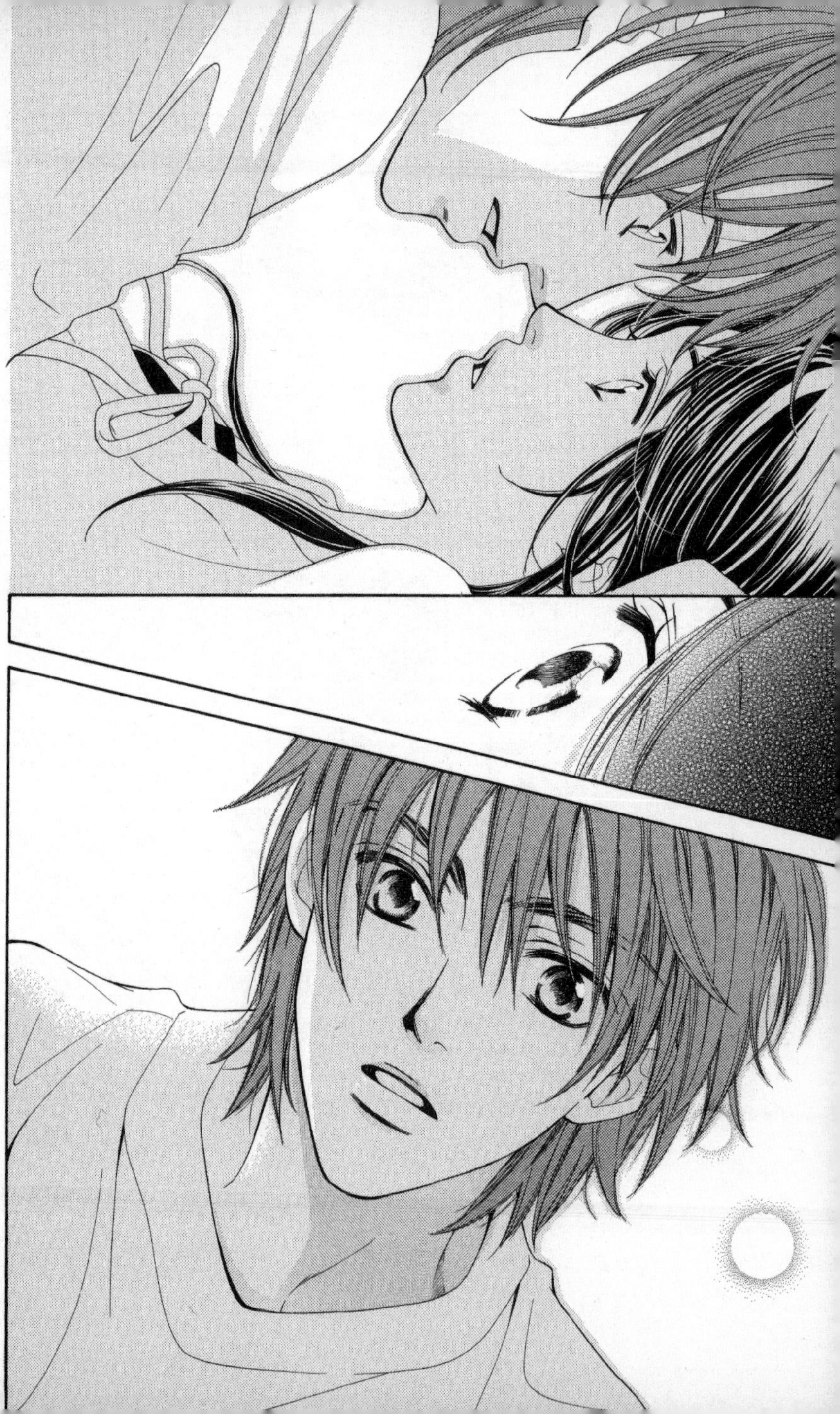

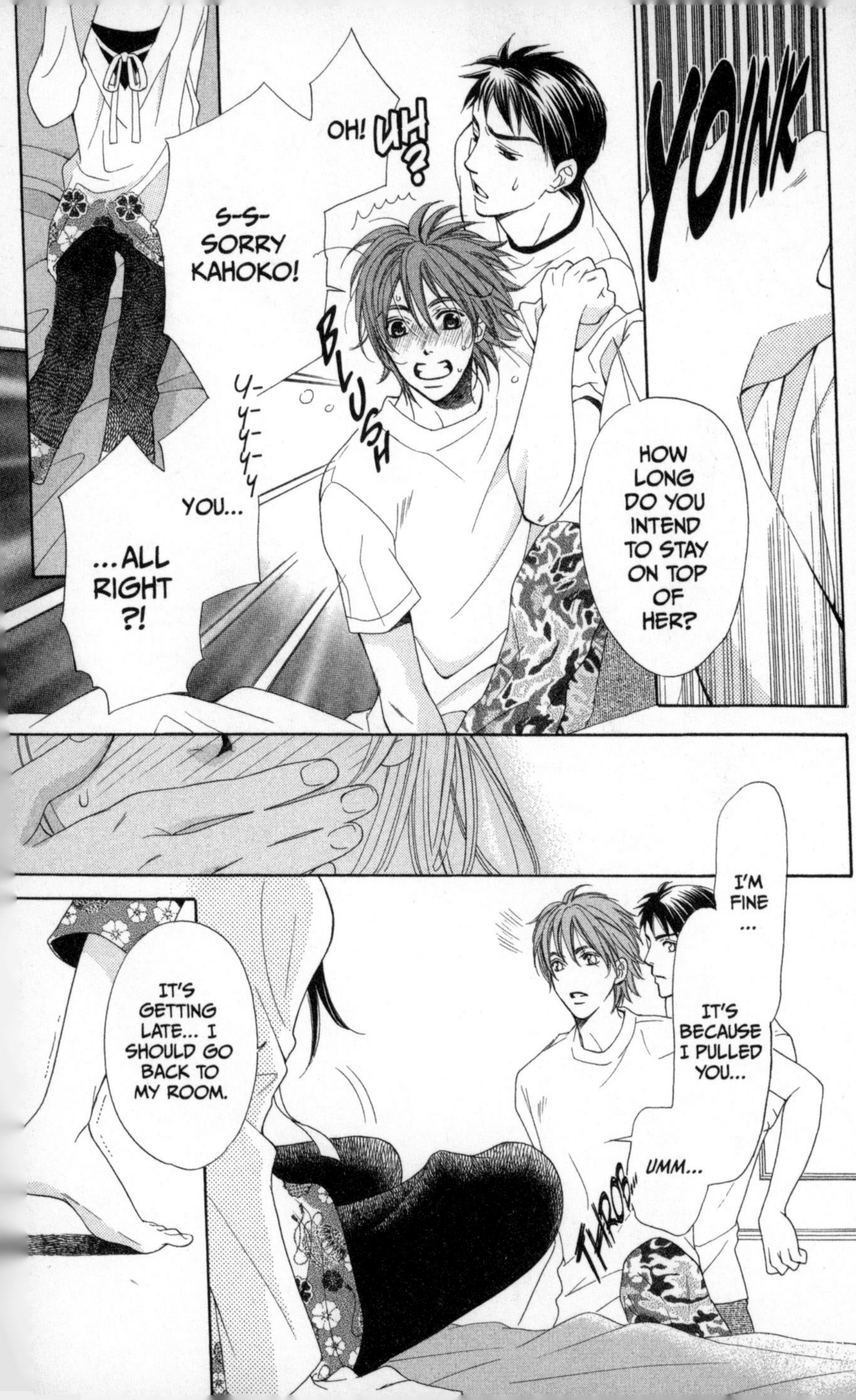
YOINK
HOW LONG DO YOU INTEND TO STAY ON TOP OF HER?
OH! UH?
S-S-SORRY KAHOKO!
BLUSH
Y-Y-Y-Y-Y
YOU...
...ALL RIGHT?!
I'M FINE...
IT'S BECAUSE I PULLED YOU...
UMM...
THROB...
IT'S GETTING LATE... I SHOULD GO BACK TO MY ROOM.

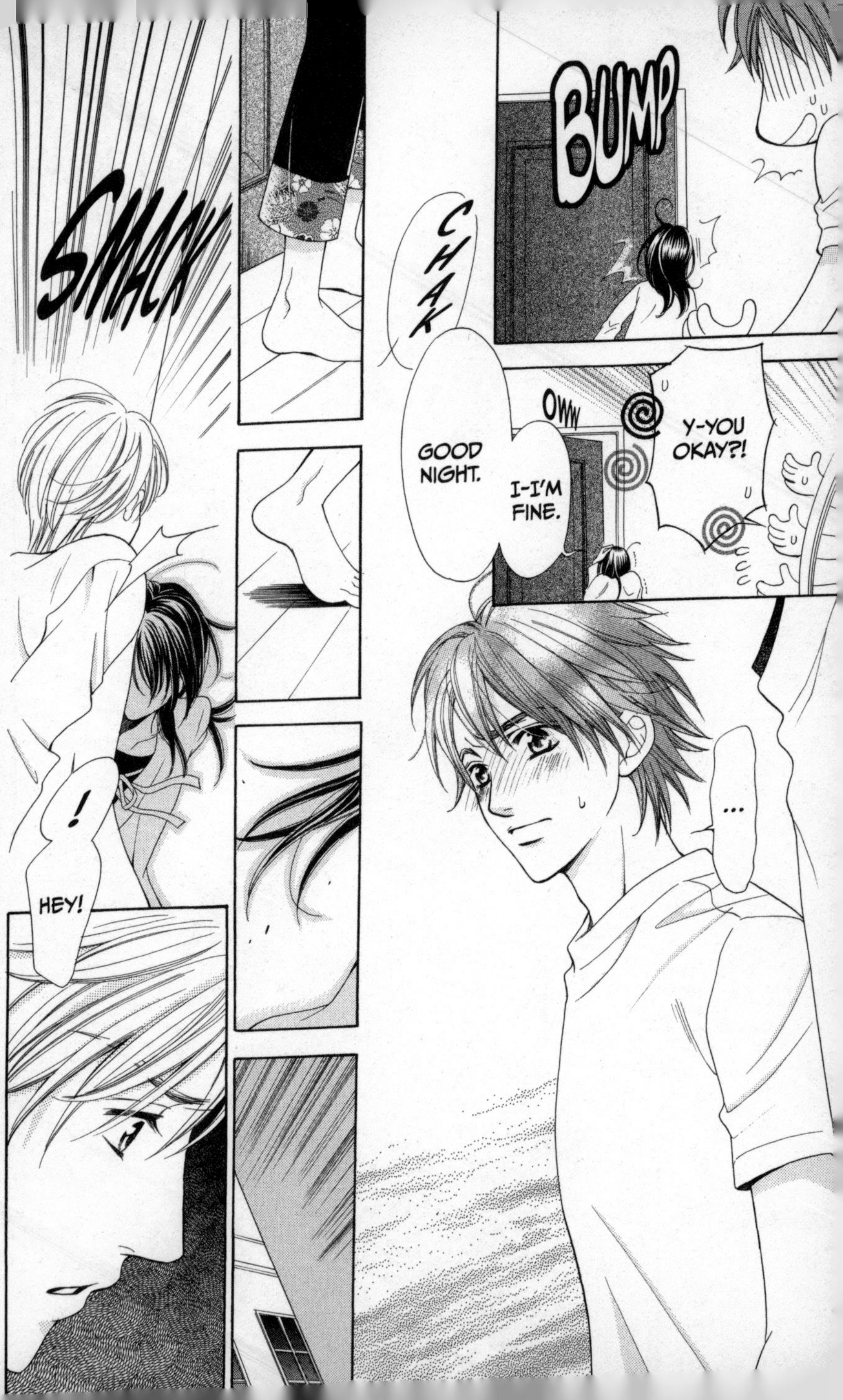
BUMP
CHAK
OWW
Y-YOU OKAY?!
I-I'M FINE.
GOOD NIGHT.
...
SMACK
!
HEY!

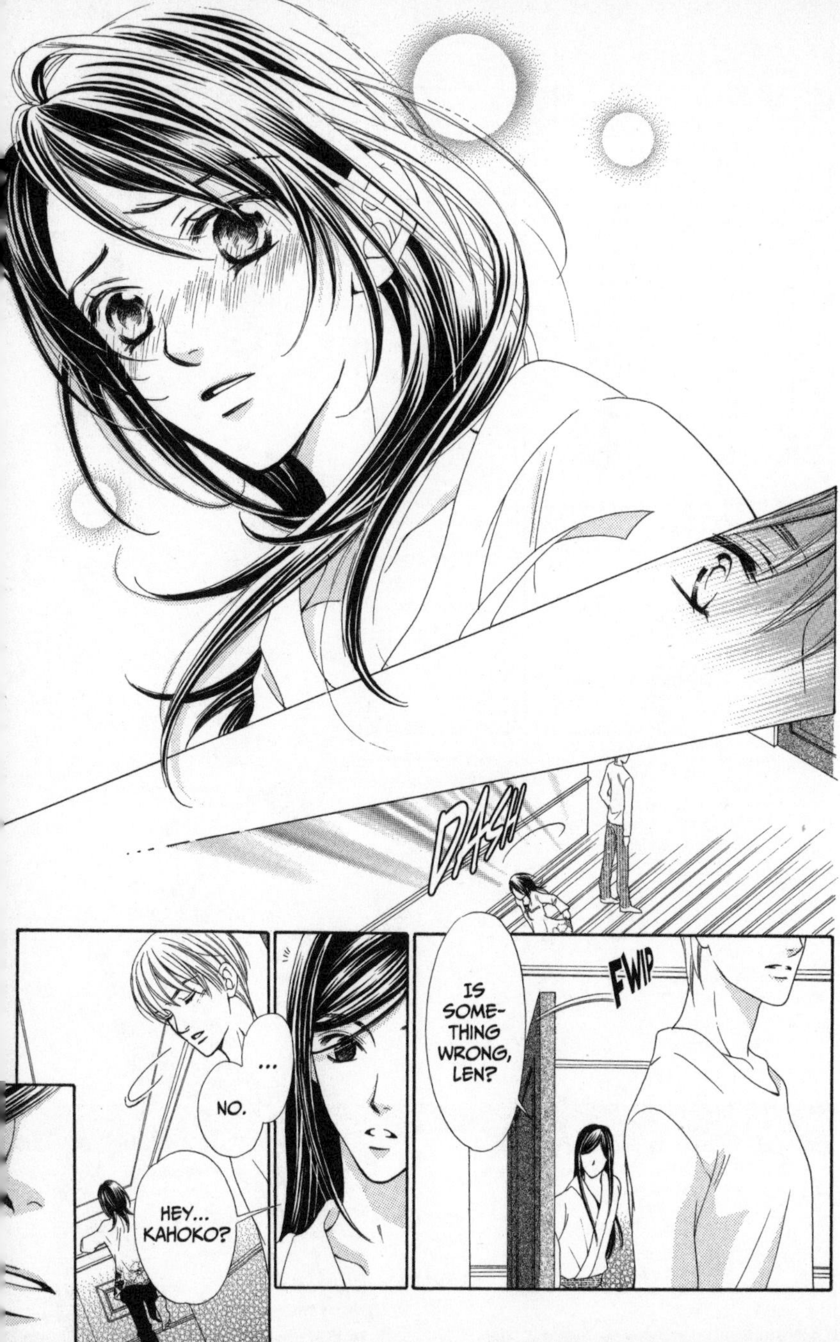
DASH
FWIP
IS SOMETHING WRONG, LEN?
...
NO.
HEY... KAHOKO?

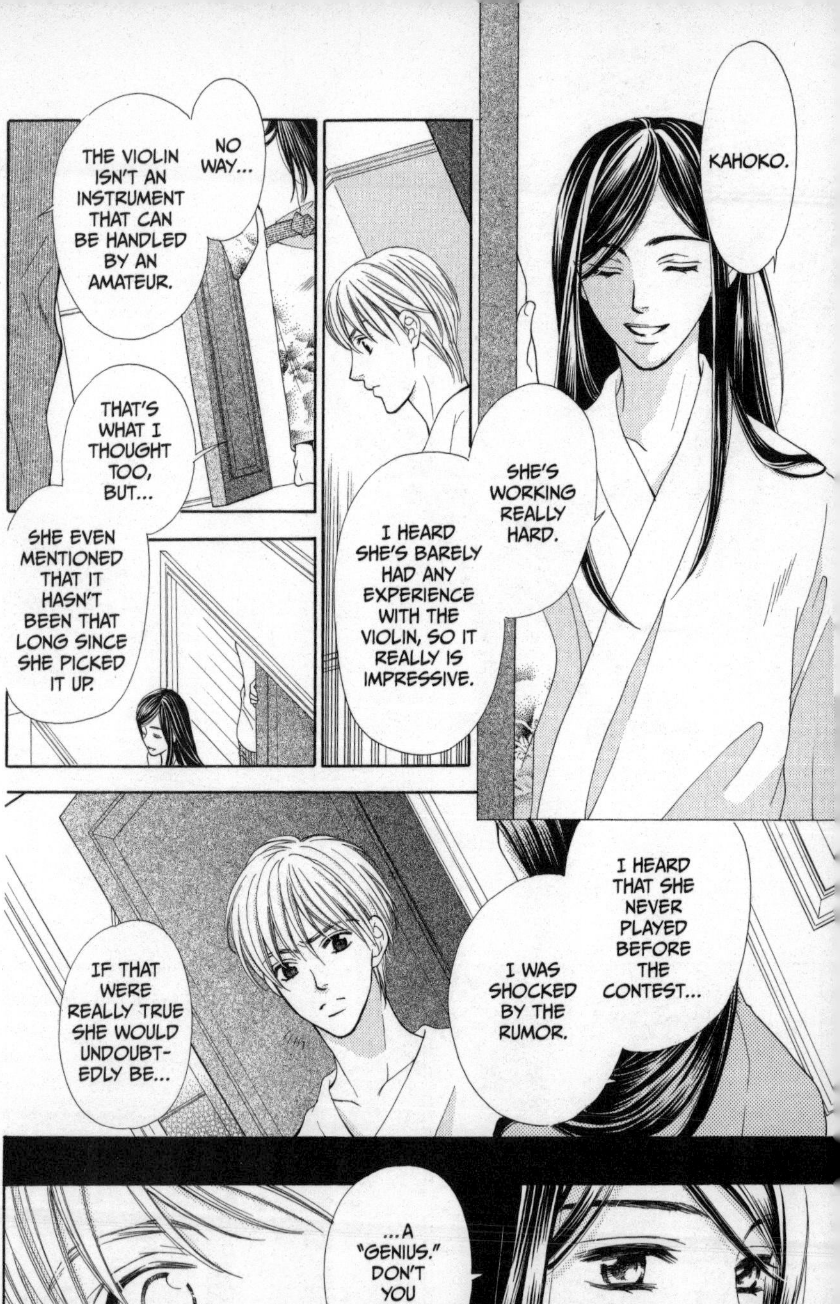
KAHOKO.
SHE'S WORKING REALLY HARD.
I HEARD SHE'S BARELY HAD ANY EXPERIENCE WITH THE VIOLIN, SO IT REALLY IS IMPRESSIVE.
NO WAY...
THE VIOLIN ISN'T AN INSTRUMENT THAT CAN BE HANDLED BY AN AMATEUR.
THAT'S WHAT I THOUGHT TOO, BUT...
SHE EVEN MENTIONED THAT IT HASN'T BEEN THAT LONG SINCE SHE PICKED IT UP.
I HEARD THAT SHE NEVER PLAYED BEFORE THE CONTEST...
I WAS SHOCKED BY THE RUMOR.
IF THAT WERE REALLY TRUE SHE WOULD UNDOUBTEDLY BE...
..."A "GENIUS." DON'T YOU THINK?

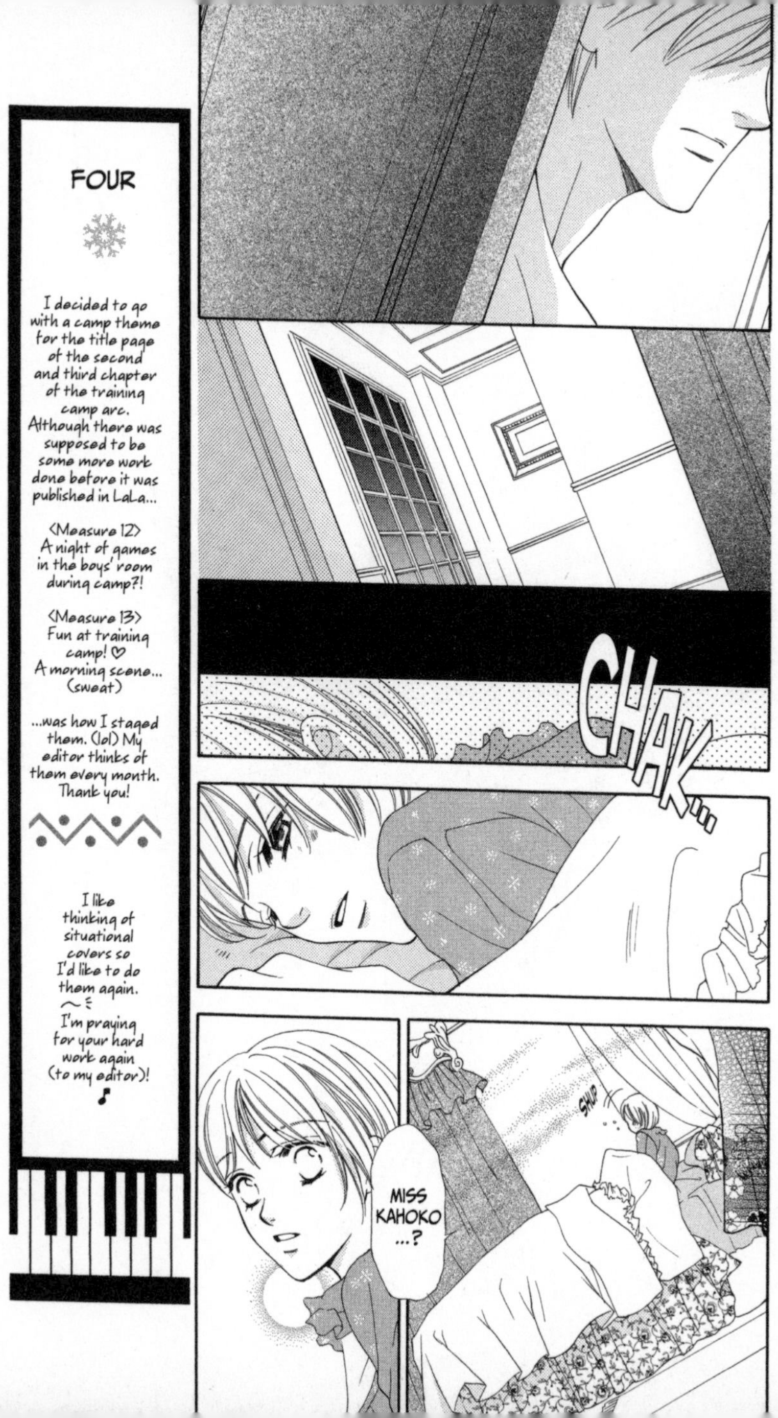
CHAK...
SHUP
MISS KAHOKO ...?

FOUR

I decided to go with a camp theme for the title page of the second and third chapter of the training camp arc. Although there was supposed to be some more work done before it was published in LaLa...

<Measure 12>
A night of games in the boys' room during camp?!

<Measure 13>
Fun at training camp! ♡
A morning scene... (sweat)

...was how I staged them. (lol) My editor thinks of them every month. Thank you!

I like thinking of situational covers so I'd like to do them again. ～ミ
I'm praying for your hard work again (to my editor)! ♪

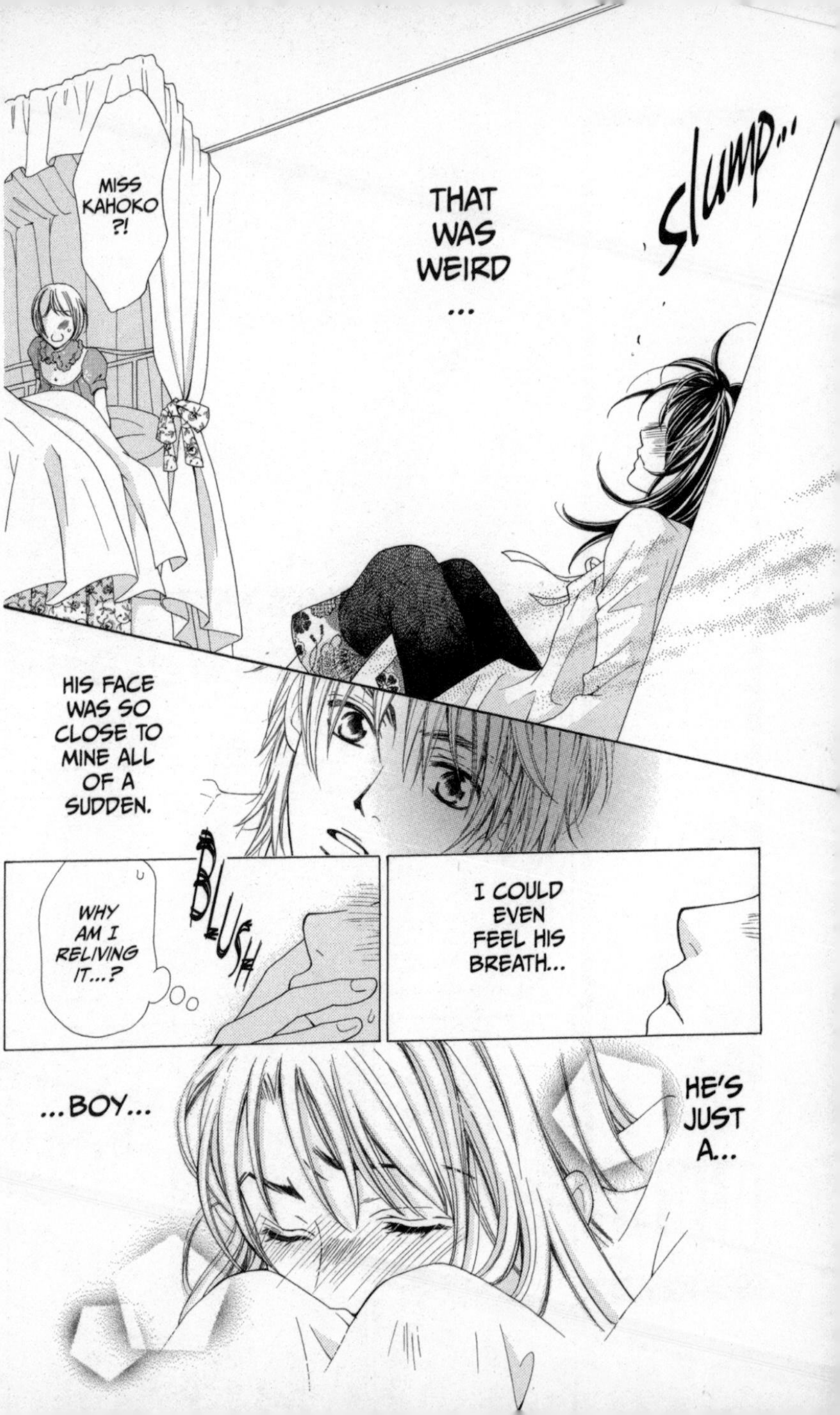
slump...
THAT WAS WEIRD ...
MISS KAHOKO ?!
HIS FACE WAS SO CLOSE TO MINE ALL OF A SUDDEN.
I COULD EVEN FEEL HIS BREATH...
BLUSH
WHY AM I RELIVING IT...?
HE'S JUST A...
...BOY...

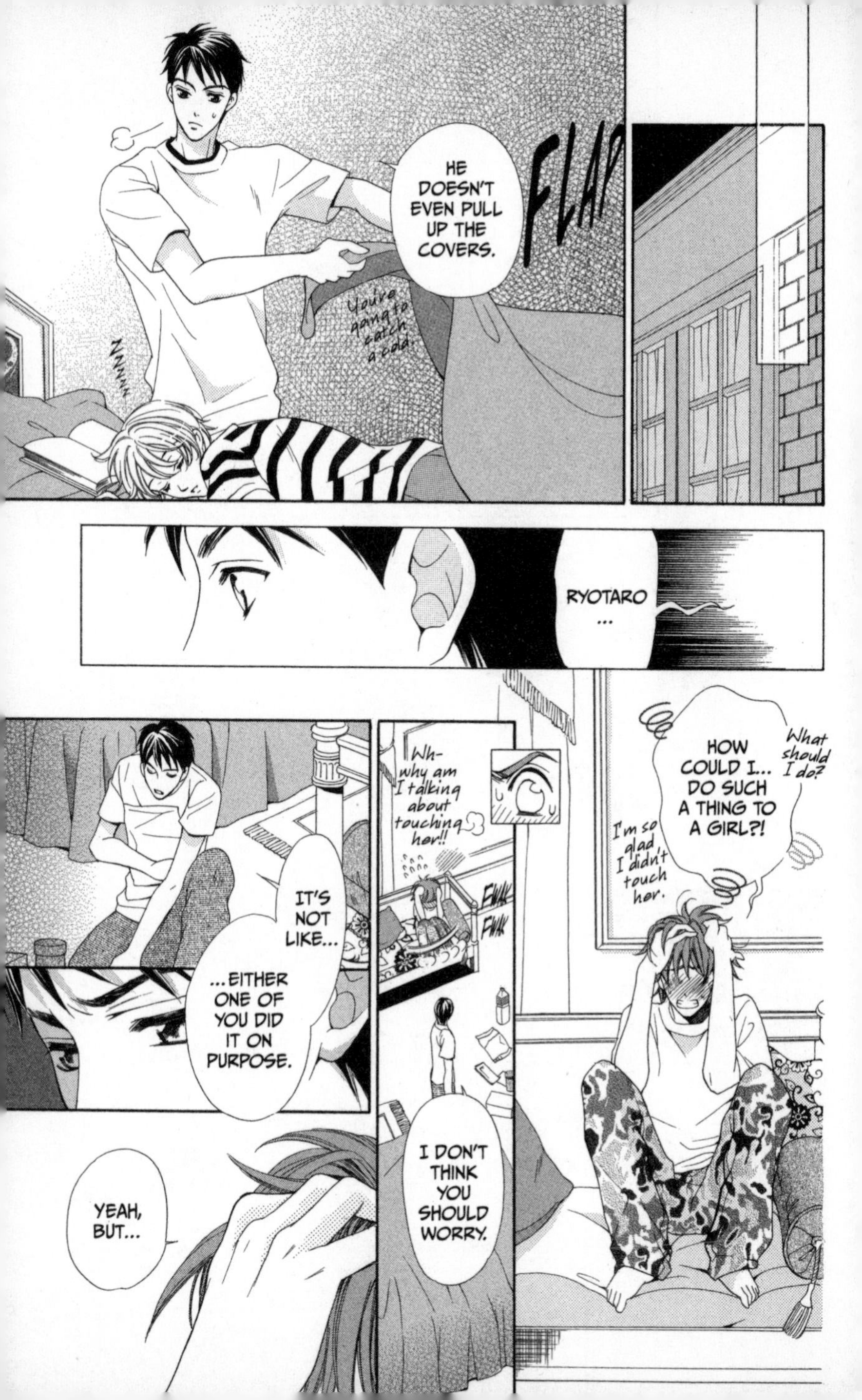
FLAP
HE DOESN'T EVEN PULL UP THE COVERS.
You're going to catch a cold.
RYOTARO ...
HOW COULD I... DO SUCH A THING TO A GIRL?!
What should I do?
I'm so glad I didn't touch her.
Wh-why am I talking about touching her!!
FWAK
FWAK
IT'S NOT LIKE...
...EITHER ONE OF YOU DID IT ON PURPOSE.
I DON'T THINK YOU SHOULD WORRY.
YEAH, BUT...

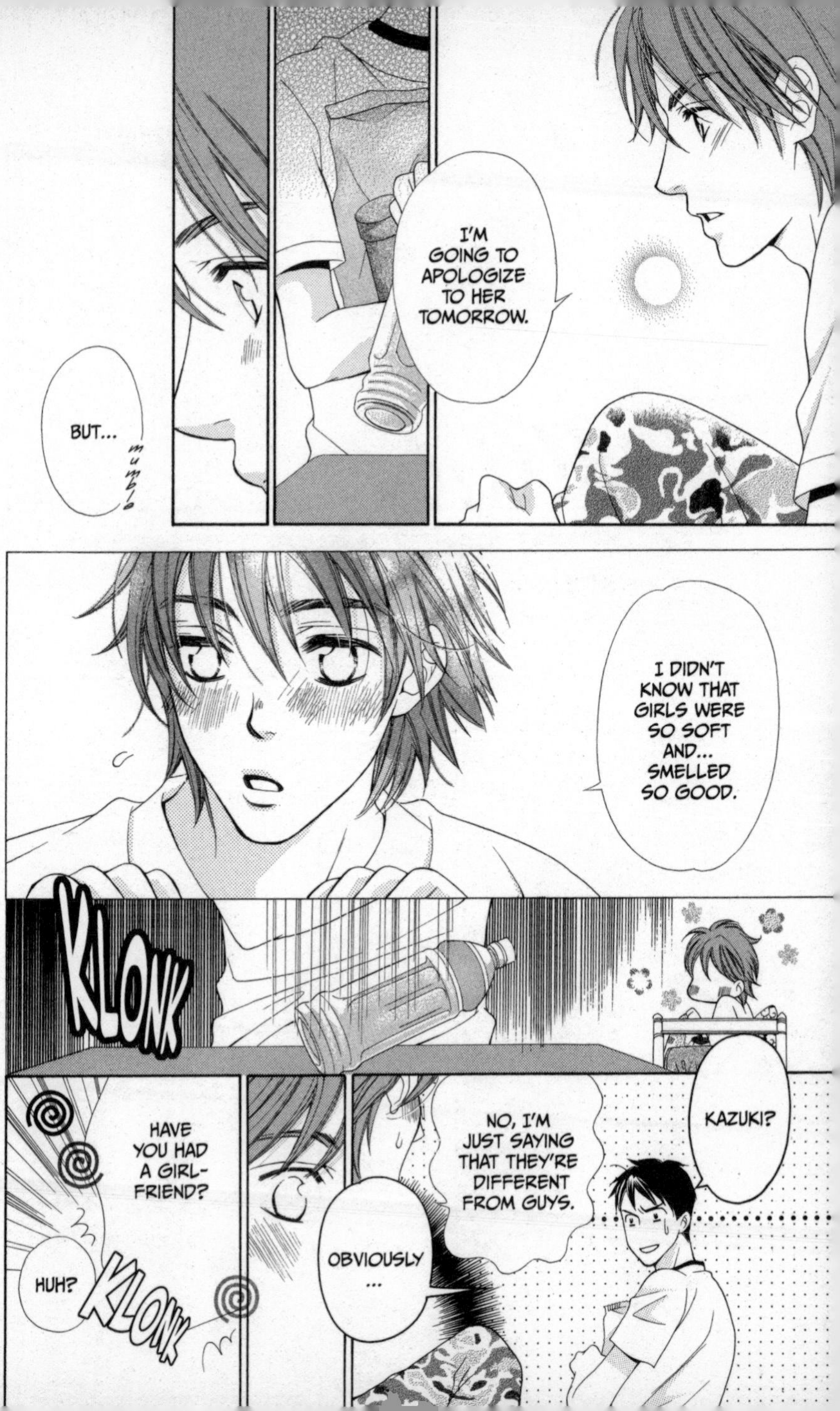
I'M GOING TO APOLOGIZE TO HER TOMORROW.
BUT...
mumble
I DIDN'T KNOW THAT GIRLS WERE SO SOFT AND... SMELLED SO GOOD.
KLONK
KAZUKI?
NO, I'M JUST SAYING THAT THEY'RE DIFFERENT FROM GUYS.
OBVIOUSLY...
HAVE YOU HAD A GIRL-FRIEND?
HUH?
KLONK

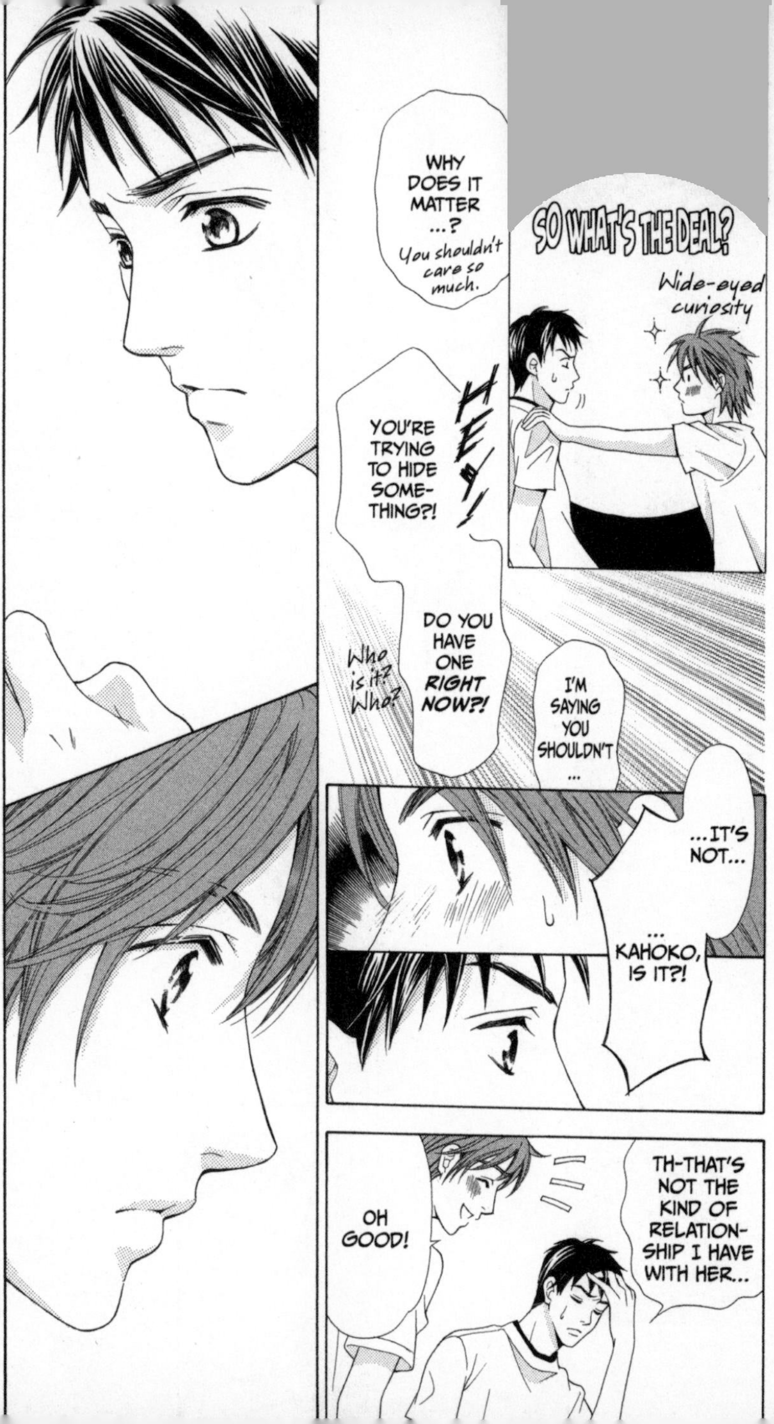
SO WHAT'S THE DEAL?
Wide-eyed curiosity
WHY DOES IT MATTER ...? You shouldn't care so much.
HEY!
YOU'RE TRYING TO HIDE SOME-THING?!
I'M SAYING YOU SHOULDN'T ...
DO YOU HAVE ONE RIGHT NOW?!
Who is it? Who?
...IT'S NOT...
... KAHOKO, IS IT?!
TH-THAT'S NOT THE KIND OF RELATION-SHIP I HAVE WITH HER...
OH GOOD!

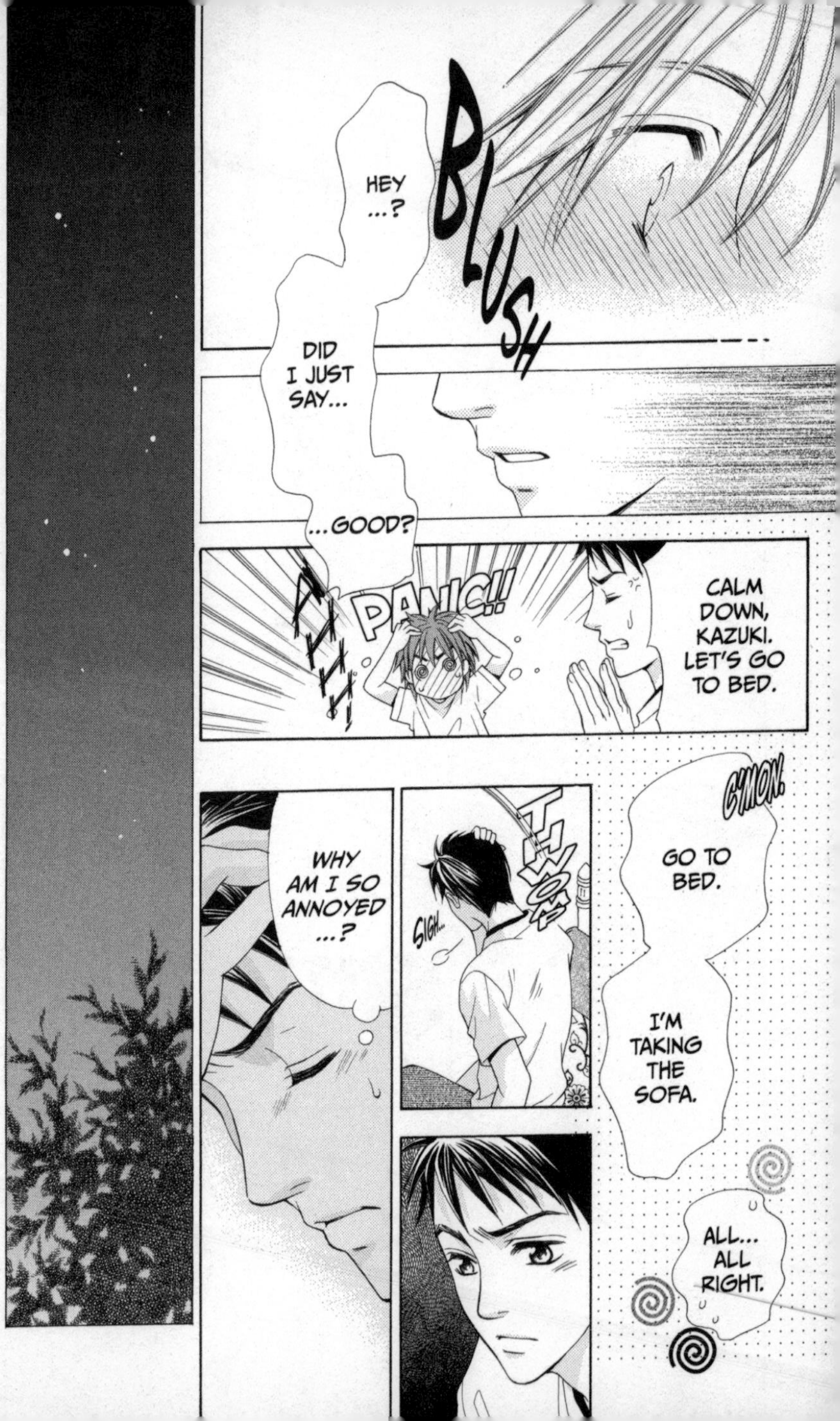
BLUSH
HEY ...?
DID I JUST SAY...
...GOOD?
CALM DOWN, KAZUKI. LET'S GO TO BED.
PANIC!!
C'MON.
GO TO BED.
I'M TAKING THE SOFA.
THWOMP
SIGH...
ALL... ALL RIGHT.
WHY AM I SO ANNOYED ...?

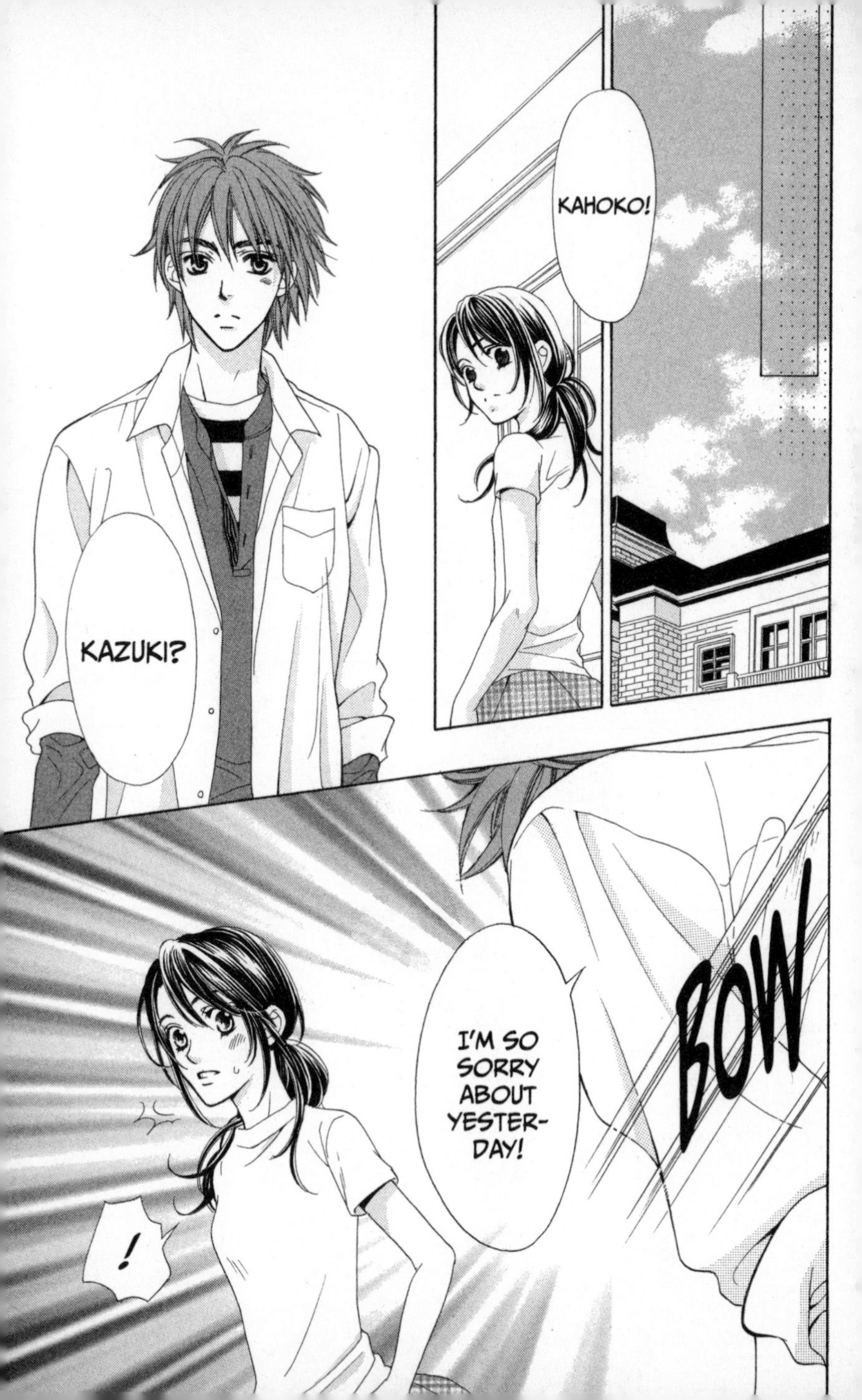
KAHOKO!
KAZUKI?
BOW
I'M SO SORRY ABOUT YESTER-DAY!
!

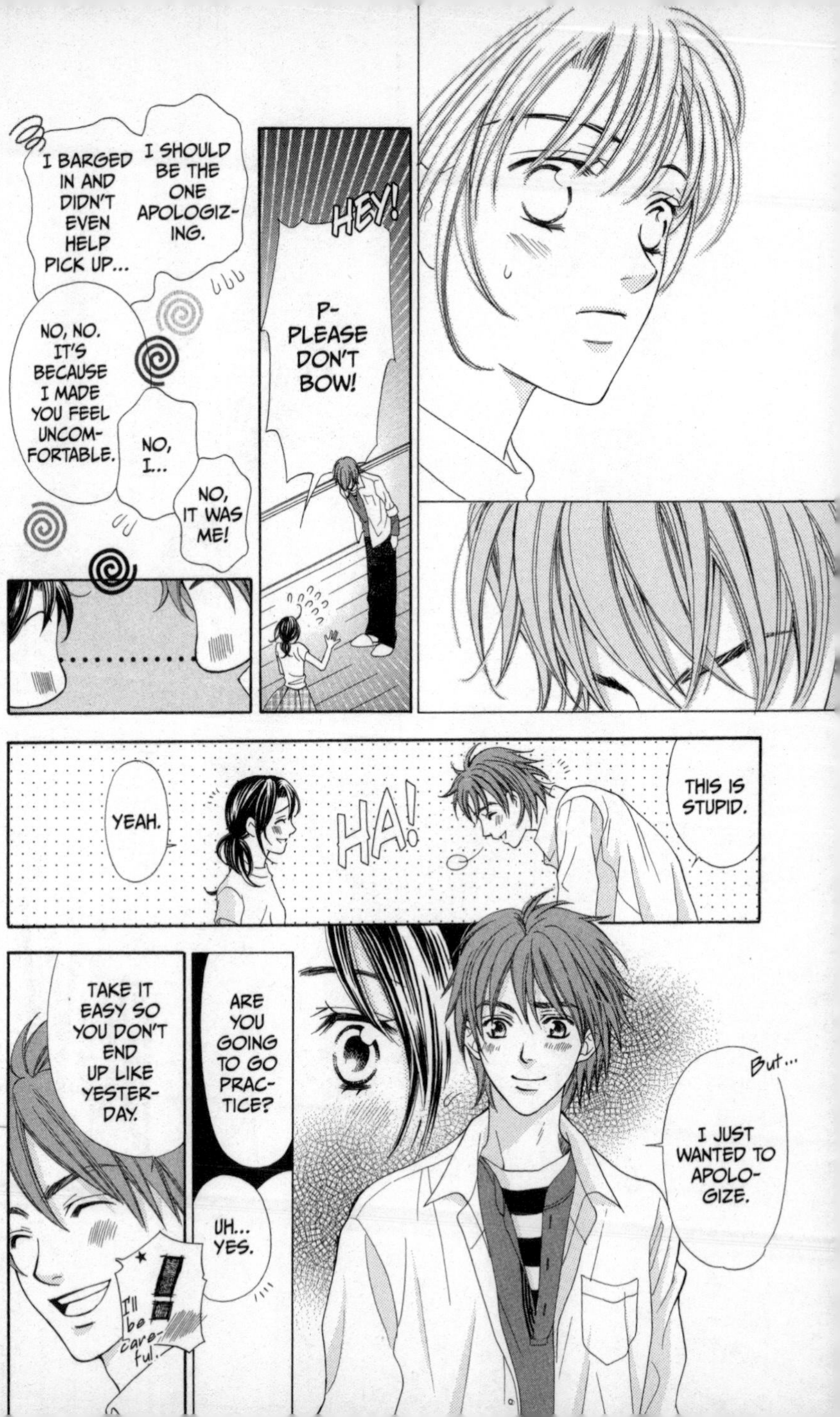
HEY!
P-PLEASE DON'T BOW!
I SHOULD BE THE ONE APOLOGIZING.
I BARGED IN AND DIDN'T EVEN HELP PICK UP...
NO, NO. IT'S BECAUSE I MADE YOU FEEL UNCOMFORTABLE.
NO, I...
NO, IT WAS ME!
THIS IS STUPID.
HA!
YEAH.
But...
I JUST WANTED TO APOLOGIZE.
ARE YOU GOING TO GO PRACTICE?
UH... YES.
TAKE IT EASY SO YOU DON'T END UP LIKE YESTERDAY.
I'll be careful.

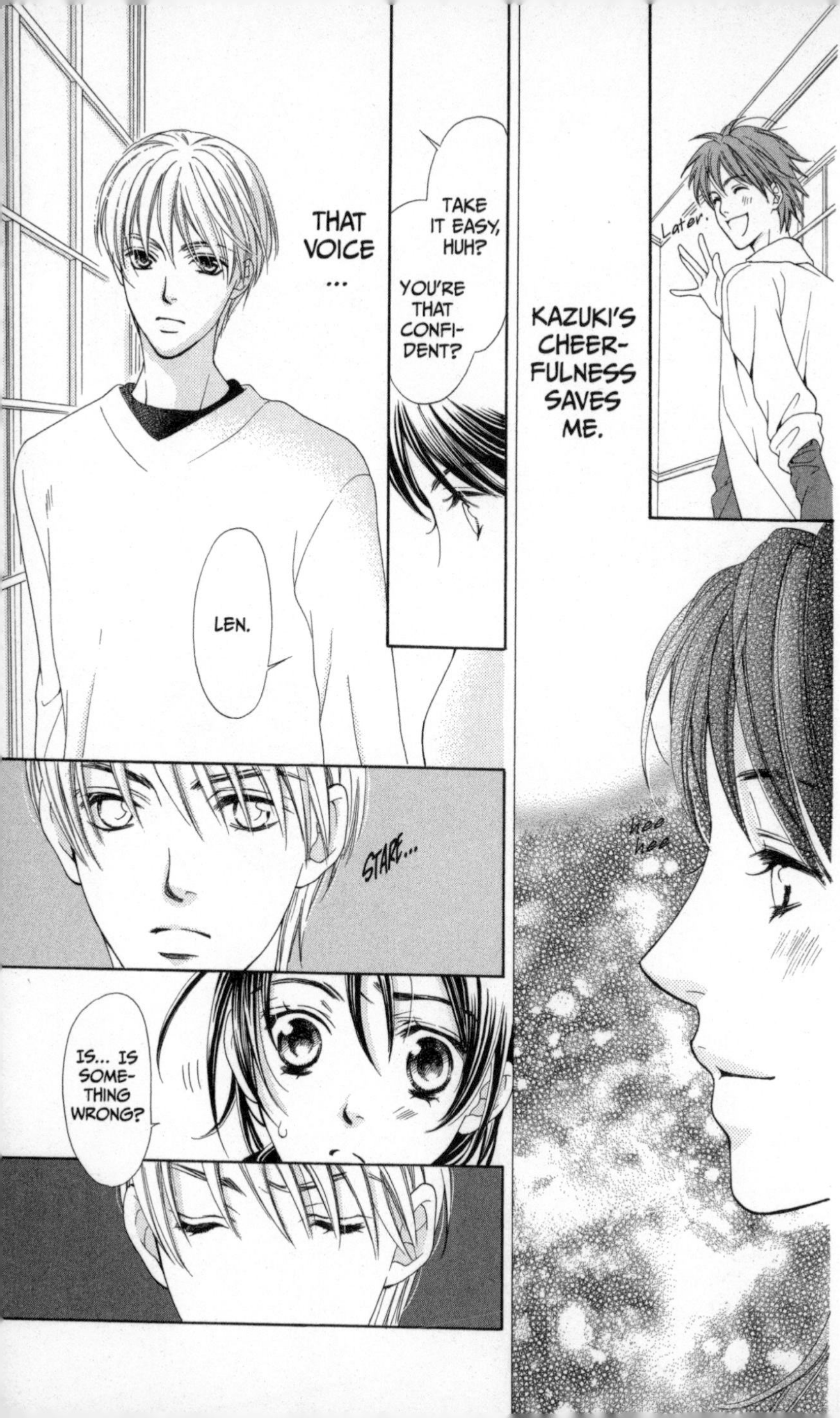

Later.
KAZUKI'S CHEER-FULNESS SAVES ME.
hee hee
TAKE IT EASY, HUH?
YOU'RE THAT CONFI-DENT?
THAT VOICE ...
LEN.
STARE...
IS... IS SOME-THING WRONG?

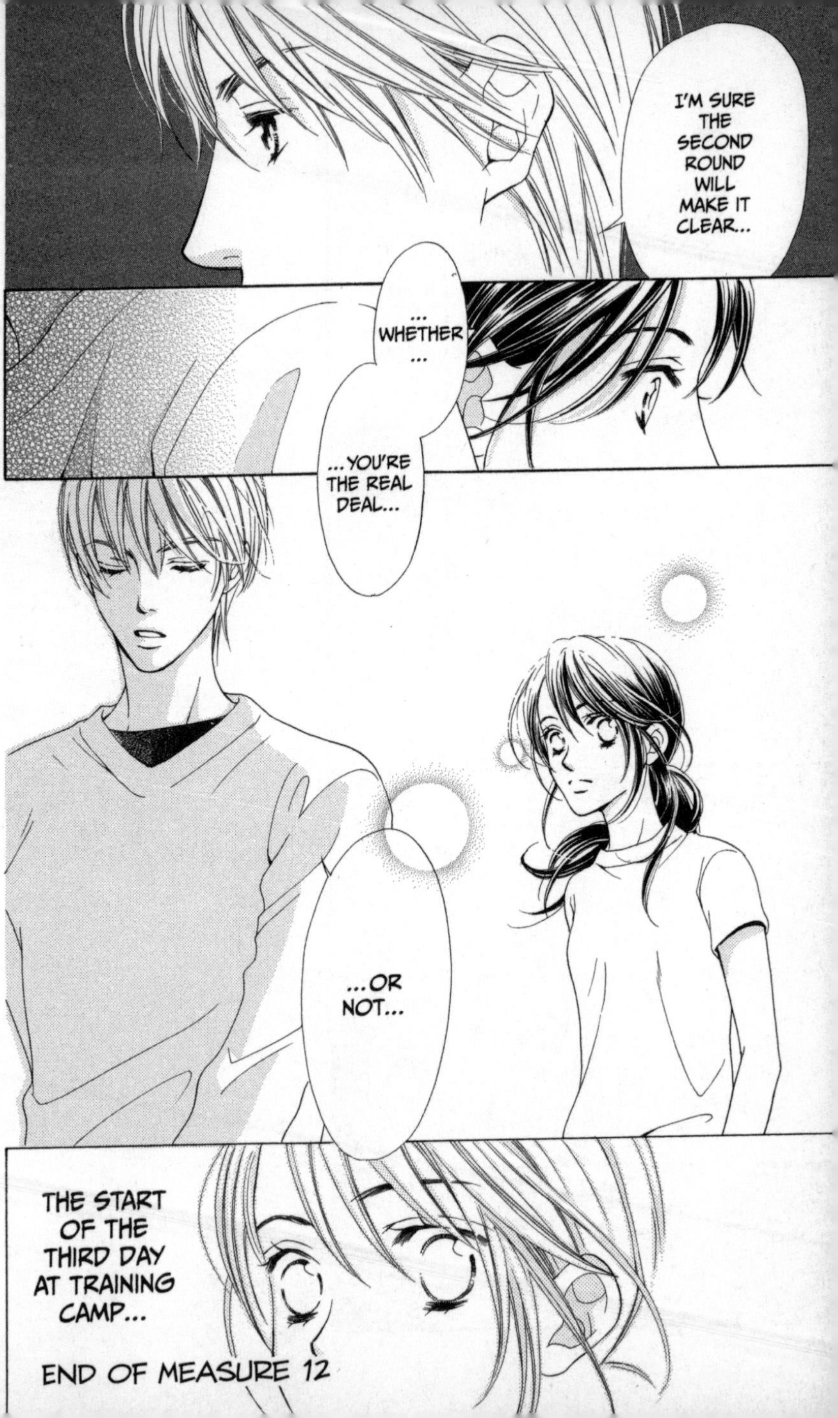
I'M SURE THE SECOND ROUND WILL MAKE IT CLEAR...
...WHETHER...
...YOU'RE THE REAL DEAL...
...OR NOT...
THE START OF THE THIRD DAY AT TRAINING CAMP...
END OF MEASURE 12

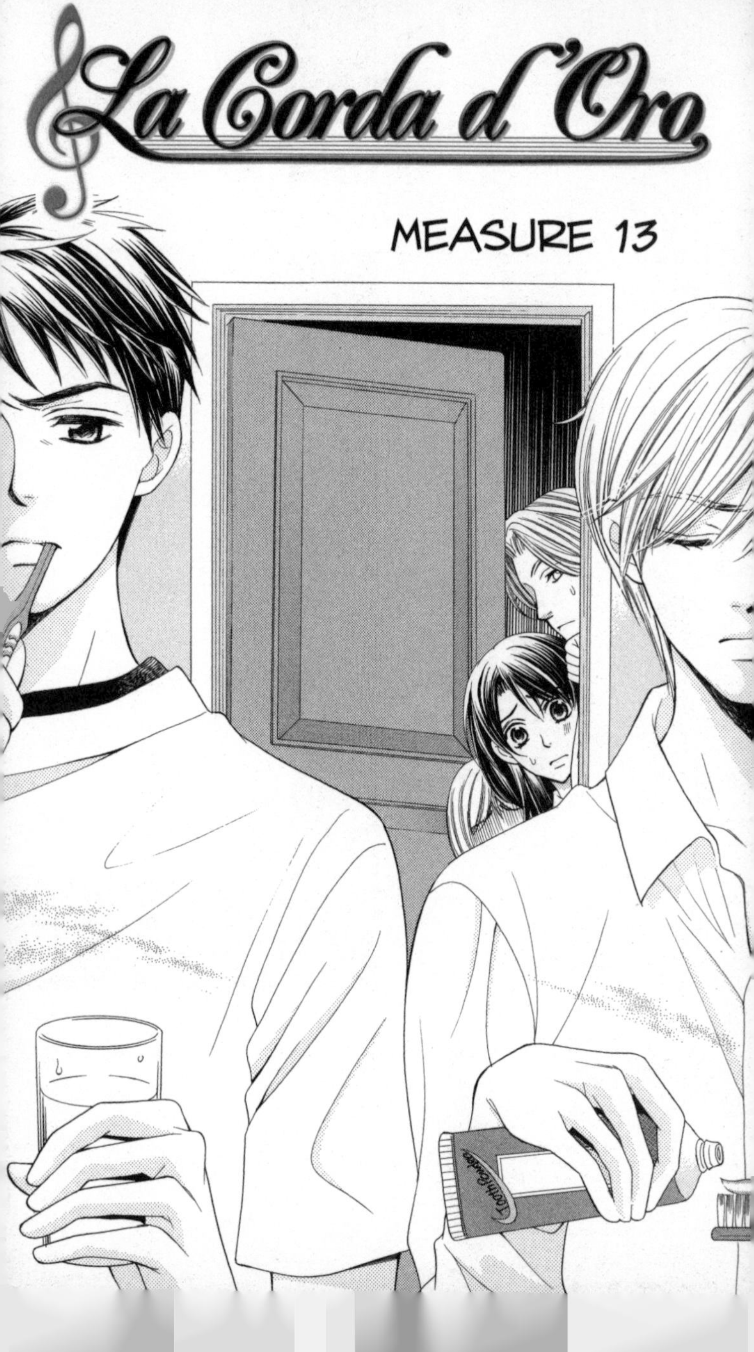
La Corda d'Oro
MEASURE 13
Tooth Paste

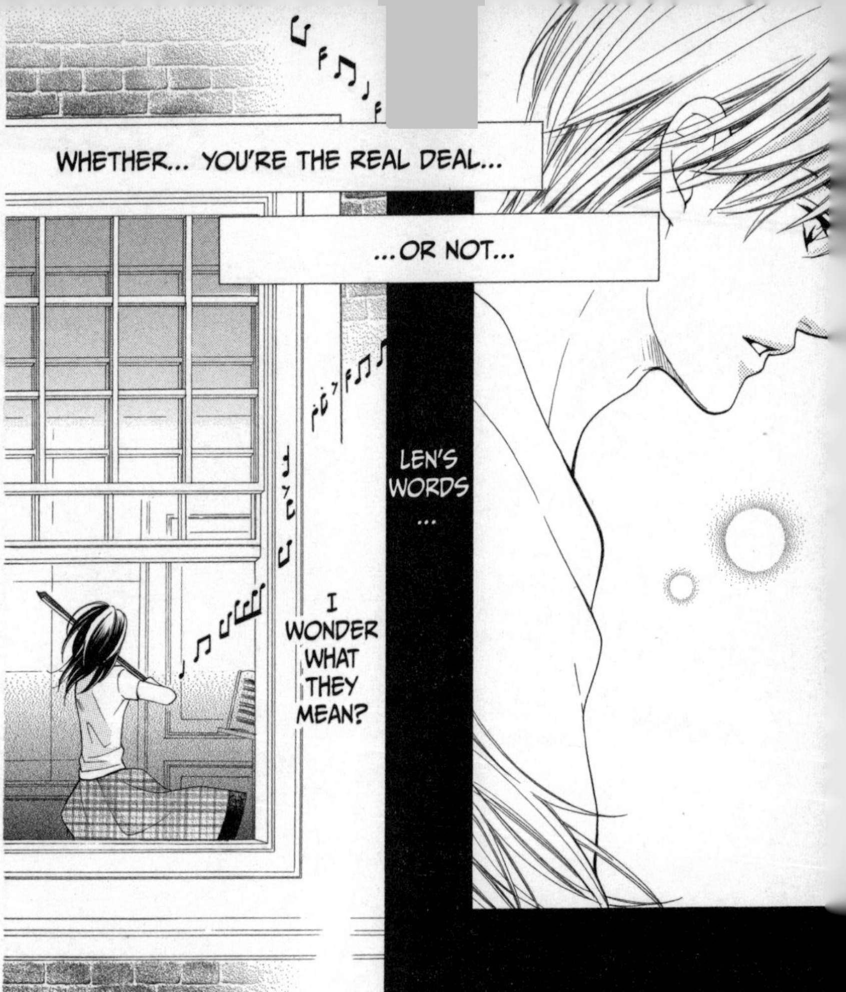
WHETHER... YOU'RE THE REAL DEAL...
...OR NOT...
LEN'S WORDS ...
I WONDER WHAT THEY MEAN?

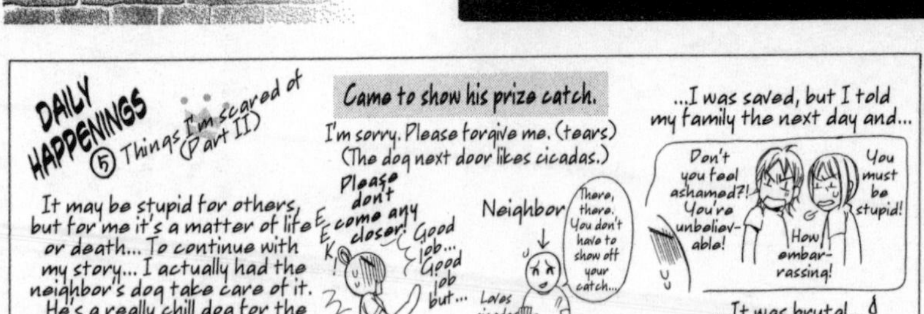
DAILY HAPPENINGS
⑤ Things I'm scared of (Part II)
It may be stupid for others, but for me it's a matter of life or death... To continue with my story... I actually had the neighbor's dog take care of it. He's a really chill dog for the most part, but this time he moved at incredible speeds to capture the bug and...
Came to show his prize catch.
I'm sorry. Please forgive me. (tears)
(The dog next door likes cicadas.)
Please don't come any closer!
EEK!
Good job... Good job but...
Neighbor
There, there. You don't have to show off your catch...
Loves cicadas
BUZZ BUZZ
WAG WAG
...I was saved, but I told my family the next day and...
Don't you feel ashamed?! You're unbelievable!
How embarrassing!
You must be stupid!
...It was brutal...
I'm sorry to ramble on about such trivial matter.

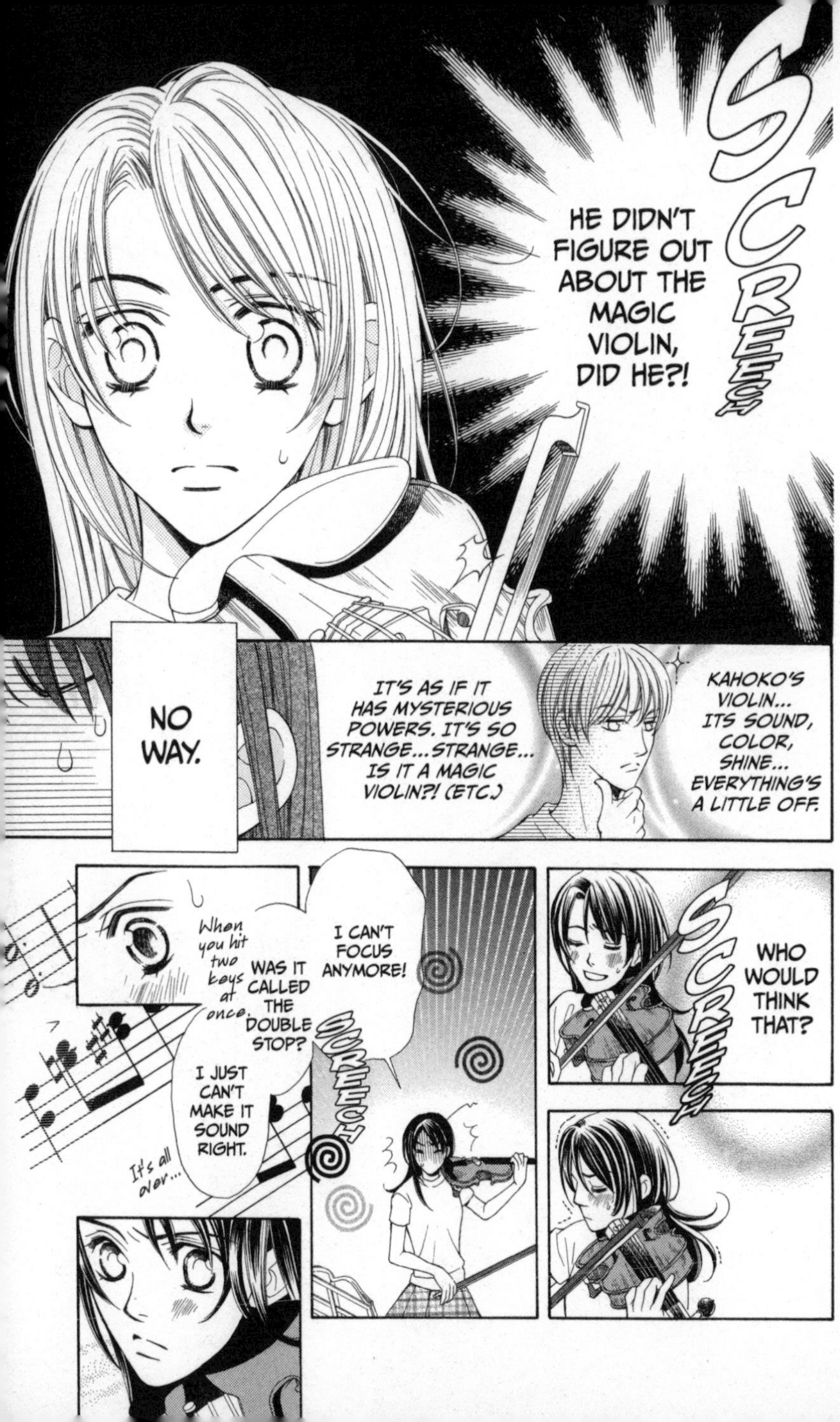
SCREECH
HE DIDN'T FIGURE OUT ABOUT THE MAGIC VIOLIN, DID HE?!
KAHOKO'S VIOLIN... ITS SOUND, COLOR, SHINE... EVERYTHING'S A LITTLE OFF.
IT'S AS IF IT HAS MYSTERIOUS POWERS. IT'S SO STRANGE...STRANGE... IS IT A MAGIC VIOLIN?! (ETC.)
NO WAY.
SCREECH
WHO WOULD THINK THAT?
I CAN'T FOCUS ANYMORE!
SCREECH
WAS IT CALLED THE DOUBLE STOP?
When you hit two keys at once.
I JUST CAN'T MAKE IT SOUND RIGHT.
It's all over...

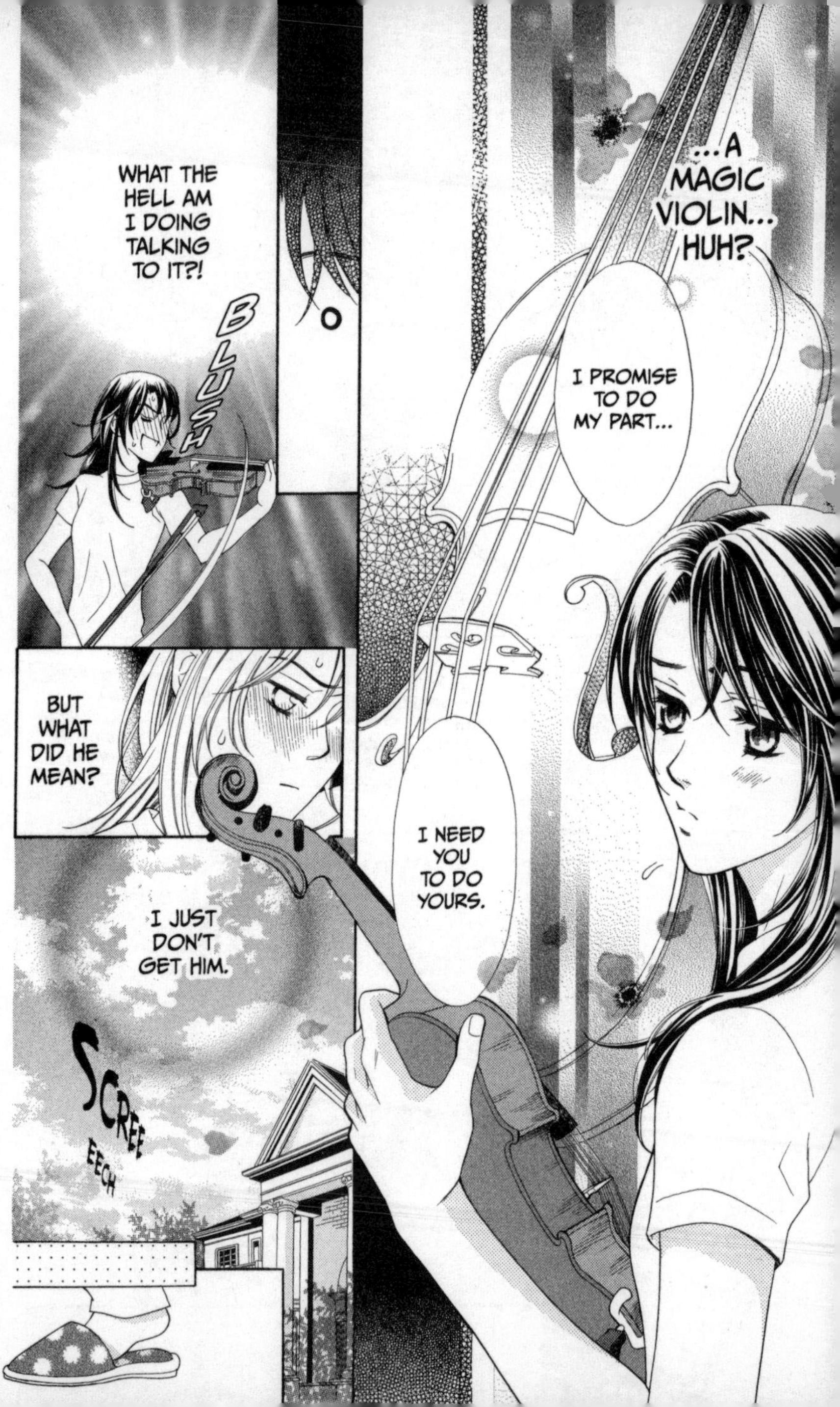
...A MAGIC VIOLIN... HUH?
I PROMISE TO DO MY PART...
I NEED YOU TO DO YOURS.
WHAT THE HELL AM I DOING TALKING TO IT?!
BLUSH
BUT WHAT DID HE MEAN?
I JUST DON'T GET HIM.
SCREEEECH

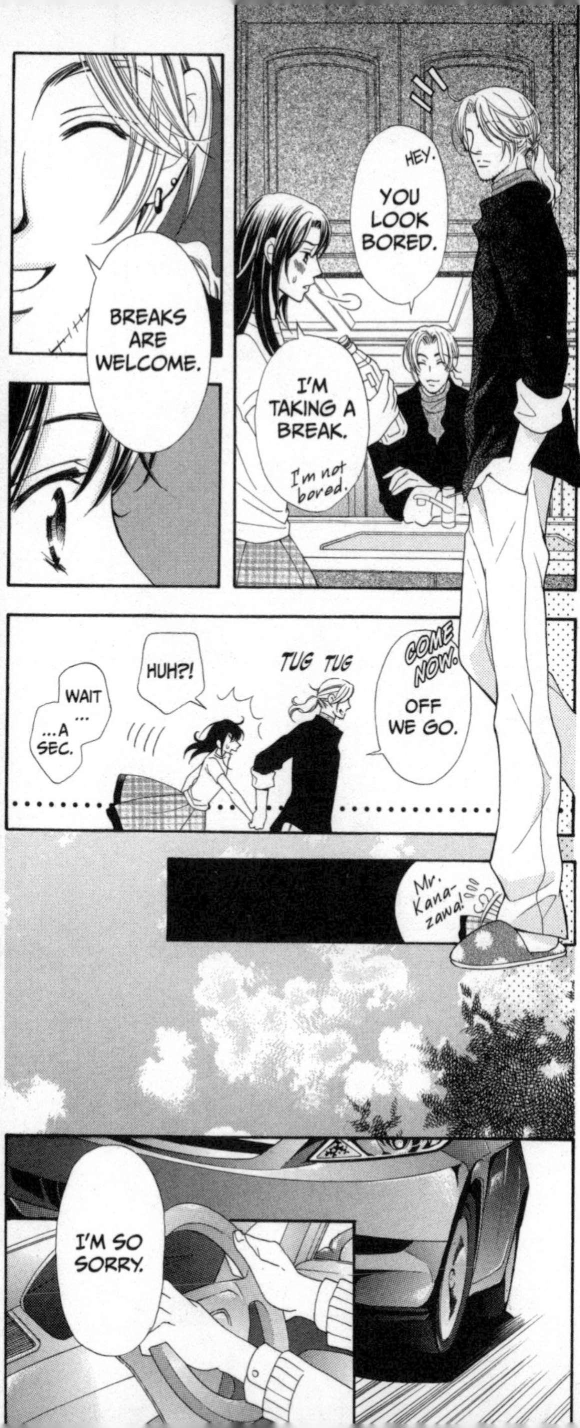
HEY.
YOU LOOK BORED.
I'M TAKING A BREAK.
I'm not bored.
BREAKS ARE WELCOME.
COME NOW.
OFF WE GO.
TUG TUG
HUH?!
WAIT... ...A SEC.
Mr. Kanazawa!
I'M SO SORRY.

FIVE

...I hope you were able to enjoy the third volume.

I tried incorporating a short story with the two boys from 3B. I'd like to do the others as well if there's an opportunity.

Now about volume 4... The plan is to increase Azuma's role a little. ...as of now... ←(totally unsure)

Thank you for reading. I'm sorry I have such poor penmanship. Until next time...

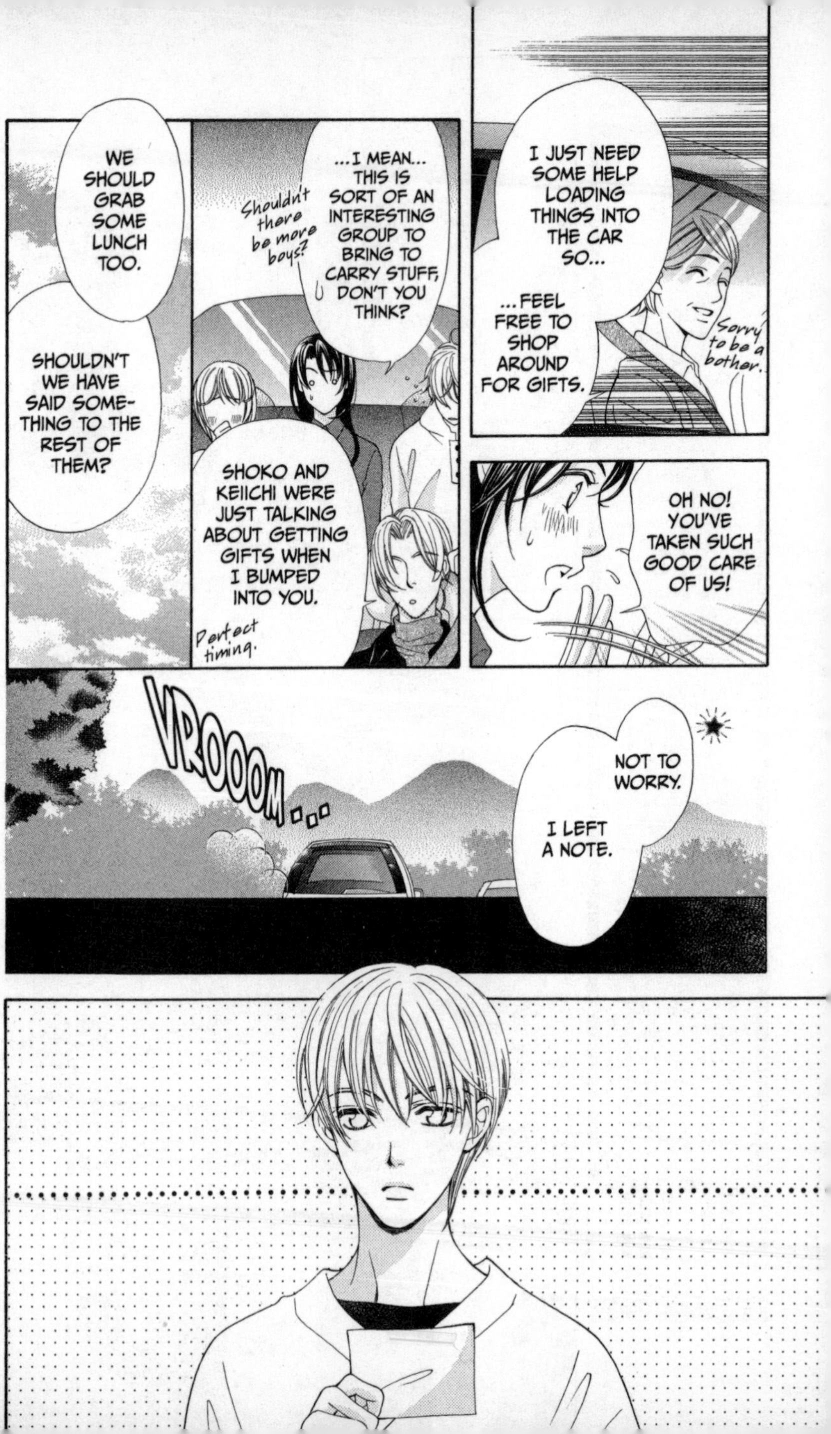
I JUST NEED SOME HELP LOADING THINGS INTO THE CAR SO...
...FEEL FREE TO SHOP AROUND FOR GIFTS.
Sorry to be a bother.
OH NO! YOU'VE TAKEN SUCH GOOD CARE OF US!
...I MEAN... THIS IS SORT OF AN INTERESTING GROUP TO BRING TO CARRY STUFF, DON'T YOU THINK?
Shouldn't there be more boys?
SHOKO AND KEIICHI WERE JUST TALKING ABOUT GETTING GIFTS WHEN I BUMPED INTO YOU.
Perfect timing.
WE SHOULD GRAB SOME LUNCH TOO.
SHOULDN'T WE HAVE SAID SOME-THING TO THE REST OF THEM?
NOT TO WORRY.
I LEFT A NOTE.
VROOOM...

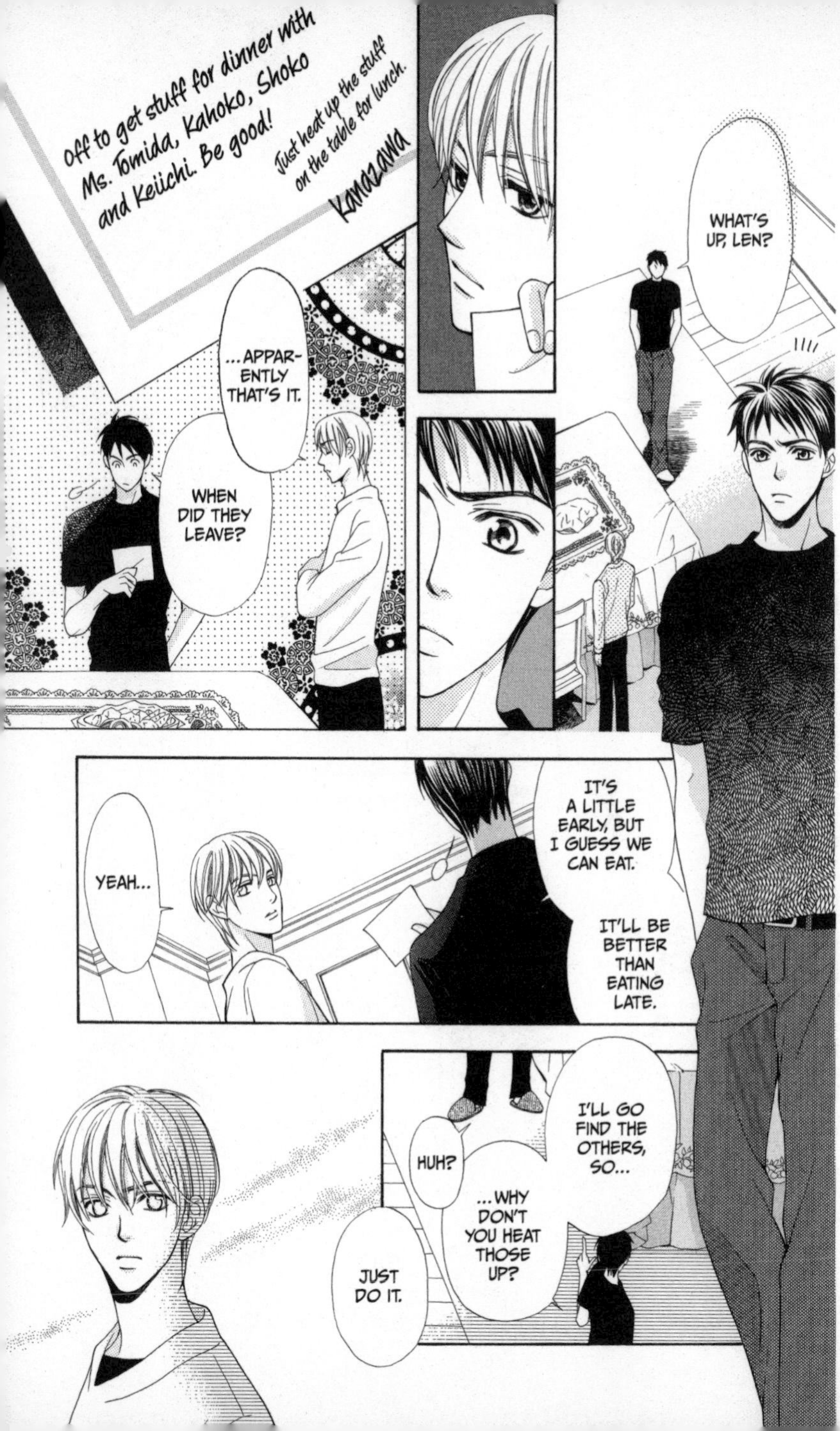
WHAT'S UP, LEN?
Off to get stuff for dinner with Ms. Tomida, Kahoko, Shoko and Keiichi. Be good!
Just heat up the stuff on the table for lunch.
Kanazawa
...APPARENTLY THAT'S IT.
WHEN DID THEY LEAVE?
IT'S A LITTLE EARLY, BUT I GUESS WE CAN EAT.
IT'LL BE BETTER THAN EATING LATE.
YEAH...
I'LL GO FIND THE OTHERS, SO...
HUH?
...WHY DON'T YOU HEAT THOSE UP?
JUST DO IT.

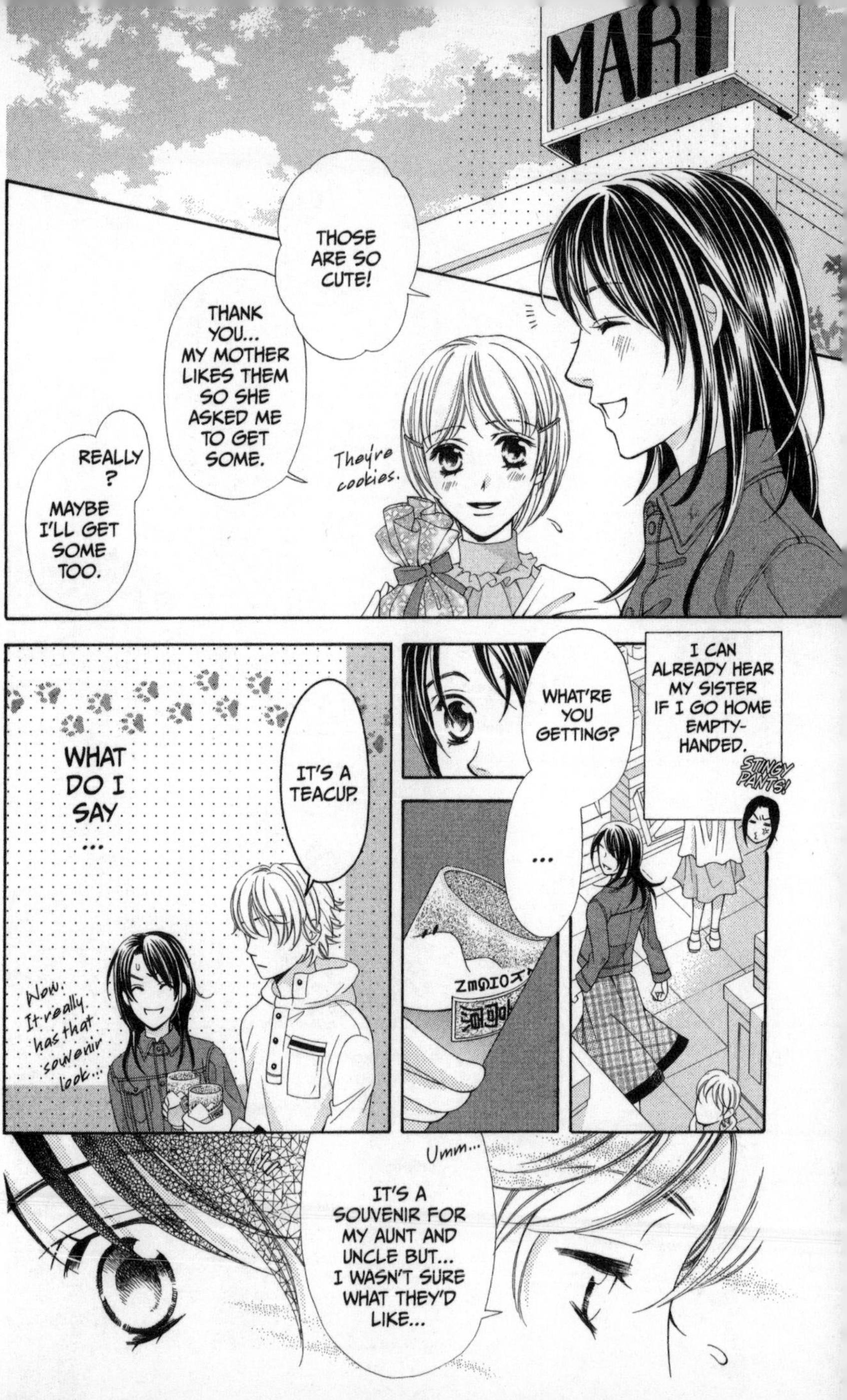
MARI
THOSE ARE SO CUTE!
They're cookies.
THANK YOU... MY MOTHER LIKES THEM SO SHE ASKED ME TO GET SOME.
REALLY? MAYBE I'LL GET SOME TOO.
I CAN ALREADY HEAR MY SISTER IF I GO HOME EMPTY-HANDED.
STINGY PANTS!
WHAT'RE YOU GETTING?
...
IT'S A TEACUP.
WHAT DO I SAY...
Wow. It really has that souvenir look...
Umm...
IT'S A SOUVENIR FOR MY AUNT AND UNCLE BUT... I WASN'T SURE WHAT THEY'D LIKE...

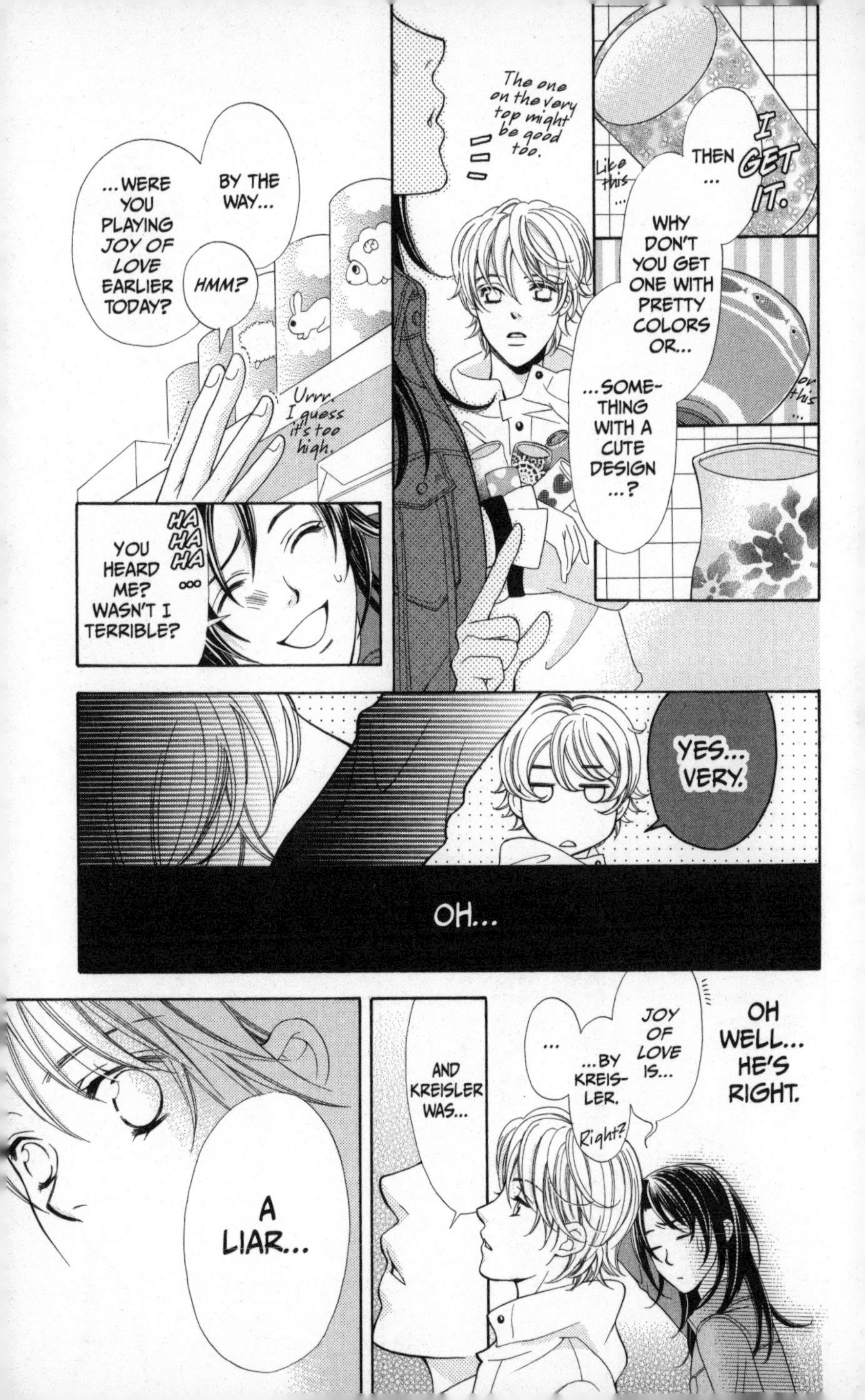
I GET IT.
THEN...
WHY DON'T YOU GET ONE WITH PRETTY COLORS OR...
...SOMETHING WITH A CUTE DESIGN...?
Like this...
or this...
The one on the very top might be good too.
BY THE WAY...
...WERE YOU PLAYING JOY OF LOVE EARLIER TODAY?
HMM?
Urrr. I guess it's too high.
HA HA HA
YOU HEARD ME? WASN'T I TERRIBLE?
YES... VERY.
OH...
OH WELL... HE'S RIGHT.
JOY OF LOVE IS...
...BY KREISLER.
Right?
...
AND KREISLER WAS...
A LIAR...

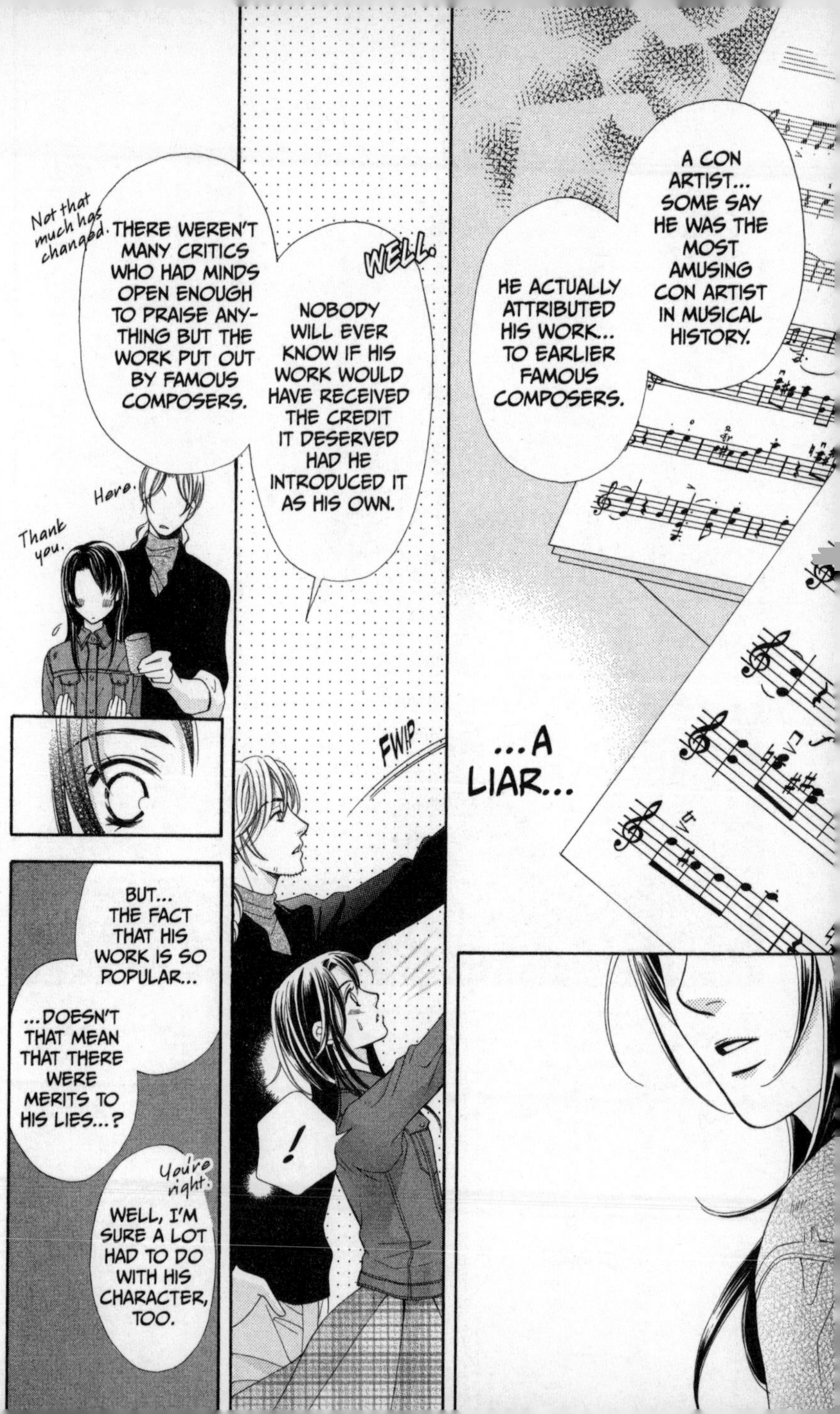
A CON ARTIST... SOME SAY HE WAS THE MOST AMUSING CON ARTIST IN MUSICAL HISTORY.
HE ACTUALLY ATTRIBUTED HIS WORK... TO EARLIER FAMOUS COMPOSERS.
...A LIAR...
WELL.
NOBODY WILL EVER KNOW IF HIS WORK WOULD HAVE RECEIVED THE CREDIT IT DESERVED HAD HE INTRODUCED IT AS HIS OWN.
FWIP
!
Not that much has changed.
THERE WEREN'T MANY CRITICS WHO HAD MINDS OPEN ENOUGH TO PRAISE ANY-THING BUT THE WORK PUT OUT BY FAMOUS COMPOSERS.
Here.
Thank you.
BUT... THE FACT THAT HIS WORK IS SO POPULAR...
...DOESN'T THAT MEAN THAT THERE WERE MERITS TO HIS LIES...?
You're right.
WELL, I'M SURE A LOT HAD TO DO WITH HIS CHARACTER, TOO.

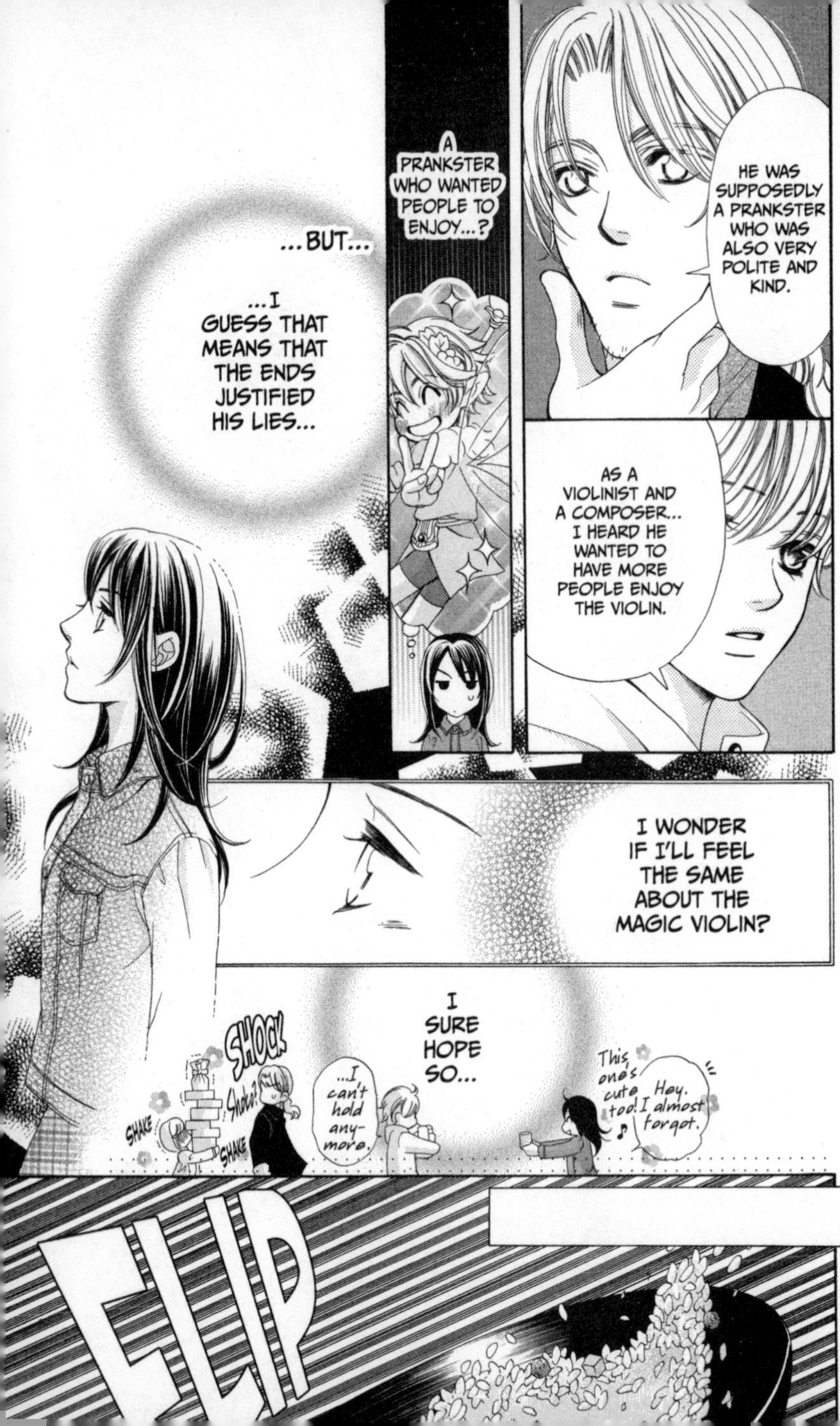

HE WAS SUPPOSEDLY A PRANKSTER WHO WAS ALSO VERY POLITE AND KIND.
AS A VIOLINIST AND A COMPOSER... I HEARD HE WANTED TO HAVE MORE PEOPLE ENJOY THE VIOLIN.
A PRANKSTER WHO WANTED PEOPLE TO ENJOY...?
...BUT...
...I GUESS THAT MEANS THAT THE ENDS JUSTIFIED HIS LIES...
I WONDER IF I'LL FEEL THE SAME ABOUT THE MAGIC VIOLIN?
I SURE HOPE SO...
Hey. I almost forgot.
This one's cute too! ♪
...I can't hold anymore.
Shoko?
SHOCK
SHAKE
SHAKE
FLIP

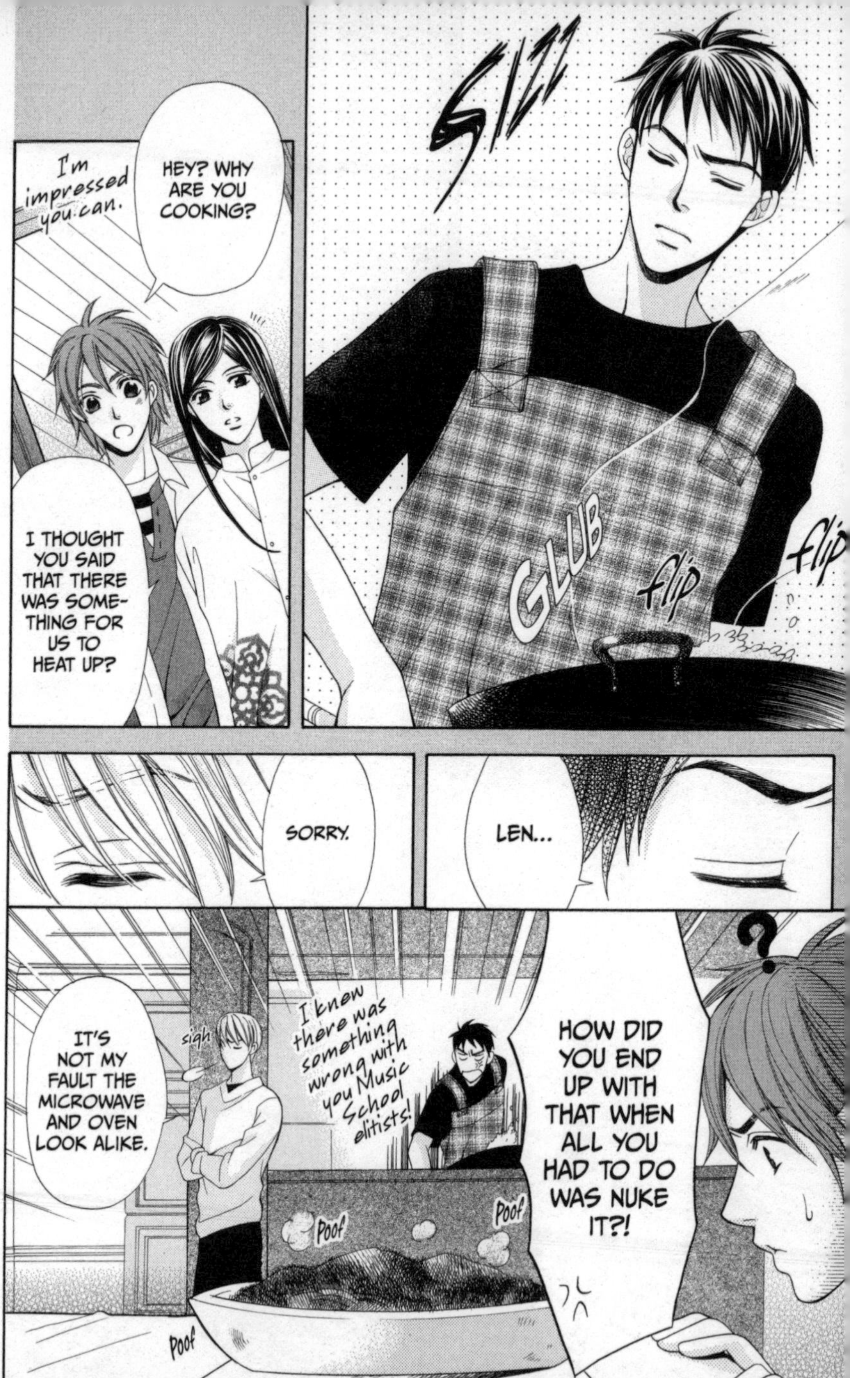
SIZZ
GLUB
flip
flip
HEY? WHY ARE YOU COOKING?
I'm impressed you can.
I THOUGHT YOU SAID THAT THERE WAS SOME-THING FOR US TO HEAT UP?
LEN...
SORRY.
HOW DID YOU END UP WITH THAT WHEN ALL YOU HAD TO DO WAS NUKE IT?!
I knew there was something wrong with you Music School elitists!
Poof
Poof
sigh
IT'S NOT MY FAULT THE MICROWAVE AND OVEN LOOK ALIKE.
Poof

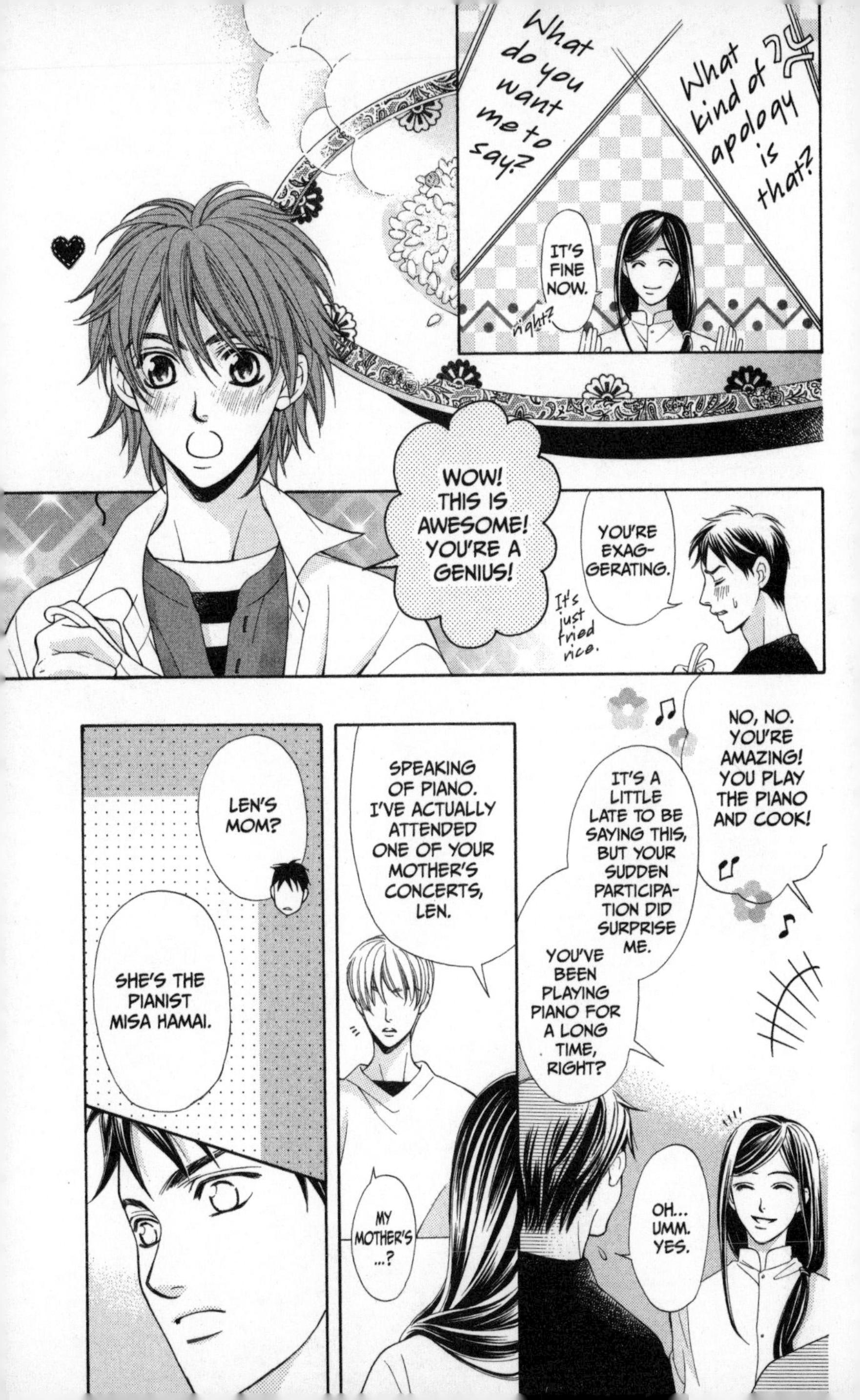

What kind of apology is that?
What do you want me to say?
IT'S FINE NOW.
right?
WOW! THIS IS AWESOME! YOU'RE A GENIUS!
YOU'RE EXAG-GERATING.
It's just fried rice.
NO, NO. YOU'RE AMAZING! YOU PLAY THE PIANO AND COOK!
IT'S A LITTLE LATE TO BE SAYING THIS, BUT YOUR SUDDEN PARTICIPA-TION DID SURPRISE ME.
YOU'VE BEEN PLAYING PIANO FOR A LONG TIME, RIGHT?
OH... UMM. YES.
SPEAKING OF PIANO. I'VE ACTUALLY ATTENDED ONE OF YOUR MOTHER'S CONCERTS, LEN.
MY MOTHER'S ...?
LEN'S MOM?
SHE'S THE PIANIST MISA HAMAI.

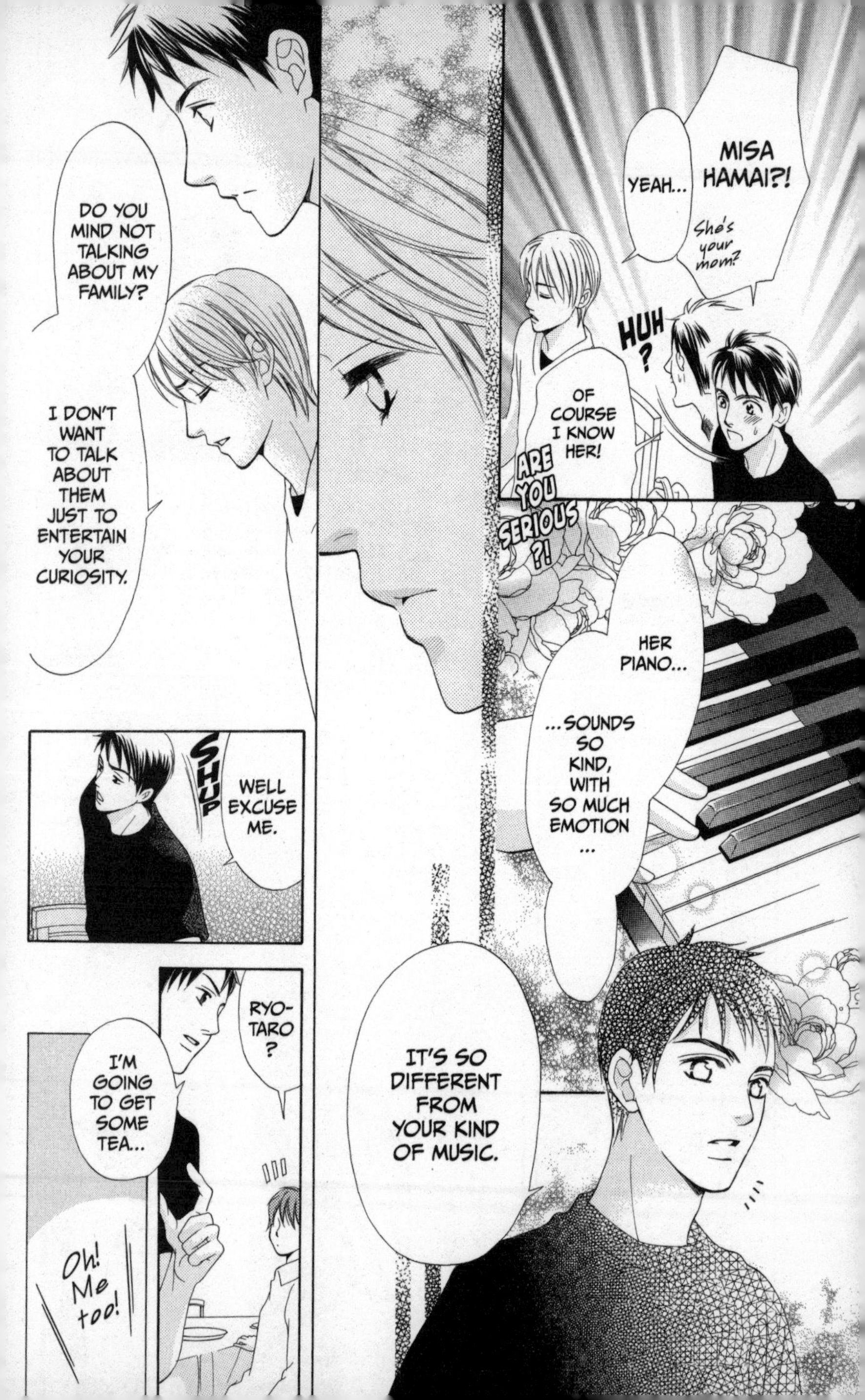

MISA HAMAI?!
She's your mom?
YEAH...
HUH?
OF COURSE I KNOW HER!
ARE YOU SERIOUS?!
HER PIANO...
...SOUNDS SO KIND, WITH SO MUCH EMOTION...
IT'S SO DIFFERENT FROM YOUR KIND OF MUSIC.
DO YOU MIND NOT TALKING ABOUT MY FAMILY?
I DON'T WANT TO TALK ABOUT THEM JUST TO ENTERTAIN YOUR CURIOSITY.
SHUP
WELL EXCUSE ME.
RYO-TARO?
I'M GOING TO GET SOME TEA...
Oh! Me too!

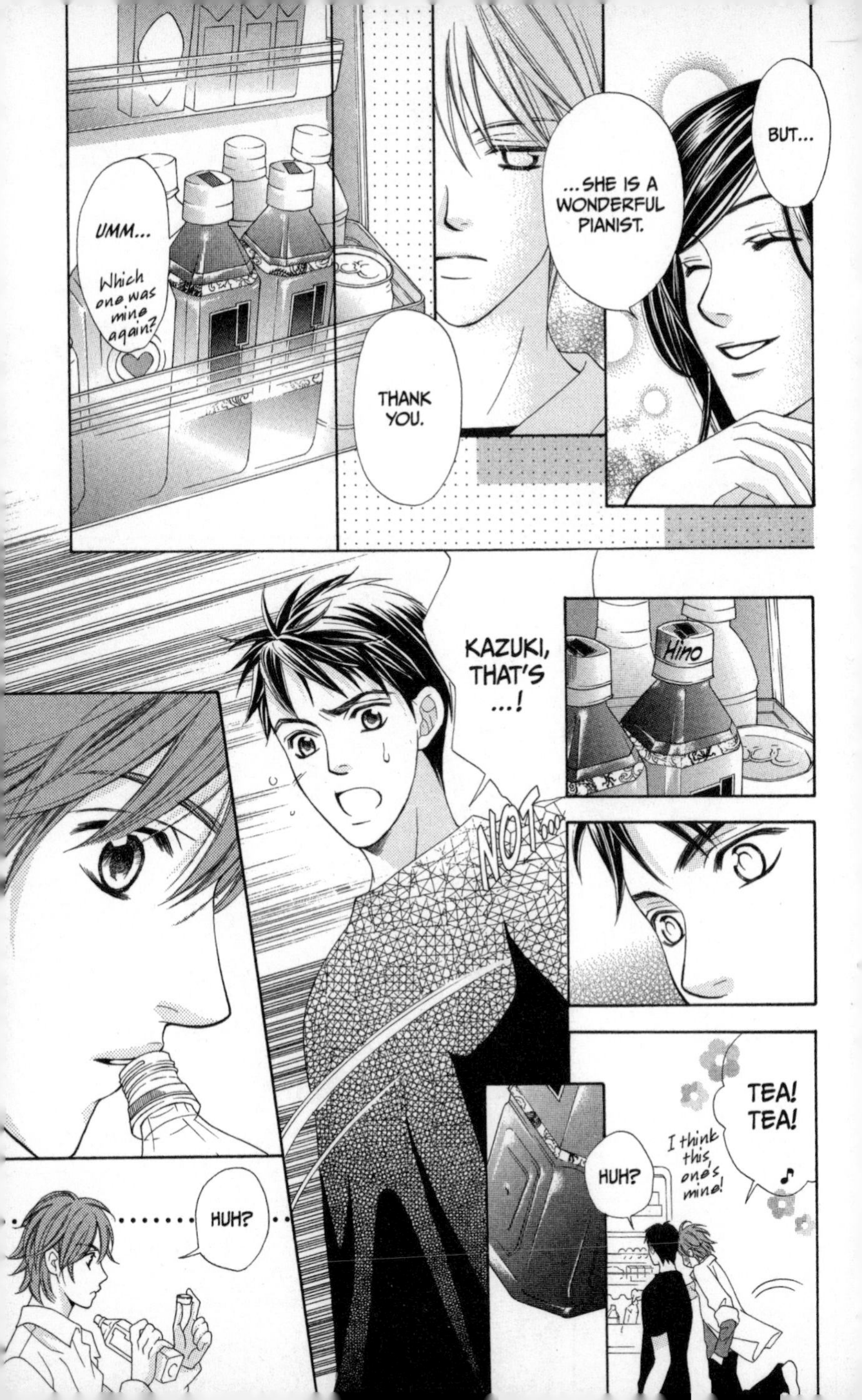
BUT...
...SHE IS A WONDERFUL PIANIST.
THANK YOU.
UMM...
Which one was mine again?
Hino
KAZUKI, THAT'S ...!
NOT...
TEA! TEA!
I think this one's mine!
HUH?
HUH?

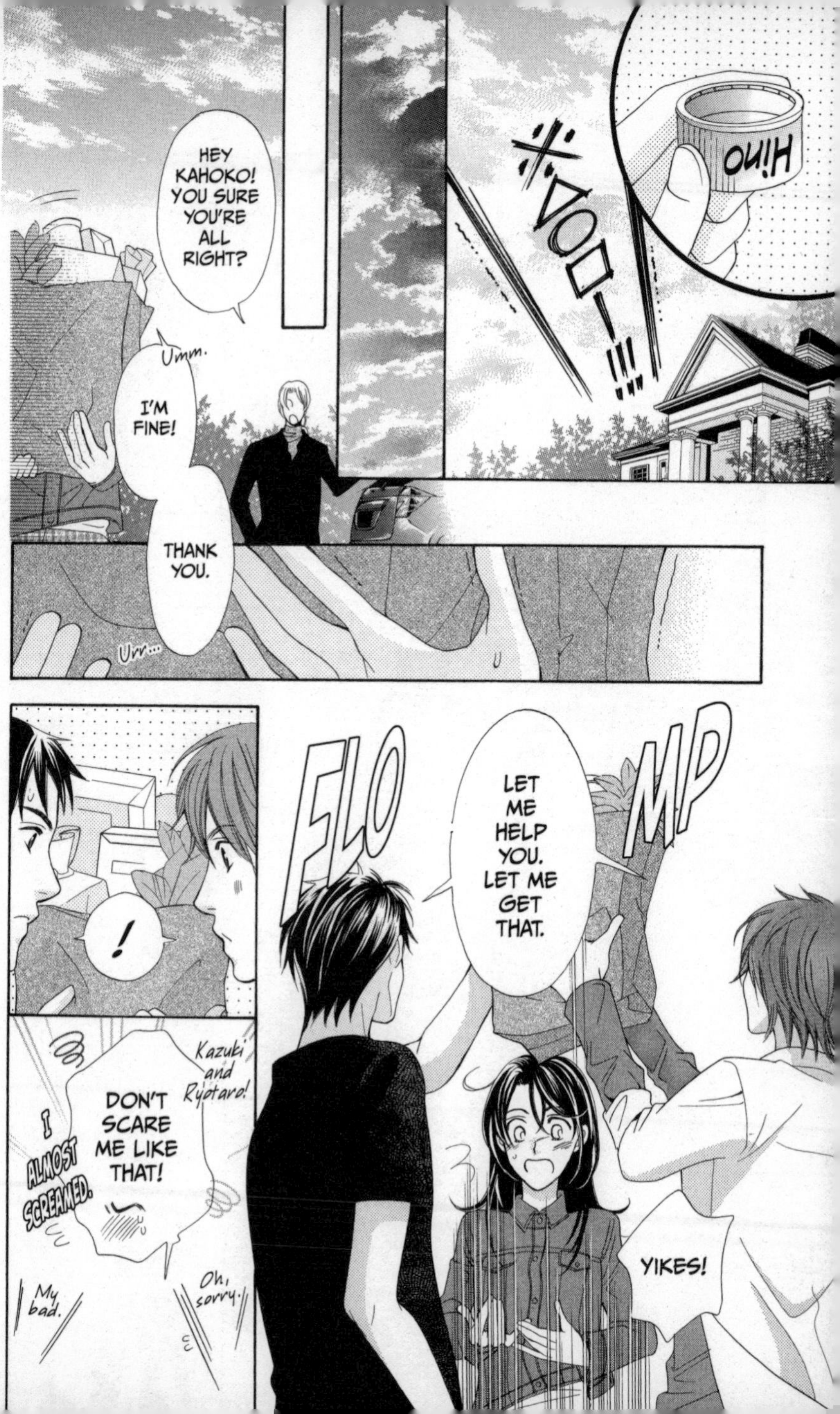
Hino
HEY KAHOKO! YOU SURE YOU'RE ALL RIGHT?
Umm.
I'M FINE!
THANK YOU.
Urr...
FLOMP
LET ME HELP YOU. LET ME GET THAT.
YIKES!
!
Kazuki and Ryotaro!
DON'T SCARE ME LIKE THAT!
I ALMOST SCREAMED.
Oh, sorry.
My bad.

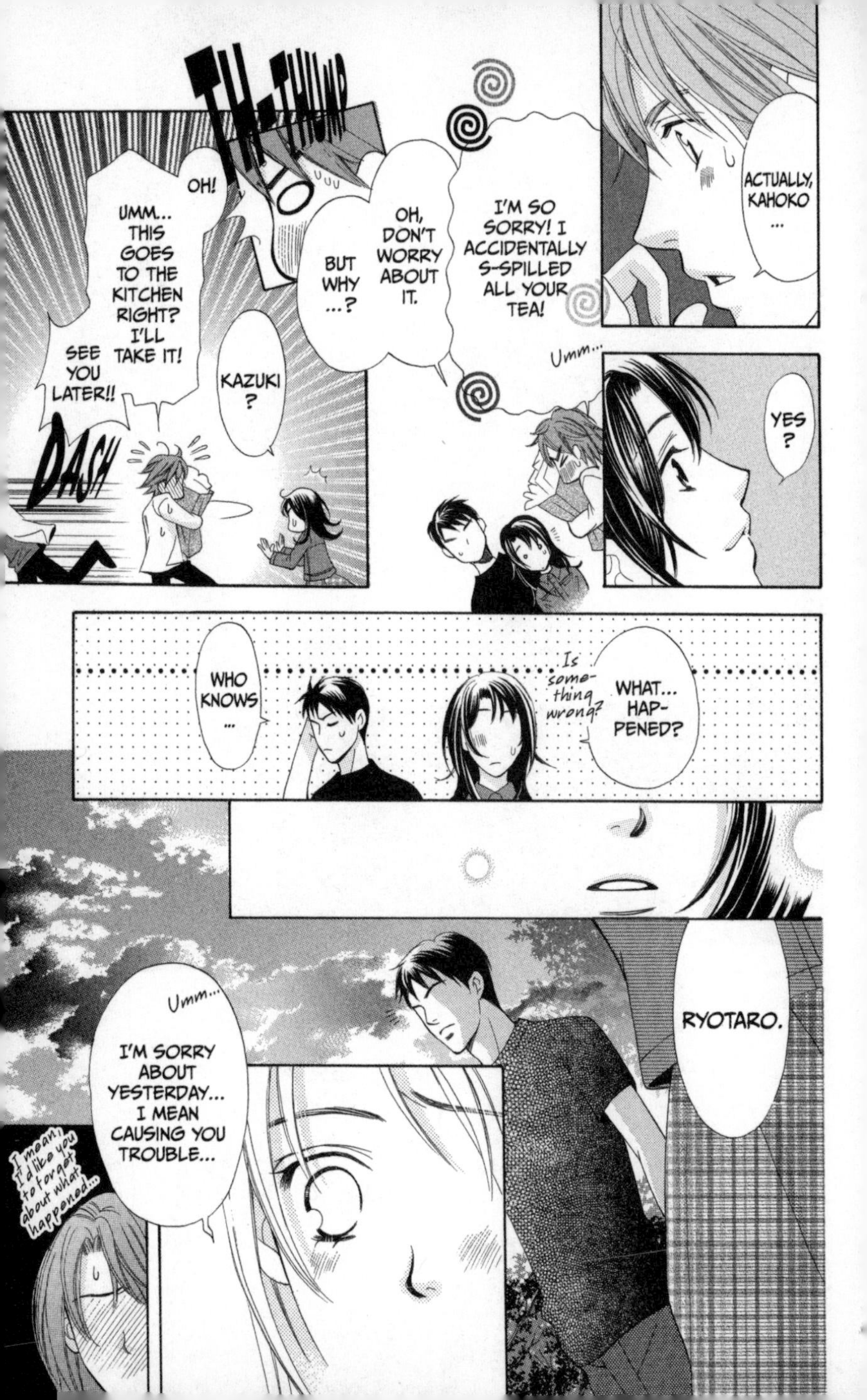
ACTUALLY, KAHOKO ...
YES ?
Umm...
I'M SO SORRY! I ACCIDENTALLY S-SPILLED ALL YOUR TEA!
OH, DON'T WORRY ABOUT IT.
BUT WHY ...?
TH-THUMP
OH!
UMM... THIS GOES TO THE KITCHEN RIGHT? I'LL TAKE IT!
KAZUKI ?
SEE YOU LATER!!
DASH
WHAT... HAP-PENED?
Is some-thing wrong?
WHO KNOWS ...
RYOTARO.
Umm...
I'M SORRY ABOUT YESTERDAY... I MEAN CAUSING YOU TROUBLE...
I mean, I'd like you to forget about what happened...

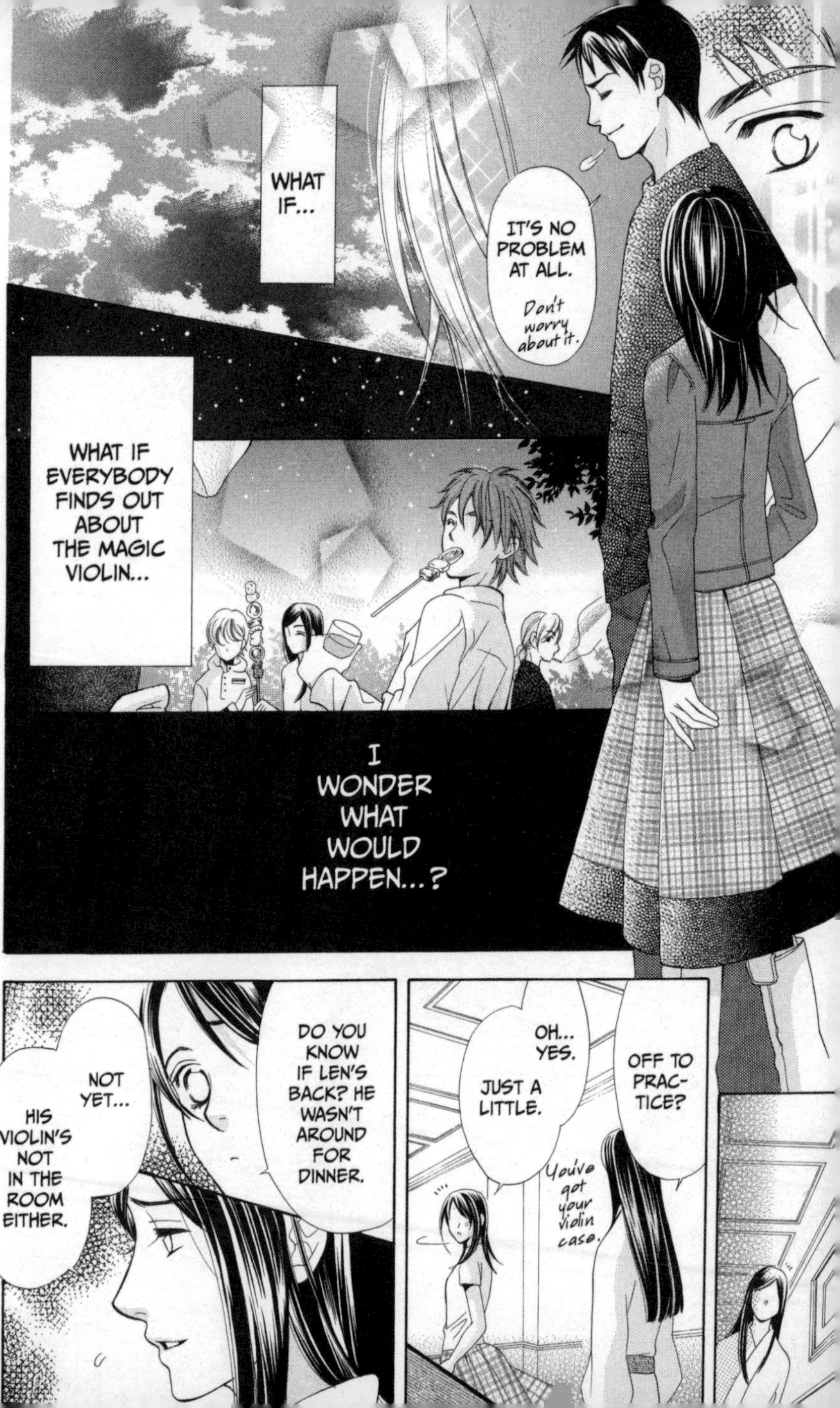
IT'S NO PROBLEM AT ALL.
Don't worry about it.
WHAT IF...
WHAT IF EVERYBODY FINDS OUT ABOUT THE MAGIC VIOLIN...
I WONDER WHAT WOULD HAPPEN...?
OFF TO PRAC-TICE?
You've got your violin case.
OH... YES.
JUST A LITTLE.
DO YOU KNOW IF LEN'S BACK? HE WASN'T AROUND FOR DINNER.
NOT YET...
HIS VIOLIN'S NOT IN THE ROOM EITHER.

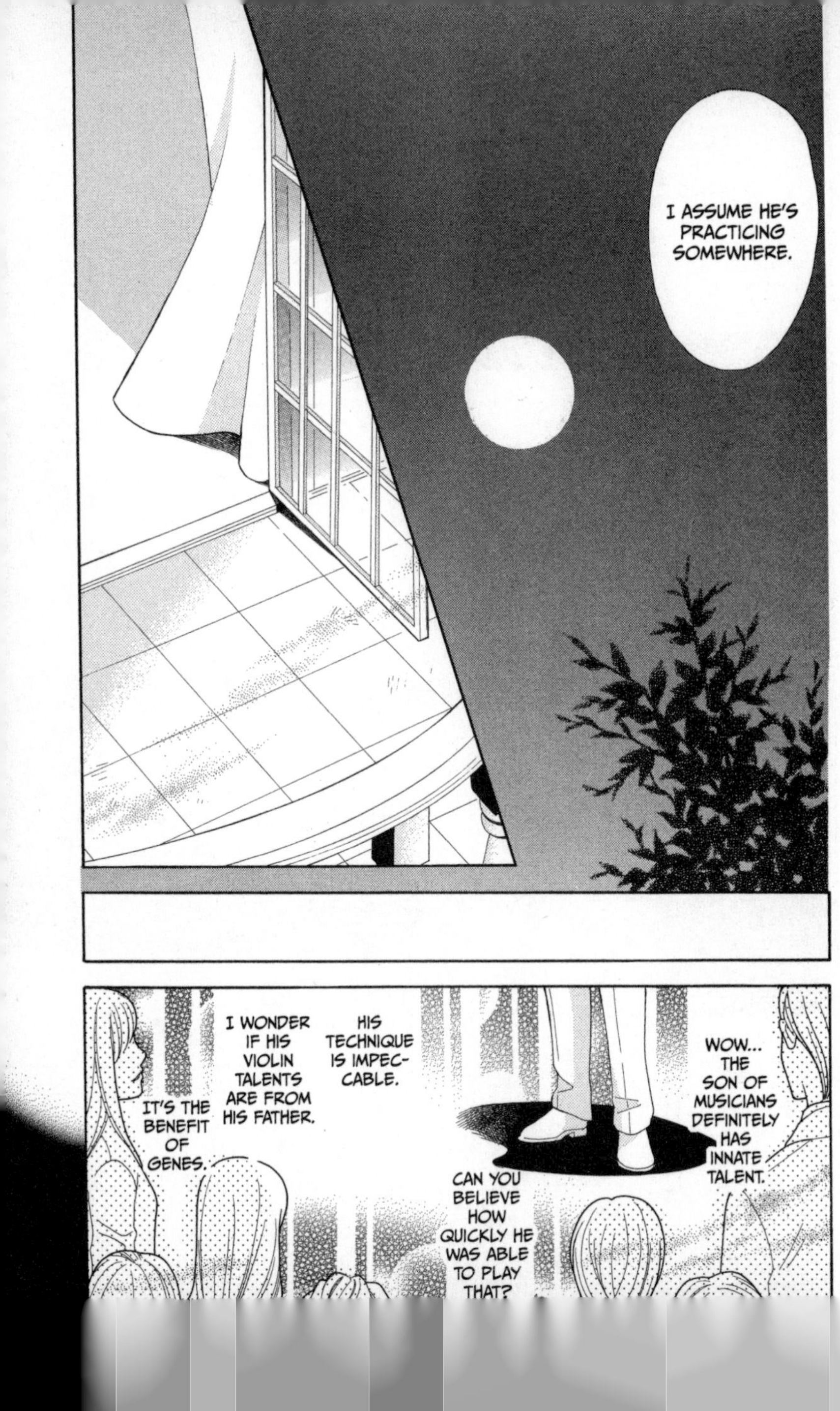
I ASSUME HE'S PRACTICING SOMEWHERE.
WOW... THE SON OF MUSICIANS DEFINITELY HAS INNATE TALENT.
HIS TECHNIQUE IS IMPEC-CABLE.
I WONDER IF HIS VIOLIN TALENTS ARE FROM HIS FATHER.
IT'S THE BENEFIT OF GENES.
CAN YOU BELIEVE HOW QUICKLY HE WAS ABLE TO PLAY THAT?

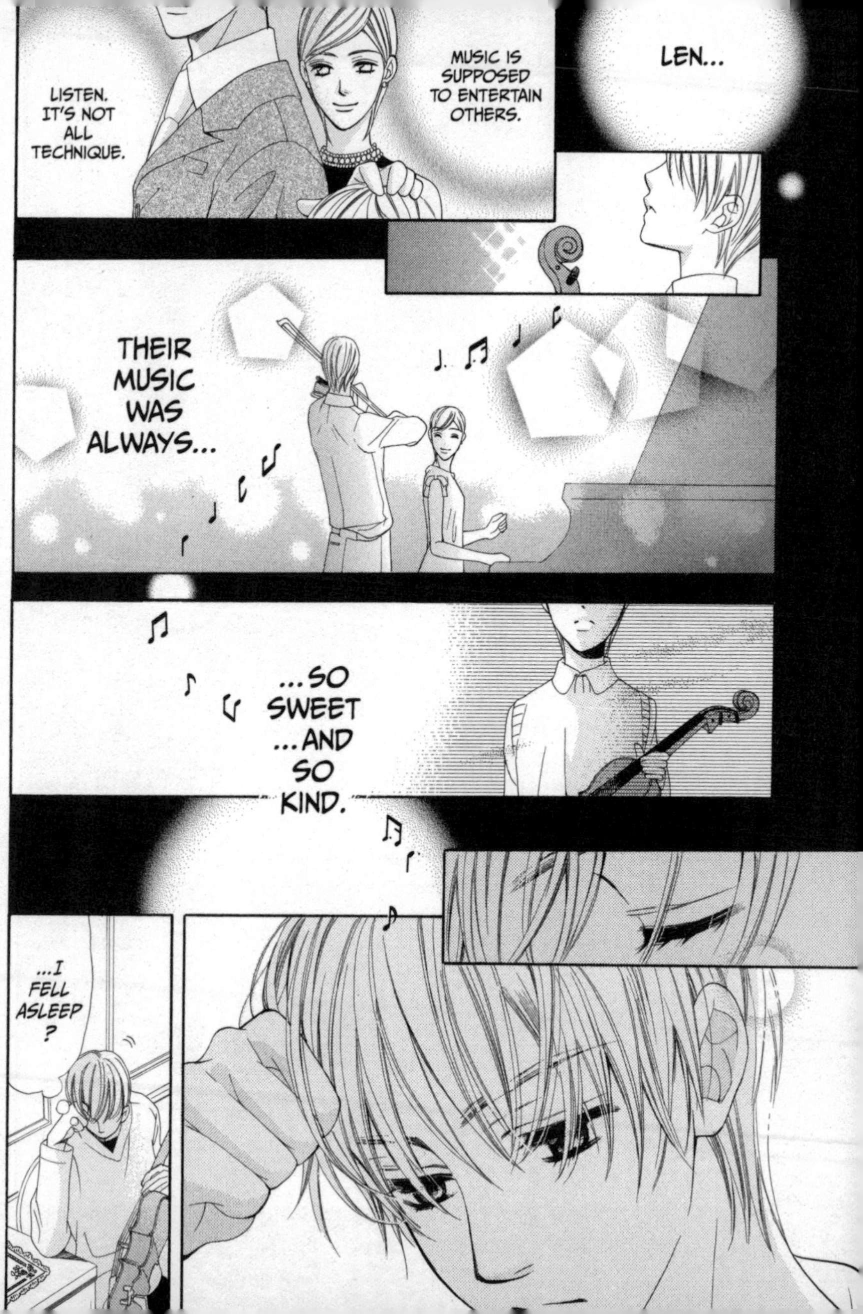
LEN...
MUSIC IS SUPPOSED TO ENTERTAIN OTHERS.
LISTEN. IT'S NOT ALL TECHNIQUE.
THEIR MUSIC WAS ALWAYS...
...SO SWEET ...AND SO KIND.
...I FELL ASLEEP?

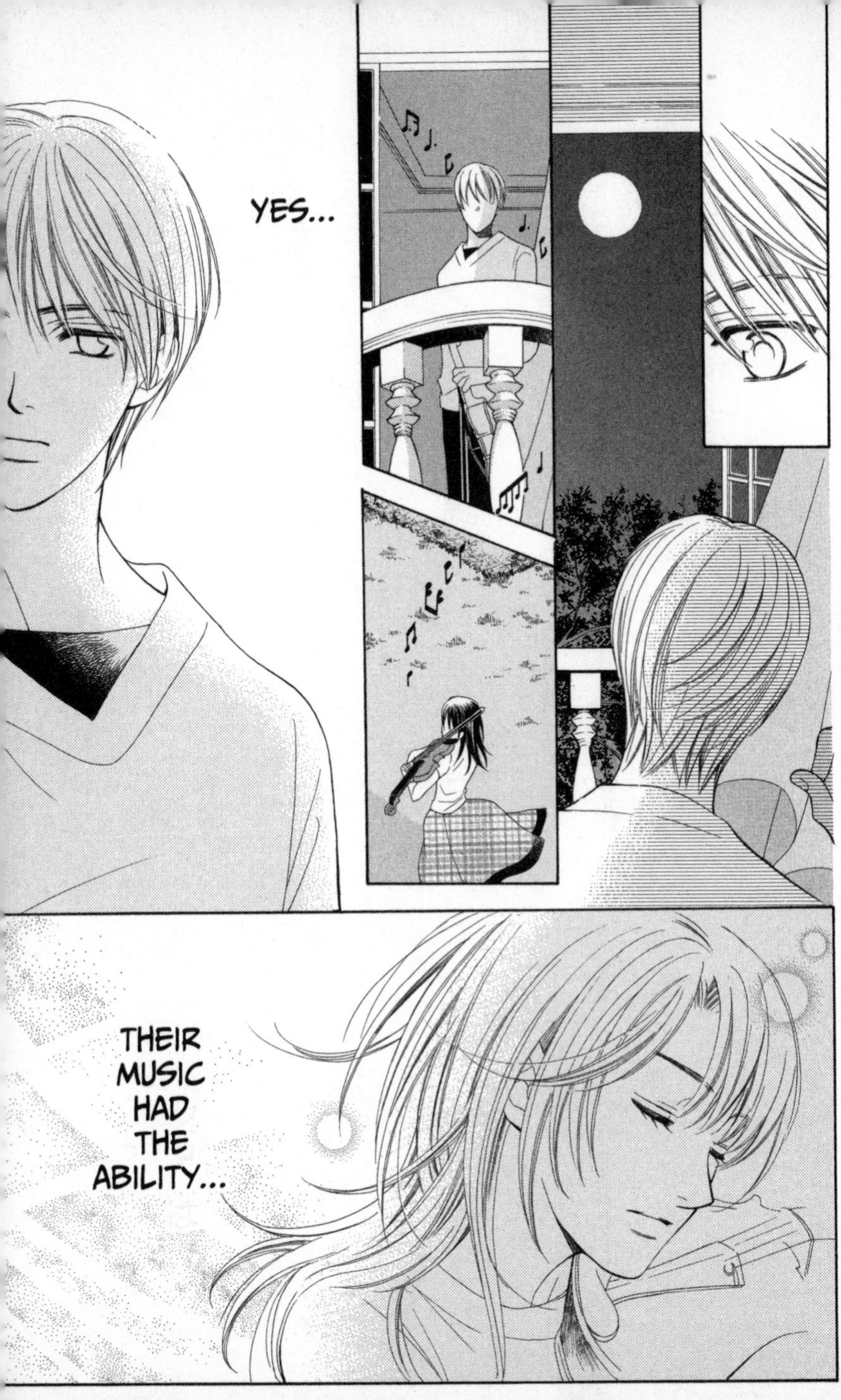
YES...
THEIR MUSIC HAD THE ABILITY...

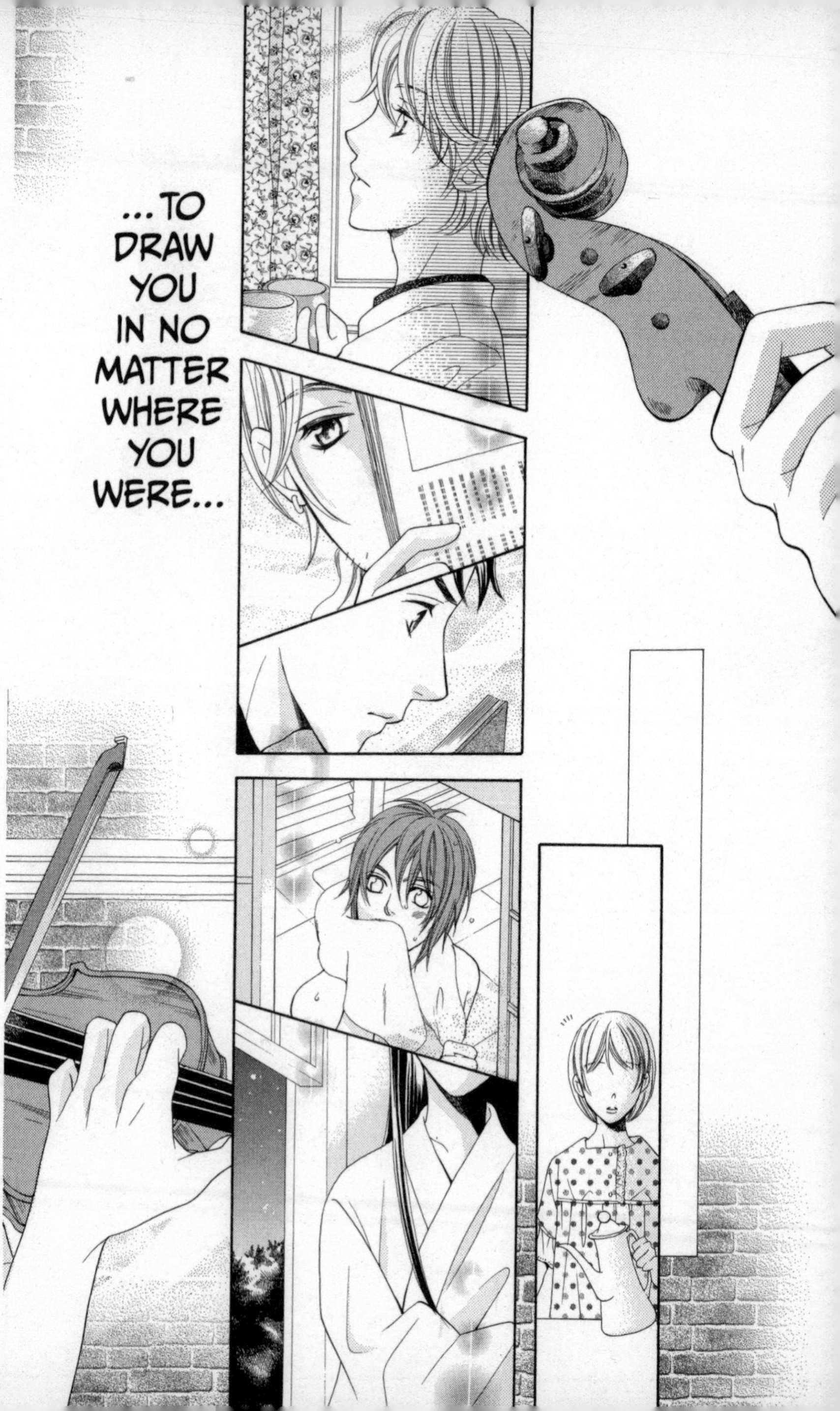
...TO DRAW YOU IN NO MATTER WHERE YOU WERE...

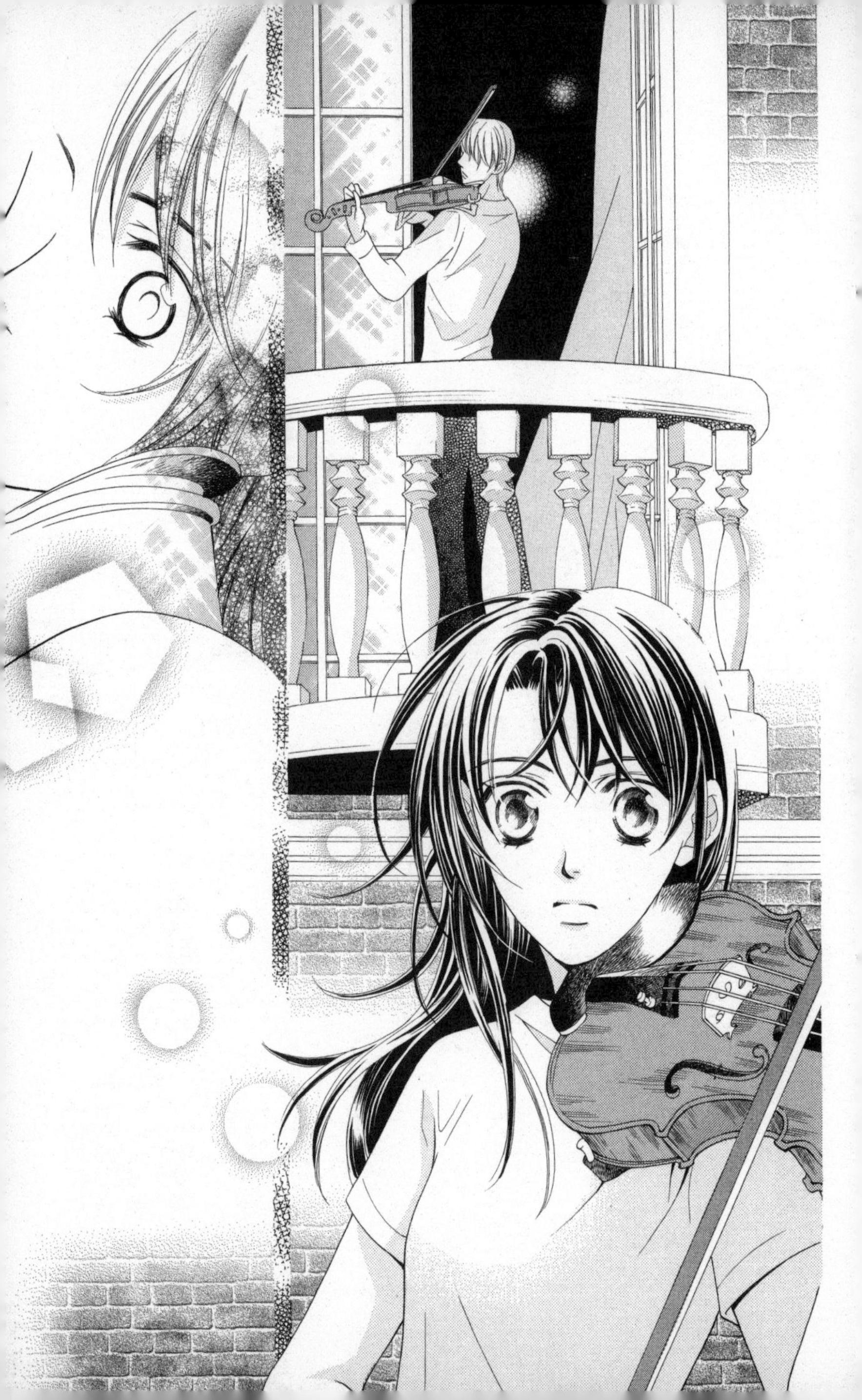

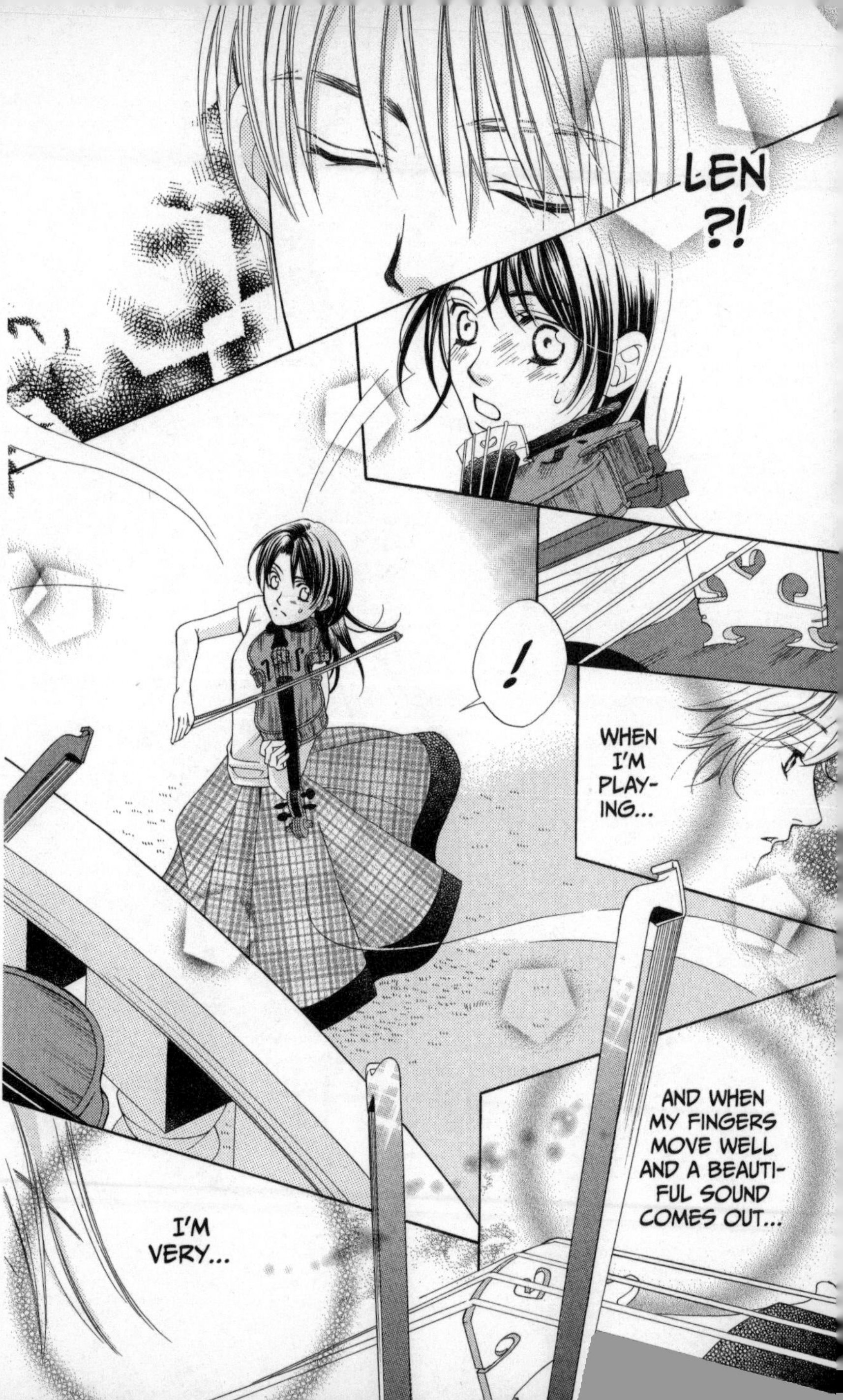
LEN ?!
!
WHEN I'M PLAY-ING...
AND WHEN MY FINGERS MOVE WELL AND A BEAUTI-FUL SOUND COMES OUT...
I'M VERY...

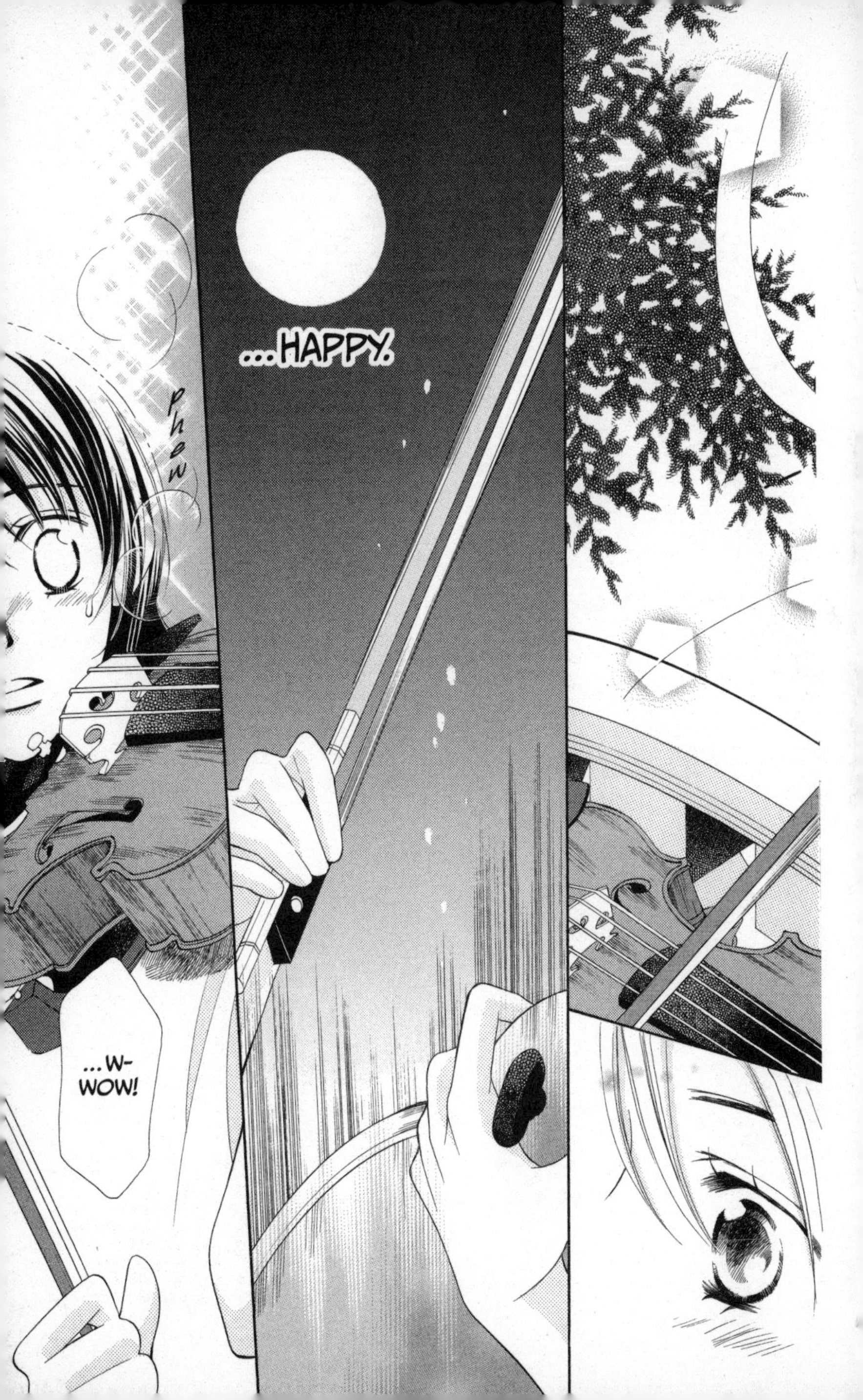
...HAPPY.
Phew
...W-
WOW!

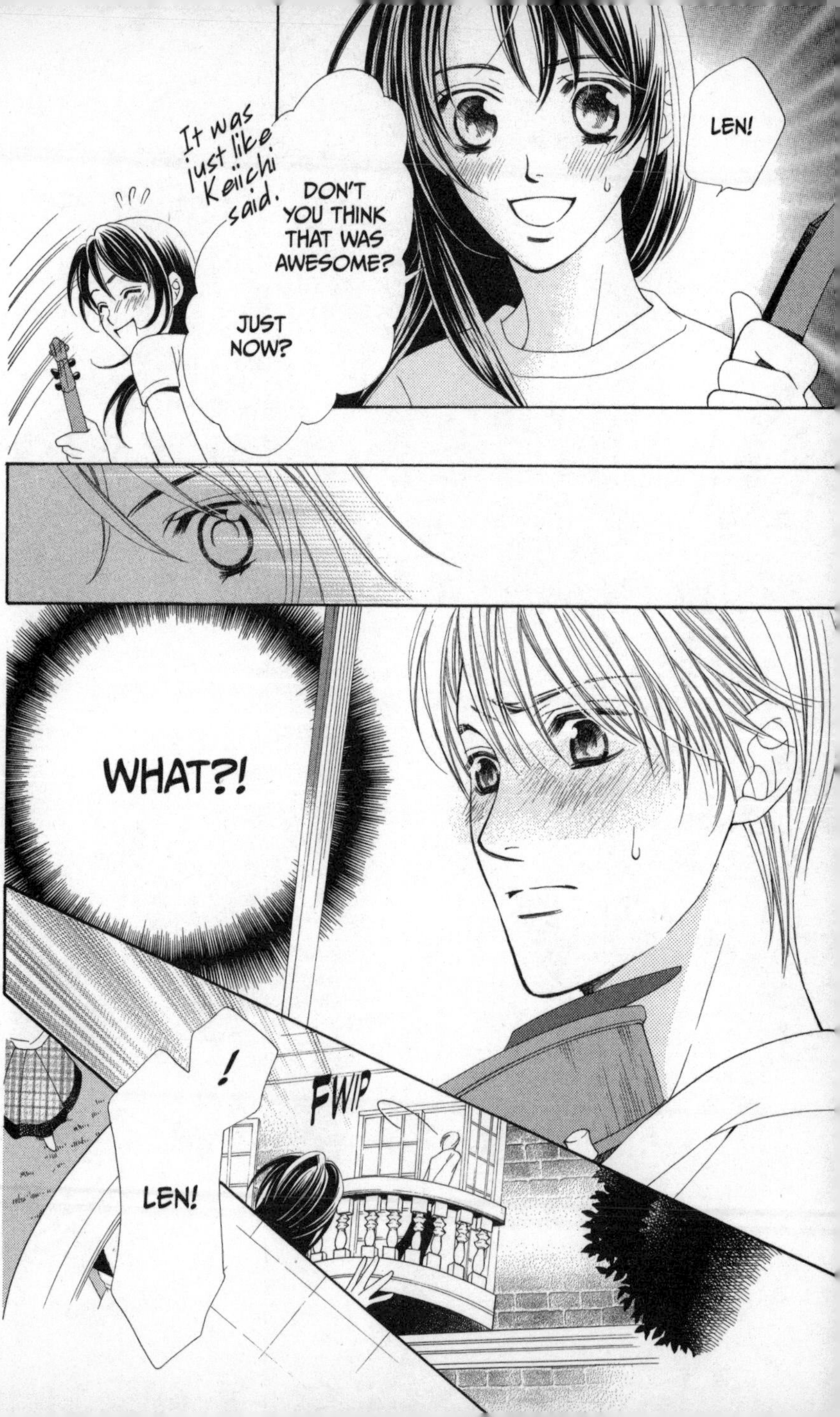
LEN!
DON'T YOU THINK THAT WAS AWESOME?
JUST NOW?
It was just like Keiichi said.
WHAT?!
FWIP
!
LEN!

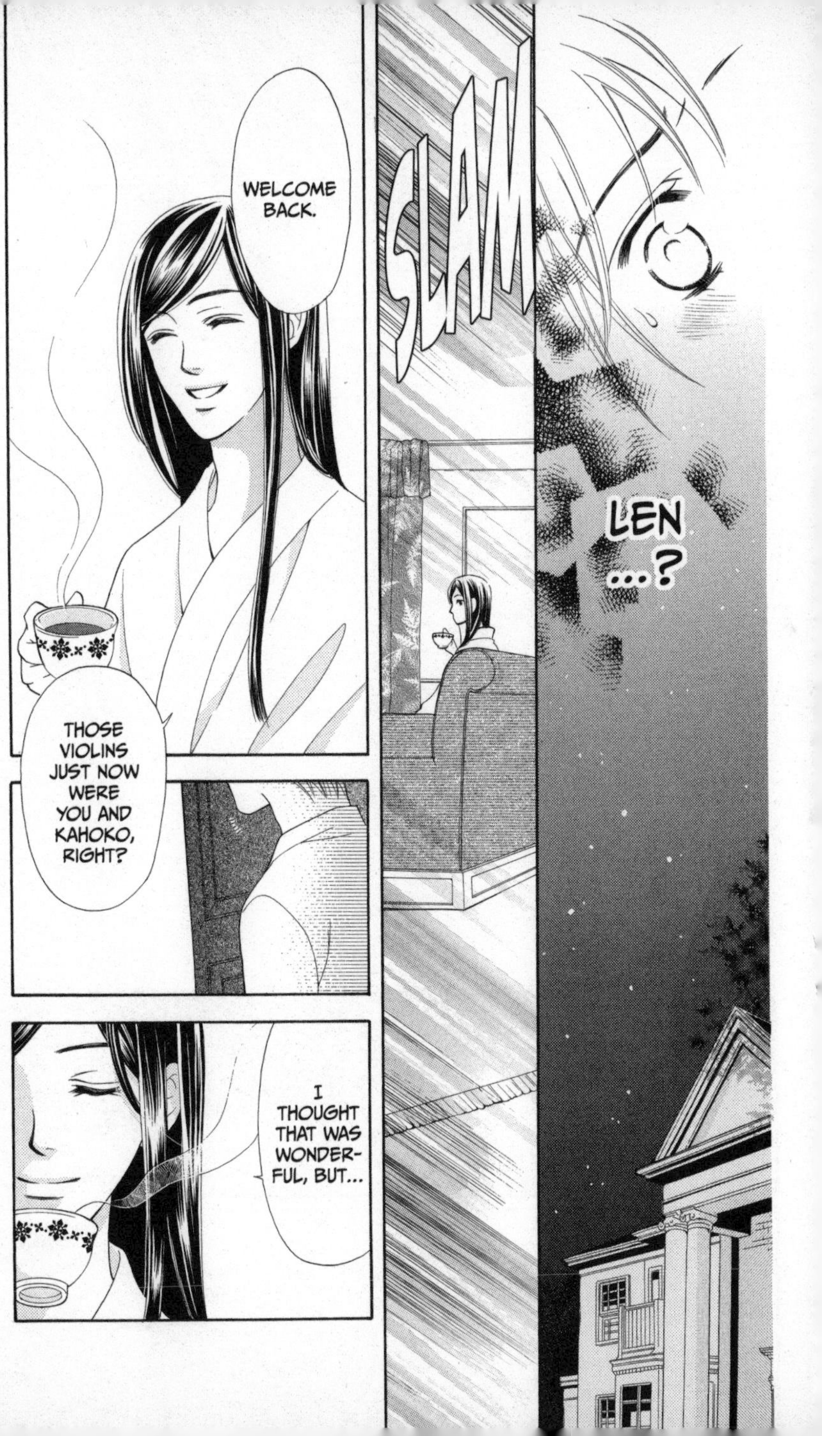
LEN ...?
SLAM
WELCOME BACK.
THOSE VIOLINS JUST NOW WERE YOU AND KAHOKO, RIGHT?
I THOUGHT THAT WAS WONDERFUL, BUT...

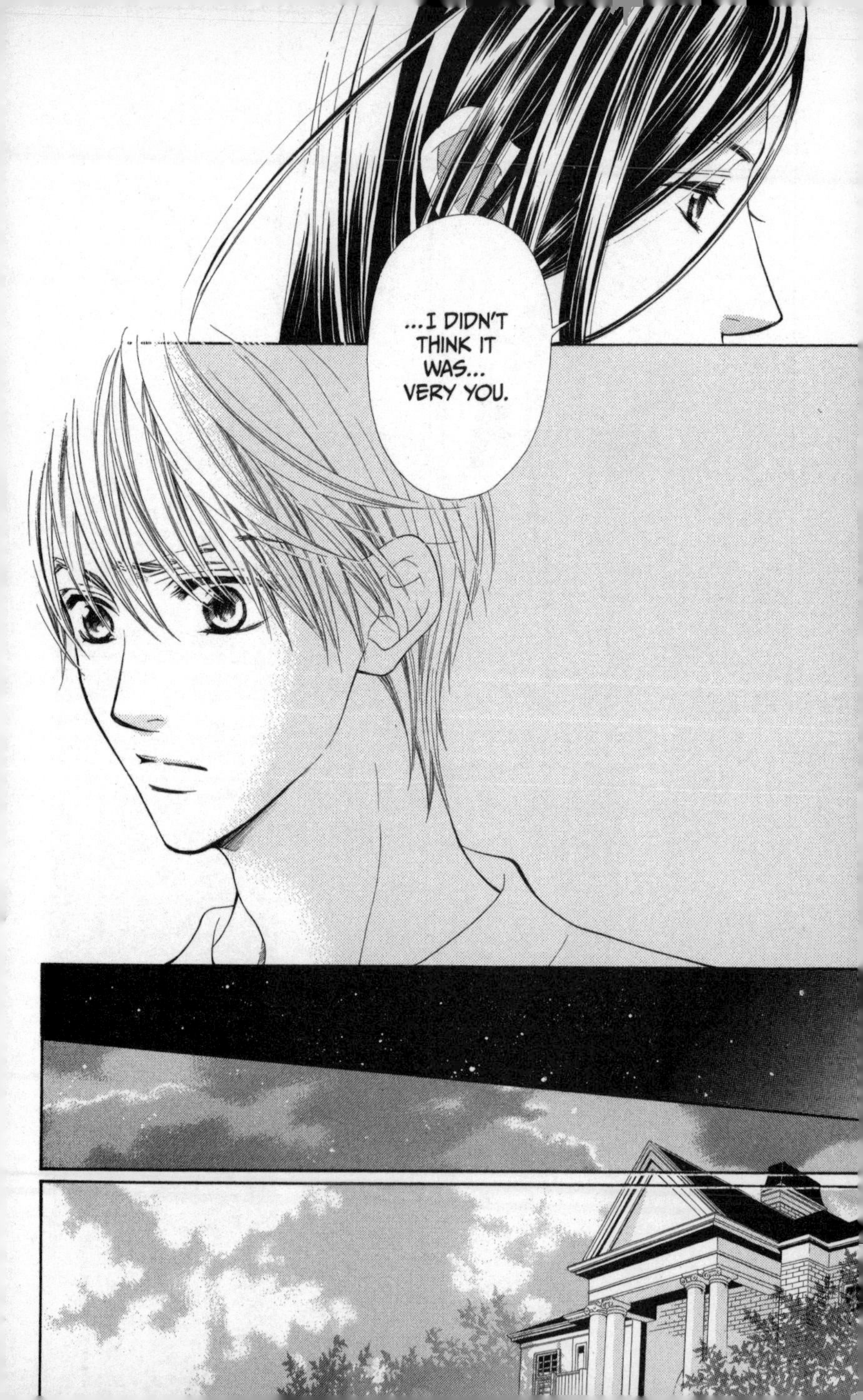
...I DIDN'T THINK IT WAS... VERY YOU.

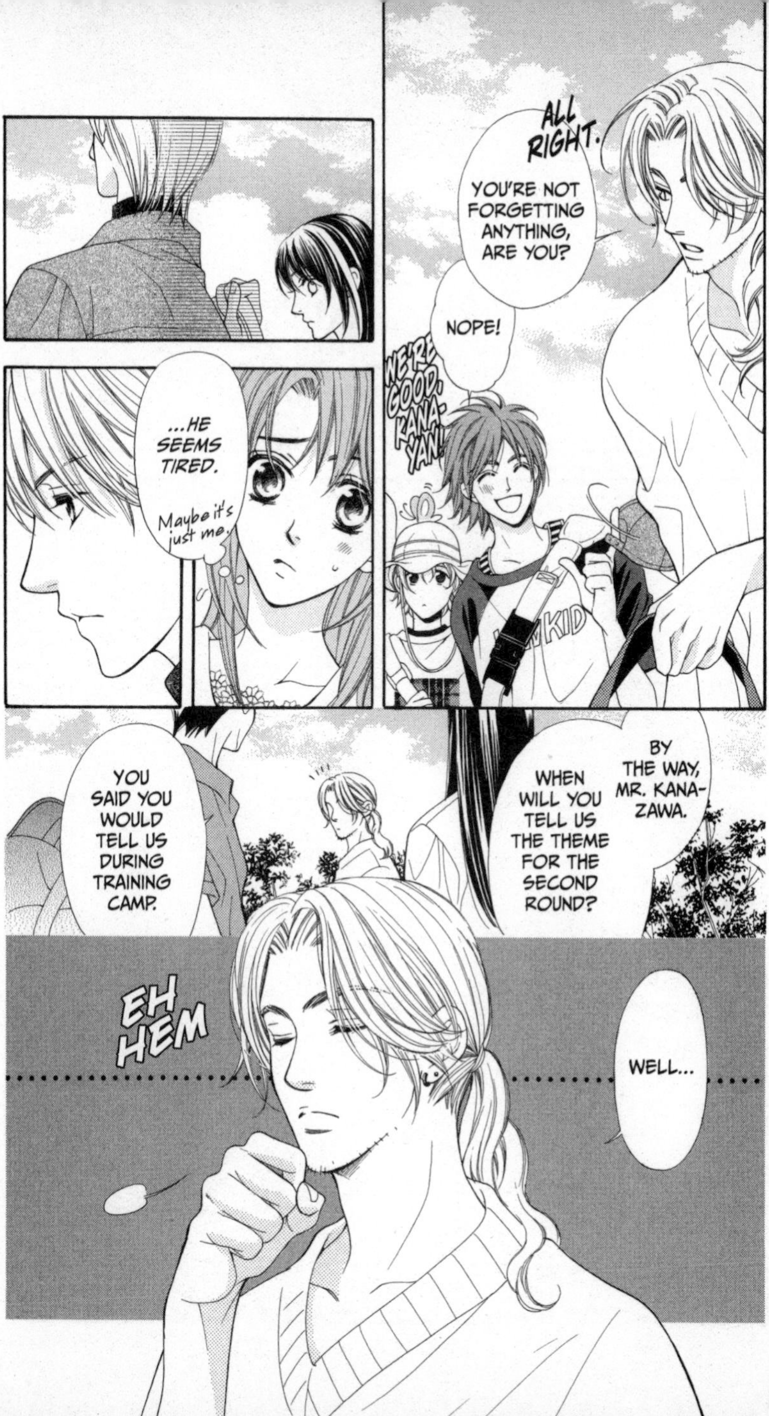
ALL RIGHT.
YOU'RE NOT FORGETTING ANYTHING, ARE YOU?
NOPE!
WE'RE GOOD, KANA-YAN!
...HE SEEMS TIRED.
Maybe it's just me.
BY THE WAY, MR. KANA-ZAWA.
WHEN WILL YOU TELL US THE THEME FOR THE SECOND ROUND?
YOU SAID YOU WOULD TELL US DURING TRAINING CAMP.
EH HEM
WELL...

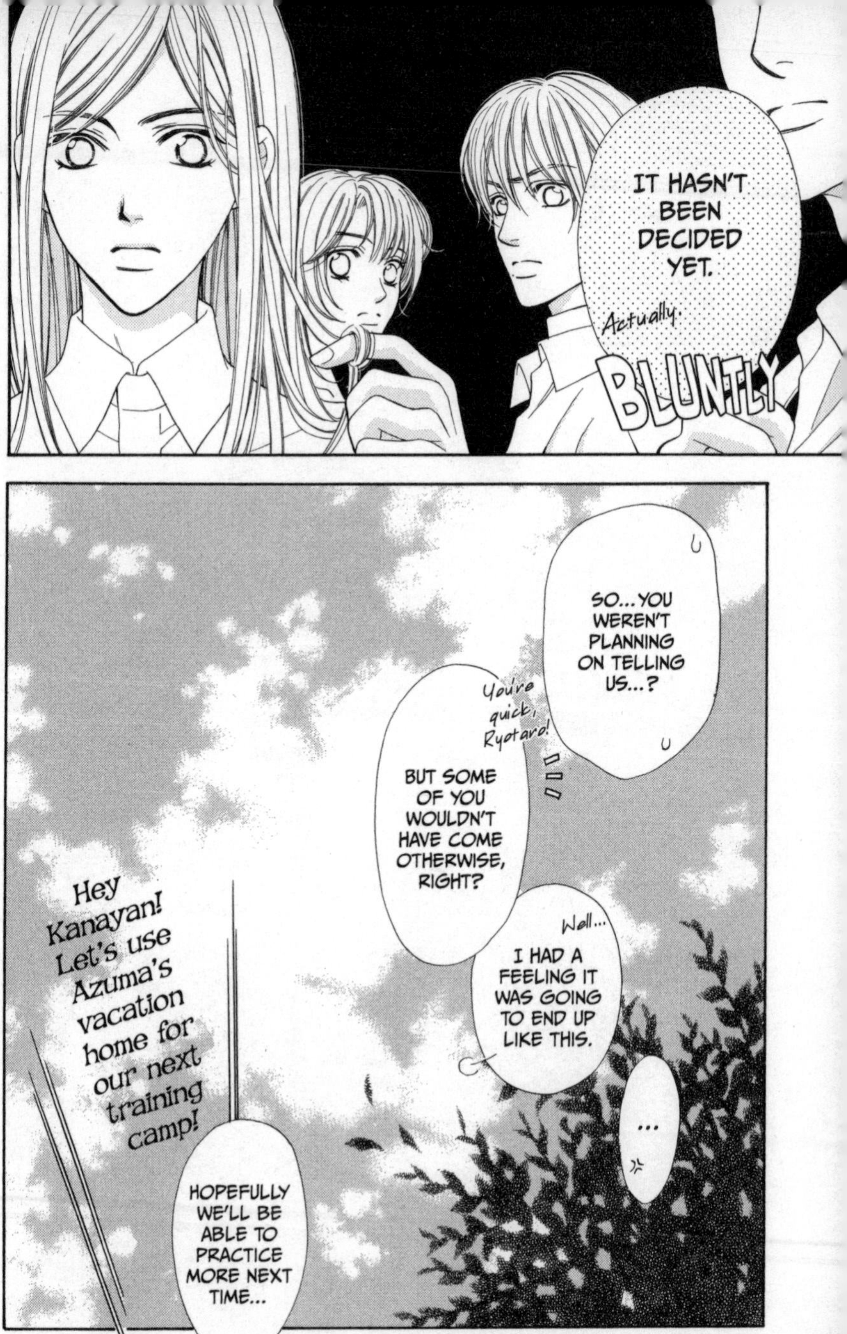
IT HASN'T BEEN DECIDED YET.
Actually.
BLUNTLY
SO...YOU WEREN'T PLANNING ON TELLING US...?
You're quick, Ryotaro!
BUT SOME OF YOU WOULDN'T HAVE COME OTHERWISE, RIGHT?
Well...
I HAD A FEELING IT WAS GOING TO END UP LIKE THIS.
...
Hey Kanayan! Let's use Azuma's vacation home for our next training camp!
HOPEFULLY WE'LL BE ABLE TO PRACTICE MORE NEXT TIME...

END OF MEASURE 13

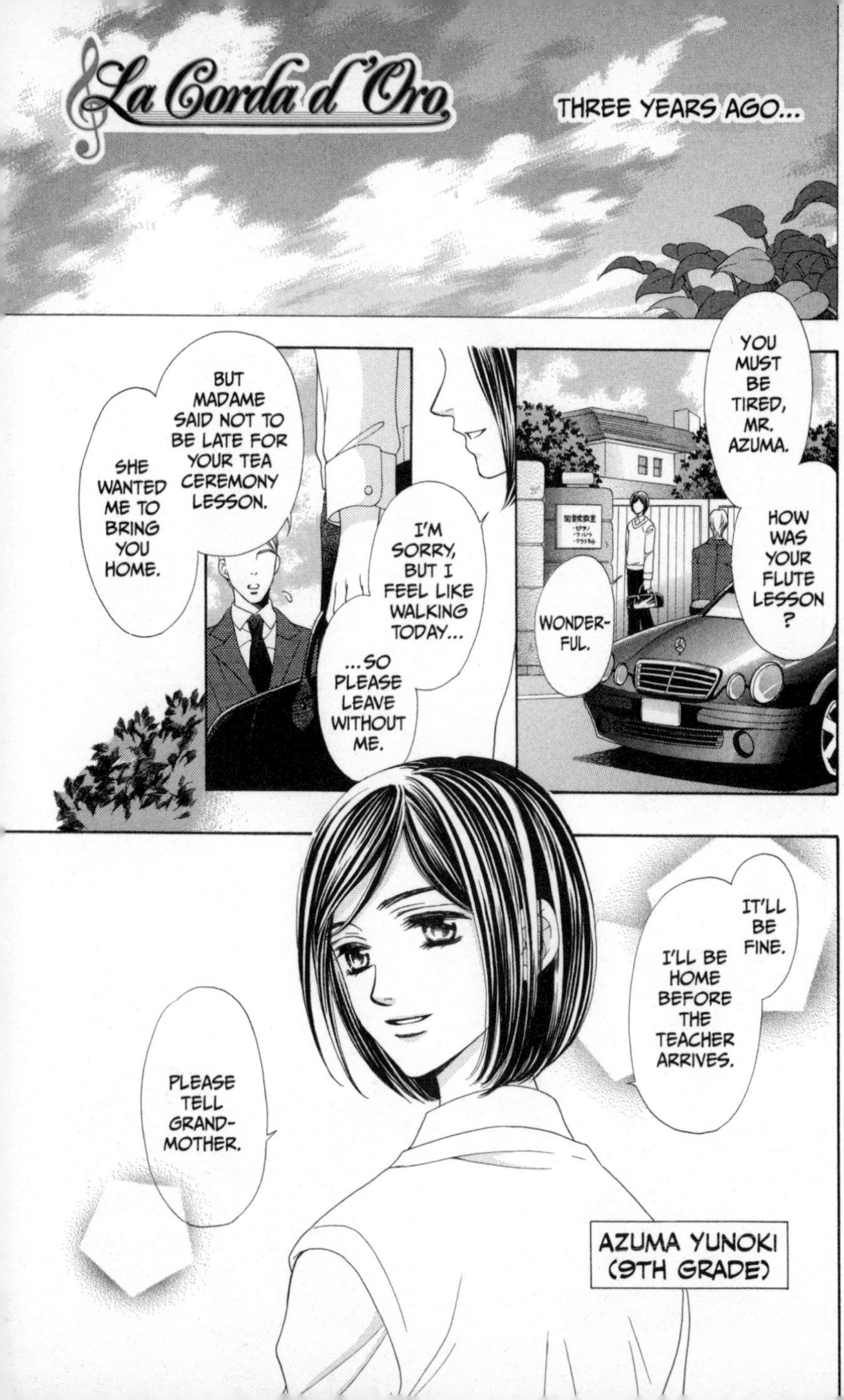
La Corda d'Oro
THREE YEARS AGO...
YOU MUST BE TIRED, MR. AZUMA.
HOW WAS YOUR FLUTE LESSON?
WONDERFUL.
I'M SORRY, BUT I FEEL LIKE WALKING TODAY...
...SO PLEASE LEAVE WITHOUT ME.
BUT MADAME SAID NOT TO BE LATE FOR YOUR TEA CEREMONY LESSON.
SHE WANTED ME TO BRING YOU HOME.
IT'LL BE FINE.
I'LL BE HOME BEFORE THE TEACHER ARRIVES.
PLEASE TELL GRANDMOTHER.
AZUMA YUNOKI (9TH GRADE)

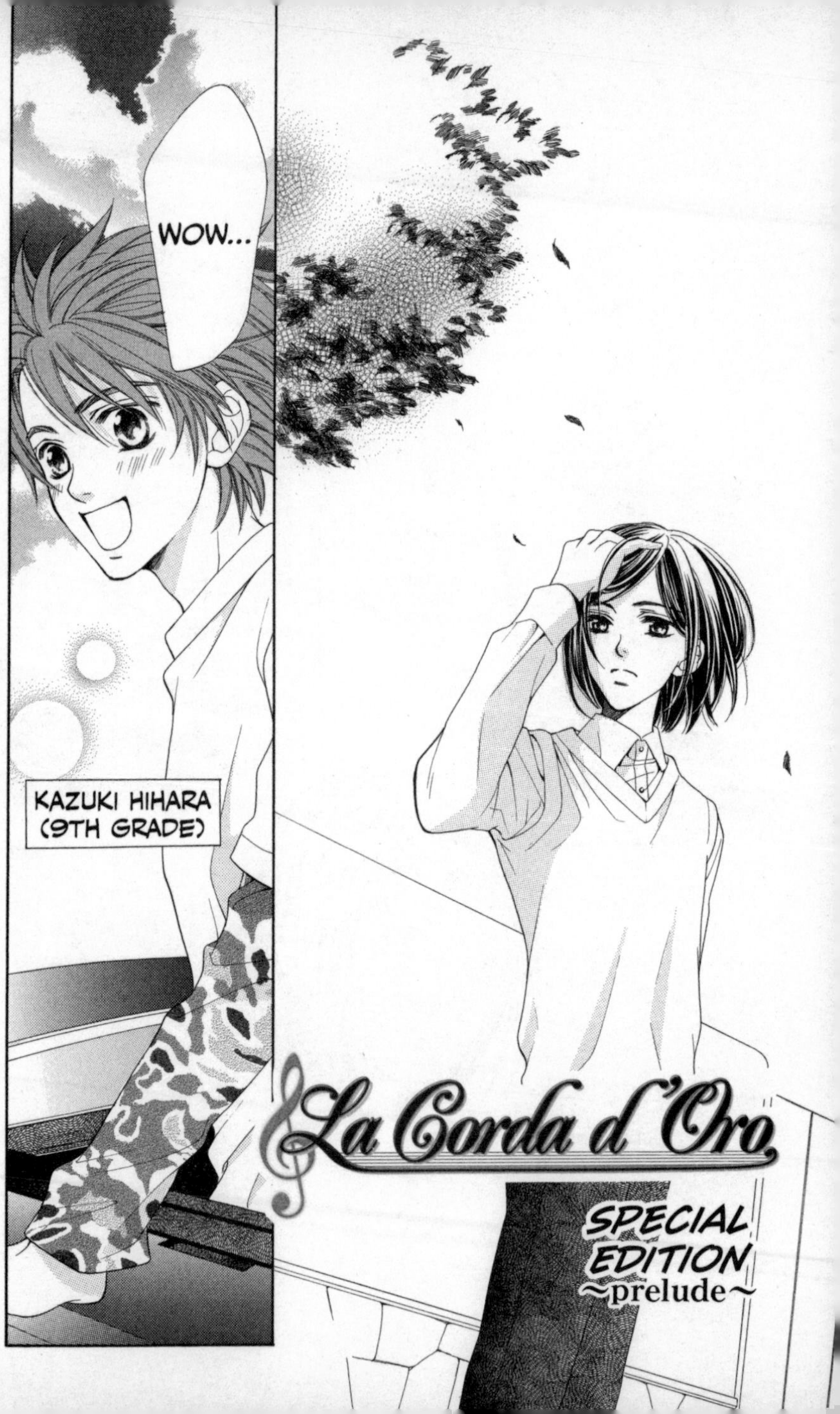
La Corda d'Oro
SPECIAL EDITION
~prelude~
WOW...
KAZUKI HIHARA (9TH GRADE)

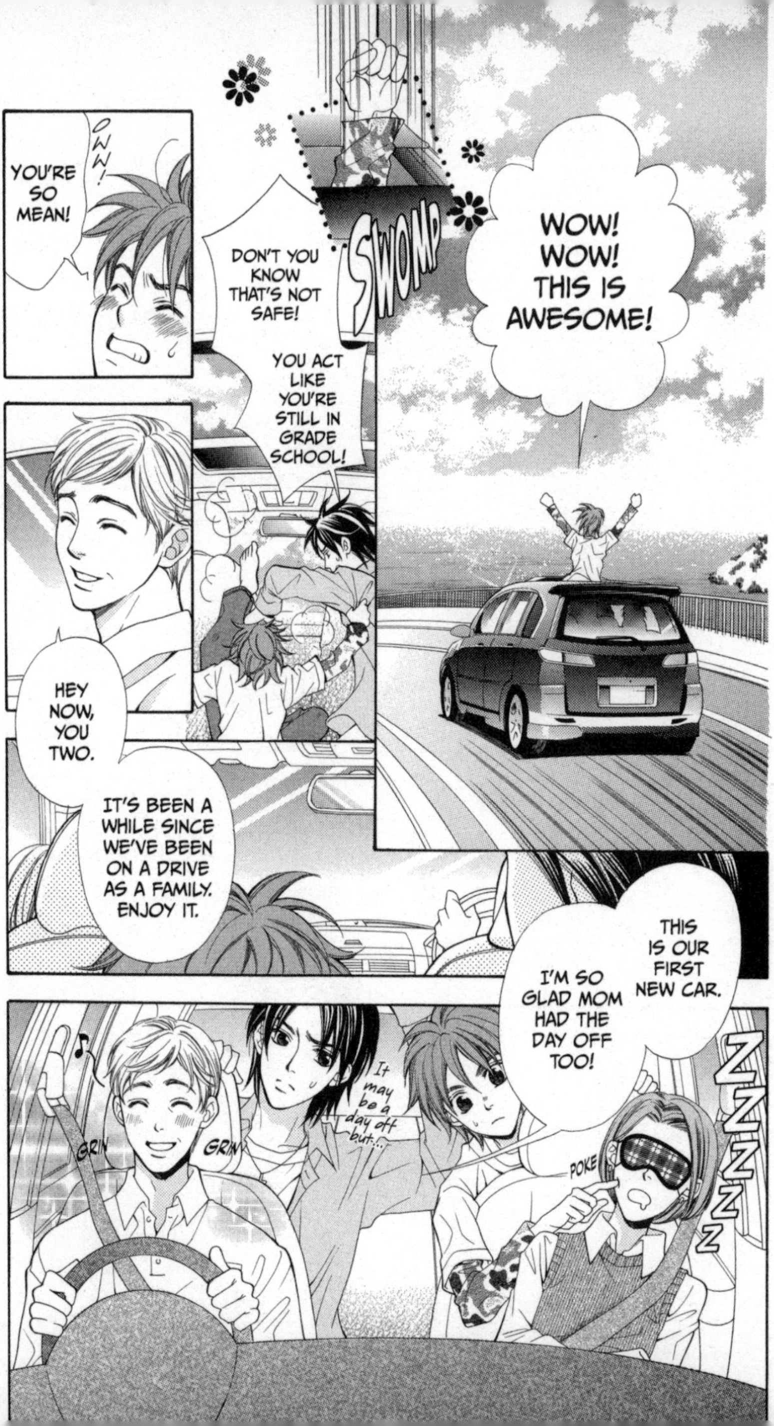
WOW! WOW! THIS IS AWESOME!
SWOMP
OWW!
YOU'RE SO MEAN!
DON'T YOU KNOW THAT'S NOT SAFE!
YOU ACT LIKE YOU'RE STILL IN GRADE SCHOOL!
HEY NOW, YOU TWO.
IT'S BEEN A WHILE SINCE WE'VE BEEN ON A DRIVE AS A FAMILY. ENJOY IT.
THIS IS OUR FIRST NEW CAR.
I'M SO GLAD MOM HAD THE DAY OFF TOO!
ZZZZZ
POKE
It may be a day off but...
GRIN
GRIN

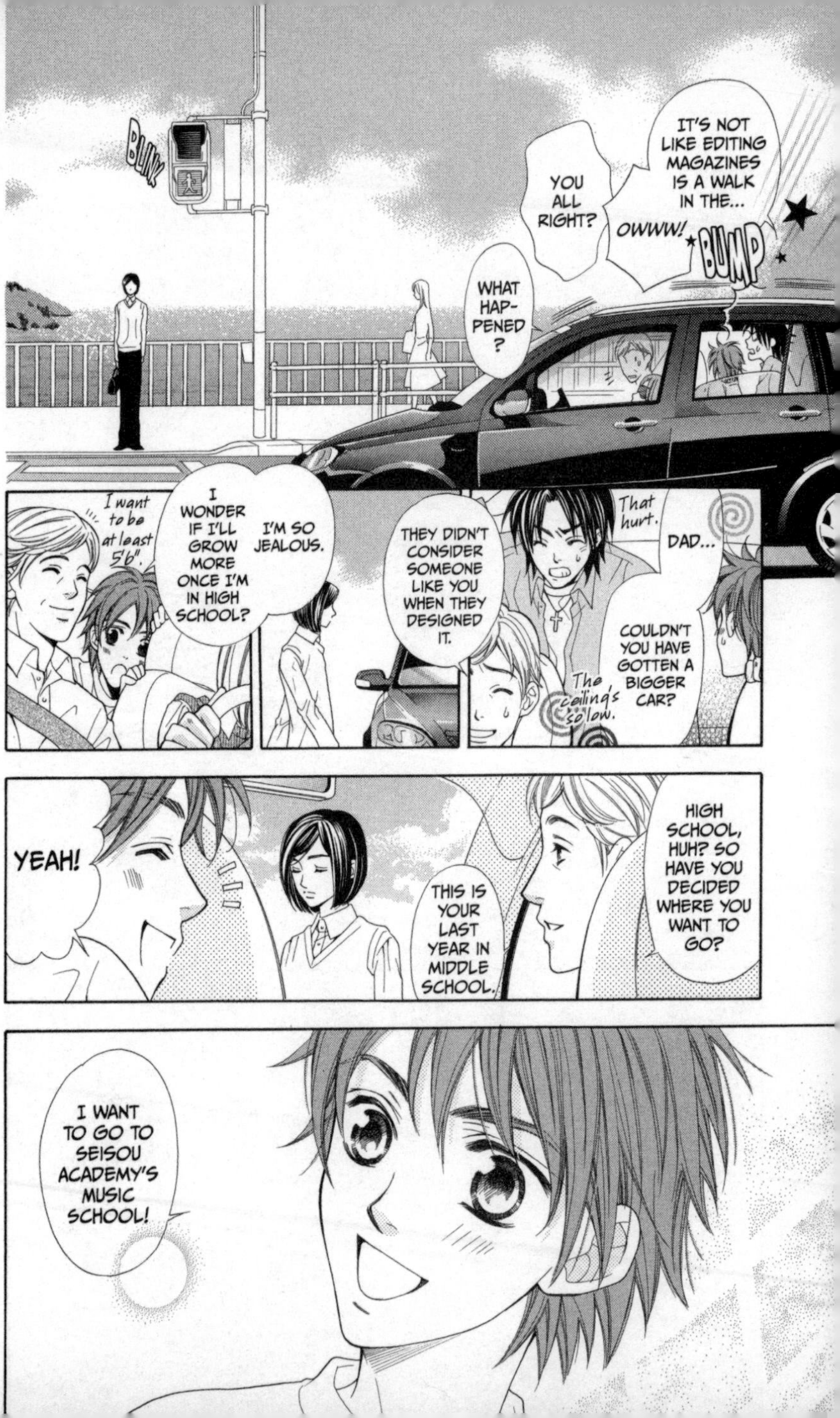
IT'S NOT LIKE EDITING MAGAZINES IS A WALK IN THE...
OWWW!
BUMP
YOU ALL RIGHT?
WHAT HAP-PENED?
BLINK
DAD...
That hurt.
COULDN'T YOU HAVE GOTTEN A BIGGER CAR?
The ceiling's so low.
THEY DIDN'T CONSIDER SOMEONE LIKE YOU WHEN THEY DESIGNED IT.
I'M SO JEALOUS.
I WONDER IF I'LL GROW MORE ONCE I'M IN HIGH SCHOOL?
I want to be at least 5'6".
HIGH SCHOOL, HUH? SO HAVE YOU DECIDED WHERE YOU WANT TO GO?
THIS IS YOUR LAST YEAR IN MIDDLE SCHOOL.
YEAH!
I WANT TO GO TO SEISOU ACADEMY'S MUSIC SCHOOL!

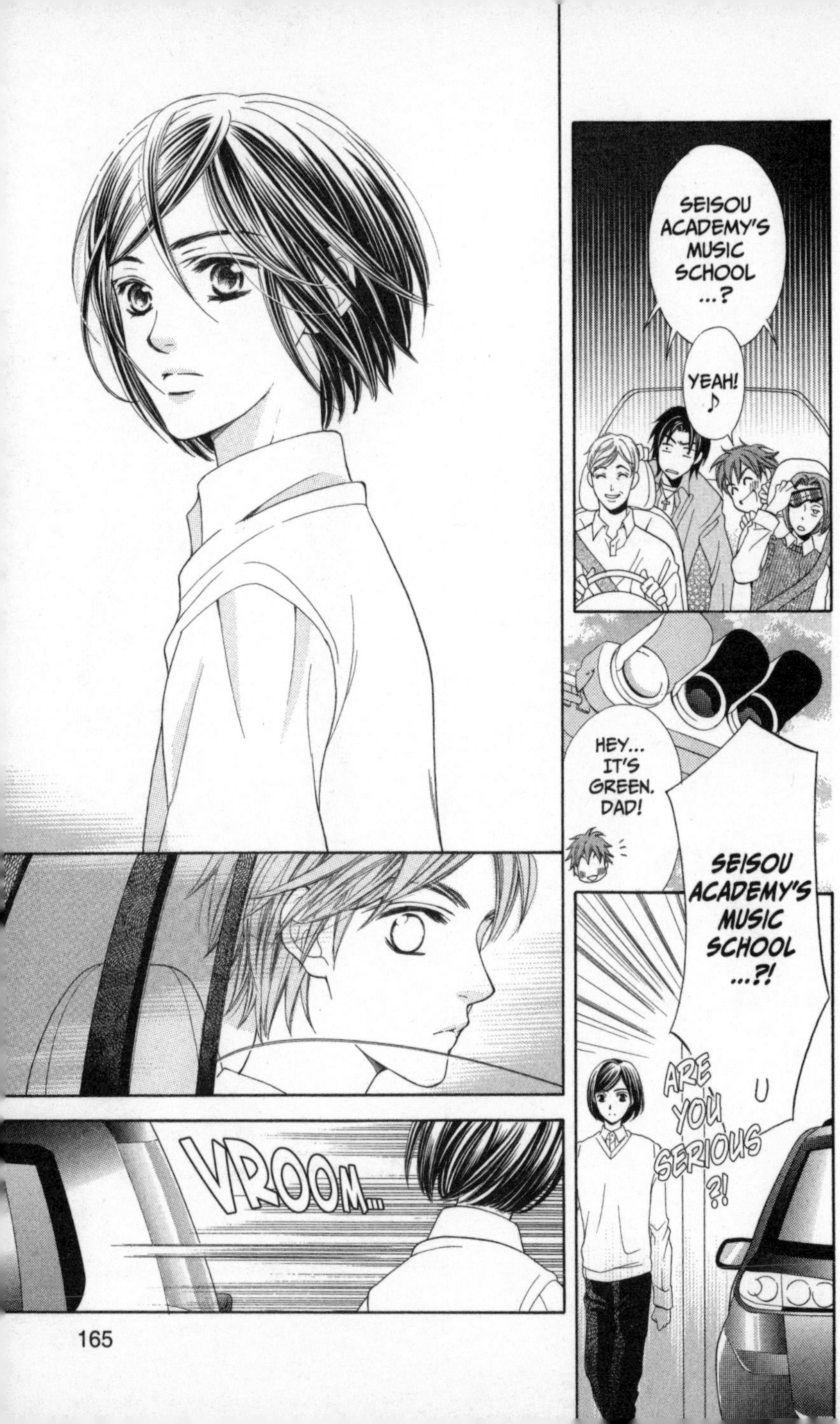
SEISOU ACADEMY'S MUSIC SCHOOL ...?
YEAH! ♪
HEY... IT'S GREEN. DAD!
SEISOU ACADEMY'S MUSIC SCHOOL ...?!
ARE YOU SERIOUS ?!
VROOM...

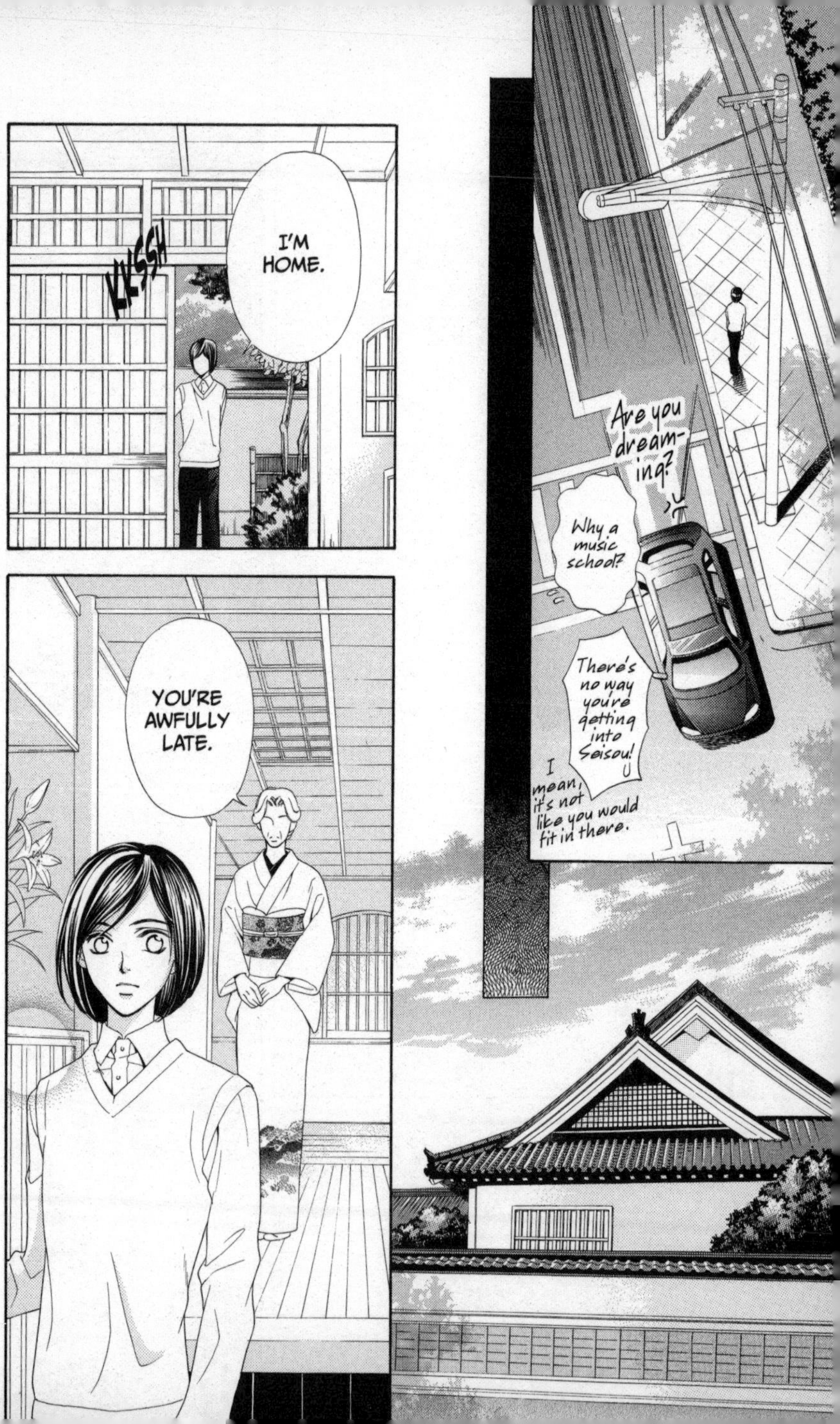
Are you dreaming?
Why a music school?
There's no way you're getting into Seisou!
I mean, it's not like you would fit in there.
KLSSH
I'M HOME.
YOU'RE AWFULLY LATE.

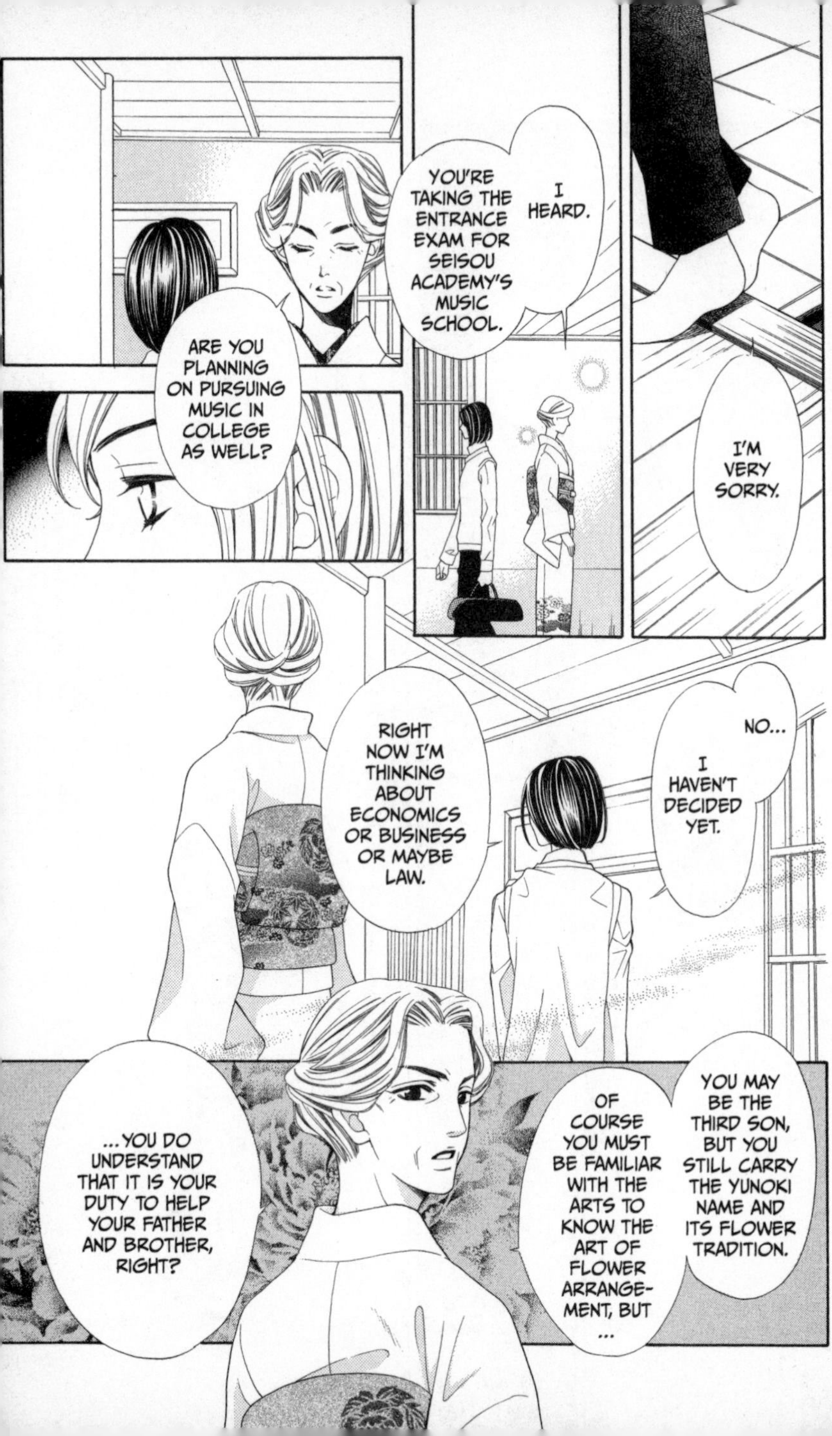
I'M VERY SORRY.
I HEARD.
YOU'RE TAKING THE ENTRANCE EXAM FOR SEISOU ACADEMY'S MUSIC SCHOOL.
ARE YOU PLANNING ON PURSUING MUSIC IN COLLEGE AS WELL?
NO...
I HAVEN'T DECIDED YET.
RIGHT NOW I'M THINKING ABOUT ECONOMICS OR BUSINESS OR MAYBE LAW.
YOU MAY BE THE THIRD SON, BUT YOU STILL CARRY THE YUNOKI NAME AND ITS FLOWER TRADITION.
OF COURSE YOU MUST BE FAMILIAR WITH THE ARTS TO KNOW THE ART OF FLOWER ARRANGE-MENT, BUT ...
...YOU DO UNDERSTAND THAT IT IS YOUR DUTY TO HELP YOUR FATHER AND BROTHER, RIGHT?

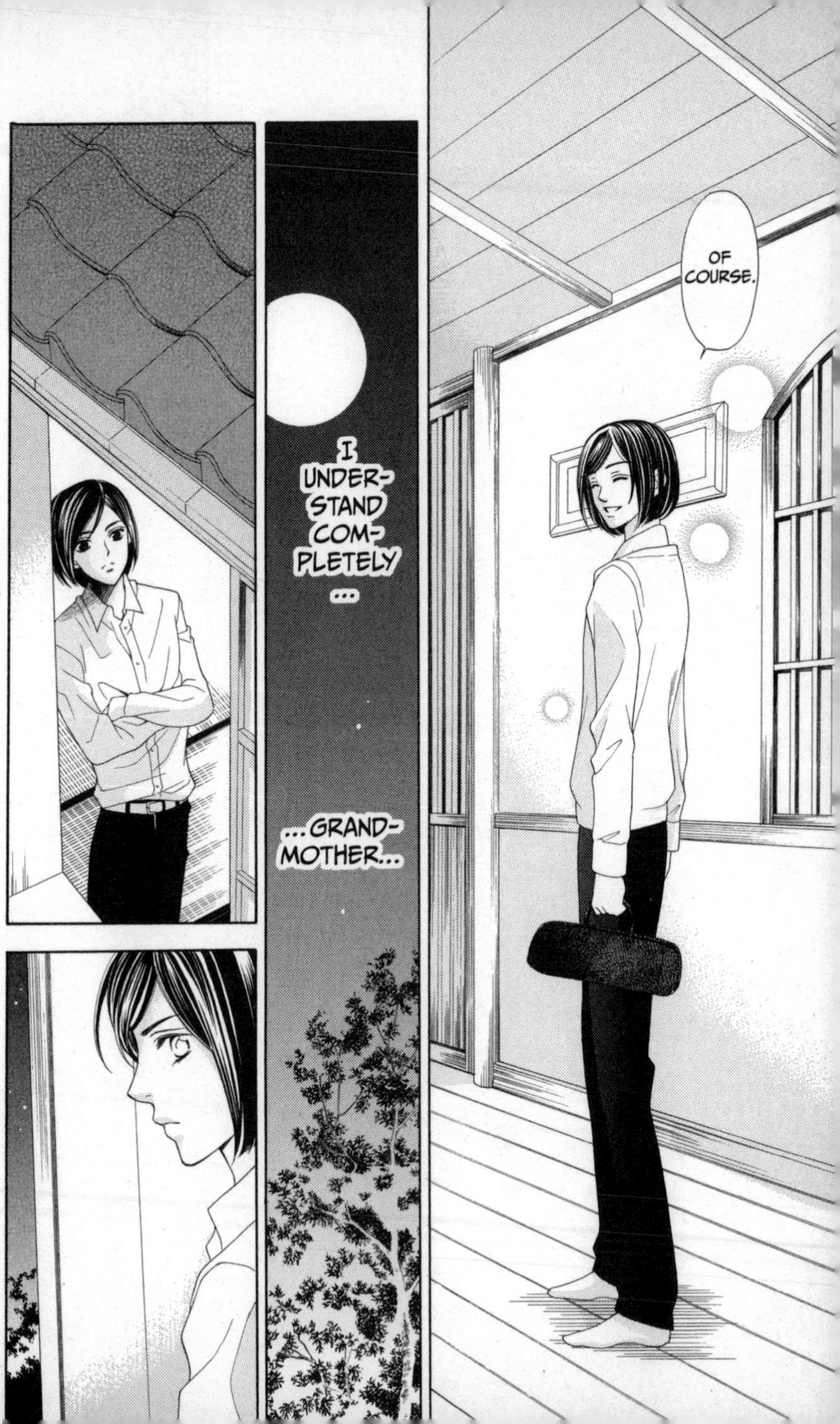
OF COURSE.
I UNDER-STAND COM-PLETELY...
...GRAND-MOTHER...

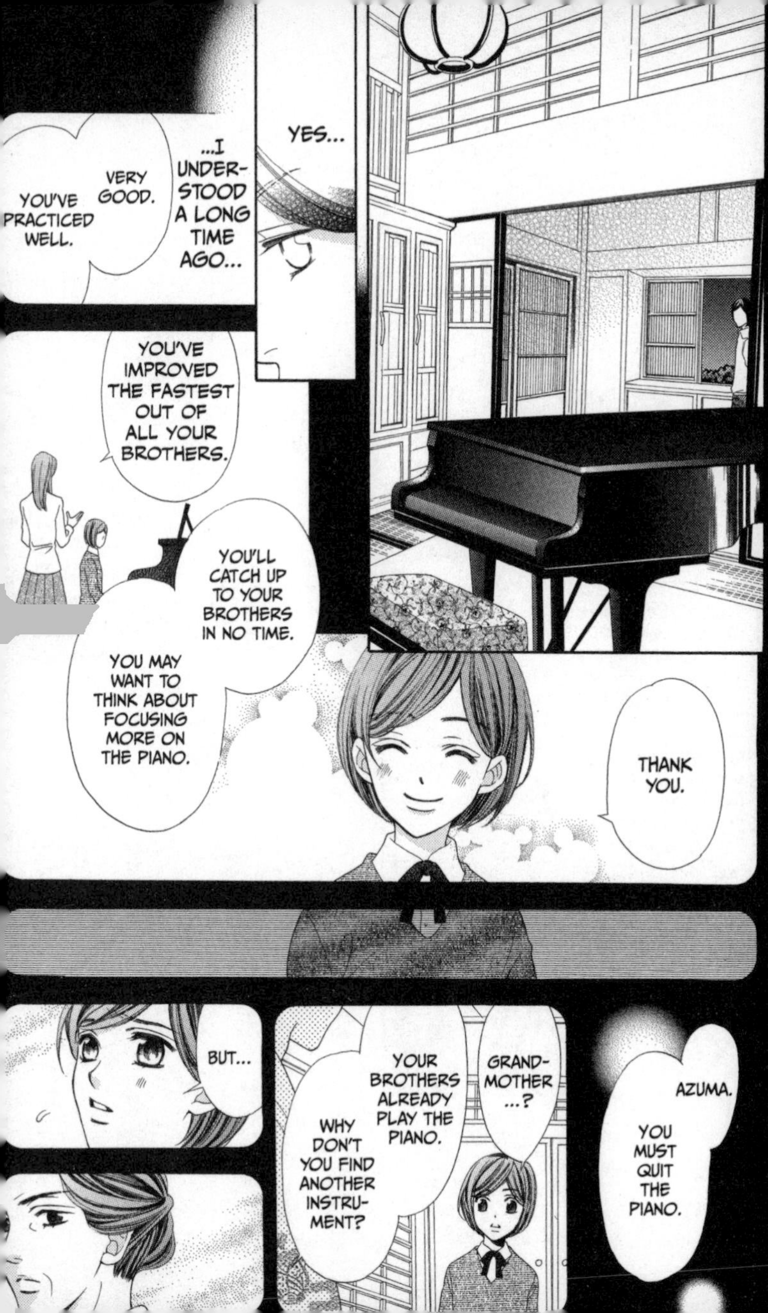
YES...
...I UNDERSTOOD A LONG TIME AGO...
VERY GOOD.
YOU'VE PRACTICED WELL.
YOU'VE IMPROVED THE FASTEST OUT OF ALL YOUR BROTHERS.
YOU'LL CATCH UP TO YOUR BROTHERS IN NO TIME.
YOU MAY WANT TO THINK ABOUT FOCUSING MORE ON THE PIANO.
THANK YOU.
AZUMA.
YOU MUST QUIT THE PIANO.
GRANDMOTHER...?
YOUR BROTHERS ALREADY PLAY THE PIANO.
WHY DON'T YOU FIND ANOTHER INSTRUMENT?
BUT...

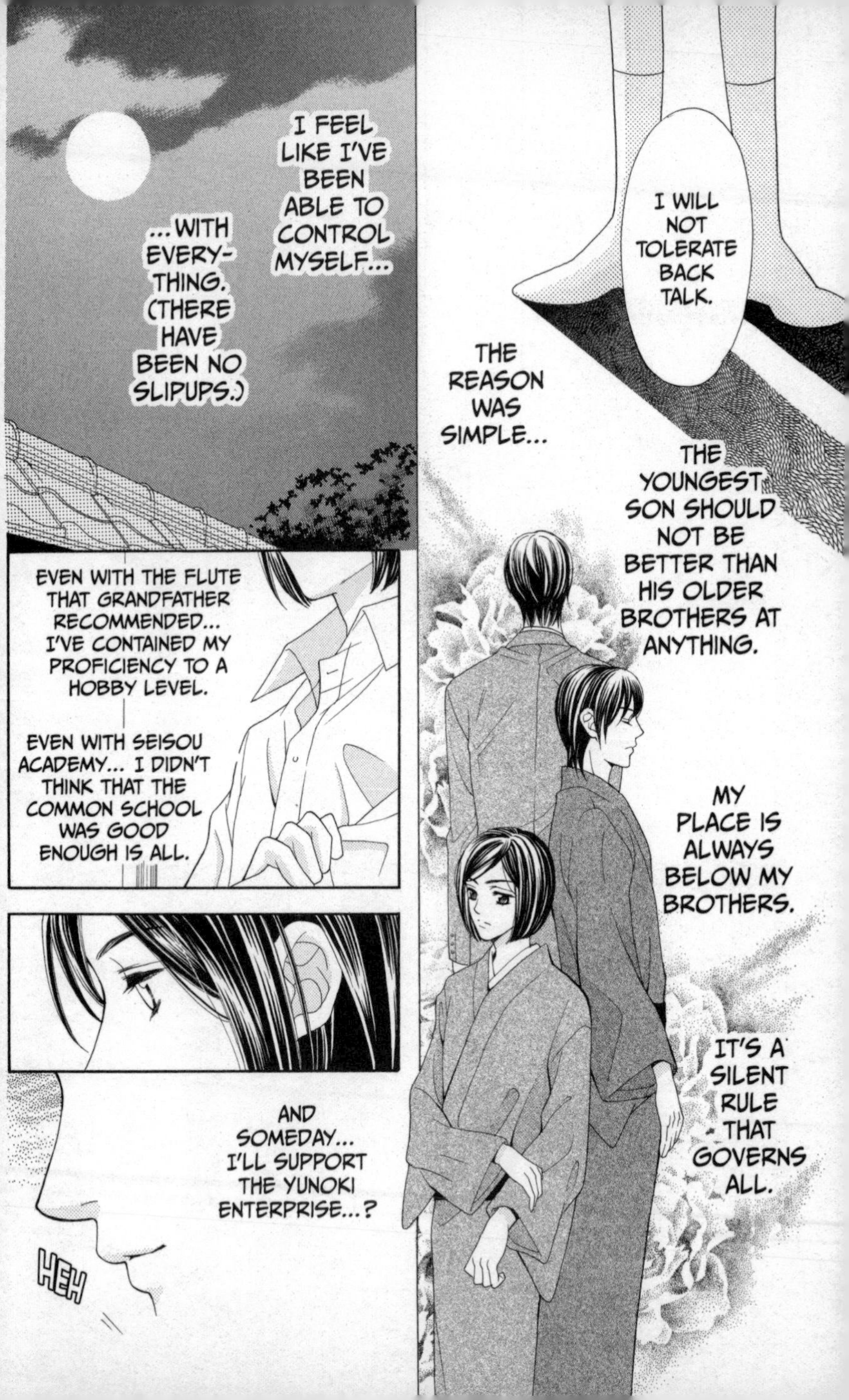
I WILL NOT TOLERATE BACK TALK.
THE REASON WAS SIMPLE...
THE YOUNGEST SON SHOULD NOT BE BETTER THAN HIS OLDER BROTHERS AT ANYTHING.
MY PLACE IS ALWAYS BELOW MY BROTHERS.
IT'S A SILENT RULE THAT GOVERNS ALL.
I FEEL LIKE I'VE BEEN ABLE TO CONTROL MYSELF...
...WITH EVERY-THING. (THERE HAVE BEEN NO SLIPUPS.)
EVEN WITH THE FLUTE THAT GRANDFATHER RECOMMENDED... I'VE CONTAINED MY PROFICIENCY TO A HOBBY LEVEL.
EVEN WITH SEISOU ACADEMY... I DIDN'T THINK THAT THE COMMON SCHOOL WAS GOOD ENOUGH IS ALL.
AND SOMEDAY... I'LL SUPPORT THE YUNOKI ENTERPRISE...?
HEH

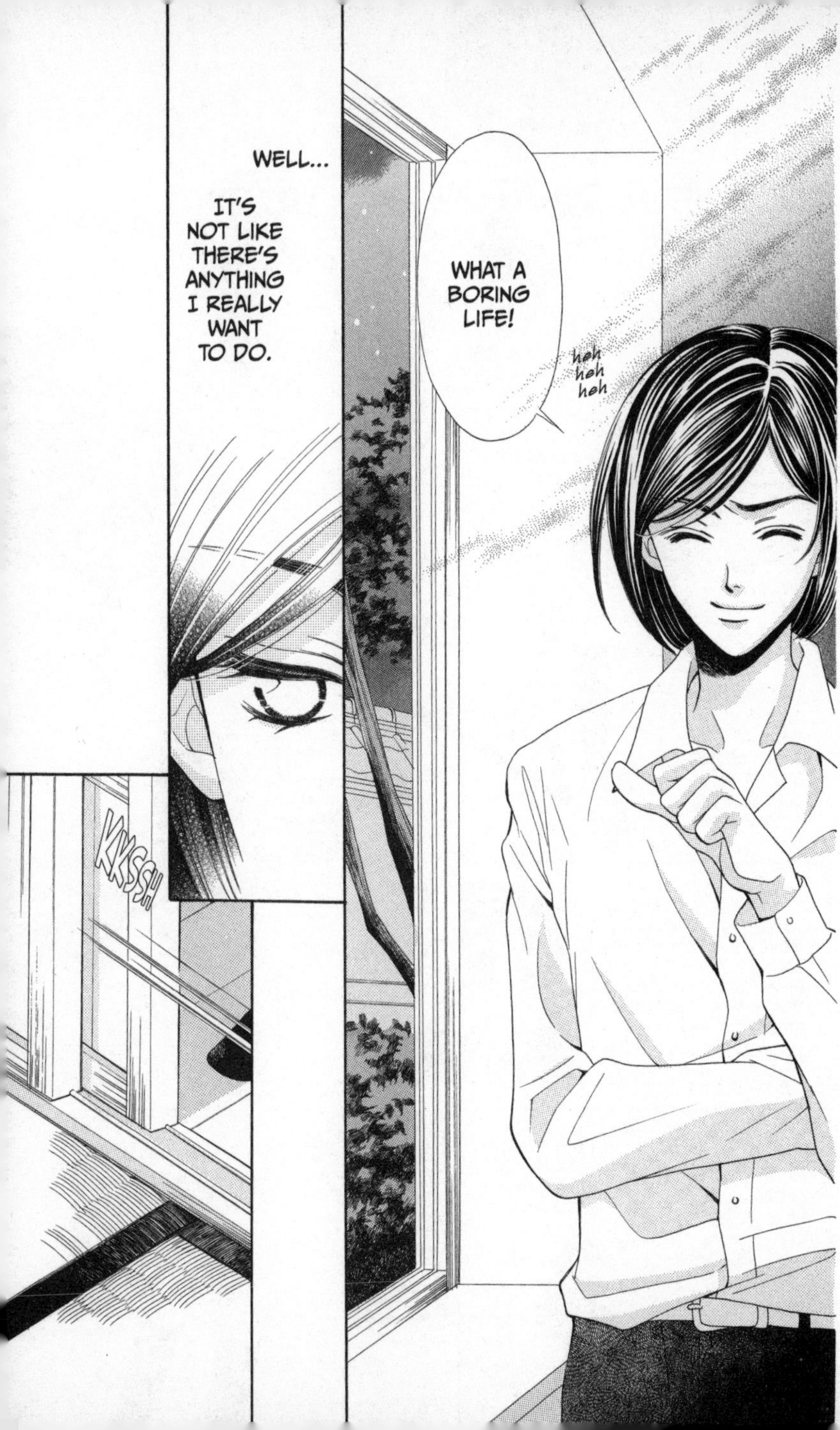
WHAT A BORING LIFE!
heh heh heh
WELL...
IT'S NOT LIKE THERE'S ANYTHING I REALLY WANT TO DO.
KKSSH

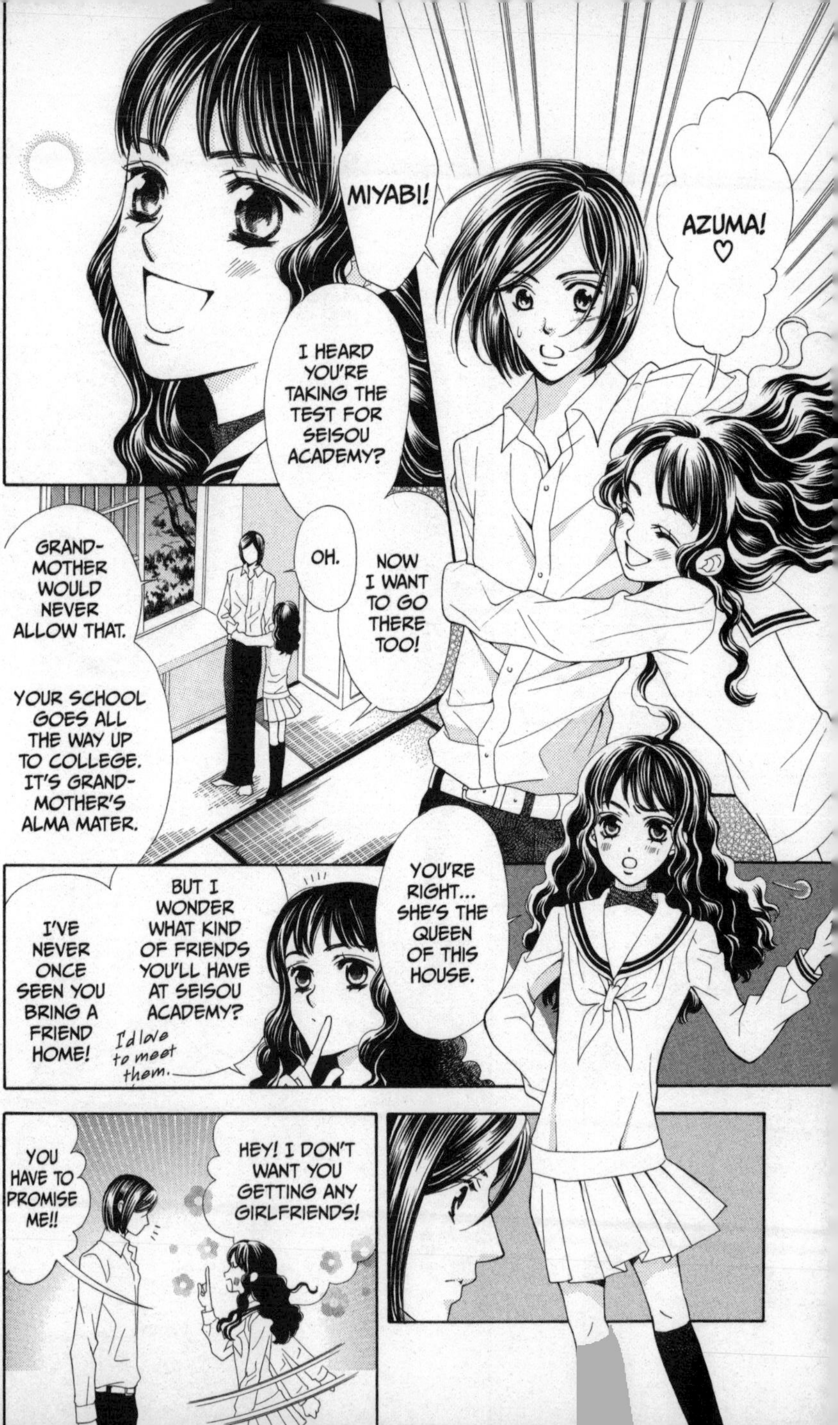
AZUMA! ♡
MIYABI!
I HEARD YOU'RE TAKING THE TEST FOR SEISOU ACADEMY?
NOW I WANT TO GO THERE TOO!
OH.
GRAND-MOTHER WOULD NEVER ALLOW THAT.
YOUR SCHOOL GOES ALL THE WAY UP TO COLLEGE. IT'S GRAND-MOTHER'S ALMA MATER.
YOU'RE RIGHT... SHE'S THE QUEEN OF THIS HOUSE.
BUT I WONDER WHAT KIND OF FRIENDS YOU'LL HAVE AT SEISOU ACADEMY?
I'd love to meet them.
I'VE NEVER ONCE SEEN YOU BRING A FRIEND HOME!
HEY! I DON'T WANT YOU GETTING ANY GIRLFRIENDS!
YOU HAVE TO PROMISE ME!!

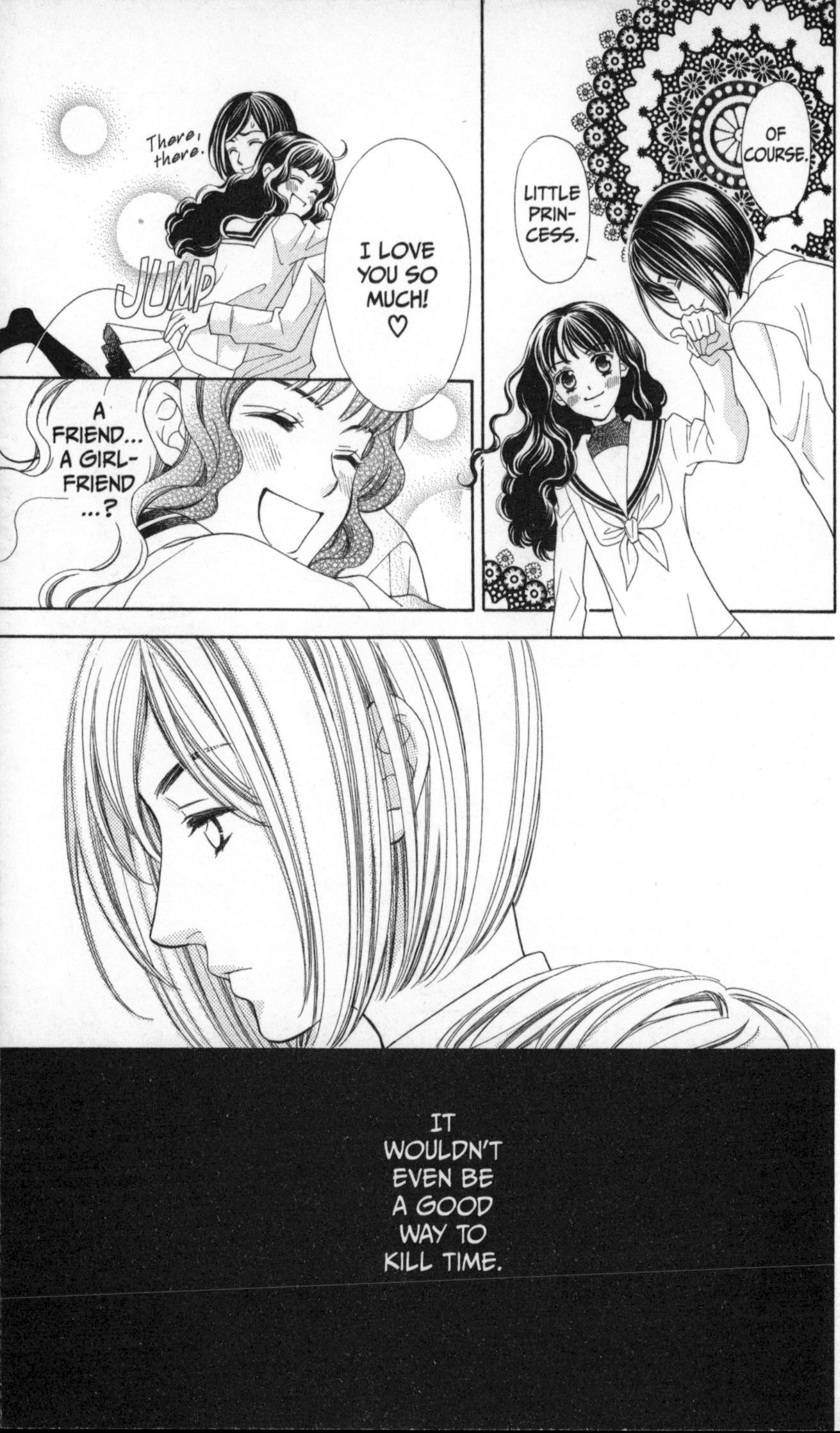
OF COURSE.
LITTLE PRINCESS.
I LOVE YOU SO MUCH! ♡
There, there.
JUMP
A FRIEND... A GIRLFRIEND ...?
IT WOULDN'T EVEN BE A GOOD WAY TO KILL TIME.

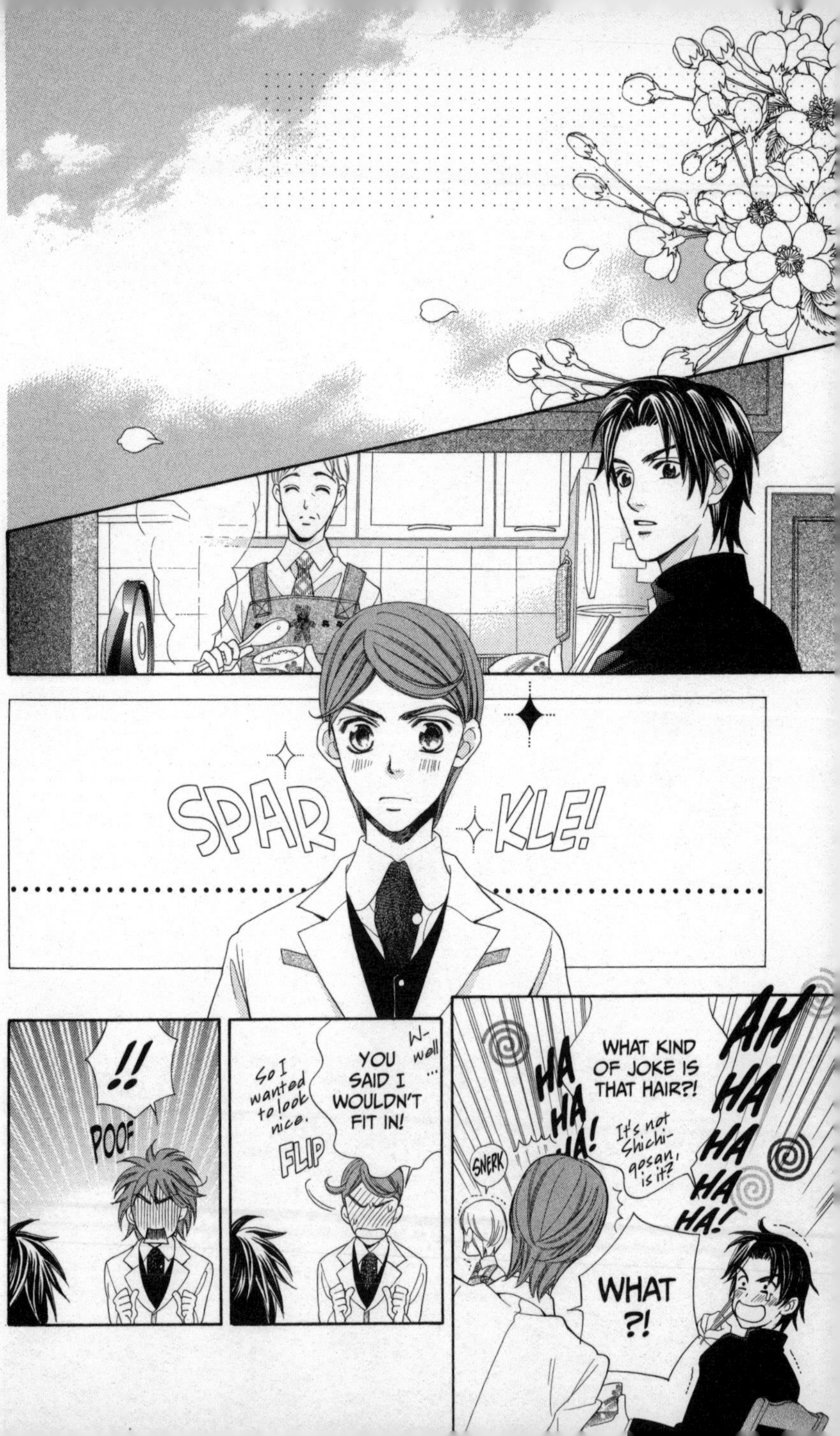
SPAR
KLE!
AH HA HA HA HA HA!
HA HA HA!
WHAT KIND OF JOKE IS THAT HAIR?!
It's not Shichi-gosan, is it?
SNERK
WHAT?!
W-well...
YOU SAID I WOULDN'T FIT IN!
So I wanted to look nice.
FLIP
!!
POOF

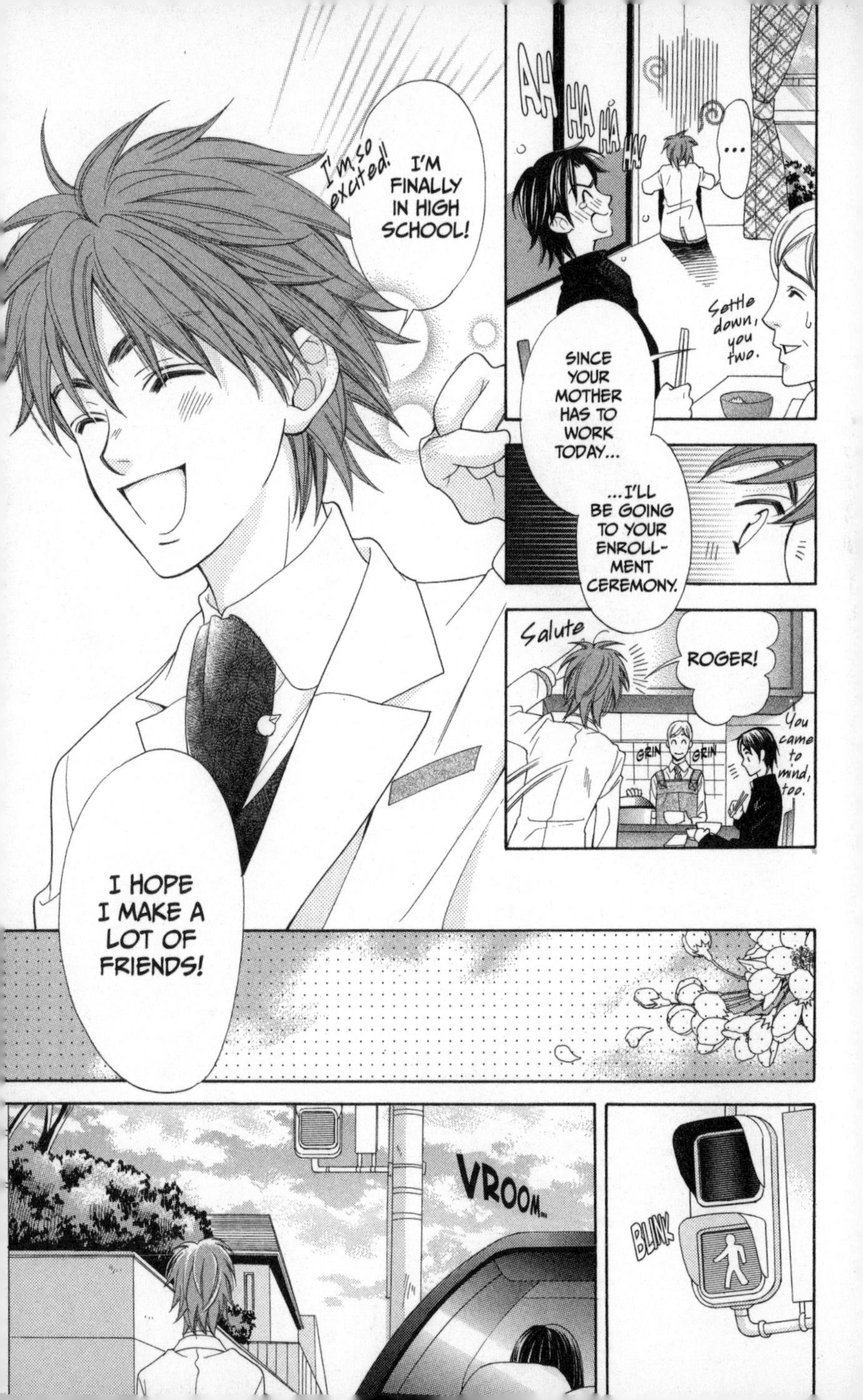
AH HA HA HA
...
Settle down, you two.
SINCE YOUR MOTHER HAS TO WORK TODAY...
...I'LL BE GOING TO YOUR ENROLL-MENT CEREMONY.
Salute
ROGER!
GRIN GRIN
You came to mind, too.
I'm so excited!
I'M FINALLY IN HIGH SCHOOL!
I HOPE I MAKE A LOT OF FRIENDS!
BLINK
VROOM...
...

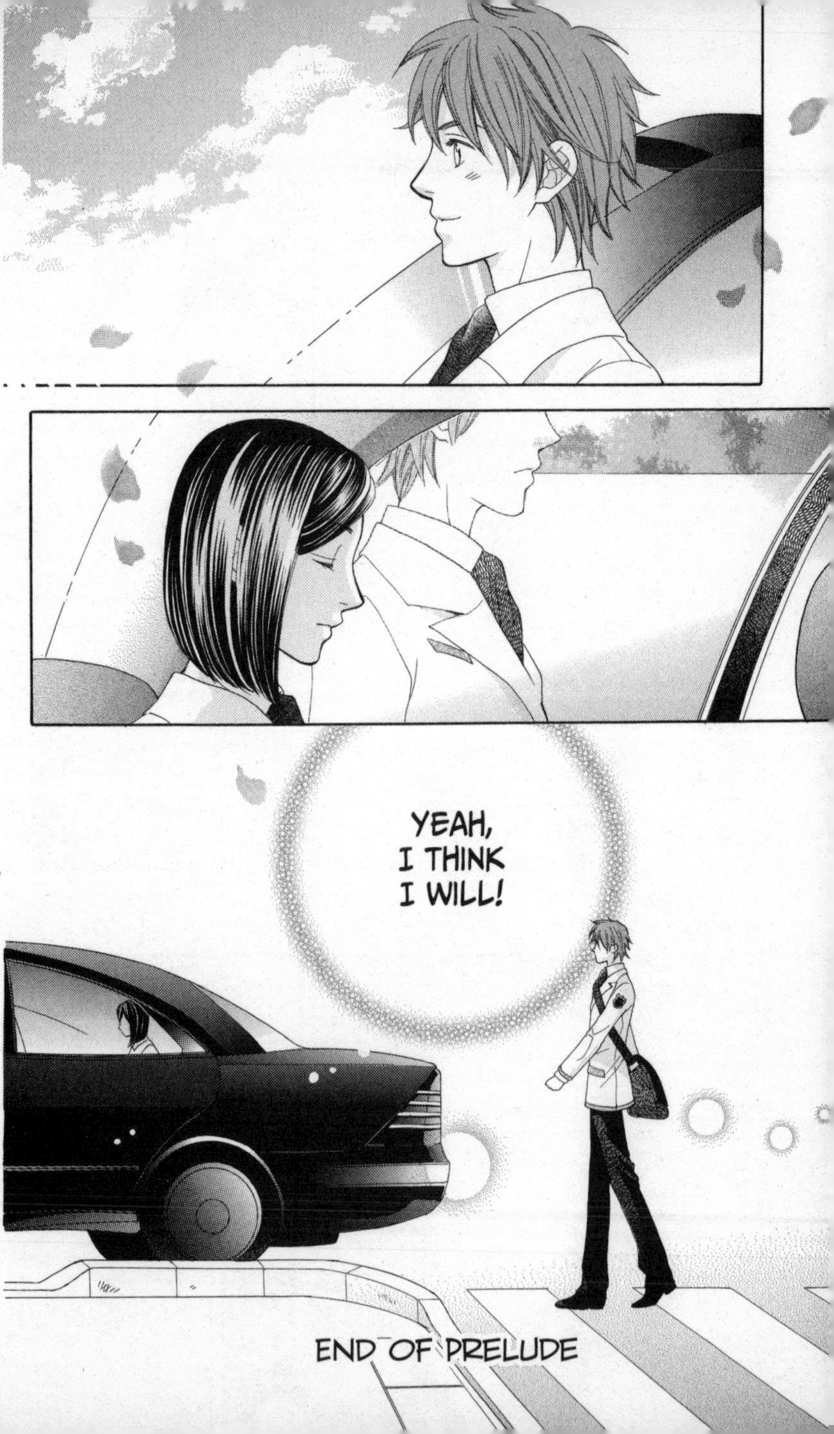
YEAH, I THINK I WILL!
END OF PRELUDE

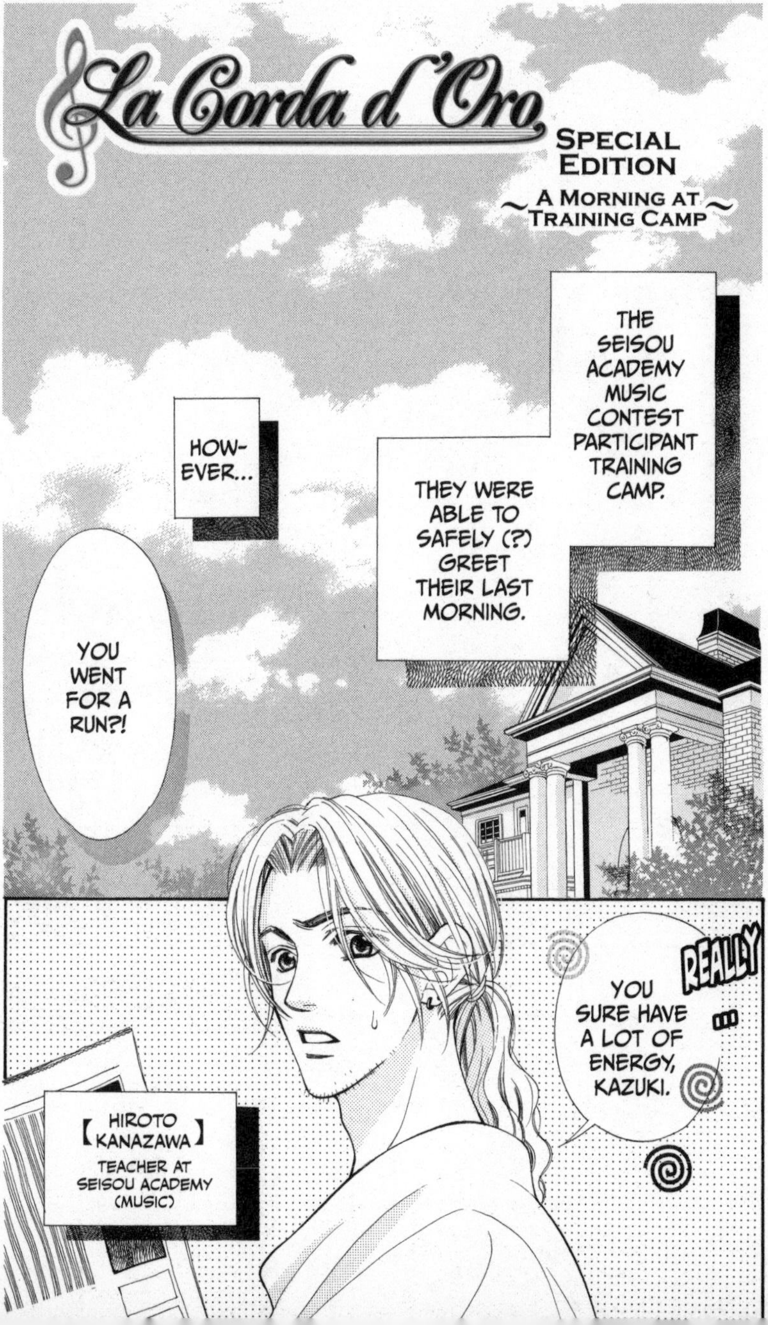
La Corda d'Oro
SPECIAL EDITION
~A MORNING AT TRAINING CAMP~
THE SEISOU ACADEMY MUSIC CONTEST PARTICIPANT TRAINING CAMP.
THEY WERE ABLE TO SAFELY (?) GREET THEIR LAST MORNING.
HOW-EVER...
YOU WENT FOR A RUN?!
REALLY
YOU SURE HAVE A LOT OF ENERGY, KAZUKI.
【HIROTO KANAZAWA】 TEACHER AT SEISOU ACADEMY (MUSIC)

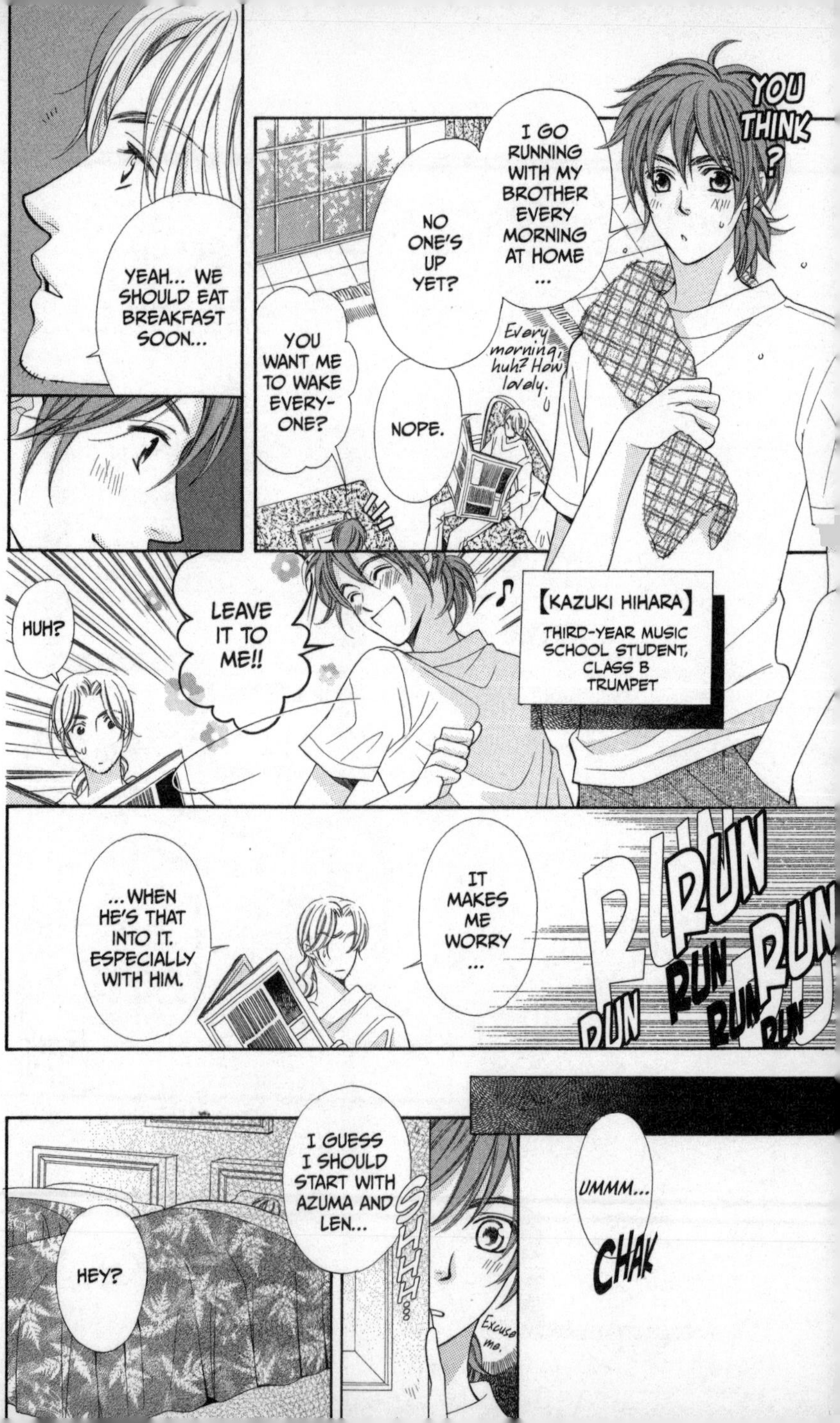
YOU THINK?
I GO RUNNING WITH MY BROTHER EVERY MORNING AT HOME...
NO ONE'S UP YET?
Every morning, huh? How lovely.
YOU WANT ME TO WAKE EVERY-ONE?
NOPE.
YEAH... WE SHOULD EAT BREAKFAST SOON...
【KAZUKI HIHARA】
THIRD-YEAR MUSIC SCHOOL STUDENT, CLASS B
TRUMPET
LEAVE IT TO ME!!
HUH?
RUN RUN RUN RUN RUN RUN RUN RUN
IT MAKES ME WORRY...
...WHEN HE'S THAT INTO IT. ESPECIALLY WITH HIM.
UMMM...
CHAK
I GUESS I SHOULD START WITH AZUMA AND LEN...
SHHH...
Excuse me.
HEY?

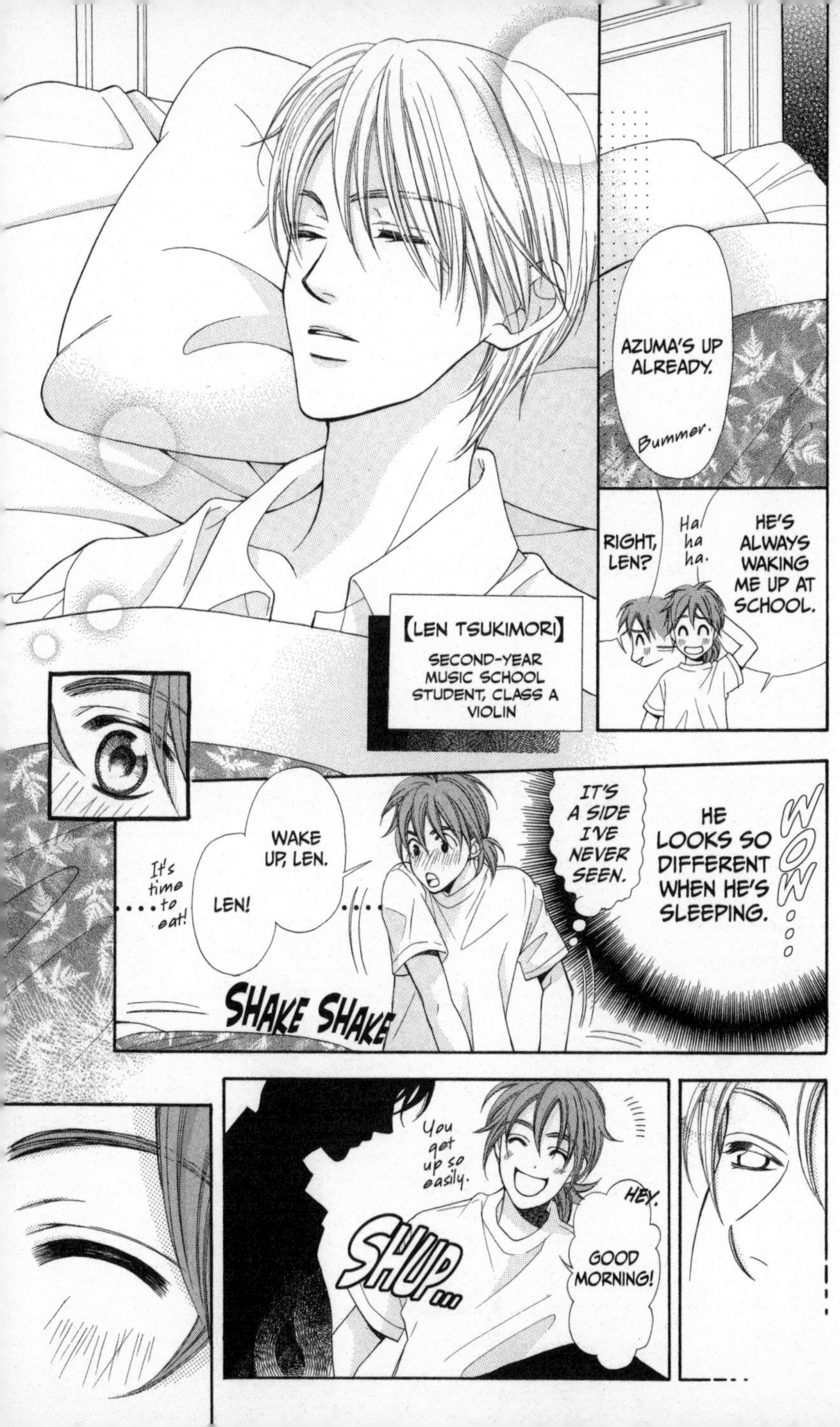
AZUMA'S UP ALREADY.
Bummer.
HE'S ALWAYS WAKING ME UP AT SCHOOL.
Ha ha ha.
RIGHT, LEN?
【LEN TSUKIMORI】
SECOND-YEAR MUSIC SCHOOL STUDENT, CLASS A VIOLIN
WOW...
HE LOOKS SO DIFFERENT WHEN HE'S SLEEPING.
IT'S A SIDE I'VE NEVER SEEN.
WAKE UP, LEN.
LEN!
It's time to eat!
SHAKE SHAKE
GOOD MORNING!
HEY.
You get up so easily.
SHUP...

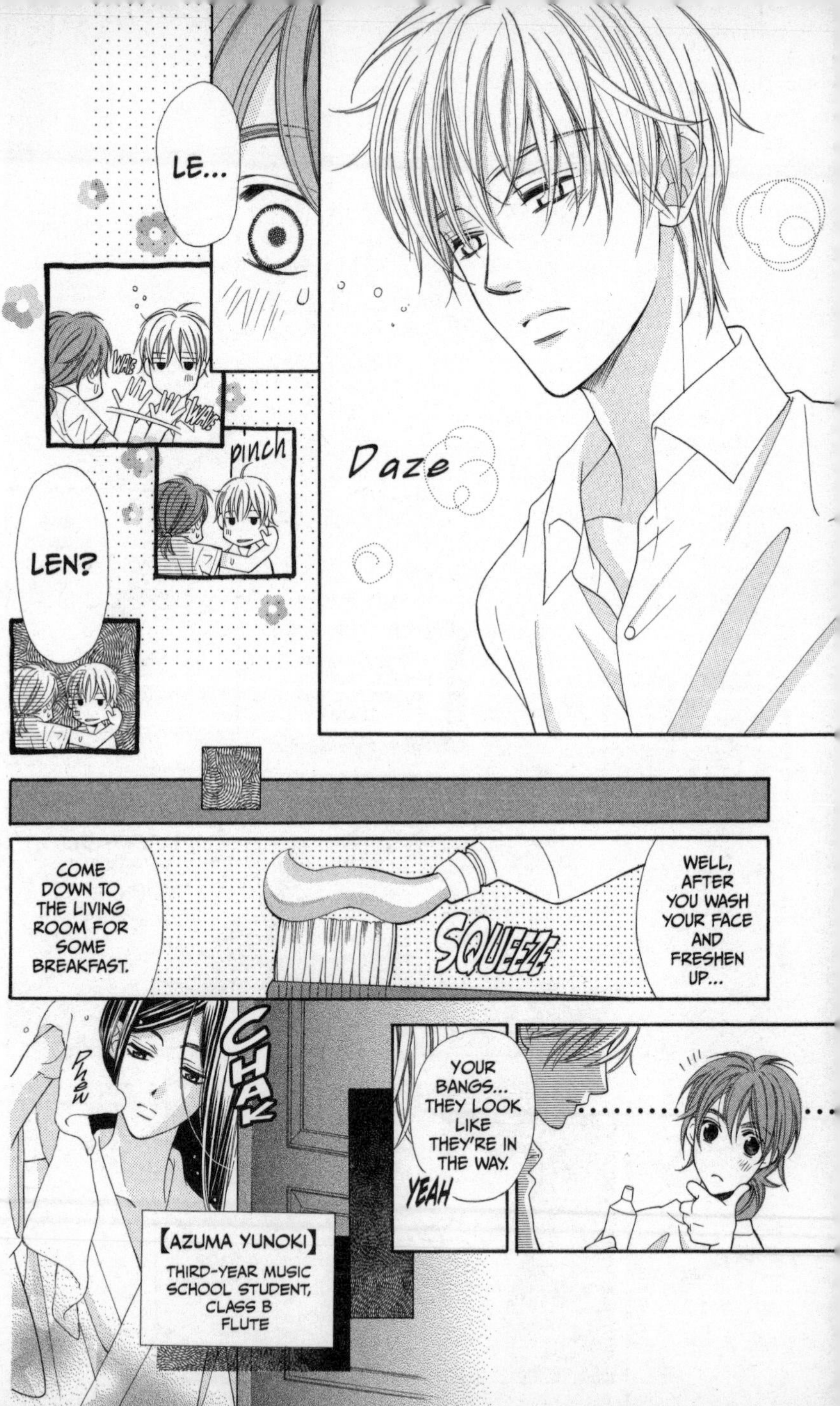
Daze
LE...
WAE
WAE
pinch
LEN?
WELL, AFTER YOU WASH YOUR FACE AND FRESHEN UP...
SQUEEZE
COME DOWN TO THE LIVING ROOM FOR SOME BREAKFAST.
YOUR BANGS... THEY LOOK LIKE THEY'RE IN THE WAY.
YEAH
CHAK
Phew
【AZUMA YUNOKI】
THIRD-YEAR MUSIC SCHOOL STUDENT, CLASS B
FLUTE

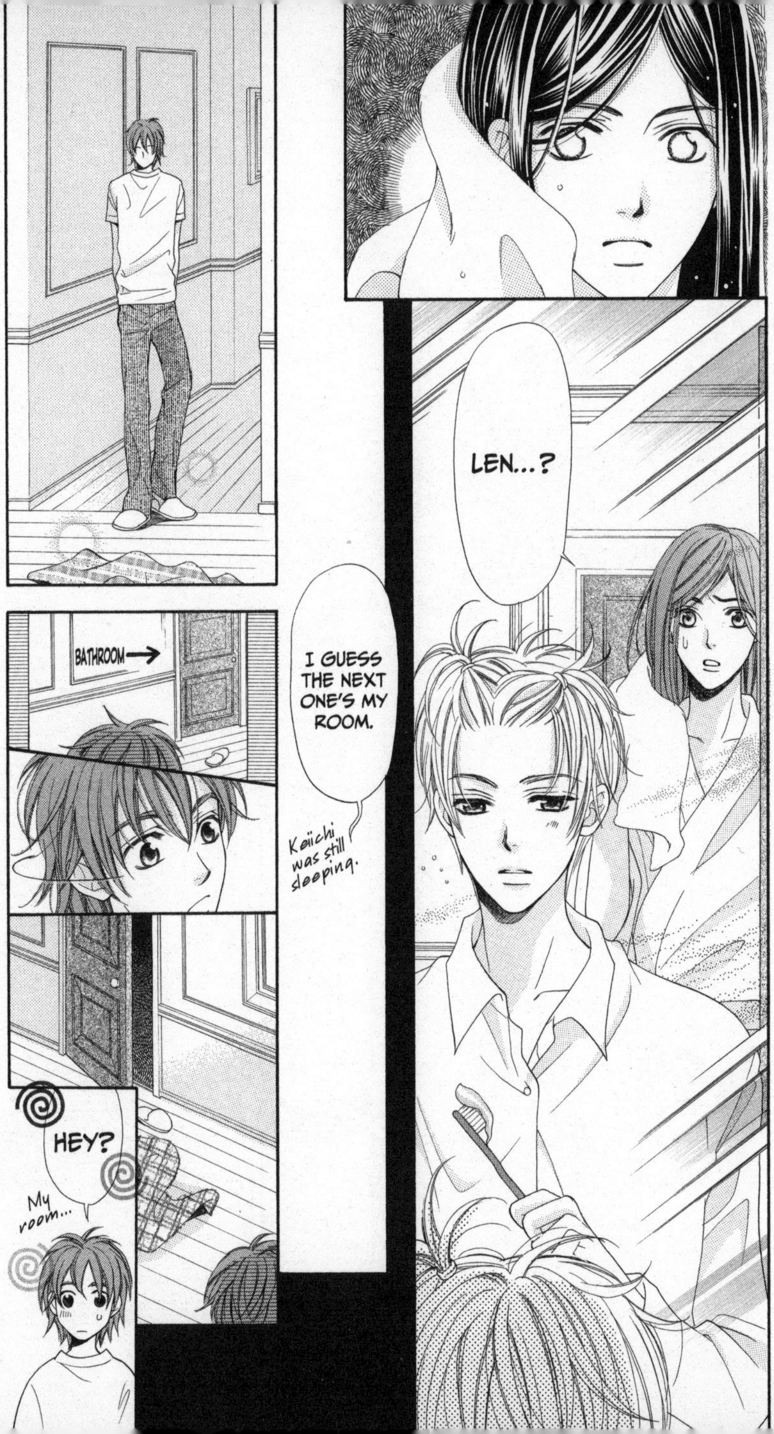
LEN...?
BATHROOM→
I GUESS THE NEXT ONE'S MY ROOM.
Keiichi was still sleeping.
HEY?
My room...

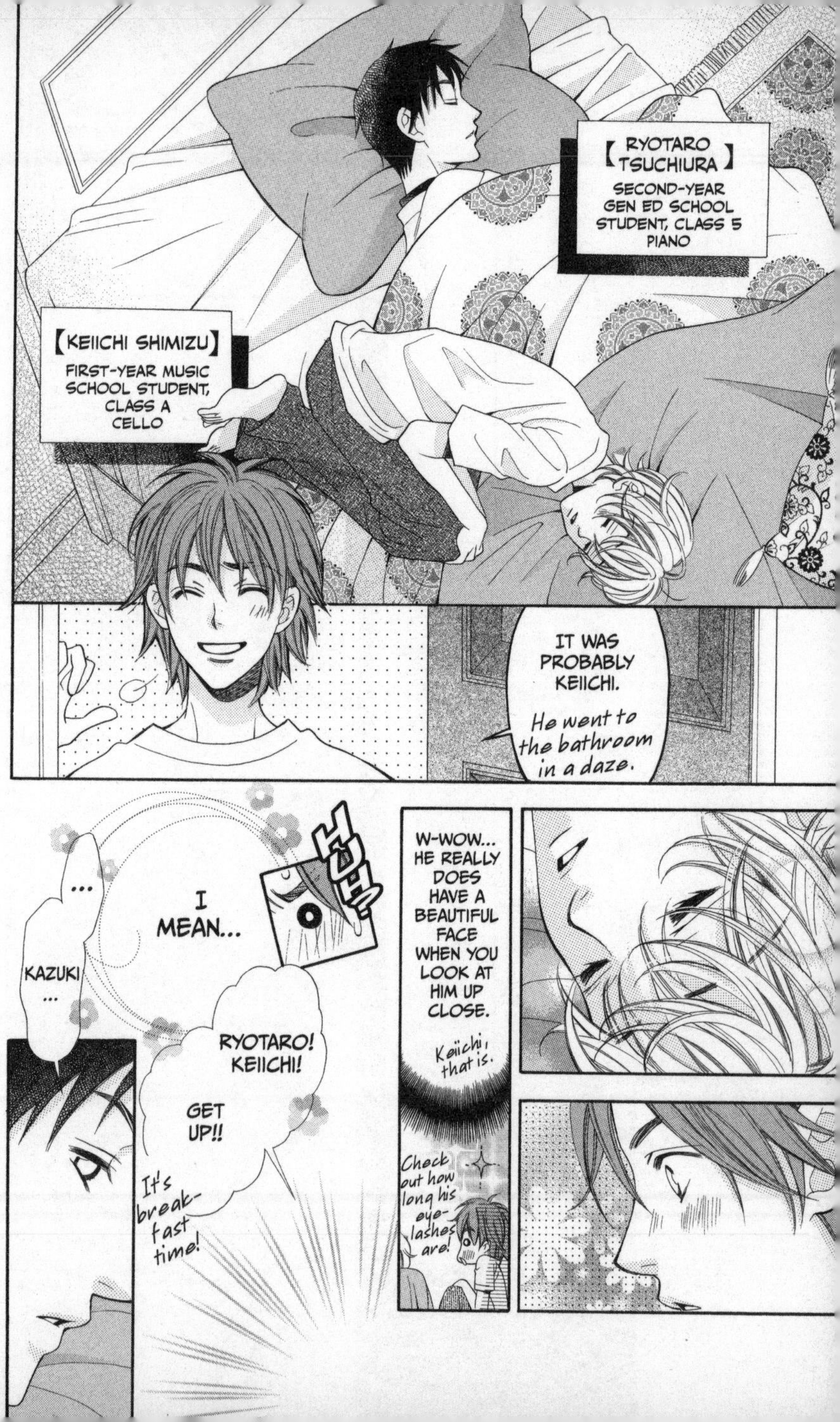
【RYOTARO TSUCHIURA】
SECOND-YEAR GEN ED SCHOOL STUDENT, CLASS 5
PIANO
【KEIICHI SHIMIZU】
FIRST-YEAR MUSIC SCHOOL STUDENT, CLASS A
CELLO
IT WAS PROBABLY KEIICHI.
He went to the bathroom in a daze.
W-WOW... HE REALLY DOES HAVE A BEAUTIFUL FACE WHEN YOU LOOK AT HIM UP CLOSE.
Keiichi, that is.
Check out how long his eye-lashes are!
I MEAN...
...
KAZUKI ...
RYOTARO! KEIICHI!
GET UP!!
It's break-fast time!

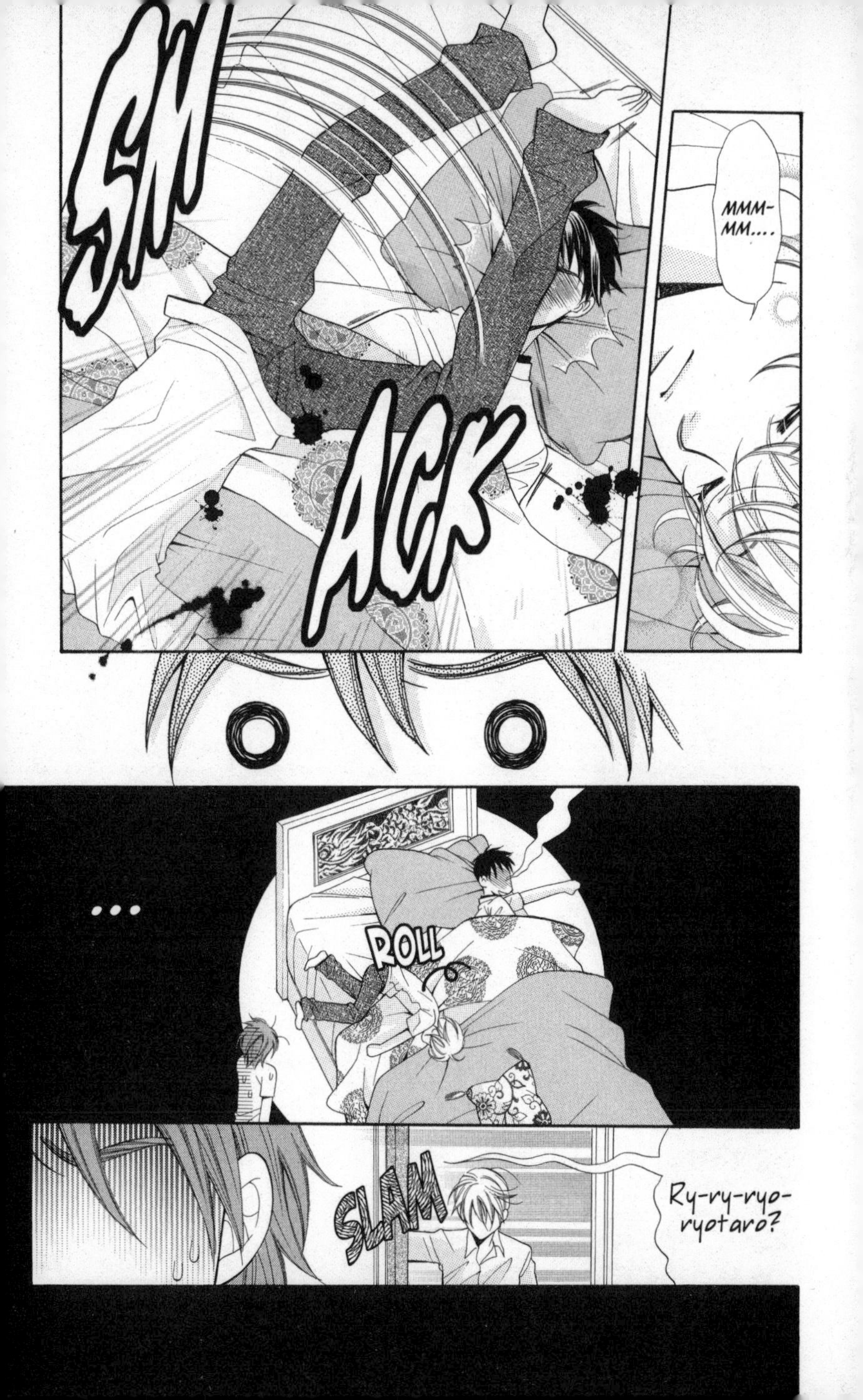
MMM-MM....
SH
ACK
...
ROLL
Ry-ry-ryo-ryotaro?
SLAM

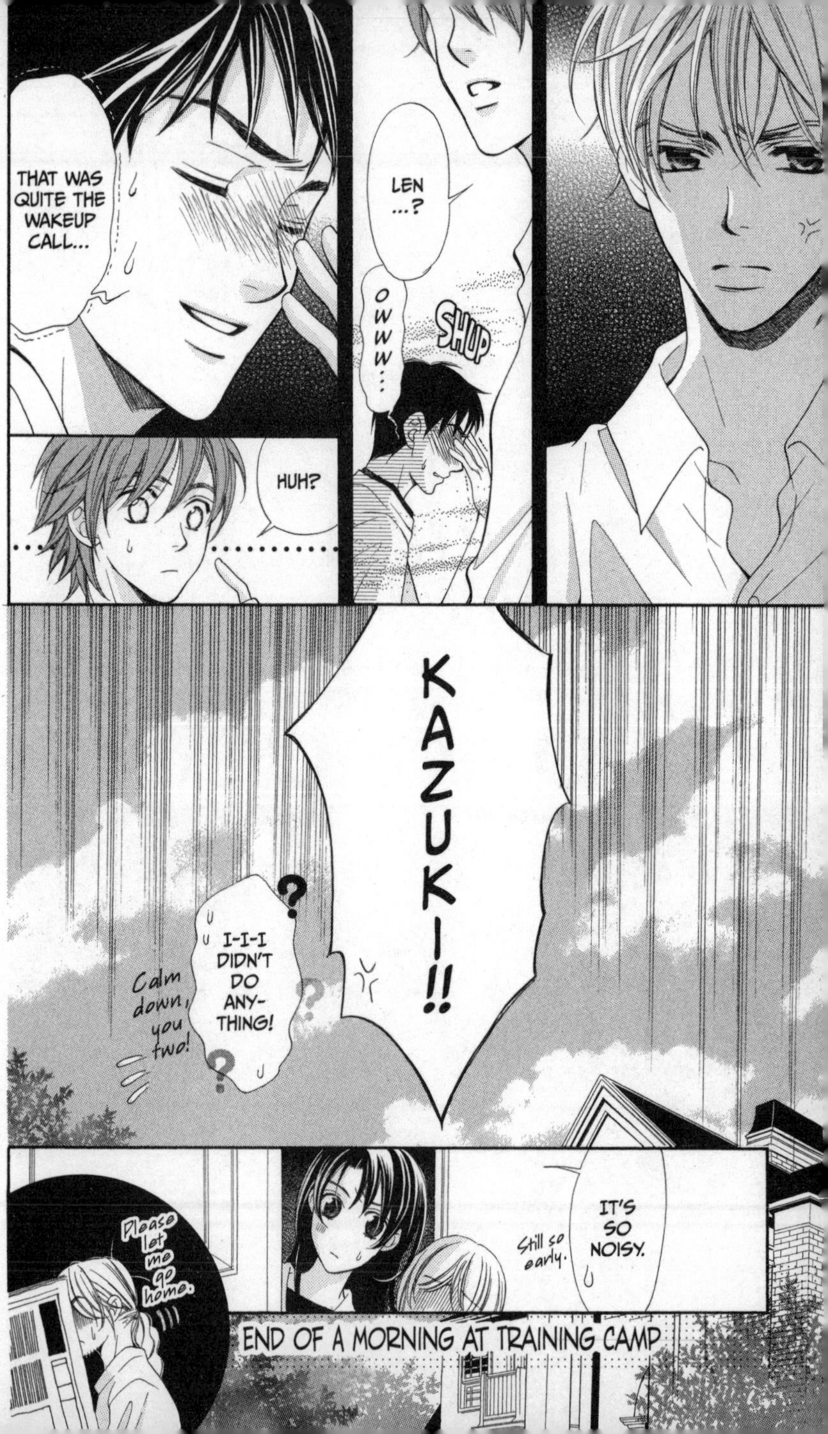
LEN ...?
OWWW...
SHUP
THAT WAS QUITE THE WAKEUP CALL...
HUH?
KAZUKI!!
I-I-I DIDN'T DO ANYTHING!
Calm down, you two!
IT'S SO NOISY.
Still so early.
Please let me go home.
END OF A MORNING AT TRAINING CAMP

TOP SECRET

BACKSTAGE WITH THE JOURNALISM CLUB #2

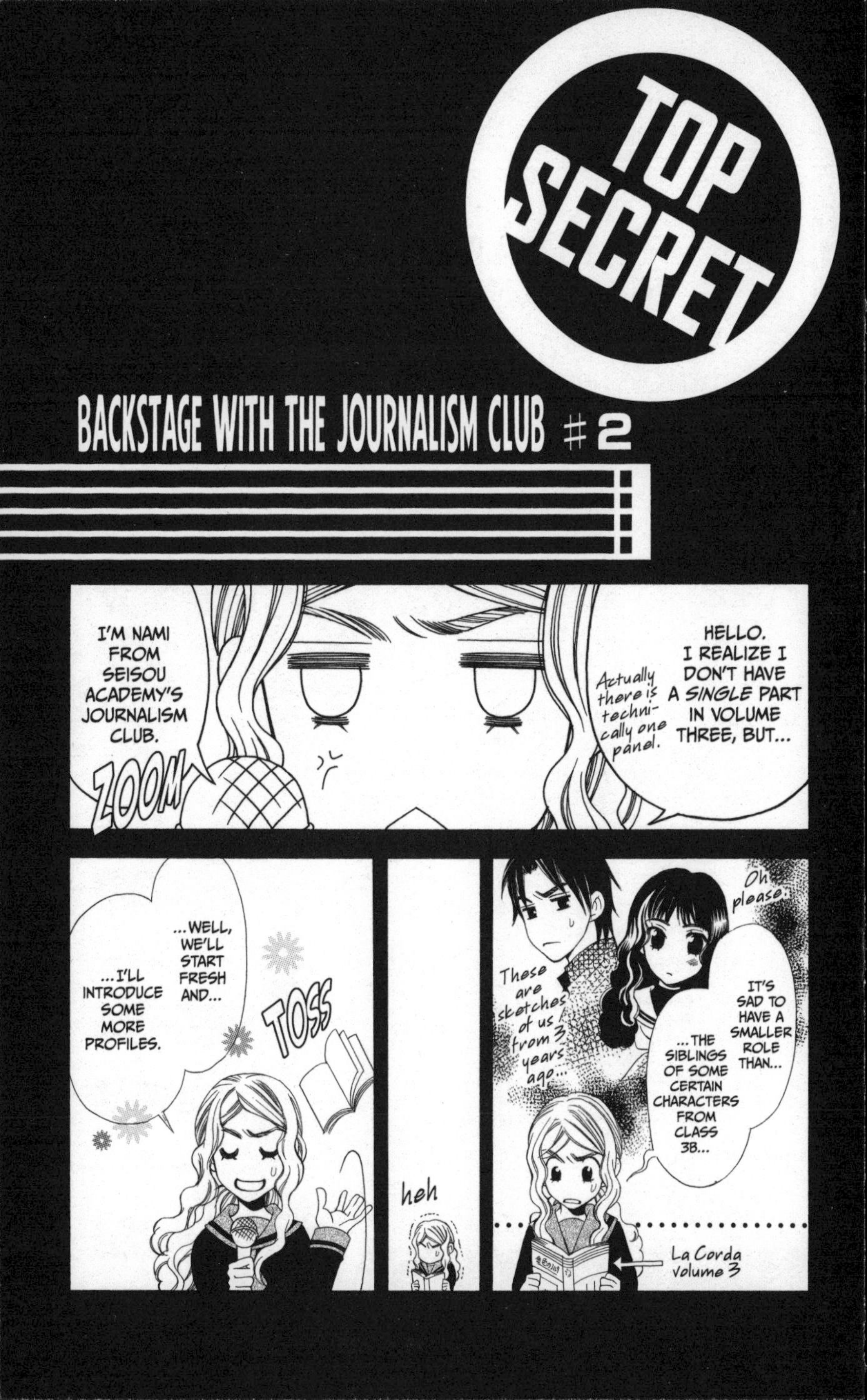
HELLO. I REALIZE I DON'T HAVE A *SINGLE* PART IN VOLUME THREE, BUT...
Actually there is techni-cally one panel.
I'M NAMI FROM SEISOU ACADEMY'S JOURNALISM CLUB.
ZOOM
Oh please.
IT'S SAD TO HAVE A SMALLER ROLE THAN...
...THE SIBLINGS OF SOME CERTAIN CHARACTERS FROM CLASS 3B...
These are sketches of us from 3 years ago...
La Corda volume 3
heh
...WELL, WE'LL START FRESH AND...
...I'LL INTRODUCE SOME MORE PROFILES.
TOSS

土浦　梁太郎

RYOTARO TSUCHIURA

GEN ED SCHOOL, SECOND-YEAR CLASS 5

BIRTHDAY:	JULY 25TH
ZODIAC SIGN:	LEO
BLOOD TYPE:	0
HEIGHT:	5'9"
FAMILY:	FATHER, MOTHER, OLDER SISTER, YOUNGER BROTHER

■ ON THE SOCCER TEAM (MIDFIELDER)

ON BOTH THE SOCCER TEAM AND TRACK TEAM IN MIDDLE SCHOOL

GOOD AT HARD SCIENCES

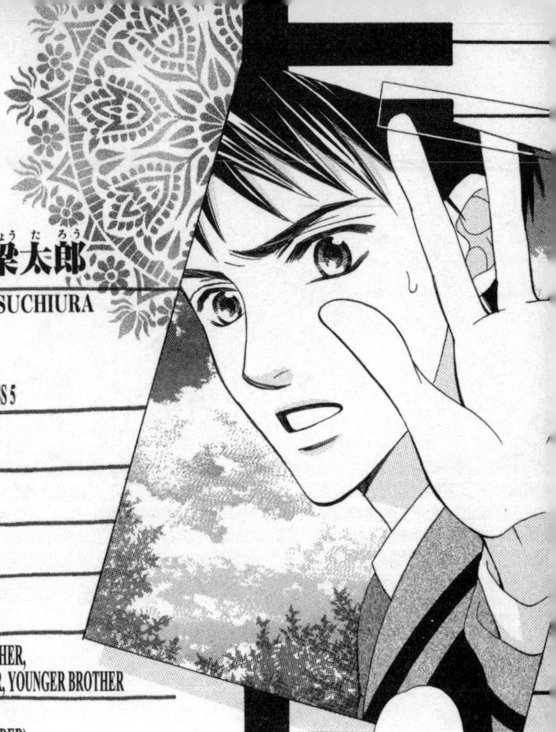

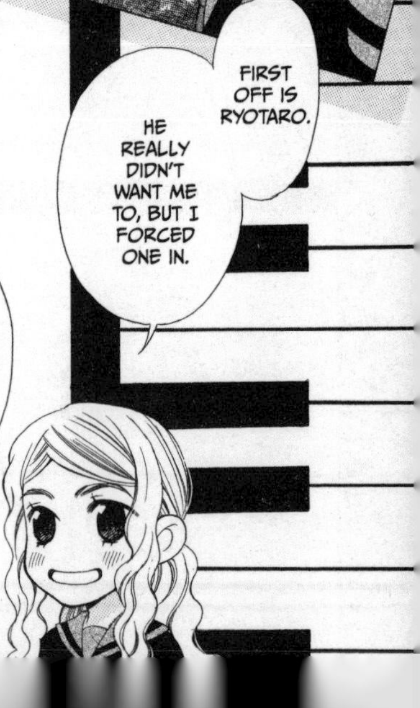
FIRST OFF IS RYOTARO.
HE REALLY DIDN'T WANT ME TO, BUT I FORCED ONE IN.
WHO KNEW HE PLAYED THE PIANO? THAT WAS A SHOCKER.
A GREAT ATHLETE AND HE'S THE KIND TYPE. ONE WOULD THINK HE DOES WELL WITH THE LADIES, BUT...
...A LOT OF THE GIRLS SAY HE'S HARD TO APPROACH. HE'S EARNED THE TRUST OF MANY OF THE GUYS AND HAS LOTS OF FRIENDS.
Apparently they think it's a bad idea to get him mad.

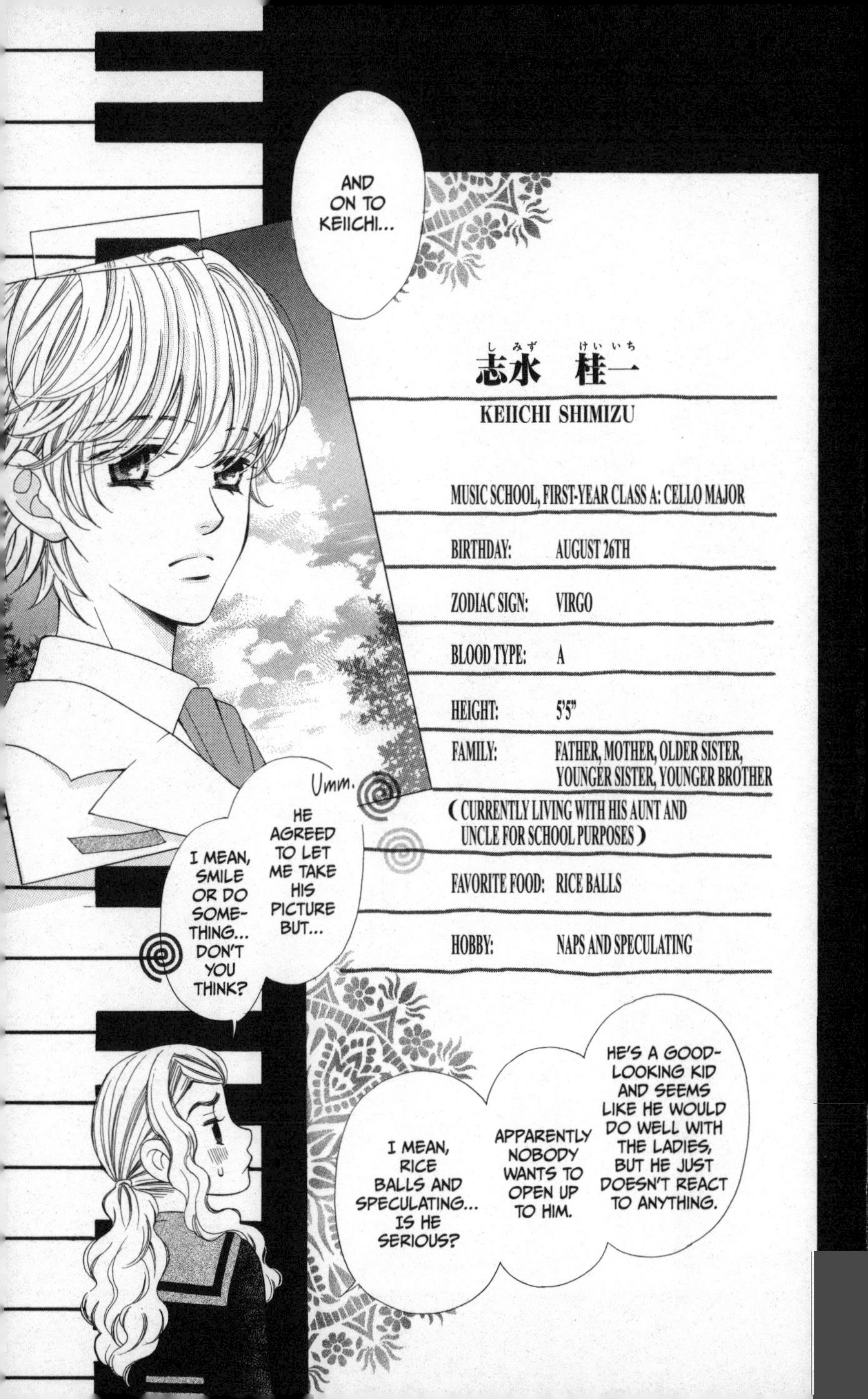
AND ON TO KEIICHI...
しみず　けいいち
志水　桂一
KEIICHI SHIMIZU
MUSIC SCHOOL, FIRST-YEAR CLASS A: CELLO MAJOR
BIRTHDAY: AUGUST 26TH
ZODIAC SIGN: VIRGO
BLOOD TYPE: A
HEIGHT: 5'5"
FAMILY: FATHER, MOTHER, OLDER SISTER, YOUNGER SISTER, YOUNGER BROTHER
(CURRENTLY LIVING WITH HIS AUNT AND UNCLE FOR SCHOOL PURPOSES)
FAVORITE FOOD: RICE BALLS
HOBBY: NAPS AND SPECULATING
Umm.
HE AGREED TO LET ME TAKE HIS PICTURE BUT...
I MEAN, SMILE OR DO SOME-THING... DON'T YOU THINK?
HE'S A GOOD-LOOKING KID AND SEEMS LIKE HE WOULD DO WELL WITH THE LADIES, BUT HE JUST DOESN'T REACT TO ANYTHING.
APPARENTLY NOBODY WANTS TO OPEN UP TO HIM.
I MEAN, RICE BALLS AND SPECULATING... IS HE SERIOUS?

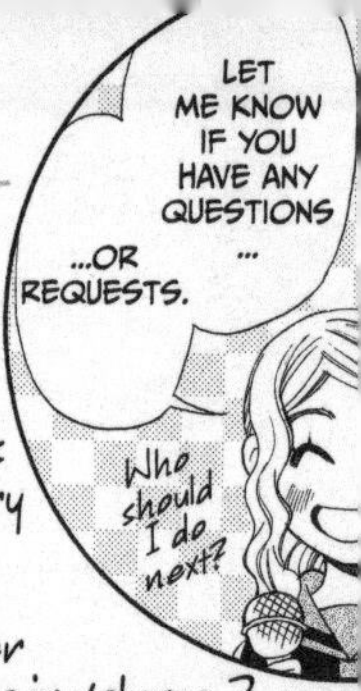
LET ME KNOW IF YOU HAVE ANY QUESTIONS ...
...OR REQUESTS.
Who should I do next?

Hello again. It's Yuki. Thank you so much for all your letters with comments and words of encouragement. I always read all of them. I'm sorry I'm so slow to respond.

I felt like there are fewer character biases starting in volume 2, but what do you think? I want to create something that you can enjoy reading, so I appreciate any feedback. Thank you again for reading through the volume.

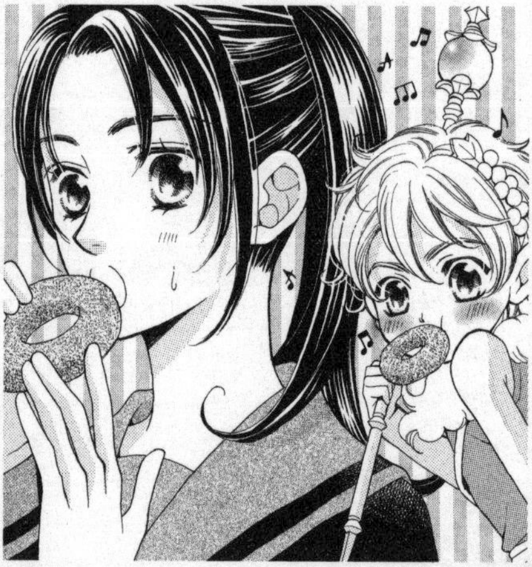

Thank you to all my readers, my editors, Koei, my family, friends, and other people who are always there when I need them.

If there's anything

Yuki Kure c/o Shojo Beat
VIZ Media
P.O. Box 77010
San Francisco, CA 94107

SPECIAL THANKS

Asuka Izumi
Ayu Kashima
Emiko Nakano
Midori Shiino
Natsumi Sato
Aki Shimaya
Kugaru

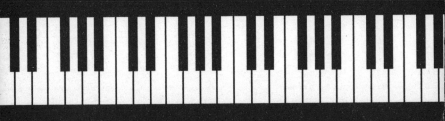

La Corda d'Oro End Notes

You can appreciate music just by listening to it, but knowing the story behind a piece can help enhance your enjoyment. In that spirit, here is background information about some of the topics mentioned in *La Corda d'Oro*. Enjoy!

Page 12, panel 1: Boccherini
Luigi Rodolfo Boccherini (1743-1805) was an Italian composer and cellist who at one time enjoyed the patronage of such worthies as King Charles III of Spain, King Friedrich Wilhelm II of Prussia, and French consul Lucien Bonapart. Boccherini was a cello virtuoso, and quite possibly the most accomplished cellist in history, but died in poverty. His *Cello Concerto in B Flat Major* is one of his most well-known works.

Page 16, panel 4: Wagner
Josef Franz Wagner (1856-1908) was an Austrian composer who specialized in marches, and is sometimes called "The Austrian March King." *Unter dem Doppleadler* (*Under the Double Eagle*) is his best-known march, and is now the official regimental march of the 1st Austrian Artillery Regiment Number 2. The march is named for the double eagles in the arms of the Austro-Hungarian Empire and was composed in 1902.

Page 20, panel 7: A fan
Often used as a prop by the *tsukkomi* (straight man in a Japanese comedy duo) against the *boke* (fool). The tsukkomi will interrupt the boke during a particularly foolish moment by bopping him on the head with a giant folded fan.

Page 24, panel 4: Reger
Johann Baptist Joseph Maxmillian Reger (1873-1916) was a German composer and teacher. He considered himself a continuation of the tradition of Ludwig von Beethoven and Johannes Brahms. *Romance in G Minor* is part of the *Second Suite in G Minor* (opus 92), composed in 1905.

Page 30, panel 1: Grieg
Edvard Hagerup Grieg (1843-1907) was a Norwegian composer and pianist who took his inspiration from Norwegian folk music. His most famous pieces include his incidental music (the theatrical version of a movie soundtrack) for Henrik Ibsen's play *Peer Gynt*, the creation of which was requested by Ibsen himself. Of the incidental music, *Morning Mood* and *In the Hall of the Mountain King* are the most well known. *Morning Mood* has been used for morning establishing shots in Warner Bros. cartoons and is also associated with Nordic scenes, although it was meant to evoke sunrise in the Sahara.

ff

Page 56, panel 7: Sarasate
Pablo Martín Melitón de Sarasate y Navascuéz (1844-1908) was a Spanish composer and violinist who performed throughout the world, and was the most famous violin virtuosi of his time. His compositions were designed to highlight his spectacular technique, and brought the spirit of Spanish dance to the violin. *Playera y Zapateado* was composed in 1880, and is actually two companion pieces. *Playera* is a grim, moody piece, while *Zapateado* (named for the heel-tapping Spanish dances) is an energetic burst that allows the violinist to draw on all the tricks of the virtuoso.

Page 71, author note: Takashi Yanase
Writer of the beloved children's anime, *Anpanman*. The main character is a man whose head is made out of a giant black bean bun. If his head is damaged, his father Jam Ojisan can bake him a new one.

Page 106, panel 3: Kreisler
Fritz Kreisler (1875-1962) was an Austrian violinist and composer, one of the most distinguished of his time, who had his first American tour by the age of 13. After being denied a seat in the Vienna Philharmonic, he tried studying medicine and painting, and even spent time in the army. He eventually moved to America and became a naturalized citizen. He often wrote in the style of other composers, and many of his works were initially attributed to them before Kreisler revealed in 1935 that he had in fact composed the pieces. His *Joy of Love* (*Liebesfreud*) and the counterpoint *Sorrow of Love* (*Liebesleid*) are his most well-known original compositions.

Page 107, panel 3: *Zigeunerweisen*
A short composition by Sarasate, also called *Gypsy Airs, Song of the Tramps*, or *Op. 20 No.1*. It is a violin solo with orchestral accompaniment that lasts between seven and nine minutes, and requires great skill.

Page 107, panel 4: *Carmen Fantasy*
Sarasate's violin fantasy of the opera *Carmen* by Georges Bizet. This piece is a favorite for concerts, and includes excerpts from the different movements of the opera. It was initially composed for a solo violin with orchestral accompaniment, but has been transcribed for the viola and trumpet.

Page 174, panel 4: Shichigosan
Celebrated on November 15, this is a special day for children ages three (san), five (go) and seven (shichi). Children get dressed up in their finest clothes to go to a shrine, and get special candy called *chitose-ame* (thousand-year candy) to promote longevity.

Yuki Kure made her debut in 2000
with the story *Chijo yori Eien ni*
(Forever from the Earth), published
in monthly *LaLa* magazine.
La Corda d' Oro is her first manga
series published. Her hobby is
watching soccer games and
collecting small goodies.

LA CORDA D'ORO
Vol. 3
The Shojo Beat Manga Edition

STORY AND ART BY
YUKI KURE
ORIGINAL CONCEPT BY
RUBY PARTY

English Translation & Adaptation/Mai Ihara
Touch-up Art & Lettering/Gia Cam Luc
Design/Yukiko Whitley
Editor/Pancha Diaz

Managing Editor/Megan Bates
Editorial Director/Elizabeth Kawasaki
VP & Editor in Chief/Yumi Hoashi
Sr. Director of Acquisitions/Rika Inouye
Sr. VP of Marketing/Liza Coppola
Exec. VP of Sales & Marketing/John Easum
Publisher/Hyoe Narita

Printed in Canada

Published by VIZ Media, LLC
P.O. Box 77010
San Francisco, CA 94107

Shojo Beat Manga Edition
10 9 8 7 6 5 4 3 2
First printing, April 2007

store.viz.com

PARENTAL ADVISORY
LA CORDA D'ORO is rated T for Teen and is recommended for ages 13 and up. This volume contains mild violence.

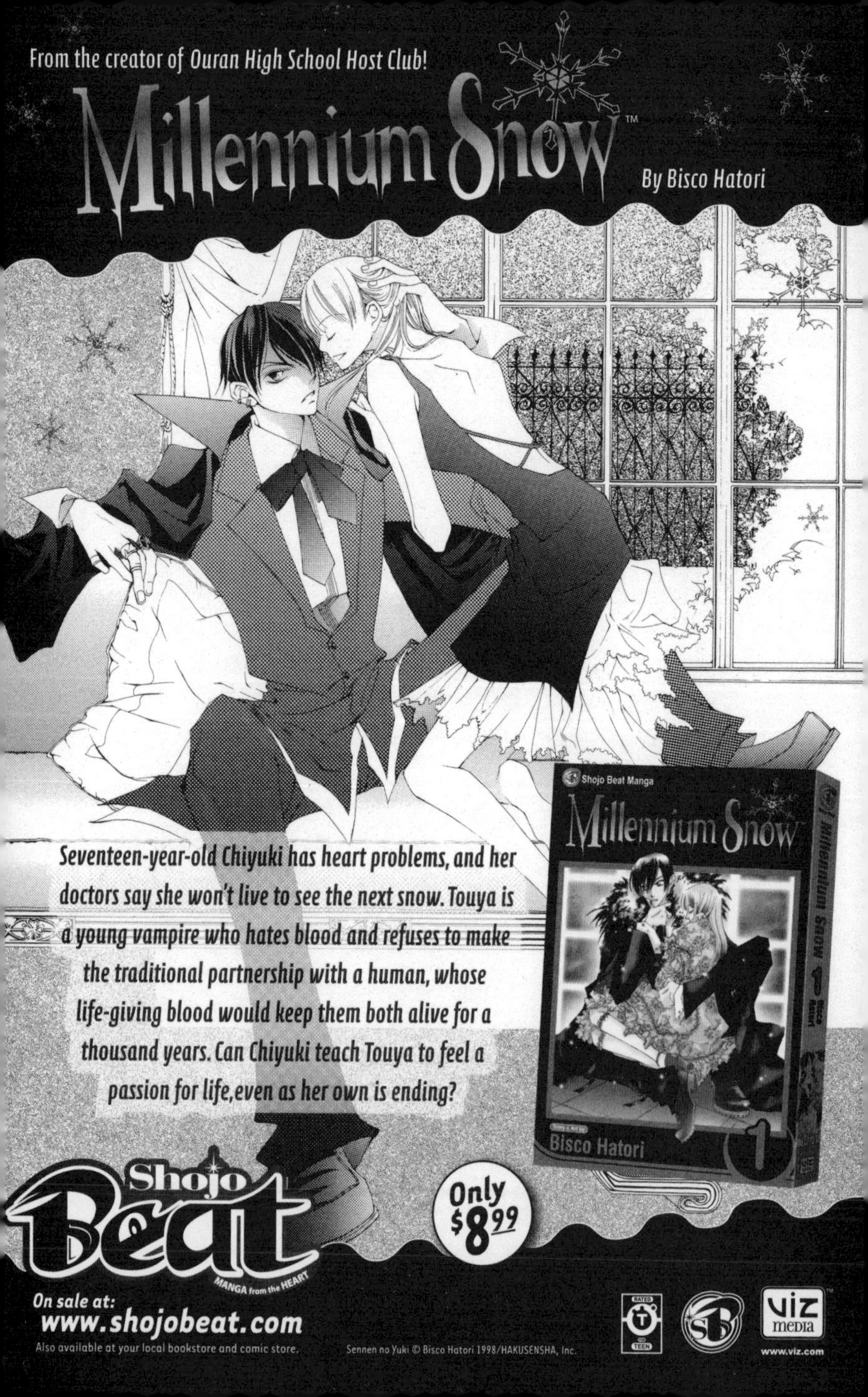

From the creator of Ouran High School Host Club!
Millennium Snow™
By Bisco Hatori
Shojo Beat Manga
Millennium Snow
Bisco Hatori
1
Seventeen-year-old Chiyuki has heart problems, and her doctors say she won't live to see the next snow. Touya is a young vampire who hates blood and refuses to make the traditional partnership with a human, whose life-giving blood would keep them both alive for a thousand years. Can Chiyuki teach Touya to feel a passion for life,even as her own is ending?
Shojo Beat
MANGA from the HEART
Only $8.99
On sale at:
www.shojobeat.com
Also available at your local bookstore and comic store.
Sennen no Yuki © Bisco Hatori 1998/HAKUSENSHA, Inc.
RATED T TEEN
VIZ media
www.viz.com

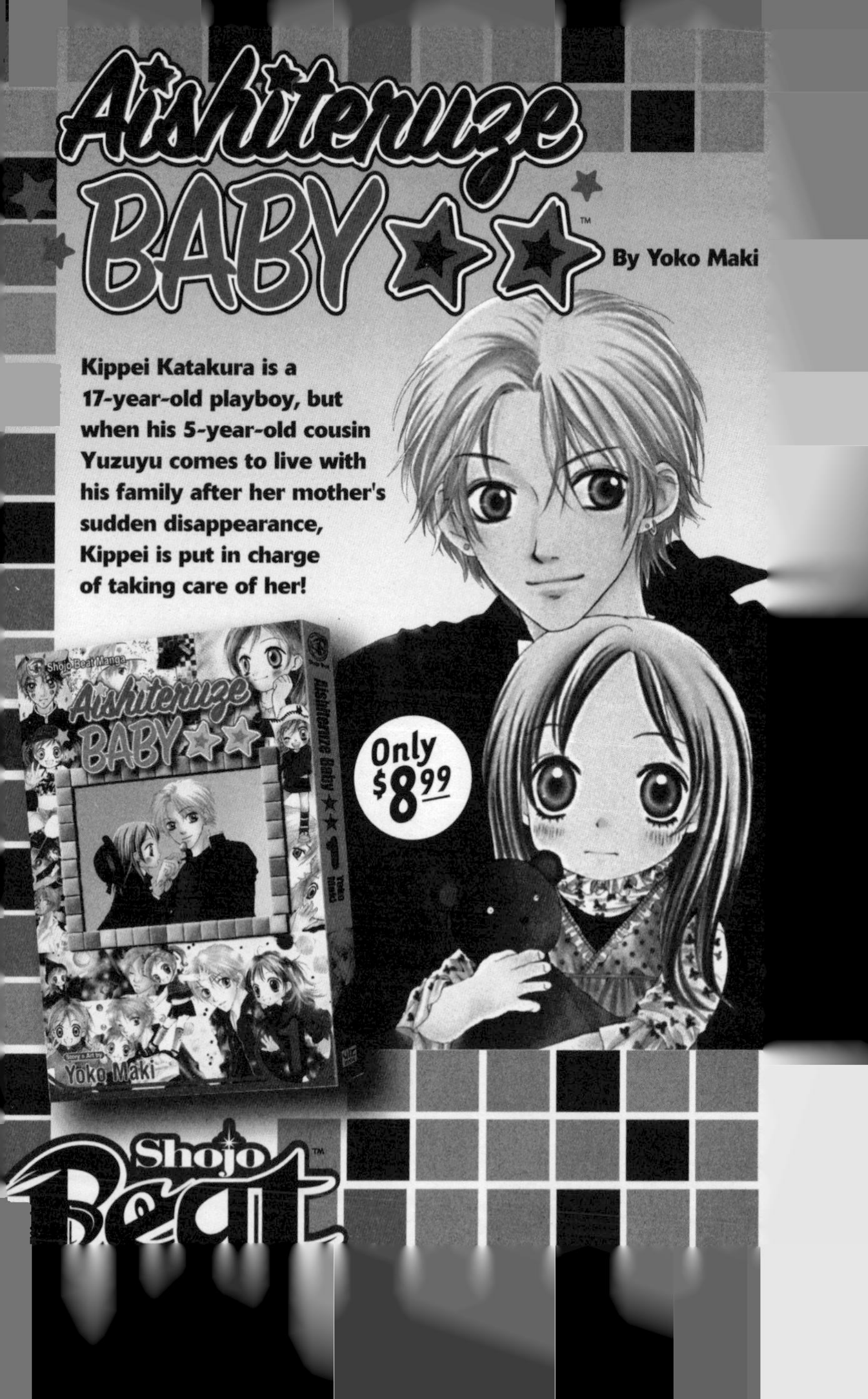

Aishiteruze BABY™
By Yoko Maki
Kippei Katakura is a 17-year-old playboy, but when his 5-year-old cousin Yuzuyu comes to live with his family after her mother's sudden disappearance, Kippei is put in charge of taking care of her!
Only $8.99
Shojo Beat Manga
Aishiteruze BABY
Aishiteruze Baby 1 Yoko Maki
Story & Art by
Yoko Maki
Shojo Beat™

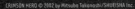

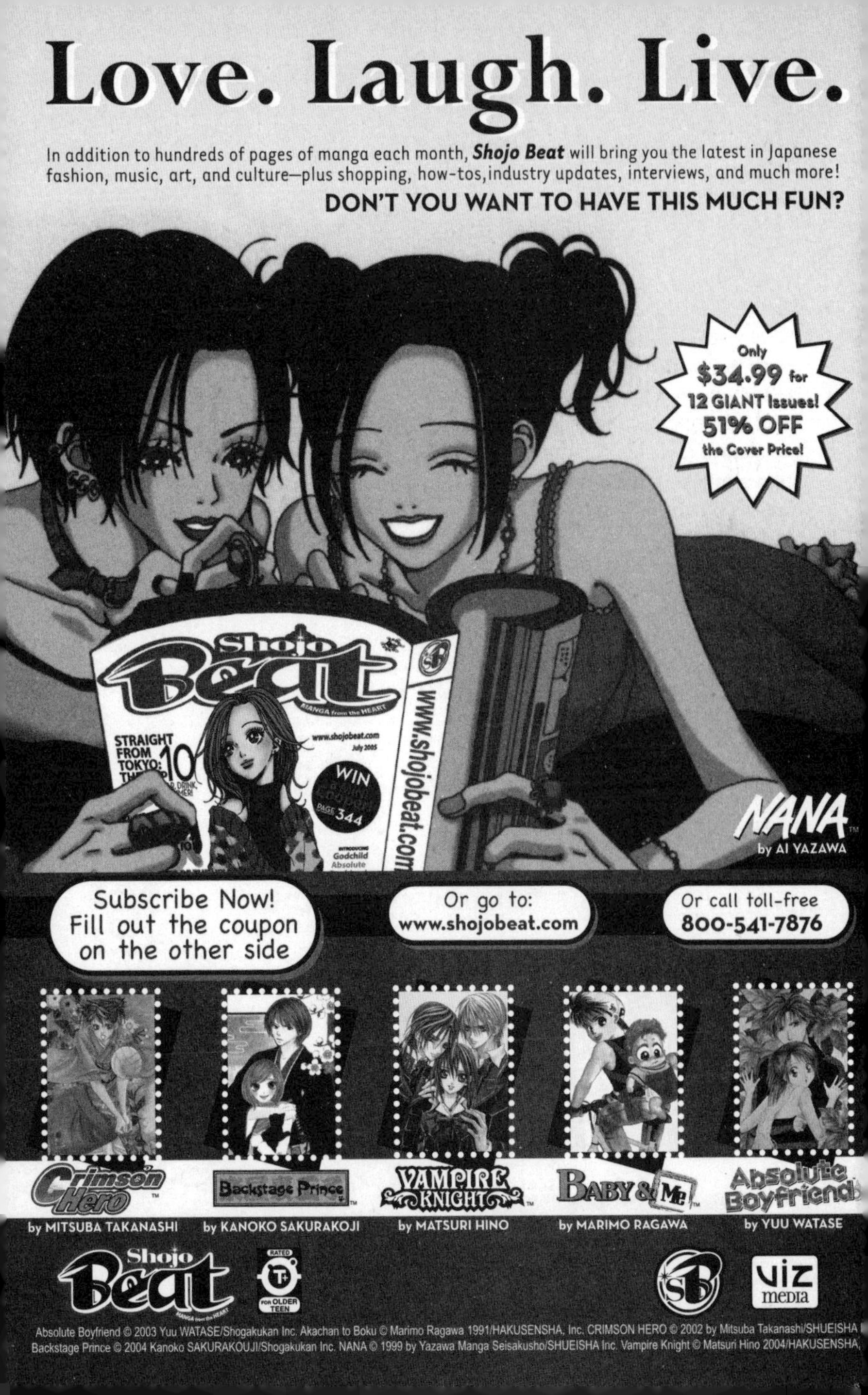

Love. Laugh. Live.
In addition to hundreds of pages of manga each month, Shojo Beat will bring you the latest in Japanese fashion, music, art, and culture—plus shopping, how-tos, industry updates, interviews, and much more!
DON'T YOU WANT TO HAVE THIS MUCH FUN?
Only $34.99 for 12 GIANT Issues! 51% OFF the Cover Price!
Shojo Beat
MANGA from the HEART
www.shojobeat.com
July 2005
STRAIGHT FROM TOKYO:
WIN
PAGE 344
Godchild
Absolute
www.shojobeat.com
NANA™ by AI YAZAWA
Subscribe Now! Fill out the coupon on the other side
Or go to: www.shojobeat.com
Or call toll-free 800-541-7876
Crimson Hero™ by MITSUBA TAKANASHI
Backstage Prince™ by KANOKO SAKURAKOJI
VAMPIRE KNIGHT™ by MATSURI HINO
BABY & ME™ by MARIMO RAGAWA
Absolute Boyfriend by YUU WATASE
Shojo Beat
MANGA from the HEART
RATED T+ FOR OLDER TEEN
viz media
Absolute Boyfriend © 2003 Yuu WATASE/Shogakukan Inc. Akachan to Boku © Marimo Ragawa 1991/HAKUSENSHA, Inc. CRIMSON HERO © 2002 by Mitsuba Takanashi/SHUEISHA Inc.
Backstage Prince © 2004 Kanoko SAKURAKOUJI/Shogakukan Inc. NANA © 1999 by Yazawa Manga Seisakusho/SHUEISHA Inc. Vampire Knight © Matsuri Hino 2004/HAKUSENSHA,